People & Events
A HISTORY OF THE UNITED WAY

People & Events
A HISTORY OF THE UNITED WAY

Library of Congress Catalog No. 76-41-88
Printed by Case-Hoyt/Atlanta, Atlanta, Georgia, U.S.A.

Dedicated to the spirit of
voluntarism which marks
America as unique.

ACKNOWLEDGMENT

This book combines the efforts of many people.

Elwood Street, a United Way pioneer, researched the early years, drawing on a United Way career that began in 1913. Mr. Street's work, recorded in over three thousand pages of manuscript, begins with the origins of organized charity and covers United Way's development through the early 1960s. That document is kept at the Information Center of United Way of America in Alexandria, Virginia. A microfilm copy is available in the Archives Center of the University of Minnesota.

Editors Helen Shenefield, Betty Lund, and the late Barbara Abel, reshaped and condensed the research material into its present form. Jeannette Coyne and the late Alice Weber were responsible for the final preparation of the manuscript and for production.

Henry Weber directed the work, first as Associate Executive Director of the national association of the United Way from 1960 until 1973. When he retired he continued to work on the project, compiling the historical illustrations and preparing the parts of the manuscript which cover the most recent period.

Literally hundreds of United Way volunteers and professionals, locally and nationally, have had a hand in this first published history of United Way.

But, more than anyone, Henry Weber brought the project to this successful conclusion and deserves the thanks of us all.

William Aramony, National Executive, United Way of America, commends Henry Weber for his services to United Way at a meeting of retired executives in Alexandria, Virginia, on November 12, 1975.

PREFACE

When a Denver priest, two ministers and a rabbi put their heads together in 1887 to plan the first united campaign for ten health and welfare agencies, they produced one of the most important social inventions in America's history. That year, Denver raised $21,700 the United Way. Ninety years later, in 1976, United Way in 2300 communities raised more than a billion dollars to support 37,000 agencies serving 34 million families.

United Way has built a proud record. For nearly a century, it has been a leading example of America's most distinctive tradition—the impulse of Americans to act on their own on the problems of their communities. United Way has become the principal life support system for the nation's growing, changing network of voluntary community agencies.

But United Way has become much more than a piece of money-raising machinery. It is a unifying force in almost every American community—a place where community problems can be seen as a whole, a place where people can decide what kind of community response is most appropriate to the need.

United Way has become the principal mechanism through which people can be most fully involved—directly and personally—in improving community life. It is the mechanism through which the human qualities essential to a good society—caring, mutual concern, compassion—can find a ready outlet.

In a field susceptible to abuse, United Way has developed and extended a stern tradition of strict accountability, rock-bottom overhead and reasonable fund-raising costs.

It has become the nation's principal training ground for informed, concerned community leaders. For all its size and scope, it has stayed flexible, able to accommodate change as new approaches to dealing with community problems displaced old ones.

United Way is the leading force in a growing movement. As the Coalition for the Public Good wrote recently in a report to the Filer Commission on Philanthropy, "the voluntary sector is not in decline, as some observers seem to believe, but growing more rapidly than ever in its history."

United Way's history falls naturally into two phases. From 1887 to 1970, United Way developed community by community. Local programs developed separately and independently; the national organization was simply a service center.

Then, in 1970, local United Ways came together to form a more truly national movement. They came to view their national association as more than a service station, but as a mechanism through which they would combine their strengths in programs of mutual support. United Way is still composed of 2300 autonomous local United Way organizations. But now they act together through the United Way of America on a growing agenda of common concerns.

Chapters 1, 17, and 18 record this rebirth and renewal. The chapters in-between tell the story from the beginning.

CONTENTS

NATIONAL HEADQUARTERS
UNITED WAY OF AMERICA,
Alexandria, Virginia
Dedicated April 30, 1972.

Ground was broken for the new national headquarters of United Way of America in Alexandria on April 7, 1971 by Bayard Ewing (left), Chairman of the Board of Governors and William Aramony, National United Way Executive.

Construction proceeded with such speed that 36 weeks later moving into the building began.

1

THE UNITED WAY...
TODAY AND TOMORROW

In 1970, an 83-year-old movement was renewed and reborn. It took a new name, developed a new sense of its possibilities and a new enthusiasm about its future.

The name change was symbolic. The national organization had been formed in 1918. Since that time, it had had five names. It began as the American Association for Community Organizations. In 1927, it became the Association of Community Chests and Councils. Five years later, it was changed to Community Chests and Councils, Inc., and in 1948 to Community Chests and Councils of America. In the Fifties, the "United Fund" designation was becoming popular across the country and in 1956, the national association became the United Community Funds and Councils of America.

The lack of a strong national identification had produced a confusing diversity of local designations. Many were called Community Chests or United Funds. But there were dozens of others: Crusade of Mercy, Joint Appeal, Golden Rule Campaign, Torch Drive, Red Feather Fund, Welfare Federation, the Big One, United Crusade, Good Neighbors, United Givers, the City City, and many more.

Attempts to adopt a common name nationally and locally had always failed.

There had been too little sense of common purpose, too little recognition of the possibilities for mutual support and reinforcement. Local organizations had understandably insisted on maintaining their locally established identification. Thus the national had had to adopt a series of designations too general for effective national use.

When the Board approved *United Way of America* as the national association's designation, it did more than adopt a new name; it affirmed a new spirit. It formalized a new recognition that local United Ways could strengthen each other without sacrificing local autonomy and initiative. It was a sign of new maturity, a new self-confidence. United Way became more than another new name; it was an accurate expression of a new reality.

The new name had a history. Twenty years before, in 1950, the phrase, "Give the United Way" had been used as a campaign theme in network television, radio, magazines and other mass media by the national organization's campaign committee in its annual program to reinforce the local fund drives.

In twenty years, over $300 million worth of contributed national media time and space, given by the communications industry through the Advertising Council, had won the phrase United Way a solid place in the national vocabulary. It was more than a familiar label; it expressed an almost universally accepted approach to charitable giving.

By 1976, nearly 904 local organizations had changed their names to United Way . . . and the trend was accelerating.

The Board's decision to adopt the new name was a clear signal that the national association had outgrown its "service station" role and had become the instrument through which the local United Ways could begin to function as a national force.

The name change was only one of many major changes. In 1969, Peat, Marwick, Mitchell and Co. completed a comprehensive analysis of the national association to redefine its role, its pattern of services, its administration and its financial structure.[1]

The major study recommendations approved in January 1970, were far-reaching: The United Way needed outstanding volunteer policymakers. It needed outstanding professional direction. It needed a more sharply focused national identity. It needed to reorder its program priorities radically.

The process began with the search for a replacement for Lyman S. Ford, the retiring Executive Director. On April 3, 1970 the national Board approved the appointment of William Aramony and he became the fourth National Executive in the association's history.

Mr. Aramony, trained in both business administration and social work, was known nationally as a leader and an innovator. He was 42 years old when he took charge on May 18, 1970—the youngest man ever to occupy the top post.

Within a week of his appointment, Mr. Aramony delivered an acceptance address to a national United Way Biennial Staff Conference in Hollywood Beach, Florida.[2]

"To justify community support, the United Way must project an umbrella that makes services available to all the people," he said.

"It must unify the community—not divide it.

"It must be community and service-delivery oriented, not agency-oriented.

"It must have powerful, representative boards.

"It must contribute to the community's ability to meet changing social conditions."

He stressed the United Way's need to develop and apply improved administrative procedures and management systems.

"And only by understanding that our own salvation lies in the well-being of every other man do we have a chance to survive as communities and as a nation," Mr. Aramony declared.

He praised his predecessor, Lyman S. Ford, "whose lifetime of service has been an example of commitment to principle . . . time will give to Lyman Ford the full appreciation of his cornerstone contributions."

The charge of building a revitalized United Way was carried a few weeks later to the Volunteer Campaign Leaders Conference in New Orleans by Keynote Speaker James R. Kerr, National Chairman of United Community Campaigns of America. He called for a renewal of personal responsibility and concern.

More changes followed in a rapid pattern. The national association moved to:

● Adopt the new name
● Create a new structure of governance
● Recruit new volunteer leadership
● Shape a new professional organization
● Move to the National Capital area
● Build a national headquarters building
● Secure new local United Way support for national services
● Propose a detailed blueprint for change.[3]

A metamorphosis was beginning . . . United Way of America was transforming itself from a trade association to a unified national movement.

With an accelerating momentum, board, executive and special committee meetings and conferences were producing major policy actions:

● A new Headquarters Site Committee was appointed.
● A Nominating Committee was selected and a governance group formed to construct new Articles of Incorporation and By-Laws.
● A new plan of staff organization was designed by the National Executive.
● A new Metro Organization of cities by fundraising results to facilitate service was structured.
● A combined fund raising, planning and allocations Volunteer Leaders Conference was organized instead of separate ones, emphasizing the unity of the movement.

The Rebirth and Renewal of the United Way had begun.

By 1976, the slogan "It's working" had become an understatement. That year:

- More than thirty-four million families were helped through the United Way.
- Thirty-seven thousand agencies were supported the United Way and spent more than three and a half billion dollars for human care services.
- Forty million individuals, companies and groups contributed money the United Way.
- The United Way, for years the world's most successful fund raiser, passed the billion dollar mark in a single campaign with the help of 20 million volunteers.

On July 9, 1975, representatives of Metro I United Way communities—those raising nine million dollars or more—were invited by C. Peter McColough, Chairman of the Board of Governors, United Way of

America, to the Alexandria headquarters to consider the future of United Way. They reviewed United Way's achievements and acknowledged a stern reality: United Way's resources were *not* growing as rapidly as its responsibilities—not nearly.

They began to act. They set in motion a process which took nearly twenty months and involved hundreds of United Way volunteers and professionals. The search for solutions proceeded in two separate directions: addressing long-range planning requirements and to impact immediately fund-raising results.

The Long Range Planning Committee was appointed, chaired by John W. Hanley, Chairman of the Board and President, Monsanto Company. When Mr. Hanley became Chairman-Elect of the Board of Governors, United Way of America, A. W. Clausen, President, Bank of America NT&SA, assumed leadership of the Long Range Planning Committee. This group, charged with the task of examining the basic issues affecting the

President Ford welcomes to the White House James R. Kerr, Chairman of the Board of Governors, United Way of America, on the occasion of his all-network and radio broadcast launching the 1974 United Way campaigns.

John W. Hanley, Chairman of the Board and President, Monsanto Company (left); C. Peter McColough, Chairman of the Board and Chief Executive Officer, Xerox Corporation (Center); and John D. deButts, Chairman of the Board and Chief Executive Officer, American Telephone & Telegraph Co. met on January 25, 1976 in New York to launch the National Corporate Development Program.

United Way movement and of determining how best to assure its viability in the future, met eight times in 1976.[4]

In March 1976, the committee wrote to United Way leaders and executives throughout the United States asking them to describe how the future looked to them and, particularly, what their principal problems were. Literally hundreds of replies poured in—mostly appeals for help. There was a common theme throughout the replies: people felt overwhelmingly that the forces that most vitally affect their health and growth were moving outside their control. They felt they needed help in five areas:

1. *The decline, in real terms, of corporate support.* With corporate decision making becoming more centralized, local communities lose access to the decision makers.

2. *The need for support for the United Way concept from the national media.* Local United Ways felt that the media in which they needed more visibility was the national media.

3. *The formation of public policy which vitally affects United Way voluntary services was being formed without United Way participation.* United Ways need a more visible, effective, aggressive

presence in the forums where public policy decisions are made. This initiative needs to be at both the federal and state level.

A. W. Clausen, President, Bank of America NT&SA, assumed leadership of the Long Range Planning Committee on October 21, 1976.

4

Bayard Ewing, Chairman of the Board of Governors, United Way of America, delivering his "Rebirth and Renewal" address to United Way Trustees at their annual meeting in Dallas on December 3, 1970. Seated at speaker's table, left, M. M. Brisco, United Way Board Member and President, Standard Oil Company (N.J.) and William Aramony, National Executive, United Way of America.

4. *The effective use of volunteers.* The major source of local United Ways' strength has been broad participation; therefore, the movement needs to find more ways to use more volunteers more effectively.

5. *The need for expanded areawide management arrangements.* Because population shifts have been drawing people away from the central cities, local United Ways felt that expanded areawide management arrangements were needed to reconcile where people give with where people live. Outposts in smaller communities should be developed to provide special services to locals which operate without professional help.

The *Program for the Future* is a specific response to these concerns expressed by local individuals, volunteers and professionals. In order to keep this continuing dialogue flowing, the committee asked each local community to name its long-range planning committee. Together, local and national Long Range Planning Committees can influence the direction of the *Program for the Future* and can track its progress.[5]

In addition to the chairman, A. W. Clausen, the Long Range Planning Committee members include: Dr. Roy Amara, President, Institute of the Future; James E. Burke, Chairman and Chief Executive Officer, Johnson & Johnson; Dr. Lisle Carter, Chancellor, Atlanta University Center; John W. Hanley, Chairman

of the Board and President, Monsanto Company; Mr. Earle Harbison, Jr., General Manager, Specialty Chemicals Division, Monsanto Company; Joseph P. Maldonado, Regional Director, Department of Health, Education and Welfare; C. Virgil Martin, Past President, Carson Pirie Scott and Company; Dr. John W. Oswald, President, Penn State University; Ralph A. Pfeiffer, Chairman of the Board, IBM World Trade Americas/Far East Corporation; Miss Flaxie Madison Pinkett, President, John R. Pinkett, Inc.; Dr. Frank Stanton, Chairman, American National Red Cross; Glenn E. Watts, President, Communications Workers of America, AFL-CIO; and Dr. Franklin D. Murphy, Chairman of the Board, The Times Mirror Company.

The other major outcome of the July 9, 1975 meeting was the formation of the National Corporate Development Program. This program headed by John D. deButts, Chairman of the Board, American Telephone & Telegraph Co., accepted responsibility for undertaking a major cultivation effort aimed at enhancing current and immediate future contributions from national corporations and their employees. The major elements of the program are: 1) to mobilize national corporate-giving decision makers in order to triple corporate giving; and 2) to conduct, for the first time, company-wide employee campaigns.[6]

The program developed by the National Corporate Development Committee has two interrelated efforts:

Serious consideration and thought was given to the Program For The Future before the Board of Governors of United Way of America gave unanimous approval to the Program on December 8, 1976.

1. A strategy for reaching *national* corporate decision-makers so there will be a national corporate policy for the support of local United Ways including the adoption of a new fair share corporate guideline.[7]

2. Encouraging national corporations and international labor to improve employee response, particularly in branch operation.

The equitable guideline for corporate support was developed by corporate executives for corporate executives. To test the program, three separate meetings were held in New York, Chicago and San Francisco. The program was beginning to work.

In addition to the chairman, John D. deButts, the committee included: Dutton Brookfield, President, Unitog Company; R. Manning Brown, Jr., Chairman, New York Life Insurance Company; E. Mandell deWindt, Chairman, Eaton Corporation; Thomas J. Galligan, Jr., President, Boston Edison Company; Philip

O. Geier, Jr., Past Chairman, Cincinnati Milacron, Inc.; W. H. Krome George, Chairman of the Board, Alcoa; Harry Gray, Chairman and Chief Executive Officer, United Technologies Corporation; H. J. Haynes, Chairman and Chief Executive Officer, Standard Oil Company of California; John V. James, President and Chief Executive Officer, Dresser Industries, Inc.; David S. Lewis, Chairman and Chief Executive Officer, General Dynamics Corporation; C. Peter McColough, Chairman of the Board, Xerox Corporation; James P. McFarland, Chairman of the Board, General Mills, Inc.; Randall Meyer, President and Chief Executive Officer, Exxon U.S.A.; Paul A. Miller, Chairman and Chief Executive Officer, Pacific Lighting Corporation; G. H. Moede, President, Wisconsin Bell Telephone Company; Thomas A. Murphy, Chairman of the Board and Chief Executive Officer, General Motors Corporation; Donald S. Perkins, Chairman, Jewel Companies, Inc.; Charles M. Pigott, President, PACCAR, Inc.; Charles J. Pilliod, Jr., Chairman and Chief Executive

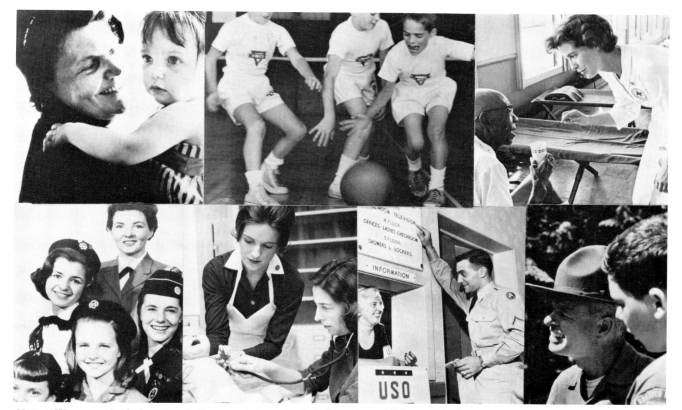

United Way agencies help not only the poor. They also help homeless children...the lonesome aged...the ill...troubled youth ...members of the Armed Forces and their families...disaster victims.

Officer, Goodyear Tire & Rubber Company; J. Stanford Smith, Chairman, International Paper Company; Augustus H. Sterne, Chairman of the Board, Trust Company of Georgia; and Frank K. Tarbox, President and Chief Executive Officer, Penn Mutual.

The conclusions of the Long Range Planning Committee and the National Corporate Development Committee resulted in the *Program for the Future*. The *Program* has five principal elements:

1. Tested National Corporate Development Program to assist local United Ways, in concert with other United Ways, to triple the total funds raised from corporations and their employees.

2. National Media Program to bring the United Way story to the people more often and more forcefully through television, radio, newspapers and magazines.

3. Federal Legislative Program to increase United Way capacity to achieve impact on human service policy decisions in all branches of the Federal government.

4. New Resources Development to tap new sources of funds, including deferred gifts, endowments and contributions from foreign firms operating in the United States.

5. Services to smaller cities to provide more intensive management assistance to United Ways in small communities.

Through long-range planning, the *Program* will be kept responsive. It was recognized that only by looking beyond the annual campaign, can United Way reduce the barriers to a strong voluntary future.

The *Program* acknowledged that United Way could only hold and enlarge its constituency of voluntary sector organizations if it grew as rapidly as the needs of those organizations grow.

It recognized that an expanded United Way presence was necessary to set standards of responsiveness and cost-effectiveness for the whole voluntary sector.

But the *Program for the Future* had a larger meaning. The voluntary sector is a crucial, countervailing force

7

to expanding centralization. Without it, there would be no alternative to impulsive, open-ended government involvement in every aspect of community life. Americans everywhere are questioning the effectiveness of a generation of headlong centralization. Now, more than ever, the United Way had to strengthen its capacity as an alternative system.

But most important, the voluntary sector has provided the principal channel through which Americans can act personally and directly on the problems they see about them. This kind of participation has been a great source of strength in our society and United Way has been for nearly a century the primary enabling mechanism for the organizations which provide these opportunities.

Probably, the United Way's growth has just begun.

The story of how United Way was born and how it grew is told in the following chapters.

NOTES

Chapter 1

1. Peat, Marwick, Mitchell & Company. *A Study of United Community Funds and Councils of America.* 1969.

2. William Aramony, *Future Directions,* Address, Hollywood Beach, Florida, April 10, 1970.

3. *Proceedings, Annual Meeting of Trustees, United Way of America, Rebirth and Renewal,* December 3, 1970.

4. *Executive Newsletter,* United Way of America, December 8, 1975.

5. John W. Hanley, Address, New York, New York, November 15, 1976.

6. *The Program For The Future, Questions and Answers,* United Way of America, December 1976.

7. John D. deButts, Address, New York, New York, November 15, 1976.

8. *The Program For The Future, Questions and Answers,* United Way of America, December 1976.

Fund-Raising Record of United Way Campaigns United States & Canada—1919-1976

Year*	Number of Campaigns	Amount	Percent of Previous Year	Year*	Number of Campaigns	Amount	Percent of Previous Year
1919	39	$19,651,334		1947	1,011	181,716,355	104.7
1920	61	22,781,834	115.9%	1948	1,153	193,307,693	106.4
1921	96	28,568,453	125.4	1949	1,319	198,120,167	102.5
1922	147	40,280,649	140.1	1950	1,499	218,421,521	110.2
1923	203	50,351,190	125.0	1951	1,501	246,813,142	113.0
1924	240	58,003,965	115.2	1952	1,561	272,257,433	110.3
1925	285	63,677,235	109.8	1953	1,691	293,898,475	107.9
1926	308	66,432,072	104.3	1954	1,859	308,303,285	104.9
1927	314	68,664,042	103.4	1955	1,940	346,270,606	112.3
1928	331	73,276,688	106.7	1956	1,962	385,240,407	111.3
1929	353	75,972,555	103.7	1957	2,042	421,683,494	109.6
1930	386	84,796,505	111.6	1958	2,105	434,567,603	103.1
1931	397	101,377,537	119.6	1959	2,148	465,801,286	107.2
1932	401	77,752,954	76.7	1960	2,187	486,114,951	104.4
1933	399	70,609,078	90.8	1961	2,190	510,181,047	104.9
1934	406	69,781,478	98.8	1962	2,205	533,904,233	104.7
1935	429	77,367,634	110.9	1963	2,208	556,004,671	104.1
1936	452	81,707,787	105.6	1964	2,232	594,135,545	106.8
1937	475	83,898,234	102.7	1965	2,217	635,570,048	107.0
1938	524	86,561,920	103.2	1966	2,250	680,145,832	107.0
1939	562	89,751,702	103.7	1967	2,272	719,639,697	105.8
1940	599	94,161,098	104.9	1968	2,268	766,870,879	106.6
1941	633	108,812,899	115.6	1969	2,255	816,576,160	106.5
1942	650	166,538,363	153.1	1970	2,241	839,990,142	102.9
1943	704	214,757,782	129.0	1971	2,236	865,300,000	103.0
1944	773	225,934,893	105.2	1972	2,224	914,622,000	105.7
1945	799	201,859,357	89.3	1973	2,192	975,158,000	106.6
1946	842	173,512,638	86.0	1974	2,353	1,038,995,000	106.6
				1975	2,354	1,086,605,117	104.5
				1976[1]	2,350	1,171,410,138	107.8

* Campaigns conducted in indicated year for allocations the following year.

[1] Projection based upon 75% of campaigns reported through January, 1977.

THE BEGINNINGS OF ORGANIZED CHARITY: 2100 B.C.-1886

The United Way of planning and financing community health and welfare services is a relatively recent development in human history. Yet the origins of charity itself are to be found in the remotest depths of antiquity where evidence lies that even most primitive man felt compassion for the poor and homeless and extended aid to the oppressed. History corroborates Aristotle's thesis that man is a social animal who must cooperate with and assist his fellow man. Charity might well be called a law of nature.

Problems of poverty, illness, and family discord are as old as man himself. But while tribes and villages were small, help came from family, neighbors, or local collective action. As society became more complex, the record reveals growing governmental concern for the wellbeing of all citizens. The "welfare state" idea, far from being a modern development, arose early in man's social life.

In the traditional site of the Biblical Garden of Eden, Hammurabi, King of Babylonia about 2100 B.C., proclaimed his concern for subjects in a code of laws carved in a diorite column nearly eight feet high. These laws called for protection of widows, orphans, and the poor, and strongly prohibited defrauding the helpless.

In neighboring Egypt it was believed that charity and good works would assist the soul to salvation after death. *The Book of the Dead,* recording many examples of charitable acts, is found in papyrus editions dating to about 1500 B.C.

As civilization spread through the Eastern Mediterranean, ancient Greece and Sparta formed public charity policies to relieve poverty. In Attica about 600 B.C. an additional fund was established for children of those killed in war. The Temples of Asclepius, son of Apollo and Coronis, became clinics and hospitals, attended by priest-physicians. The staff of Asclepius, entwined by a snake, is the well-known symbol of modern medicine.

Other societies similarly provided for the sick. Buddha, the great Indian leader who died about 483 B.C., exhorted his followers to alleviate the pains and miseries of human life, and is credited with erecting the first hospitals.

The sick in Rome were cared for in their Temples of Asclepius, with strangers and wayfarers sheltered in public guest houses. As Rome grew, attracting dispossessed peasants, private and public philanthropy expanded to meet their needs. Tiberius Gracchus, elected Tribune of Rome in 133 B.C., directed a large scale distribution of grain, first at half price and later free. But reformers then, as now, were not always popular; Tiberius Gracchus was murdered during a riot.

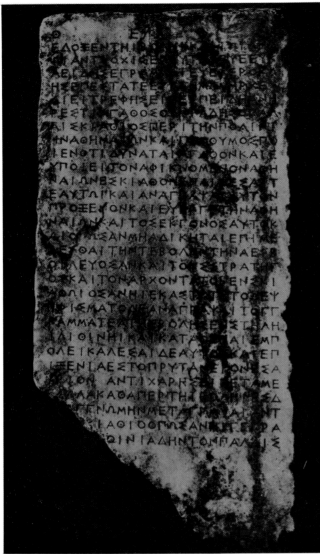

Inscribed Marble Slab found on the Acropolis of Athens. It records a decree of the Council of the Athenians, honoring one of history's first known volunteers to aid travelers. Translation: "Gods... since Oeniades of Old Skiathos is... eager to do whatever good he can and helps any Athenian who arrives in that city... the Council decrees that he—and his descendants—be registered as honorary consul and benefactor of the Athenians. Further, Oeniades is to be invited to dinner in the Town Hall tomorrow." Photograph, the German Archaeological Institute, Athens. Published and translated in "The Greeks Until Alexander" by R. M. Cook.

The Good Samaritan not only gave emergency assistance to the victim of the robbers but also gave a demonstration of planning and allocating for human need. Leaving money with the Innkeeper for care of the injured man he said that if more should be needed he would provide adequate funds upon his return.

Despite his death, distribution of free grain to the hungry and often greedy citizens continued. Lists of citizens eligible for relief were inscribed on bronze tablets and maintained by appointed officials, becoming perhaps the world's first charity records. The public officials assigned to determine eligibility may be thought of as ancestors to modern social workers in public assistance. Under Augustus, first Roman emperor, 28 B.C.-14 A.D., some 200,000 citizens received public aid.

Romans recognized not only hunger and poverty as social problems, but the lot of children suffering from broken family life. A special child-caring institution was founded, supported first by voluntary and then by imperial funds. It may be thought of as a precursor to the child welfare agencies of modern America.

Side by side with public charity, private philanthropy was developing. The "sportula," a form of charity bestowed by a patron, was widely abused, demonstrating what modern social work reaffirms, that indiscriminate charity, when administered without skill or understanding, defeats itself and tends to destroy both recipients and donor.

Contributions of the Ancient Hebrews

In the Old Testament is found the first written injunction of humanity going beyond the narrow bounds of family, the command to "Love your neighbor as yourself." (Leviticus 19:18) This principle and a high sense of responsibility for the needy were maintained by the Jews through years of adversity, along with their religious and racial identity, and their unique belief in one God.

The period from the ninth to twelfth centuries has often been called the Golden Age of the Jews' literary and cultural flowering. In this period Moses Maimonides, Jewish rabbi, scholar philosopher and physician, presented the "Golden Ladder" or code of charity, describing steps toward the highest summit of enlightened giving. Born in Spain in 1135, Maimonides gave the world a code which has guided men of many faiths for centuries.

The Golden Ladder of Maimonides

First.
In the duty of charity the first and lowest degree is to give—but with reluctance or regret. This is the gift of the hand; but not of the heart.
Second.
The second degree is to give cheerfully, but not proportionately to the distress of the sufferer.
Third.
The third is to give cheerfully and proportionately but not until we are actually solicited.
Fourth.
The fourth is to give cheerfully, proportionately, and even unsolicitedly; but to put it in the poor man's hand, thereby exciting in him a painful emotion of shame.
Fifth.
The fifth is to give charity in such a way that the distressed may receive the bounty and know their benefactor without their ever being known to him.
Sixth.
The sixth, which rises still higher is to know the objects of our bounty but remain unknown to them.
Seventh.
The seventh is still more meritorious, namely, to bestow charity in such a way that the benefactor may

not know the relieved persons, nor they the names of their benefactors, as was done by our charitable forefathers during the existence of the temple. For there was in that holy building a place called the Chamber of the Silent, wherein the good deposited secretly whatever their generous hearts suggested, and from which the poor were maintained with equal secrecy.
Eighth.
Lastly, the eighth and most meritorious of all is to anticipate charity by preventing poverty; namely to assist the reduced brother by a considerable gift, or a loan of money, or by teaching him some trade, or by putting him in the way of business, so that he may earn an honest livelihood; and not be forced to the dreadful alternative of holding up his hand for charity. And to this Scripture alludes when it says: And if thy brother be waxen poor, and fallen in decay with

Moses Ben Maimon, (1135-1204) usually called Maimonides advanced a high concept of charity. In the eighth step of his Golden Ladder he enunciated the principle that the highest level of philanthropy is "to help people to help themselves," a tenet always held by the United Way.

thee, then thou shalt support him; Yes, though he be a stranger or a sojourner, that he may live with thee. This is the highest step and the summit of charity's Golden Ladder.[1]

In summarizing early Jewish thought and activity in the area of charity, a modern Jewish historian says, "What . . . did the Biblical period and its chief creation, the Holy Scriptures, have to pass down to the subsequent generations in the way of philanthropic teaching and action? First, a warm glowing feeling for charitable deed, which amounts almost to a passion . . . Second, it was the Jewish Biblical law that first made charity a human obligation incumbent on every person . . . Third, definite measures of relief to those in want and regulations of a preventive nature were evolved and set in motion . . . Fourth, during this period there was made clear for all time the chief, the basic causes of poverty and misery, namely, economic maladjustment and injustice due to human greed." [2]

Early Christian Charity

Whereas Judaism centered in the family and tribe, with care for the needy primarily a family responsibility, early Christianity was marked by a spirit of brotherhood for all. The Christian church extended its ministrations to all in need, whether or not they were members of the faith. Hospitals, leper homes, hospices for travelers, and orphan asylums were established under Church auspices, and in 325 A.D. the Ecumenical Council of Nicea commanded the establishment of such institutions in every town. Bishop Ambrose of Milan who set out to establish a sense of balance and reason in the administration of charity, ordered that relief be given not too freely to the undeserving, yet not too sparingly to those in real need. In any case, none were to be refused. Research into causes of need still was unheard of, since it was accepted that "the poor ye shall always have with you."

When Constantine the Great became emperor of the Roman Empire, he made Christianity the official religion and in 321 A.D. authorized the contribution of money to the Church. From then on great endowments accumulated for the Church and its charitable institutions.

When the Western Empire broke into fragments following the fall of Rome to the Gauls in 476, poverty became the lot of the common man. He was a slave-like serf, attached to the land and the will of his feudal lord. Civilization itself seemed crumbling, and the period has often been called the Dark Ages.

Outside the Church there was little organized aid for the needy—no tithing, no committees or institutions at the community level. Most often the victim of misfortune was helped by friends who took it for granted that he should receive their help. Merchant and craft guilds provided spontaneous and unorganized aid, and the feudal lord assumed responsibility for protecting and aiding his serfs.

In 1096 the first Crusade started for the Holy Land, initiating 200 years marked by bloody battles as the Christian forces of Western Europe sought to recover the Holy Land from the Moslems. When Crusaders took Jerusalem in 1099, the military religious order

The 850-year-old award of the Order of the Hospital of St. John of Jerusalem, bestowed in 1961 by Queen Elizabeth II, "for conspicuous service in the cause of humanity" upon John H. Yerger, then Executive Director of the Toronto United Way is presented by Canada's Governor General, George P. Vanier.

of Friars of the Hospital of St. John was formed to establish and protect hospitals for the sick and the wounded. During its 800-year lifetime the order not only served its own hospitals, but stimulated the development of hospitals throughout the western world. Some of history's first "benefits" were staged by the order, which used jousting tournaments and sporting events as fund-raising devices.

The Crusades opened new horizons and set the mood for change. To some, the growing wealth of the monasteries and their frequent isolation from people seemed outmoded. So it appeared to Francis of Assisi who held that the Christ-like way of life was that of "evangelical poverty." Born around 1182, he founded the Franciscan order of friars with a philosophy of living among the people, knowing their needs, sharing their lives and ministering to them.

Broader concepts of charity than those of almsgiving and church poor funds were coming into men's minds. Charitable fraternities, an elementary form of community organization, were established by laymen. In the later Middle Ages guilds of merchants, master craftsmen and their journeymen made contracts with hospitals and almshouses, established institutions and collected funds for the needy. They had a particular interest because of the barriers between different grades of workmen whereby conditions of apprenticeship were made hard and journeymen were hindered from becoming masters. There were many problems which the guilds could not handle, however, and responsibility for those caused by famine, pestilence, and the

Illustrations from the "Book of the Very Active Life of the Nuns of the Hotel—Dieu of Paris," Fifteenth Century, Musée De L'Assistance Public, Paris." Photograph, New York Public Library.

Martin Luther, a founder of the Common Chest for various charities in Leisnig in 1523.

growing number of beggars was transferred to the cities.

By the fourteenth century municipalities in England, Germany, and France were struggling with the old problem of indiscriminate relief-giving creating its own evils of pauperism and vagrancy. The Statute of Laborers, passed shortly after the Black Death in England in 1349, decreed that no alms be given to beggars refusing to work, on pain of imprisonment. This, and further repressive enactments including whipping, mutilations, branding, and compulsory labor all apparently failed in their purpose as they were unable to meet the

spreading problems of poverty. With the crumbling of the feudal system, poverty grew and the ever-greater number of charitable endeavors became chaotic, conflicting, and inadequate, for they aimed at meeting needs rather than removing their causes.

Private foundations grew in number and size, and by the time of the Reformation there were more than 460 in England. Money was willed for almshouses, hospitals, colleges, bridges, and other public works. The Church continued to provide the major part of relief, however, incorporating the concepts of poverty as a way to receive grace, and almsgiving as a meritorious deed. One third of Church funds was to be set aside for the poor, but as the Middle Ages advanced, this principle was neglected.

The Old Order Changes

After the Protestant Reformation in the 16th century, it was soon discovered that the needs of the poor and afflicted continued whether in a Catholic or Protestant society. The new Lutheran Church was not organized to handle the widespread charities of recently dispossessed Catholic churches and monasteries. Many German cities, therefore, with already-established systems of relief, expanded their services. Control of former Catholic hospitals was taken over by boards of laymen, and thus began the secularization of charity and the development and management of social agencies by laymen.

Martin Luther, called on by the citizens of Leisnig, Saxony for advice regarding various problems, especially vagrancy and poverty, helped to set up the Com-

13

St. Vincent dePaul was renowned for his humility, benevolence and interest in children. The Society which bears his name now participates in the United Way.

mon Chest in 1523 with a communitywide, unpaid citizen responsibility. It was a form of centralized operation and control of various public and private charities rather than a federation of autonomous participating agencies. Financing came from church offerings, legacies, and a compulsory rate levied on all parishioners. Ten elected supervisors, including three from the common burgesses of the town, two "honorable men" of distinction, two of the governing council, and three peasants administered the Chest.

Secrecy regarding beneficiaries was a point in ethics then, as now. Other features which persist in modern philanthropy include: the annual election of laymen as overseers, annual contributions from all, and "new pennies" collected quarterly from workers by employers, an early example of payroll deduction.

In England, following his excommunication in 1533, Henry VIII expropriated the monasteries, breaking up the Catholic charitable system. This resulted in great distress and poverty among the people, for no substitute was immediately provided. But the strengthening of Parliament as a central authority paved the way for a uniform national relief program under the Elizabethan Poor Law.

Until the Poor Law was enacted in 1601 the government's approach to poverty had been punitive and

American Revolution Hospital. Replica of crude log hospital used by the Continental Army in Jockey Hollow, near Morristown, New Jersey, during the winters of 1777 to 1781. Photograph, New York Public Library.

repressive. Begging was the accepted form of seeking help although the guilds, private foundations, and churches tried to alleviate poverty according to their means. The Poor Laws recognized the obligation of the state, through the local municipality to the needy; established poorhouses financed by local taxes where the sick, aged, and insane were housed together; made relatives liable for needy kinsmen, and threatened jail to those who refused either to work or pay their poor rates. In 1662 the Poor Laws were made more rigorous when amended as part of the Law of Settlement.

These laws had a vital effect on American practices, for in the early settlements at Jamestown and Plymouth the laws of the Mother Country prevailed. In Virginia, Massachusetts, and other colonies the parish or town was made responsible for the levying of poor rates.

As time passed in colonial America, it became evident that the indigent were flocking into localities where relief was generous, and thus the Settlement Act was enacted in 1701 to restrict relief to those with legal residences. Those who seemed likely to become a burden on a parish to which they had recently come could be ejected at any time within 40 days.

The Settlement Act of Charles II in 1662 became part of the legal apparatus of the American colonies and while England made modifications, it prevailed until the Depression of the 1930's. State and federal sharing of responsibility was established then, but even yet the repressive spirit of English Poor Law persists in many states where migrants and non-residents still have difficulty when in need of public assistance.

In England, dissatisfaction with the Poor Laws and rising administrative costs led to restrictive measures such as the "workhouse test" which ordered that "no poor who refuse to be lodged and kept in such houses (poor houses) should be entitled to ask for parochial relief." Later the "allowance system" abolished this test and decreed that only the aged and infirm, unmarried mothers and young children should be sent to the poorhouse. In 1834 the Poor Law Reform Act was passed, providing for local administration under central regulation.

In addition to England's governmental agencies there was a plethora of voluntary societies which had resulted from attempts to meet the new problems of poverty and squalor. With a growing need for cooperation between agencies and for new fund-raising methods since the dole had become inadequate, Charity Organization Societies came into being. In London between 1860 and 1869 the number of persons as-

The Cincinnati City Work House in the 1880's. People of all ages inhabited the Work House and it was the focal point of service from many social agencies, including the Home for the Friendless, German Widows Society, the City Mission and Associated Charities.

15

sisted by official charity rose from 85,000 to 120,000 and expenditures rose from $4 million to $7 million annually.

Charity Organization Societies Are Formed

It was the Rev. Henry Solly, a Unitarian minister of London, whose paper, "How to Deal with the Unemployed Poor," spurred action. Its message of social evangelism was like a trumpet call, resulting in a committee of influential men who formed an association and developed a far-reaching policy for organizing all charities. Their plan for cooperation was not popular with the agencies, however, and at the first conference of representatives of nearly 400 London charities, they flatly opposed the whole idea. Despite this resistance the London Charity Organization Society (COS) established an office in 1869 and employed a secretary. Its program was soon put into effect. District committees were organized, volunteers recruited for friendly visiting, and full-time employees hired. They worked to avoid overlapping with Poor Law recipients and stressed the need for cooperation. Their idea of a central registry to prevent duplication and fraud had to be given up, however, because of the size of the job. Each district raised its own funds.

In Liverpool a Central Relief Society, formed in 1863 with similar purposes and methods, added a further feature: the central collection of contributions. Perplexed by the number of meritorious appeals, Liverpool citizens conducted a study which showed the 38 leading charities were being supported by about 6,600 of an estimated 20,000 potential contributors. The organization then persuaded 98 Liverpool agencies to let it raise funds for them, using a common pledge sheet.

In 1877 the world's first successful plan for central financing raised what amounted to $125,000 in American money for the 98 agencies. No attempt was made for a central budget or over-all goal, and agencies were free to make their own separate solicitations.

This plan, with groundwork started in 1873, was the beginning of central financing of community health and welfare services, as the London plan was the beginning of central planning. The London COS provided the working model for the first American Charity Organization Society established in Buffalo, N.Y., in 1877. The Liverpool plan of combined charity organization and joint financing was largely copied in Denver, Colorado in 1887. Liverpool has continued its plan in modified form until the present day. While historically significant, the Liverpool plan had little impact on the development of joint financing of social agencies in the United States.

American Charities Blaze a Trail

Social service needs in America differed from those in England because the new nation offered free land and wide opportunity, a theoretically classless society, and an economy still largely agricultural. The human problems caused by industrialization and urbanization came later.

Relief in New England was administered by the towns, with appropriations to the poor decided at town meetings where local farmers made bids for use of their homes as "poorhouses" and where infants, widows, infirm, and other "impotent" persons were committed to them. Any person receiving public aid could be indentured or apprenticed, and orphans were often bound out to apprenticeship which most often proved to be hard labor. Public auctions were social occasions, complete with alcoholic refreshment. It was a harsh period in our history, a time when the committed insane were exposed for the entertainment of those paying a fee. Public aid was limited to legal residents. Non-residents were shipped back to their places of legal residence, or if they had none were "passed on."

In the first part of the 19th century efforts were made to correct social evils, particularly to bring about "women's rights," abolish slavery, effect greater religious tolerance, provide free public education, introduce prohibition, and provide better care for the insane and other unfortunates, and to separate the deserving and undeserving poor on the basis of those who could be "elevated." Specialized institutions were established to separate the various kinds of persons in almshouses. In 1841 Dorothea Lynde Dix began a crusade to improve care of the insane and other unfortunates. Results of her work included the establishment of state hospitals and improved county poorhouses and jails. For six years she struggled to obtain federal financing for care of the insane. A bill finally was passed by Congress in 1854 only to be vetoed by President Franklin Pierce "on the ground that the federal government should not become involved in financial responsibility for any welfare program . . ." This veto set a precedent for refusal of federal assistance to the states for welfare programs which was not altered until the 1930's. [3]

In Virginia and other southern states, county (originally parish) administration prevailed rather than town as in New England. Both plans continued in almost undiluted Elizabethan style until the Federal Social Security Act of 1935 brought about shared responsibility of local, state, and federal governments for public assistance.

As floods of new immigrants came into seaport cities, more adequate services were needed. Churches still provided help, but usually to members only. Private philanthropies began to spring up and secular voluntary agencies were formed to fill the gaps and inadequacies. Nationality groups set up benevolent organizations. The new organizations flourished and multiplied, fertilized by the flood of well-meant dollars. Wealth was coming to the cities as world trade developed following the Treaty of Ghent in 1814. By 1820 the larger cities had an embarrassment of benevolent associations.

America's benevolent affluence greatly influenced a French traveler, Alexis de Tocqueville, whose book *Democracy in America* published in 1835 has been widely quoted ever since. "Americans are an unusual people," he wrote, "when they see a problem come up, they immediately form a group or committee—whatever is necessary to get the job done."

Joint planning and action for community health and welfare had its first expression in America in 1817 when John Griscom, pioneer chemistry teacher, advocate of free, universal public education, and philanthropist, led in the organization of the Society for the Prevention of Pauperism in the City of New York. He sought to enlist "all the spontaneous charities of the town" to "flow in one channel," but the idea did not take hold and his society languished and died. The idea of cooperation, however, was planted in the American mind.

In Philadelphia the economist and publisher, Mathew Carey in 1829 attempted to interest Philadelphians in a single campaign for 33 benevolent societies. He, too, failed.

In 1833 a Board of Missionaries was formed in Boston under the direction of Joseph Tuckerman, a Unitarian minister, to discuss possibilities for more cooperation by relief agencies. A plan was finally accepted and the Association of Delegates from the Benevolent Societies of Boston formed. Objectives were to remedy and prevent the abuse of alms, and to bring about the most effectual relief of the suffering poor. They helped stimulate the establishment of the Society for the Prevention of Pauperism which later merged with the Boston Provident Association and finally, in 1953, with the Associated Charities, to become the Family Service Association of Greater Boston.

The ideas for cooperation kept reappearing in various guises. A New York Association for the Improvement of the Condition of the Poor (AICP) was widely copied. With a broad plan covering the entire city this association proposed not to supersede any other agencies but to supply what was lacking. One difficulty was a conspicuous lack of cooperation among agencies. Another was its sectarian nature, for it was inaugurated, controlled and supported solely by Protestants. The movement also suffered from lack of a democratic base, the volunteer leadership coming invariably from wealthy families.

While not serving as a coordinator, AICP did succeed in its appeal to the Legislature to make the State responsible for the care, training and education of neglected children and did represent a new approach to the problems of giving aid to the poor and preventing pauperism.

This plan was widely copied and during the 1850's similar societies (generally called Societies for the Improvement of the Condition of the Poor) were organized in nearly all large cities. Their stated purpose was "to find work for all willing to do it, to investigate all cases thoroughly, to raise the needy above the need for relief, and incidentally to relieve directly such want as seemed to require it." [4] The latter function soon submerged all others, but while almsgiving was profuse (and chaotic) for the next 50 years, it still did not meet the demands.

Among the many other organizations formed in the 1840's were Mutual Benefit Societies set up by immigrants. Some of these societies accumulated substantial funds which they used to establish and support their own hospitals, orphanages, and homes for the aged.

Various philanthropies rose spontaneously when groups of individuals noted particular needs and established organizations to take care of them. This weed-like growth soon choked up the social welfare landscape with confusing activities and vexatious appeals for funds. There was a growing demand for scientific cultivation of this field, but effective cooperation and coordination were still more than half a century in coming.

This picture of Clara Barton (1821-1912), founder of the American Red Cross was taken in the mid 1860's by Brady, premier photographer. Approximately 90% of Red Cross funds are now raised through United Way campaigns. U.S. Signal Corps photo.

The Post Civil War Period

With the return of peace after the Civil War, new problems accompanied new opportunities. Agencies were numerous, kaleidoscopic in variety, purpose and method. They sprang from no common, generally agreed-on purpose, and were not related to known needs of the community as a whole. Rather, they were often the products of philanthropic whim, or emotional reaction to partly-known needs. Many duplicated others, while the needs of many persons in distress were met inadequately, if at all. There were no common standards of performance.

In 1865 the American Social Science Association was launched, the first organization of size to deal with the over-all problems of charity and corrections. Its membership included a sparse number of officials from state public welfare and penal institutions and the recently-organized state boards of charity, plus professional and lay members. Its plan was to provide opportunity for discussions. In 1874, the organization served as co-convener (with the Mass. State Board of Charities) of the First National Conference of Charities, from which developed the National Conference on Social Welfare. One of the major national organizations in the field of social work, its Annual Forums are attended by more than 8,000 professionals and laymen from governmental and voluntary agencies.

Boston in 1869 took an important step to bring more contact and hopefully better communication between agencies by housing them under one roof for the first time. Boston thus pioneered in central housing as it had in central registration of relief applicants in 1834.

The Panic of 1873, when the extended financial structure of post-war America came down with a crash, speeded the development of the Charity Organization movement. Failure of the banking house of Jay Cooke in Philadelphia brought a slump in the stock market followed by one of the longest and most severe periods of industrial depression in American history. Unemployment and suffering were unprecedented in extent and degree. Multitudes were thrown out of work, their ranks augmented by Civil War soldiers who had not yet found a place in the nation's growing industrial life. Tramps increased in number; unemployment was a national problem for the first time.

Philadelphia tackled its problem in the 22nd ward by districting the ward (Germantown) into eight divisions with a central office and a paid superintendent. No relief was given except in emergency, but each division availed itself of soup houses, fuel societies, churches and municipal relief in getting help to those in need. The Germantown Relief Society became the first full-fledged society for organizing charity in America, bringing local charitable operations into unexpected unison and gaining the confidence of all denominations.

Boston, through its central registration of needy persons and families, took action to make relief more effective, and in 1875 established the Cooperative Society of Volunteer Visitors. The following year the Boston Registration Bureau was formed, the first real Social Service Exchange. Such Exchanges became valuable in promoting cooperation between social,

health, and recreation agencies and are still part of many Community Welfare Councils, though their popularity has waned in recent years.

Problems in New York were more complex and a Bureau of Charities which proposed to register persons receiving outdoor relief (administered in the recipient's home) was frustrated by the refusal of the largest relief-giving society in the city to cooperate.

Following the depression, industrialization grew and an old problem in new form began to spread. Because industry needed labor—cheap labor—the doors were opened and people streamed in from Europe. In 1880 half a million poured in; 25 years later the rate was one million per year.

"This rapid transfer of people from an older way of life to a new one caused problems in social adjustment of immense range and complexity. The attempts to solve these problems, through the advance of education and the application of scientific methods, formed the background for the development of many present-day social welfare services and philanthropies.

"During the last three decades of the Nineteenth Century the secular private welfare agencies began to avoid 'direct relief' cases, hopeless cases, and those requiring permanent institutional care; these they left for government agencies. The private agencies began rather to specialize in services for families and children." [5]

First American Charity Organization Society

With a great number of immigrants flocking into Buffalo, western terminus of the Erie Canal, the Rev. S. H. Gurteen, an Episcopalian, was distressed by the poverty and suffering he saw. After visiting England to study London's charity organization, he returned to draw up a plan for a Charity Organization Society which he succeeded in selling to the community. The new society was launched in 1877, administering no relief funds of its own, but investigating needs and referring cases to appropriate agencies. It pledged to recognize all forms of religious beliefs, political affiliations, nationalities and to be impartial—an indication of the greater liberality of religious thought then beginning to prevail. This Society was the first actual, communitywide body of its nature, and the similar societies which followed led 30 years later to all-inclusive community planning for community health and welfare services by Community Welfare Councils.

The Reverend S. Humphreys Gurteen, assistant rector of St. Paul's Cathedral was the Founder of the Charity Organization Society of Buffalo, the first of its kind to be established in the United States.

Poster by Urquhart Wilcox used in Buffalo in 1920 for the Joint Charities and Community Fund Campaign.

In Indianapolis a Congregational minister, the Rev. Oscar McCulloch, led in establishing the COS in 1879, and later advocated establishment of a "united treasury" to be set up on the basis of proven need by affiliated groups. His idea was not put into effect, though central housing was effected and telephonic communication arranged with all public institutions so that every case of need, begging, or accident could be reported to the central office. This arrangement shows the alertness of Indianapolis citizens, for it was just three years after Alexander Graham Bell's telephone was patented.

In the same year, 1879, in New York a "united treasure" was established, the country's first plan for joint money raising for hospitals. The organization flourished, and today is known as the United Hospital Fund.

By 1883, 25 cities had adopted the central principles of the charity organization movement: investigation of applicants, central registration, cooperation of all relief agencies, and the use of volunteer friendly visitors. By 1892, a total of 92 cities had COS agencies.

Within 10 years after Buffalo's COS was established in 1877 the waves of cooperative organization had swept as far across the country as the Rocky Mountains. In Denver something further was added to the cooperative theories and practices of the COS: that is, a United Appeal for Funds. Such an attempt had been made through the central collection plan in Liverpool; it had been proposed by the Rev. Mr. McCulloch of Indianapolis in 1879; it had been advocated by the Boston Associated Charities; it had been successful for the hospitals in New York City. Now Denver was to take another step.

NOTES

Chapter 2

1. Boris Bogan, *Jewish Philanthrophy,* N.Y., Macmillan Company, 1917, pp. 22-23.
2. Ephraim Frisch, *Historial Survey of Jewish Philanthrophy,* N.Y., Macmillan Company, 1924, pp. 21-23.
3. Russell H. Kurtz (ed.), *Social Work Year Book.* (Albany and New York; Boyd Printing Company, Inc. 1960, copyright by National Association of Social Workers) p. 25.
4. Amos G. Warner, Stuart Alfred Queen, and Ernest B. Harper, American Charities, fourth edition (New York; Thomas Y. Crowell Co. 1930) p. 204.
5. *Ibid.,* p. 16.

UNITED WAY PIONEERS: 1887-1917

Denver in 1887, having grown from less than 5,000 citizens in 1870 to 100,000, was enmeshed in a tangle of relief problems. As the Denver Community Chest later recalled in its Golden Anniversary program, "Many of its people were health seekers, some were wealth seekers who had lost their stake in search of gold and silver and a great many others were unemployed 'soldiers of fortune' who had come West because of the glamour that might be found. Denver was prosperous in many ways but these classes of people brought a serious charity and relief problem to the community." [1]

Recognizing their city's welfare problems and the need for cooperative action, four Denver clergymen got together to work out a plan for organization: Rev. Myron W. Reed, who had worked in Indianapolis with the Rev. McCulloch in establishing the COS; Msgr. William J. O'Ryan who had worked in England and was familiar with English fund-raising methods; Dean H. Martyn Hart of St. John's Episcopal Church, and Rabbi William S. Friedman.

Their activities and plans resulted in establishment of the Charity Organization Society, launched in 1887 at a public meeting of agency representatives and other interested persons. The Rev. Mr. Reed was elected president.

The new organization of 22 agencies had two functions and apparently two names, one official, the other unofficial. As the COS (the legal name) it coordinated relief services, counselled and referred clients to co-operating agencies, and made some emergency assistance grants in cases which could not be referred. In addition it served as agent in collecting funds for charities of a diverse nature, including itself. These fund-participating agencies were unofficially called Associated Charities, a name first used in 1879 by Boston for its local COS.

With the power structure of the city giving leadership and backing, the COS got off to a good start. Ten agencies participated in the first joint appeal, which raised $21,700 in November 1888. Of this, $17,880.03 went to the organizations, the balance to the COS for its expenses and emergency relief work.

Denver was aware, however, that more was involved in a united campaign than raising money. The first annual report said, "Your Executive Committee must not only be a means to the collection of a fund and disburse the same, but must also act in an advisory and supervisory direction in securing greater efficiency in the various societies; carefully examine the financial reports of the different institutions, prevent waste and extravagance; establish such particular branches of

Dean H. Martyn Hart, St. John's Episcopal Cathedral.

Monsignor William J. O'Ryan, St. Mary's Roman Catholic Cathedral.

The Reverend Myron Reed, First Congregational Church.

Rabbi William S. Friedman, Temple Emanuel.

Recognizing their community's health and welfare problems, and the need for cooperative action, these four Denver clergymen joined together to launch the first United Way at a public meeting in 1887.

22

charities as may from time to time become necessary and aid the growth of those now in existence; and on the whole give the public a better understanding of the entire charity dispensation in our city." [2]

This new federation was popular, active and influential. It persuaded the city council to construct a large hospital, secure the creation of the state department of charities, organized a state conference of charities, brought the annual meeting of the National Conference on Charities and Corrections to Denver in 1892 and secured needed legislation in both city and state.

The Federation continued to increase in favor and influence during its first five or six years. Then Congress demonetized silver and the panic of '93 followed. Banks and business houses failed on every hand. Probably this new experiment in joint financing would have collapsed had not the city fathers come to the rescue with substantial appropriations during those dark years. Even with this help the Society found increasing difficulty in meeting the growing needs of its agencies. Some of them withdrew; others put on strenuous individual efforts to raise funds. Federation officials became discouraged and on two occasions recommended that the organization be dissolved, but fifteen loyal agency members would not consent.

Despite the pioneering nature and initial success of the Denver plan, it had little effect on other communities. Later comment was critical of Denver's initial efforts toward central financing. When in 1924 the Chicago Council of Social Agencies considered some sort of Community Chest, a spokesman commented, "The (Denver) plan had its roots almost exclusively in a desire for economy and the saving of the giving public from annoyance. It did not sufficiently stress cooperation, community planning, and high standards of work." [3] Further judgment was added by William J. Norton, director of the Detroit Community Fund, in his book, *The Cooperative Movement in Social Work* published in 1927. "Although the Denver people were seeking a charity organization society, they visioned a financial federation at the same time; and the thing that they created was in part an association of agencies, in part an association of people interested in philanthropy, and in part a family welfare society . . . The plan lacked financial power, partly because of the time and the setting, partly because there was no driving responsibility, and partly because of the intimate association of the office with one of the major portions of the field of social work, family welfare and relief . . . Because of its financial weakness it did not correct duplication, at least in money raising, or lower

Surviving members of the founding Board of Directors of the first United Way campaign in Denver in 1887 are honored on the occasion of its 50th Anniversary by the Mile High United Way, Denver, 1937. (Left to right) Thomas B. Croke, William R. Howland, Mrs. A. L. Doud, A. L. Doud, Dr. Robert Levy, Mrs. L. E. Leman, Rabbi William S. Friedman, Mrs. Owen LeFevre and Monsignor William O'Ryan.

administrative costs, or command the necessary respect to enable it to steer the development of the field." [4]

While Denver was developing its pioneer plan for united financing, other social services throughout America were moving toward joint planning and financing of community health and welfare services. From 25 Charity Organization Societies in 1883 there were about 100 in 1895, most of them in the North. These societies became very influential in American social service and "developed in many . . . communities a kind of 'overlordship of charity.' The dominating position which they came to occupy came from the fact that the business community frequently turned to such organizations for protection from imposters. It was a natural step for them to add supervisory powers which were to eventuate into the work of charities endorsement." [5]

The depression of 1873-80 had impressed upon many the need for cooperation in relief measures. Charity Organization Societies had helped substantially in raising relief funds and directing their distribution. While soup kitchens and bread lines were to be found in many communities, more constructive measures were also being taken. Even while the depression was at its height, thoughtful social workers were pressing for more cooperation in social service.

Surplus wealth from industrial and business expansion following the depression added to charitable funds. But while benevolence was increasing, so were needs. Industrialization reached a high point and there were myriad problems of child labor, employment of women, low wages, long working hours, bad and crowded housing, poor sanitation, tuberculosis, delinquency, crime and other social ills. Many voices were raised for reform and social justice. Prevention as well as treatment of human ills became the purpose of many health and welfare organizations.

Reform was not to take place overnight, however. A long tradition of harshness, the prevailing theory of laissez-faire, fear that aid would encourage laziness, and widespread misunderstanding ruled against rapid change. Pauperism was considered a character defect, hereditary and probably due to intemperance. Almshouses were deliberately kept undesirable in order to discourage people from seeking admission. There was great need for consolidation of charitable efforts.

At the annual meeting of the National Conference on Charities and Corrections in 1893, Charles D. Kellogg, chairman of the Section on Charity Organization,

pointed out, "Cooperation is one of the most difficult (goals) of attainment . . . In some cities there exists a distinct hostility in the older charity societies to charity organization. They resent the implication that their work may need a mending or they are unwilling to submit to any outside judgment." [6]

While national conferences had begun in 1874 with the Conference of Boards of Public Charities, regional and state conferences now were being organized. The first State Conference of Charities and Correction was held in Wisconsin in 1881. At the same time national health and welfare agencies were being established: the Young Men's Christian Association in 1854, American Red Cross in 1881 and others. Between 1870 and 1919 a total of 97 national voluntary welfare agencies were organized. A handbook published in 1892 for the Illinois Conference of Charities and Correction listed 450 charitable societies and state institutions.

Social settlements were coming into prominence, adding to the American scene the concept of living among those to be helped. Jane Addams founded her famous Hull House in Chicago in 1889, three years after Neighborhood Guild, the first, was established in New York.

In 1893 the International Congress of Charities, Correction and Philanthropy was held in Chicago during the World's Fair, bringing delegates from all over the civilized world. One of the speakers was Francis G. Peabody of Boston who had made a study of English social service. He spoke on the value of the Liverpool plan for joint fund raising. "Scattered and disconnected organizations are enormously extravagant. There is more than one institution today in most of our cities calling itself a charity where at least half of the total income goes to support the person who collects the funds . . . Still further, this very multiplicity of demands makes many persons shrink altogether from their duty. They are never safe from these irregular appeals, their giving becomes unsystematic and spasmodic, and finally they begin to harden their hearts to the whole subject." [7] He then recommended inauguration of joint financing plans in America.

Until this time agency campaigns had been long, drawn-out affairs, but in 1893 the Omaha, Nebraska YMCA used a short-term campaign for new members, and the YMCA in New Westminster, British Columbia obtained pledges for $6,000 in two weeks. From 1902 to 1904 the Washington, D.C. YMCA raised $200,000, the last $85,000 in a short time. These successful plans were later adopted by many Community Chests and United Funds.

Charitable institutions were given a great boost in 1894 and an important precedent was set when they were exempted from the first federal act imposing a tax on "all corporations organized for profit." The exemptions for charitable, religious, and educational organizations have been continued in every subsequent Federal Income Tax Law. By 1894, similar exemptions were well established in the property tax laws of the various states, the origin of such exemptions dating back to medieval days.

In several cities, Jewish agencies formed their own independent federations, starting with Boston in 1895, and followed by Cincinnati, Chicago, Philadelphia, Cleveland, St. Louis, Kansas City, Detroit, Denver, New York, Baltimore, San Francisco, Los Angeles and Pittsburgh. Reasons for this early recognition of federation's advantages by Jewish organizations included the compactness and mutual concern of the Jewish com-

TAG DAY in Minneapolis. Volunteer fund raisers for the Visiting Nurse Association "tag" a contributor before the organization of the first United Way campaign in 1918.

munity, and the rapid increase in Jewish immigration following Russia's persecutions. Then "the simple, leisurely pace of helping an occasional immigrant could not be maintained . . . Some farsighted leaders and generous contributors . . . (decided) to bring together the various agencies engaged in separate fund raising and to concentrate on a single annual, combined subscription appeal." [8]

The Twentieth Century Begins

The Twentieth Century opened with increasing material progress and wealth, but intensified social problems as well. There was no minimum age for child labor, no regulation of hours and wages, few standards of safety for workers. Efforts of social reformers were concentrated on easing hardships rather than changing the basic social structure.

An awakening of social conscience was at hand, however, resulting in a rise in social movements and a tremendous multiplication of social agencies. Opposition continued to governmental assumption of responsibility for welfare programs even though "in 1898 the United States Supreme Court, reflecting the rising liberal trend, affirmed that it was the duty of the state to protect the health and morals of its citizens through its police power, thus making it constitutional to limit the hours of labor in dangerous occupations." [9]

The vast number and diversity of appeals brought about a new system for protecting the contributor. In 1900 the Cleveland Chamber of Commerce formed a Committee on Benevolent Associations, followed in 1902 by San Francisco and soon thereafter by New York City. Standards were established such as: limiting solicitors' fees to 15 percent; requiring solicitors to show identification cards and give receipts; and forbidding charities from lending their names to benefit entertainments. In New York contributors were furnished a complete confidential report without endorsement or recommendation.

Foundations were organized in great numbers after the turn of the century as men of great wealth recognized the opportunity for providing social services not likely to be supported by either government or private individuals. The thought was that such funds would be the venture capital of philanthropy. They were bold enterprises, dedicated not to direct relief but to the advancement of knowledge and human welfare. Their great weapon against human misery was research, and their purposes included prevention and discovery. Between 1901 and 1913 the following, among others, were established: Rockefeller Institute for Medical Research, Carnegie Foundation, Milbank Memorial Fund, Russell Sage Foundation, Carnegie Corporation, and Rockefeller Foundation. A directory of charities published in Chicago in 1905 listed 3,000 agencies, including churches, and carried an epitome of laws affecting health and welfare.

Cooperation among agencies continued to be a major concern of the 143 Community Organization Societies then in existence, focusing, as Miss Mary E. Richmond of the Philadelphia COS explained, on "the restoration of poor families." Today the emphasis is on the well-being of the entire community and overall planning. Feeling a need to exchange information with other professionals, several COS secretaries attending the 1905 National Conference of Charities and Correction annual meeting in Portland, Oregon agreed to exchange form letters and printed matter each month through a central agency.

At the 1907 annual meeting of the National Conference in Minneapolis, 10 of the 16 secretaries belonging to the COS Exchange decided to employ a field secretary and undertake work on a national scale. Francis H. McLean, Superintendent of the Brooklyn Bureau of Charities, was hired for the job. The Russell Sage Foundation made a one-year grant of $7,500 and the new department went to work with Miss Richmond as Chairman.

At the 1906 annual meeting of the National Conference Dr. Walter S. Ufford, general secretary of The Baltimore Federated Charities asked, "Do we not need a financial clearinghouse to assume responsibility for the support of our local charities? Let there be in every city and town a representative body or committee to review annually the charitable needs of the community. Let this committee receive and act upon all separate budgets of existing charitable agencies. Let it issue an annual appeal . . . Let the committee's campaign be an educational one . . . Let this committee also pass upon the merit of existing charitable agencies, seeking to coordinate their work, to reduce duplication . . . Here is a chance for some bold spirit to make history, for the rest of us to follow or to avoid." [10]

In five years such bold action was to be taken and history to be made. But it was preceded by bold action in joint planning.

America's First Council

Pittsburgh is generally held to have organized America's first Council of Social Agencies in 1908, action brought about as the result of a survey after the industrial depression of 1907 by the new Russell Sage Foundation.

When Russell Sage, an American financier, died in 1906 he left nearly all of his $65 million fortune to his wife. One of her earliest gifts was that of $10 million for the establishment of the Russell Sage Foundation for "the improvement of social and living conditions in the United States of America." The Foundation was incorporated in 1907 and one of its first projects was the Pittsburgh survey which was "expected to be not merely research but 'an object lesson not only to the city of Pittsburgh itself but to American industrial cities of which it is a type.'" [11]

Conducted by Francis H. McLean, the survey had an explosive impact on the economic and social structure of the city. "The survey shocked the community out of any complacency it might have had by its description of the deplorable conditions found among the less privileged residents." [12] It told of poor working and living conditions and revealed that social agencies were duplicating services to a shocking extent. At this time Pittsburgh had a myriad of agencies but alone among large cities had no COS.

As a result of Mr. McLean's report and recommendations, Associated Charities of Pittsburgh was established in 1908, largely through the efforts of the Civic Club of Pittsburgh. It was an association of charities which appointed delegates to a central council. Purposes were to form a social service exchange, conduct monthly meetings, hold conferences on case problems and in other ways develop cooperation. It was intended as a general relief organization, but tried to enlist material relief from other agencies where needed.

All did not go well at first. Some of the agencies to be coordinated objected and an investigation was launched by the Chamber of Commerce. A committee of the Chamber gave Associated Charities a clean bill of health and also gave the premise on which it was founded an enthusiastic endorsement.

In 1909 the nation's second joint planning body for community health and welfare services was organized in Milwaukee, Wisconsin and another in Elmira, New York where agencies were housed under one roof and supported by one annual campaign conducted by the Women's Federation.

Formation of Milwaukee's Council of Social Agencies also followed a study by Francis McLean of the Russell Sage Foundation. It consolidated the efforts of 36 local organizations. In its first four years the Council counted among its achievements: appointment of a County probation officer, development of social centers, establishment of standards for relief, breaking up a notorious baby farm, passage of a law limiting night messengers to men over 21, installation of social workers in hospitals and the Juvenile Court, and efforts toward laws requiring licensing of child placing organizations.

At the 1909 meeting of the National Conference on Charities and Corrections the 23 COS organizations which had been exchanging information monthly selected a committee to establish a national organization. This was accomplished in 1911 when the National Association of Societies for Organizing Charity was formed, with 60 of the 129 Charity Organization Societies joining. It assumed the duties of extension work, while the COS Department of the Russell Sage Foundation retained the tasks of research, publishing a journal and offering a short course for training COS workers. In 1911 Francis McLean became general secretary of the new organization, which continues today, through several name changes, as Family Service Association of America. It is now a federation of more than 300 local Family Service Agencies, providing field service information, conducting research and publishing topical materials and reports.

President Theodore Roosevelt called the first White House Conference on the Care of Dependent Children in January, 1909. It had a tremendous effect on improving standards of child care, including establishment of the Federal Children's Bureau in 1912. Proceedings of the Conference pointed out the necessity for overall planning and cooperation. "The most important and valuable philanthropic work is not the curative but the preventive . . . To secure these ends we urge efficient cooperation with all agencies for social betterment." [13]

In Columbus, Ohio in the fall of 1910 a Council was formed, growing out of Associated Charities which had been established in 1899 to prevent overlapping of services and mutiplicity of solicitations. Associated Charities actually served as a community planning group, becoming more and more involved in family

service. During the depression of 1908 unemployment was so great that Associated Charities launched a one-day campaign for funds to pay the unemployed to clean city streets. A team of women in one day raised $9,359.92 with which a dispensary was established. Provisions, coal and clothing were given to the unemployed in payment for work on the streets at the rate of 15 cents per hour, probably the first citywide "work relief" program.

In 1910, Francis McLean, still working as field secretary for the national Exchange, wrote a booklet in which he warned of the danger when churches or charities took the initiative in Council formation because of consequent limiting of scope. He urged that Councils be representative of the entire community and warned that they might not succeed in communities with antagonisms and jealousies among agencies. [14]

Some communities organized informal groups called Social Workers' Clubs, several of which actively promoted central Councils and later financial federations and Community Chests. One such group was in St. Louis, Missouri, organized in 1907. It studied the problems of overlapping and duplicating services. A committee was named and came up with resolutions to form a Central Council, initiate more complete registration of cases, and organize a charities committee of the Businessmen's League to supply contributor information and endorse approved appeals. For the first 10 years the Central Council operated on a small budget, but as work increased pressure built up in favor of hiring a full-time Council secretary. In 1921 Elwood Street, who had been with the Louisville Welfare League (now Community Chest), was hired as Executive Secretary and that fall the organization name was changed to the St. Louis Community Council. A year later the Community Fund was formed.

In all these early ventures into joint planning the idea of central registration of clients was important. The Russell Sage Foundation in 1912 published a pamphlet containing recommended standards and administrative practices for such bureaus.

Joint financing was also becoming a matter of growing interest. In Cleveland a special committee of the Chamber of Commerce made studies and reports which would lead to the establishment of the first modern Community Chest in 1913. Hearing of this, Chamber leaders in San Antonio went ahead and organized a federation without waiting to see how Cleveland organized and put its plan into operation. This organization never really functioned and soon disbanded for lack of support. This failure was explained in 1913 at the National Conference on Charities and Corrections by J. J. O'Connor, secretary of Associated Charities in Minneapolis. He said the abortive attempt was made "by a body of businessmen who seem to have been ignorant of both the needs of social service and of the proper methods to accomplish their own aims. . . . A Chamber of Commerce can very well initiate a Federation of Social Agencies, but no greater blunder can by any chance be made than to have such a body dictate completely the control of the Federation after its creation." He also had this advice to offer: "It is not enough for social agencies to refrain from saying disagreeable things about each other . . . (There is) present pressing and quickly increasing need for some coordinator of social service activities, some eliminator of social service waste, some developer of effective charity, some corrector of defective charity, some methods of making eccentric charity concentric." [15] Mr. O'Connor made an effective plea for organizing central Councils of Social Agencies and was careful to deny that it should have any part in central financing.

The First Modern Community Chest

Growing out of ideas that had been germinating for a long time, the first true financial federation was organized in Cleveland in 1913. As far back as 1873 there had been concern over the haphazard pattern of charitable giving, and the influential Cleveland and Bethel Relief Association had recommended that there should be only one organization or channel in the city for investigation and distribution.

Several years of organization work followed and a plan developed by 1881, a plan that might have worked but for indifference and lack of full representation. Thus the Council never functioned as an instrument of cooperation in the way its founders had intended. In many communities during subsequent years it was to become a known fact that it is easier to get names than active participants in joint planning.

Crises have often brought important changes. So too in Cleveland where hard times had hit in 1883-84 and throngs of applicants sought work and relief. Public pressure for consolidation built up and in 1884 the COS and Bethel Associated Charities consolidated, the union becoming permanent in 1886 when the idea of the innocuous Central Council was abandoned. Repre-

sentatives from other agencies were added and began making reports on their work at BAC annual meetings. An annual conference of Cleveland Charities was instituted. In 1900 BAC voted to incorporate and change its name to the Cleveland Associated Charities. Among those joining and working actively with the new association was the Chamber of Commerce.

By 1906 the Chamber committee had begun to think about the possibility of financial federation, but a subcommittee concluded that contributors would be entirely unwilling to relinquish their vested interests in their various "pet" institutions and substitute an impersonal participation in support of all agencies.

Still, the idea did not die and the following year another subcommittee had recommended organization of financial federation. This committee's study made it shockingly clear that the giving public had little interest in or understanding of the broad needs of charity and supported it unevenly. Backed by strong contributor endorsement, the committee started plans for a federated campaign, but then depression hit the city and the idea was postponed until 1908.

New studies, continuing into 1909, showed that budgets had increased while the number of contributors decreased. Not only this but there was great disparity in development of agencies. "It is apparent," read a report in 1910, "that unless some equitable force is brought into play properly to distribute charitable funds, it will be only a question of time when many institutions doing reliable and efficient work will be in a state of bankruptcy, while others will be laying up a surplus and enlarging their work along lines not warranted." [16]

The report went on to explain at length the pros and cons of federation, citing the successful experience of Jewish Federations in various cities, and listing safeguards against undue influence or dictatorial control. It concluded with recommendations for establishing a Federation.

Further consideration was given when the committee called on larger givers to secure their commitment if possible. Among these were Samuel Mather, capitalist and philanthropist, and John D. Rockefeller of Standard Oil fame. Both men warmly approved.

Finally, in 1911 the Chamber's Board of Directors gave a tentative "go ahead" to the committee which set out on a hunt for a qualified executive secretary.

"Hop Right In, Sis. I'm Goin' Your Way."
—Cartoon by Donahey,

**One of the most effective bits of publicity in behalf of
The Cleveland Federation for Charity and Philanthrophy, 1913.**

*This cartoon by Donahey in support of the first United Way
campaign in Cleveland in 1913.*

It was no easy task, and it was not until November 1912 that Charles Whiting Williams, who had been assistant to the president of Oberlin College, began work in this capacity. Organization proceeded rapidly with a Board of Directors composed of 10 persons elected by member organizations, 10 by contributors, and 10 appointed by the president. No paid employee of constituent organizations was eligible for board membership.

An "open door" policy for agency membership was clearly stated; designated gifts were recognized; agencies were free to solicit donations from persons who had not contributed through the Federation; benefit bazaars, balls, and other entertainments were eliminated; and member agencies were required to present reports on activities to the board and open their books to it.

In presenting the plan to Chamber members, Chairman Martin A. Marks, prominent in Jewish charities, said, "The proposals put before you seem to the Committee not only reasonable but positively inevitable if the problem of philanthropy in Cleveland is to be solved. The plan proposed differs in essential points from any devised or practiced in any other city. It is not a federation of institutions alone as in Denver, not of givers alone, nor of both together. It is a federation for the advancing of charity and philanthropy, of institutions, of givers and of citizens. It does not intend to be a mere collecting agency, as is the Liverpool project. It will hope to produce its results in the way of a wiser distribution mainly through a better-educated giver rather than through its own action. It does not, furthermore, plan to do away with the financial activities of the various constituent organizations, but to direct these activities toward the non-giver.

"For the institution, for the donor and for the citizen, the plan is proposed. For the institution, it should mean a larger life because of more money and because of broader, deeper public interest. For the donor, it should mean broader social knowledge and larger satisfaction, without the pleasure of one gift being spoiled by the unhappiness of ten refusals. For the citizen, it should mean a better Cleveland." [17]

On March 1, 1913 the nation's first modern Community Chest came into being, and its first board meeting was held. Reported the *Cleveland Plain Dealer:* "Twenty thousand donors to charity within the next two years is the slogan of the board of the Cleveland Federation of Charity and Philanthropy, which met Saturday and completed its organization . . . A meeting of the executive committee will be held at the Chamber of Commerce tomorrow afternoon to arrange for reaching the donors, now numbering 6,000 . . . 'The eyes of the universe are on Cleveland,' declared Clinton Rogers Woodruff, secretary of the National Municipal League, in speaking of the work undertaken by the Federation, which is the first of its kind in the country." [18]

Cleveland avoided two mistakes made in Denver, recognizing the necessity for an able staff and the need for a steady campaign of public education and interpretation. A speaker's bureau was formed. Much resistance was avoided by letting contributors designate gifts if they wished. Prestige was enhanced by a feature story in the Sunday *New York Times* of April 6, 1913 in which the Federation's advantages were emphasized, particularly research and statistics.

Membership was limited to organizations receiving endorsement from the Chamber of Commerce, with each agency free to decide whether or not to accept the invitation. A total of 53 joined during the first year, representing a wide range of Cleveland interests.

The first United Campaign had no goal. The aim was to get as many contributors, old and new, as possible and to obtain larger gifts if possible.

Despite all the advance preparation and interpretation, financing during the first seven-month year was touch and go. A variety of agency fiscal years, past inadequacies of their financing, slowness in setting up money-raising procedures, and increased budgets reflecting high hopes, all contributed to financial uncertainty. Yet at the close of the fiscal year on September 30, Whiting Williams reported that the Federation had provided nearly one third of the agencies' receipts, and that there was a net improvement of $33,715 for the agencies. Fund-raising costs were but 10.17% of the money handled despite initial expenses, compared to 25% or more before federation.

One of the problems the Federation soon turned to was that of rigidly limited bequests and endowments that had outlived the human needs of their original times. The dilemma was described by Whiting Williams in a *Saturday Evening Post* article.[19] He envisioned establishment of an endowment fund within the Federation and accordingly a Committee on Bequests was set up. On January 2, 1914 the Cleveland Trust Company announced establishment of the Cleveland Foundation for the same general purpose.

This Foundation, the nation's first Community Trust, was administered by the Cleveland Trust Company with a distribution committee composed of five citizens selecting the organizational beneficiaries. In succeeding years, many other Community Trusts were organized in the United States and Canada. Today there are over 250.

Another problem facing the Federation centered around agency executives, who felt they did not have enough influence in the Federation's social decisions, and thought the Federation was too concerned with money raising. Then, when Mayor Newton D. Baker established a Department of Public Welfare in 1914 and invited creation of a citizen group to advise the Department, the Welfare Council was organized. Representation included practically all local organizations, plus representatives from the Federation and Department of Public Welfare. The Council soon achieved a "functional" committee structure typical of Councils of Social Agencies in other communities. One of the Council's first activities was to join with the City Council in asking the Cleveland Foundation to study relief agencies. Results of this study included complete reorganization of relief activities.

An active public relations program was launched by the Federation and a house organ called the *Social Bulletin* was published, starting in 1914, with the purpose "to make benevolence interesting." Weekly posters were distributed, and when President Martin A

(Left) Newton D. Baker, World War I Secretary of War and a founder of the Cleveland United Way campaign (in 1913), was instrumental in formation of the United War Work Campaign for seven charitable agencies which raised $205 million in 1918.

Marks gave his annual report to the Chamber of Commerce, a feature was the use of a "talking motion picture" with Andrew Carnegie speaking on "The Duties of the Man of Wealth." The film was coordinated with a record of his talk. This apparently was the first use of a talking motion picture by a social agency.

When the "guns of August" boomed out in Europe in 1914, Cleveland immediately felt the impact of World War I. Depression and unemployment hit, but somehow the Federation and its agencies staggered through the year. In September at the end of the Federation's first full fiscal year, Executive Secretary Williams reported 3,000 new givers with an increase of $104,695 in contributions. In 1916 business boomed, agency budgets increased, and again the campaign results were up—by 33 percent.

The Federation's *Social Year Book,* published in December 1916, revealed that the Federation would henceforth correlate all welfare work in Cleveland. Its charter was modified and changes made to enable it to perform the larger function of an active clearinghouse for both public and private welfare work. The new Welfare Council would have representation from the Welfare Department and the Federation plus other organizations such as Chamber of Commerce, Federation of Labor, Board of Education and others. This new plan was similar to that of Cincinnati where the Council of Social Agencies was organized on a widely representative basis in 1913, and of Milwaukee where joint financing became a function of joint planning.

Both these cities had adopted centralized budget plans.

Whiting Williams resigned on January 1, 1917 after the Federation had successfully demonstrated that joint financing of community health and welfare services could be done, and that joint planning must go hand-in-hand with joint financing. At this time the Welfare Council merged with the Federation. The new organization name became the Cleveland Welfare Federation.

Twenty-five years later, Allen T. Burns, executive director of the National Association of Community Chests and Councils, former director of the Cleveland Foundation and witness of the early Federation organization, looked back and observed, "This quest for a balanced ration of welfare services, this endeavor to see the problem whole, has become accepted as a necessary foundation for modern Chest Policy. But the Cleveland Federation ventured into unproved ground in believing that givers would welcome such a unified, systematized service and finance program." [20]

Harry Wareham, (on phone at upper right desk) Manager of the Community and War Chest of Rochester, N.Y., working with staff and volunteer leaders (standing upper left) during this United Way's first campaign in the spring of 1918.

NOTES

Chapter 3

1. Allen D. Breck, Chairman, Department of History, University of Denver, letter to Kenneth W. Miller, Exec. Dir., Mile High United Fund, May 28, 1962.

2. Guy T. Justis, "After Fifty Years, Denver Looks at Federated Financing," *News Bulletin,* CCC, September 1937.

3. *The Financing of Social Agencies,* a Fact-Finding Report, Chicago Council of Social Agencies, 1924, p. 113.

4. William J. Norton, *The Cooperative Movement in Social Work* (New York: The MacMillan Company, 1927), p. 135.

5. Frank D. Watson, *The Charity Organization Movement in the United States* (New York: The MacMillan Company, 1922), p. 222.

6. Charles D. Kellogg, "Report of the Committee on History of Charity Organization," *Proceedings, National Conference of Charities and Corrections,* 1893, pp. 72-74.

7. Francis G. Peabody, "The Problem of Charity," *The Charities Review* (Vol. III, No. 1, November 1893), pp. 10-12.

8. Max Herxberg, Presidential Address, 1904 National Conference of Jewish Charities, as quoted in Harry F. Lurie, *The Heritage Affirmed: The Jewish Federation Movement in America* (Philadelphia: The Jewish Publication Society of America, 1961), pp. 47-52.

9. See note 3 (referred to in *Chapter I*), p. 33.

10. Francis H. McLean, *The Family,* Vol. XXVII, No. 1, March 1946, Introduction, p. 3.

11. John M. Glenn, Lillian Brandt, and F. Emerson Andrews, *Russell Sage Foundation, 1907-1946* (New York: Russell Sage Foundation, 1947), pp. 3, 11, 12, 34.

12. *Two Hundred Years of Health and Welfare Planning and Coordination,* Health and Welfare Assn. of Allegheny County, September 1959.

13. *Proceedings of the Conference on the Care of Dependent Children* (Washington, D.C.: Government Printing Office, 1909), p. 14.

14. See note 10, pp. 12, 28-29.

15. J. J. O'Connor, "Cooperation Between Agencies," *Proceedings, National Conference of Charities and Corrections,* 1913, pp. 340-344.

16. *The Cleveland Federation for Charity and Philanthropy,* as proposed by the Committee on Benevolent Associations of the Cleveland Chamber of Commerce, January 7, 1913, a booklet by the Chamber, pp. 8-27.

17. Martin A. Marks, "The Cleveland Federation for Charity and Philanthropy," comments on the Report of the Cleveland Chamber of Commerce, presented at a membership meeting, January 7, 1913.

18. *The Cleveland Plain Dealer,* March 2, 1913.

19. *Saturday Evening Post,* December 20, 1913, pp. 17, 18, 31-34.

20. Allen T. Burns, "25 Years of Chests and Councils," *The Survey Mid-monthly,* April 1938.

THE WAR CHESTS: 1913-1918

While Cleveland was making its pioneer demonstration in financial federation, Cincinnati was organizing a Council of Social Agencies. As far back as the nineties, Cincinnati had experienced a quickening interest in social work. Its Federation of Jewish Charities was organized in 1896; its Associated Charities became a repository of information regarding community agencies; a Business Man's Advisory Committee had been organized to investigate any proposed new piece of social work and explore the possibilities for financing such work; and it had organized the Monday Evening Club of social workers, clergymen, educators, and other interested citizens. In 1909 the Monday Evening Club developed into the Social Workers Club, representing 104 agencies and groups of all kinds. By 1911 the conviction had grown that discussing problems was not enough, that there was need for a federation of social agencies strong enough to act. A committee, chaired by the Rev. Samuel Tyler, was organized to formulate a plan for organization, and a Conference of Charities and Philanthropies was proposed.

The idea lay practically dormant for two years, though the Bureau of Municipal Research was persuaded to organize a department for the study of social work in Cincinnati. William J. Norton, a long-time social work leader in Cleveland, was called to Cincinnati to head the survey. This study revealed more than 100 agencies conducting separate, competing campaigns for money, with fund-raising costs ranging from 15 to 60 percent; showed that child care was almost wholly institutional; that relief rather than reconstruction was the main concern of organizations; that there was practically no provision for training the handicapped; and no unified health program.

In the spring of 1913, the Miami Valley Flood hit the area, creating a great emergency that underlined the need for cooperation, as the Norton report had stressed. A Citizens Flood Committee saw the community through the acute emergency, raising funds for flood victims. But it had to admit that it did not have the information or knowledge of relief methods to spend the funds efficiently and wisely, and therefore recommended that funds be immediately supplied to an organization composed of representatives of all philanthropic and charitable agencies in Cincinnati.

The Conference of Charities and Philanthropy met the next day, voted to reorganize, changed its name to the Council of Social Agencies, and assumed responsibility not only for immediate needs but for subsequent reconstruction of social work in Cincinnati. Mr. Norton became director and thus the Cincinnati Council became the first to have a full-time, paid professional executive.

The Council took over the Confidential Exchange which had been serving Associated Charities agencies only, and created a Bureau of Endorsement for all agencies soliciting funds. With an immediate need for money, the Council decided to restrict its budget to absolute necessities and to approach only a dozen or so large contributors until it could demonstrate the need for its services.

Always in the minds of Council leaders was the conviction that joint fund raising was needed to support the agencies. In December 1914, pressed by rising unemployment which hit many cities at the outbreak of war, the Council resolved to enlarge its work to the point of federating the organized philanthropies of Cincinnati.

There was one significant difference between the Cincinnati and Cleveland plans for joint financing. While Cleveland had started with a givers' study (the business men's concern), Cincinnati started with budgeting the amounts needed (the social workers' concern), and viewed financing as one of many aspects of joint planning.

In March 1915 the Council voted for action and set up a campaign and budget committee. From the start the Budget Committee permitted givers to designate funds, believing that designated gifts were less mechanical, that they encouraged live and intelligent interest, revealed attitudes of the giving public, and gave assurance that contributions would go where the givers wanted. It was also felt that proper use of the designation sheet would have educational value and be effective in securing increased contributions. This plan worked well in Cincinnati, though later Community Chests and United Funds did not stress it, primarily because of the needs of "unglamorous" agencies whose programs, though not easily dramatized, were just as important. The right of designation continues as an option in the majority of campaigns even today.

The first campaign was held in May, 1915, with 12 participating agencies. It was the first of the federated whirlwind campaigns, following the successful experience of the YMCA with such brief, concentrated drives. It contained in embryo almost every feature of today's United Fund campaigns: campaign headquarters, advance solicitation of larger givers, solicitation by teams, and regular report meetings. The campaign raised $46,286, a six-month budget for the agencies, and obtained 457 new givers.

At the close of the campaign C. M. Bookman, who had served as a volunteer assistant, was named assistant director. When Norton resigned in 1917, Bookman took over the director's reins. A second campaign was held in November, raising $124,000 for the full year of 1916. The following campaign raised $215,000 for use in 1917, with contributors increasing from 3,900 to 10,500.

By 1915 the full force of war in Europe was making itself felt in every phase of American life. A burden of service was laid upon the social work of the city. Endorsement of the many campaigns was then divided up, with the War Council considering patriotic drives, the Council of Social Agencies, those for social service, and the Federation of Churches considering all Protestant projects. The Council of Social Agencies placed all its equipment and personnel at the service of the Social Service Committee of the Cincinnati War Council and the Confidential Exchange was enlarged so as to include war relief cases.

This first "Community Chest" poster for Cincinnati in 1920 marked that city's adoption of that name for its United Way campaigns which had been conducted since 1915.

The Miami Valley Flood of 1913 had hit neighboring Dayton as well, similarly inspiring a spirit of community cooperation which resulted in a flood control system, the beginnings of a progressive and liberal Chamber of Commerce, the Greater Dayton Association, and the drawing together of religious groups and social agencies.

Possibilities of joint financing were studied by the Greater Dayton Association, and in 1914 the Dayton Federation for Charity and Philanthropy was organized "to make charitable giving more systematic and intelligent, more effective and more pleasurable by cooperation in benevolence." In the first campaign the number of donors increased from about 500 to 1,162 and in the second, to 1,599. Since Dayton's joint financial campaign got under way a year before its big neighbor, Cincinnati, it is credited with producing the second modern Community Chest.

Another Federation for Charity and Philanthropy appeared in 1914, though it was actually only a new label for the country's first experiment in joint financing, the Denver Charity Organization, organized in 1887. For 25 years this organization had found the going very rough, with unsuccessful fund-raising campaigns, dissatisfied agencies, and little public confidence. According to Guy T. Justis, who became its director in 1917, the Denver Federation had three serious weaknesses: it was prematurely born, before sound fund-raising techniques had been developed; it did not have a plan for budgeting or allocating funds; and it did not have paid staff. In 1917 $56,250 was raised on a $75,000 goal. In 1918 with the country at war and citizens primarily interested in war appeals, $76,000 was raised and each year thereafter both the number of givers and amount raised were increased.

In October 1914 South Bend, Indiana had organized a financial federation, the Federation for Social Service, sponsored by the Chamber of Commerce. During the same year London, Ontario organized the first Canadian Federation and another was attempted in Salt Lake City but did not long survive. It had tried planning by agencies alone and fund raising by business interests only. Both failed. Baltimore in 1915 became the first metropolitan area in the East to organize a Federation, and it did well until the war came. The Cleveland plan was followed by Erie, Pennsylvania in 1915 and other federations were formed that year in Oshkosh, Wisconsin; Richmond, Indiana; and St. Joseph, Missouri. All have continued to the present day. Two large Southern cities, New Orleans and Birmingham, tried Federation but failed apparently because of misunderstanding among church-sponsored agencies of the Federation as an avowed "non-sectarian" organization. Some felt excluded, not realizing that agencies were excluded not because of name of creed, but only on the basis of acceptable services.

Birmingham's attempt at Federation was "doomed from the beginning," it was later explained by William C. White, president of the Milwaukee Centralized Budget of Philanthropy, "for the reason that it attempted to unite dissimilar or rival organizations without first having eliminated the dissension between them." [1]

Houston's financial federation was organized in 1916 and soon abandoned, only to be revived in later years. Dallas organized a small federation and named it the Welfare Council. Milwaukee formed a financial federation as part of the Central Council of Social Agencies, and Minneapolis followed suit the next year. Two main purposes were to protect the community from exploitation by fraudulent or unworthy charities, and to help agencies provide better services and more coordinated action. Deciding that the latter function could best be provided by a separate organization, Minneapolis then organized a Council of Social Agencies.

Growth of Planning Organizations

The Minneapolis Council stands as an example of the slow but steady trend toward joint planning which was then taking place in many larger cities. Speaking at the annual meeting of the National Conference on Charities and Corrections in 1916, Otto W. Davis, secretary of the Minneapolis Council, stressed the role of the Chamber's Endorsement Committee, but pointed out that the endorsement role was distinct from that of the central Council in determining standards and matters of policy.

At the same conference, C. M. Hubbard, one of the promoters of the St. Louis Central Council of Social Agencies formed in 1911, said, "Central Councils of Social Agencies are, by nature of their organization, the local agencies for the formulation of standards.

"Several reasons why standardization has not been attempted have been given by different Councils . . . It is feared that some societies would withdraw their membership in the Councils if an attempt should be made to interfere with the way they do their work. It would be embarrassing for social workers to act as critics of their fellow workers. There is a feeling that

Hamilton, Ohio held its first United Way campaign in 1918. Two years later it used this campaign poster.

not much would be gained by formulating standards as there would be no power to enforce them . . . The St. Louis Central Council seems to be the only one that has set itself directly to the task of formulating standards." [2]

The St. Louis plan featured detailed questionnaires, tabulation of replies, formulation of tentative standards by each group, discussion and revision, and finally more discussion and revision by the Executive Committee. "This plan has several good features," Mr. Hubbard continued, "The filling out of the questionnaire leads to searching self-criticism. The group discussion of proposed standards has the highest educational value. And when standards are finally adopted under such a plan each society feels that it has a part in their formulation. They will not come to it as a law imposed by some alien and unsympathetic authority." [3] In obtaining compliance with the standards, the Council had the backing of the Business Men's League, the local endorsing agency, which agreed not to endorse campaigns by societies with unapproved standards.

Almost unnoticed at the 1916 annual meeting of the National Conference was the seed being planted for organization of a national body that would eventually have tremendous influence in development of joint planning and financing, the group known today as United Way of America. William J. Norton and C. M. Bookman invited anyone interested in federated financing to get together to exchange ideas and consider organization. Only seven showed up, but this small group decided to hold additional information meetings from time to time, and Norton was elected convenor.

1917

Important developments were taking place in local communities. After several years of discussion, Chicago organized a Central Council of Social Agencies in 1917, to be a medium through which the social service forces of the community could be marshalled for the most effective service. It was supported by nominal membership fees from organization members and by contributions from understanding men and women. There was no paid director and it was not until 1933 that Chicago moved into a modified form of financial federation.

Five other cities did begin financial federations that year however: Grand Rapids, Mich.; Louisville, Ky.; Elyria, Ohio; Mt. Vernon, N.Y.; and Des Moines, Iowa.

Late in 1917 Louisville became the first community south of the Mason-Dixon Line to establish a full-fledged, continuing Federation of Social Agencies. Fifty thousand recruits were training for the Army at nearby Camps Knox and Taylor, and the city was flooded with trainees seeking recreation. Community leaders sought to provide for their needs, and thus embarked on studies of the city's total welfare needs and engaged in social planning.

During the 1917 annual meeting of the National Conference of Social Work, a second attempt was made to create a national organization for mutual exchange of information on federated financing. There was much argument about financial federations at this conference, with COS executives tending to look down their noses at the idea. William J. Norton, once of the Cincinnati Council and then working to establish a financial partner for the Detroit Community Union, flew to the defense of fund raisers. In a speech on "The Progress of Financial Federation" he reported the success of pioneering campaigns both in money raised and in spreading the principles of social service and bringing about better conditions and social order. [4]

In October 1917 the ill-concealed opposition to federation by many COS executives became manifest in "Financial Federations," a report of a special committee of the American Association for Organizing Charity. Charged with evaluating the Chest method of financing, it damned some federations with faint praise ("Yes, but!"), quoted adverse opinions, and made much of federations that had failed. Its chief criticism was that whirlwind campaigns "do not build up as stable a constituency as most organizations in non-federated cities now have." It expressed doubt regarding the system for apportioning funds, feared loss of interest and contact between givers and agencies, and said the fact "that so many federations have neglected social work indicates a tendency which grows out of the imperative character of the financial program which it is the federation's first duty to solve." In conclusion the report said, "Our recommendation . . . is very positively against any adoption of the plan at present. Fourteen cities are now experimenting with it under quite varying conditions and with several different types of organization. We feel strongly that is experimentation enough." [5]

The aggrieved adherents of federation, while biding their time for an effective comeback, organized their own forces and at the meeting called by William J. Norton in Chicago on February 22, 1918, twelve men met in three busy sessions. These men may well be considered the founding fathers of the national organization now known as United Way of America. They were: Charles R. Cooper, head resident, Kingsley House, Pittsburgh; Wilfred S. Reynolds, president of Chicago Central Council of Social Agencies; Sherman C. Kingsley, executive director, Cleveland Welfare Federation; William C. White, president, and Robert L. Frost, secretary, Centralized Budget of Philanthropies, Milwaukee; Robert E. Bondy, manager, Social Service Bureau, Chamber of Commerce, Columbus, Ohio; William J. Norton; C. M. Bookman, executive director, Cincinnati Council of Social Agencies; Elwood Street, executive director, Louisville Federation of Social Agencies; Allen T. Burns, director, Cleveland Foundation; George F. Widman, director, Federation for Social Service, South Bend, Indiana; and W. Clifton Howell, financial secretary, Federation of Charities Finance Association, Dallas.

Mr. Norton was elected temporary chairman and Mr. Bookman, secretary. The name selected was American Association for Community Organization, and its object was "to encourage and stimulate collective community planning, and the development of better standards in the work of community organization for social work." The founding group felt that the first concern should be to standardize the work of financial federation. Various suggestions were recorded. One was that the best method for organizing a financial federation was through a central organization of the city's charities. This implied a shift in sponsorship of Councils from the American Association for Organizing Charities to affiliation with their group, AACO, and recognition that joint financing is merely one aspect of joint planning and action.

Another suggestion was that Councils develop functional divisions made up of agencies performing similar types of services. Budget committees were recommended to include both laymen and agency board members. No campaign committee was proposed, probably because the idea of a concerted community campaign had not yet made any large-scale impact on the financial federations.

The founders felt that Councils of Social Agencies could not always be relied on to initiate financial federations, so they suggested that sometimes it might be advisable to start a financial federation as an independent organization. Where this was done, care would be taken to follow the general principles outlined for financial federations under central Councils and to work closely at all times with the Councils.

At the business meeting of the new American Association for Community Organization, held during the 1918 annual meeting of the recently renamed National Conference of Social Work, it was voted to organize formally and to formulate elementary principles of community organization. Allen T. Burns was elected president. Although he had earlier expressed his doubts about the value of financial federations, the huge success of the War Chests and other joint financial efforts had changed his mind. He was destined to become mentor and chief architect of the Chest-Council movement from that time until his retirement in 1942.

During the 1918 National Conference, the forces of federation trained their artillery on the American Association for Organizing Charity report critical of federation. William C. White, of Milwaukee, who had served as temporary president of the AACO until its

Jane Addams (1860-1935), pioneer social worker and founder of Hull House in 1889, a settlement house, still operating and now a United Way agency which set the pattern for today's settlements, neighborhood houses, community centers and similar United Way supported services.

business meeting, presented a strong rebuttal. He answered with factual information, explaining authoritatively the reasons some cities had failed, and listed factors in the success of continuing federations.[6]

U.S. Enters War

On April 6, 1917 the United States had entered the war, bringing about a mushrooming of appeals for war relief and the armed forces. These new agencies represented the polyglot sympathies and interests of the nation's ethnic groups. Their nationwide appeals for funds were made with varying intensities and by diverse methods. A total of 130 were already active when neutrality ended their activities ranging from sewing for Belgian refugees to providing YMCA services in prisoner-of-war camps. These appeals, worthy though most were, suffered from every variety of duplication, extravagance, mismanagement, inadequate financial control, and sometimes foolish or fraudulent purposes.

No national body corresponding to local charity endorsement committees existed. While the Council of National Defense seemed the logical body to undertake the job, its leaders showed no inclination to assume responsibility for endorsement of war charities.

Already performing this service on a local basis, the Bureau of Advice and Information of the New York City COS reluctantly became convinced that it must itself undertake the task. It drew up certain very elementary requirements and began investigations. It could not, however, investigate programs abroad which limited its usefulness, although it did issue bulletins on approved war charities from time to time.

Between April 17 and June 1, 1917 the YMCA raised $5,102,000 in a $3 million campaign to support its recreational and morale-building services in training camps and overseas. In November it made a second nationwide appeal with a goal close to $36 million. Quotas were assigned to state committees and these in turn were apportioned among local communities. The campaign won tremendous support from executives and directors of the largest business institutions in the United States and raised approximately $54 million.

The American Red Cross scheduled its first war-time drive for funds in June, 1917, with a $100 million goal, a tremendous amount for those days. There was immediate need and the money had to be raised quickly, so Red Cross fund raisers knew that passing the hat, writing letters and ordinary fund-raising techniques

would not do. Noting the success of the first YMCA campaign, Red Cross leaders brought in YMCA workers to help apply the intensive campaign principle which had worked so successfully for them.

In Cleveland the Red Cross campaign was combined with the Mayor's War Commission drive and that of the Welfare Federation. Not only was the $2,250,000 goal reached—it was doubled.

Cleveland's example was not lost on the nation. Many other communities asked, "Why shouldn't we federate all meritorious war appeals?" Three upstate New York communities were the first to organize War Chest associations: Syracuse, Ilion and Mohawk. Next were Kenosha, Wis., Granville, N.Y. and Rome, N.Y.

Cincinnati, following Cleveland's example, launched a joint campaign for the National YMCA and YWCA with the Council of Social Agencies. In South Bend, Ind. the Welfare Federation budgets were included in the War Chest campaigns of 1917 and 1918.

As the armed forces moved to the battlefields in France, the number of War Chests increased. In January 1918 there were 45 and by May, an additional 44. By the end of the war there were nearly 400.

The War Chest movement was a grass-roots enterprise, springing up spontaneously, as the financial federation movement had, out of the needs and visions of people in local communities. The "grass" caught fire from the spirit of patriotism and spread quickly across the nation, fanned by the flames of war-time urgency. By the time the war was over in 1918 nearly 400 War Chests had raised far more than $100 million.

War Chests were important in many ways. They provided, in general, an economical and effective means of financing war relief appeals. In several communities which already had financial federations, local agencies were included in War Chests, to their benefit. War Chests established the pattern of concerted community-wide campaigns which were later adopted as standard practice by Community Chests and United Funds. To promote giving to War Chests, the first War Revenue Bill was passed by Congress, establishing the legal right to deduct charitable contributions from taxable income. War Chests, with communitywide volunteer participation, were valuable in uniting people in other phases of the war effort. A considerable number of Community Chests were organized directly out of War Chests and others were established in succeeding years. Further, the success of World War I War Chests led to their prompt and practically universal reestablishment during World War II. They had made manifest the advantages of financial federation, pushing the previously slow-moving program into rapid acceptance.

Perhaps the most conspicuous and influential of the new War Chests was that in Columbus, Ohio where local agencies were not included. Workers were asked for one day's pay per month. With 7,000 volunteer workers, more than $3 million was raised.

In Elyria, Ohio at the prompting of E. F. Allen, who later founded the National Society for Crippled Children and Adults, local all-time agencies were included in the War Chest because of his belief that much money could be saved in a combined appeal.

The Red Cross, planning its second appeal for $100 million, felt that since its organization was unique, it should not merge its appeal with other agencies in War Chests. In some communities, however, volunteer leadership was practically identical with that of the War Chests and joint campaigns did take place. The Cincinnati campaign of May 1918 included the Red Cross, though it was not until November of that year that an organized campaign was put on in the name of the War Chest.

Rochester, N.Y. devised a new way of handling the multiple appeals problem and formed a Community and War Chest in 1918 at the prompting of George Eastman, President of Eastman Kodak Company. A membership organization of representative contributors was set up. Agencies neither managed nor controlled the Chest. This organization had a tremendous impact on the financial federation movement which followed the war, and provided the generic name Community Chest.

Despite the growth of War Chests, the public became confused because of the rapid growth in war organizations. President Wilson and the Council of National Defense accordingly called for organization of Community Councils of National Defense to promote teamwork for all kinds of local war services. These local Councils employed many of the procedures developed by Councils of Social Agencies, stimulated their growth after the war, and became prototypes of the Defense Councils organized during World War II.

As the war continued, joint financing on the national level was suggested by the Secretary of War, Newton

D. Baker, former mayor of Cleveland who had been active in formulating plans for Cleveland's first Community Chest. In 1918 President Wilson issued an order directing a joint appeal for funds on behalf of seven organizations: YMCA, YWCA, War Camp Community Service, Knights of Columbus, Jewish Welfare Board, American Library Association, and Salvation Army. When the armistice was signed on November 11, this United War Work Campaign was merged

Typical of the "War Chest" appeals was this 1919 campaign poster of the first United Way drive in Minneapolis.

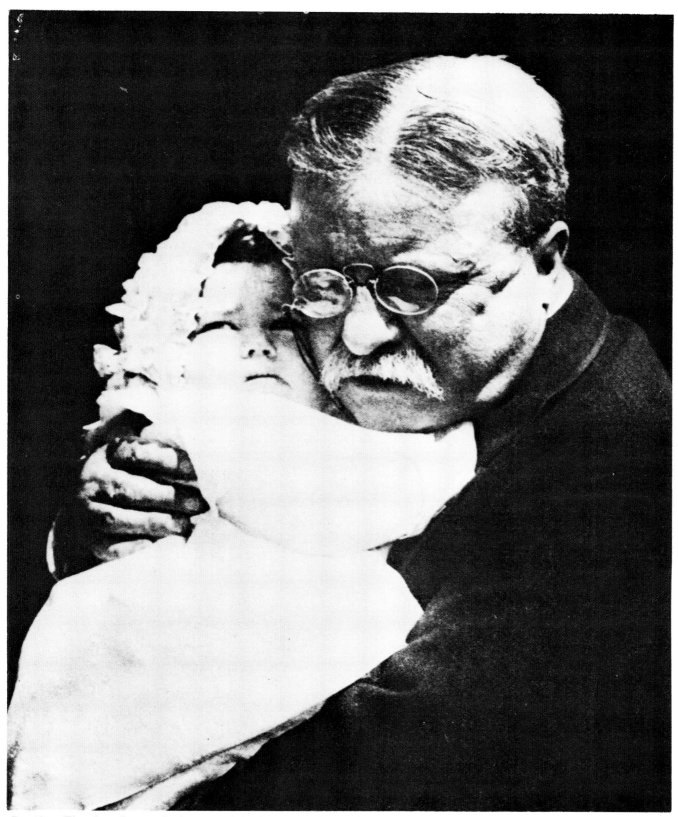

President Theodore Roosevelt, founder of the first White House Conference on Children in 1909, which continues to be held every decade. In this photograph taken shortly before his death in 1919 he is holding his granddaughter.

in many communities with War Chest campaigns. In Minneapolis which never had financial federation before, the drive combined foreign, national and local appeals, raising $3,300,000 on a $3 million goal.

With the armistice, the War Chest movement had about run its course. Already scheduled campaigns were held with emphasis on "finishing the job." By then it had become clear that War Chests had both faults and virtues. The faults were described by C. M. Bookman in an address at the 1925 Annual Meeting of NCSW. "While the War Chests undoubtedly accelerated the growth of federations, they followed certain practices that have been detrimental. Although certain well-defined standards were adopted for the determination of budgets, war agencies generally received what they asked without too-careful scrutiny of needs . . . War Chests were interested almost solely in finances. They did not undertake in any way to coordinate with social work, leaving that entirely to the separate agencies." [7]

The virtues of War Chests were described by William J. Norton in his book, *The Cooperative Movement in Social Work*. "The War Chest . . . picked up a scheme of reorganizing philanthropy that had been struggling exceedingly hard to gain a foothold; and it spread the ideas making up that scheme rapidly and comprehensively the length and breadth of the land. There is no doubt that the federation movement gained a momentum in one year that would have required possibly ten years of peacetime activity . . . National agencies living in splendid isolation in large measure prior to the war discovered all at once some of the elements of cooperation among themselves, and of cooperation with givers . . . A final consequence that can be attributed only in part, however, to the War Chest, was the acquisition by the American people of a new standard of giving." [8] He also pointed out strongly that federation, while offering membership to any qualified agency, could not and should not attempt to stop all independent solicitation for social work.

War Chests and Defense Councils, products of the "war to make the world safe for democracy," were graphic illustrations that joint financing and planning of health and welfare services were not only possible but salutary. They paved the way for the rapid growth of Community Chests and Councils. Thanks to them, federation was no longer on trial. It had become a part of the American way of life.

In December 1918 a new organization was initiated on a national scale, answering a long-felt need for investigation of national organizations. It was designed to perform the same service to the nation that Chamber of Commerce charities endorsement committees had been doing for local communities since 1900. During the war a multitude of foreign relief and local patriotic societies had been born with representatives going across the country collecting funds in communities knowing very little about them. At the instigation of the Cleveland War Chest, a meeting was called and representatives from Columbus, Toledo, Indianapolis, Detroit, Rochester, Philadelphia, Syracuse, and Cleveland founded the National Investigation Bureau, now known as the National Information Bureau.

The NIB was of tremendous importance in the development of joint planning and financing of community health and welfare services. It gave War Chests and later Community Chests invaluable information for dealing not only with war relief agencies but others. It was a factor in the establishment of the National Social Work Council and was a close ally of the American Association for Community Organization. It was a useful partner of the National Budget and Consultation Committee, and still provides useful information about more than 500 national organizations.

NOTES

Chapter 4

1. William C. White, "When Shall Financial Federations Be Started?" *Proceedings, National Conference of Charities and Corrections*, 1916, pp. 606-607.

2. C. M. Hubbard, *Proceedings, National Conference of Charities and Corrections*, 1916, pp. 326-329.

3. *Ibid.*

4. William J. Norton, "The Progress of Financial Federation," *Proceedings, National Conference of Social Work*, 1917, pp. 505-507.

5. *Financial Federations*, The Report of the Special Committee, The American Association for Organizing Charity, 1917, pp. 63-66.

6. See note 1, p. 613.

7. C. M. Bookman, "The Community Chest Movement, an Interpretation," paper read at annual meeting of National Conference of Social Work, 1924, distributed by American Association for Community Organization (United Way of America).

8. See note 4 in *Chapter II*, pp. 120-121.

THE RISE OF COMMUNITY CHESTS: 1919-1925

Rapid military and domestic demobilization followed the close of World War I. Most of the nearly 5 million who had served in the armed forces quickly returned to homes, families and jobs. Factories shifted to production of peacetime machines and commodities, and abundant prosperity followed a brief period of post-war adjustment. The people were absorbed by technological advances such as the automobile, movies, radio, and mechanical gadgets, but also made efforts to extend education, experiment in social welfare, and enforce prohibition.

War Chests disappeared rapidly, though many had final campaigns in the midst of victory celebrations. In many cases there was enough money left over to make unnecessary any appeal during 1919 by local agencies. But when the balances were spent and it came time again to plan ahead, more and more of the 400 War Chest communities asked, "If we could raise charitable funds together in wartime, can't we do it in peacetime?"

The result was that joint financial campaigns were held in at least 20 communities of the United States and Canada in 1919, with the number rising steadily in succeeding years. Most of these joint financing operations were now called Community Chests (the name originated in Rochester) although some followed the lead of Cleveland and Detroit and called theirs Community Funds. The movement was characterized by the intensive, limited-time, communitywide campaign by volunteer workers in appeals to individuals and corporations. Using this tested and proved campaign technique, Community Chests raised unprecedents sums of money at minimal cost. The example was contagious.

Then as now, actual operation and policy determination of Community Chests lay in the hands of lay leadership, elected to the boards of directors which appointed campaign leadership, organized the budgeting programs, and resolved major policy issues. Most communities felt the need for ongoing staff direction. Agencies eligible for membership were generally those providing services in the areas of health, social welfare, group work, and recreation. All agencies were nonprofit and supervised by boards of volunteers. Chests exchanged ideas with each other during inter-city visits, through national and regional meetings, and through papers and discussions at the Annual Meetings of the National Conference of Social Work.

Harry Wareham, manager of the first organization calling itself a Community Chest, is credited with inventing the name which he correctly predicted "would become a household word in the United States." He handled Rochester's campaigns so competently that laymen and Chest executives came from all over the country to study his methods.

During the war when attention was focused on fund raising, several new Councils of Social Agencies had been formed, and now in postwar campaigns Cincinnati, Dayton, and Minneapolis conducted appeals as functions of their planning bodies. Canada's first postwar Community Chest was formed in Toronto during 1918.

There were 39 federated community campaigns in 1919 which raised a total of $19,651,334. Cleveland decided to incorporate its Community Fund, the largest in America, and, for the first time, social agencies and government were represented on its governing body while Chamber of Commerce representation was cut. It was decided to separate the Welfare Federation from the Fund, and employ an executive secretary for each. They have remained distinct ever since, with the Federation serving as the general social planning body for the community.

That same year a new concept of joint planning took form with creation of the Ohio Council of Social Agencies which differed from the numerous state conferences which had been organized following the first in Wisconsin during 1881. These conferences were essentially forums for information and discussion whereas the Ohio Council functioned as a coordinator and policy maker.

One of the most striking developments of the Ohio Council of Social Agencies was its County Case Committee which became an important factor in constantly keeping before agencies the needs of the particular community rather than the extension of any one agency's program. Despite its initial success, the Council's leadership changed, promotion languished, and by 1923 it withered on the vine. Nevertheless, its pioneer demonstration of the possibilities of statewide planning was of great significance.

Other 1919 Council developments included new joint planning bodies in Winnipeg and for all of Canada. In Chicago, the Council assumed new purposes; to further cooperation and prevent duplication among agencies; to serve as an advisory Council to social service organizations; to make recommendations concerning citywide needs; to encourage development of needed agencies; and public education.

During the National Conference annual meeting in 1919 C. M. Bookman, director of the Cincinnati Council, presented a plan for a Council to operate a Chest as well as to carry on planning activities.[1]

During its annual meeting, the American Association for Organizing Charity recommended that, as a method of coordination in community programs, member societies should invariably encourage the organization of Central Councils in communities where there were ten or more social agencies with trained leadership. Where there were less than ten such agencies, informal conferences on community problems, meeting when required, should be encouraged. Another significant action of the AAOC was to limit charity organization service to family case work and accordingly to change the organization name to American Association for Organizing Family Social Work.

1920

In its 1920 campaign, Rochester came up with a widely-adopted slogan, "Suppose Nobody Cared." Originally proposed by George Eastman of Eastman Kodak Company, the slogan was copied by other cities from coast to coast.

At least a dozen new Chests appeared in 1920, including the reorganized United Welfare Fund Association of London, Ontario which, in its first campaign sought, in addition to operating funds, $35,000 in capital funds for the YMCA, YWCA, and Salvation Army. Then, as now, this was unusual.

Not only were new Chests being formed, but due to the efforts of the American Association for Organizing Family Social Work, at least half a dozen Councils were added to the roster. Statewide planning found a second recruit in Dallas where the Texas Council of Statewide Social Work was spearheaded by the local Civic Federation.

One of the great problems of Councils was trying to operate without paid staff. In larger cities special funds were often obtained for this purpose, but the major development of councils did not come about until Community Chests and United Funds provided money for staff, for shared staff, or for specific Council activities.

Social service exchanges continued to grow in number, and at the 1920 annual meeting of the National Conference of Social Work, Aaron M. Lopez of the Brooklyn Bureau of Charities reported the existence of 159 in the United States and Canada, of which 135

a communitywide program," executive secretary Guy T. Justis reported. "Four outside agencies felt the pressure of public opinion and joined the Chest for participation in the second year . . . A Council was created at the same time as a part of the Chest organization." [6]

As a result of the increase in Chests and Councils, then numbering 96, there were new faces and voices speaking for federation at the 1922 N.C.S.W. Annual Meeting. Harry Wareham, manager of the Rochester Chest, encouraged other Chests to include sectarian agencies. "Social work in religious groups is ordinarily very much under-financed. Through central financing these same contributing members receive a fuller knowledge of social needs, a better understanding of the cost of social work, a finer appreciation of the standards to be followed, and a better knowledge of the difficulties of social workers. All this is added without detracting one whit from the religious motive that first prompted them to give." [7]

The increasingly worrisome problem of national agency relations with local communities was described by Ralph J. Reed, secretary of the Public Welfare Bureau of the Des Moines Chamber of Commerce. "Financial federations are slow to include quotas of national and state agencies in their campaigns. The chief reason is that even the leading backers of social work in the local community know almost nothing about such national agencies, or what they do or what they need." He said most financial federations included budget items of national and state agencies with participating local units, and that other national agencies with no local branches increasingly were being supported after enlisting local support in direct appeals. He said that one community fund required influential local committees in such instances, and added, "We believe this is a sound and desirable requirement both in the point of view of the community and the national agency." [8]

Direct services of federations were discussed by Sherman Conrad, executive director of the Wilkes-Barre Community Welfare Federation. He had made a survey showing that very little direct service was being offered by Chests or Councils. Five federations operated central buildings, three federations and one Council promoted social service training; one federation operated a joint hospital social service department; two conducted summer outings and distributed Christmas baskets; 15 federations and four Councils ran Social Service Exchanges. He concluded that the general feeling of the federation executives was opposition to direct service by federations. [9] That opinion stands today except with respect to common administrative services.

Raymond Clapp, associate director of the Cleveland Welfare Federation, addressed himself to budgeting; his advice is still considered sound. "Control of contribution funds gives the budget committee great power, so long as the actions of the committee merit the confidence of the contributing public . . . It is especially necessary for such a committee to recognize the fact that it is dealing with individual agencies whose independent authority and initiative must be conserved." [10]

In its annual business meeting during that June conference, the AACO took one of the most important steps in its history by voting to acquire professional staff and an office. Recognizing the need to provide more services but realizing its limitations, the AACO proposed that the NIB enlarge its activities to include information service about Community Chests. Accepting the invitation, the NIB assumed responsibility in August of that year with Allen T. Burns giving three-fourths of his time to NIB business and one fourth to AACO. Mr. Burns had taken over as executive of the NIB when Barry Smith resigned June 30, 1922.

Thus dawned a new day for the struggling national office. The whole character of the community organization movement changed. Chest and Council leaders now began to receive a steady flow of information and to profit by a growing body of knowledge and skilled advisory services.

At the AACO meeting during the 1923 NCSW annual meeting, a precedent was established when a layman was elected president. He was Attorney Benjamin F. Merrick, president of the Grand Rapids Social Welfare Association. Lay participation in all phases of AACO work and that of its successor organizations has continued increasingly to the present day.

Financing was on the agenda of this 1923 meeting. The old dues of $25 per year from 40 members obviously would not suffice, so the group decided to recommend contributions of one-tenth of one percent of the total amount raised by each during the preceding fiscal year. That principle of proportionate voluntary contributions has continued through the succeeding years, although the formula has changed.

It was reported at this meeting that two groups

wished to become affiliated with AACO, the American Association of Social Service Exchanges and the Social Work Publicity Council. The staff secretary Pierce Williams, was instructed to investigate the matter and report to the December meeting. Mr. Williams had been added to the NIB staff in February to give full time to AACO work. Nothing came of the Publicity Council request, however, and the organization retained its identity aided by grants from the Russell Sage Foundation. Now it is the National Communication Council for Human Services and serves governmental and voluntary social, health, and civic agencies as well as Chests and Councils.

During the summer of 1923, the new executive secretary, Allen Burns, plunged into lively activity. Handbooks were prepared and distributed; inquiries from 90 cities considering Chest organization were answered; and 43 Chest cities were visited, beginning the field service program which has become one of the major activities of today's United Way of America. A beginning was made at organizing regional conferences when 20 to 25 southern Chest executives met informally in Atlanta that December.

In those days of modest beginnings the national office operated on a budget of $21,290 which covered the full-time service of Pierce Williams and a general assistant, one-fourth time of Allen Burns, plus office assistance and travel. The staff now began considering ways to earn income through service to Chests and others.

That year the Chamber of Commerce of the United States described the growth of federation in a pamphlet which served to stimulate Chest organization. Many Chamber secretaries served also as part-time Chest executives.

Many new Chests were launched in 1923, the ranks growing from 96 to 147. Their number now exceeded that of Councils. In Birmingham, Alabama an informal group called Associated Charities was formed. It did no budgeting or fund raising, but simply offered those interested in community service a chance to meet and discuss mutual problems. After a thorough study, the group reorganized as a Community Chest, holding its first campaign in 1923.

In Columbus, Ohio, the city with the most highly publicized War Chest in 1918, a Council study of eight Chest cities led to the conclusion that central financing had been administered with manifest and substantial advantage and with promise of continuing good effect upon the progress and development of social services.

On the national level, joint planning of health and welfare services became a reality through formation of the National Social Work Council, predecessor of the present National Assembly of National Voluntary Health and Social Welfare Organizations. One reason it was needed was the tremendous growth in number of national voluntary social welfare agencies with local units. Seven of them had worked together closely during World War I to provide services to the armed forces and raise funds for expansion of their programs through the United War Work Campaign organized in 1918.

David Holbrook, secretary of the Council from its beginning until it became the National Social Welfare Assembly in 1945, has described its goals. "Two basic motives brought the original group together in 1920: 1. to continue acquaintance and satisfactions of working together which had been greatly enhanced during World War I, and 2. to bring to bear some considered thought on opportunistic proposals then being made for mechanical coordination of national and local organized effort in the general welfare field. Service to the whole field of social work was the aim of the group rather than special advantages to national agencies as such . . . The fundamental principle of organization was the autonomy of the national agencies . . . The membership was deliberately limited to national organizations (23 originally) that had been accustomed to work closely together. Only a relatively few were added during the years. The most conspicuous widening of the circle was the admission of the Association of Community Chests and Councils after their mutual interest became sufficiently clear." [11] The organization by 1960 included representatives of more than 70 affiliated national voluntary and governmental social welfare organizations and four associate groups. In 1967 a reorganization changed its goals, name, membership, and structure.

The forward push of the Chest movement, so notable in 1923, continued during 1924. New federated campaigns numbered 56, for a total of 203. Most new federations were in relatively small communities. One exception was Los Angeles, where 125 agencies joined the first Chest, including practically every eligible organization, from the Society for the Prevention of Cruelty to Animals, to the Red Cross. In the year before federation, separate appeals had raised $1,548,178

THE FIRE TRUCK RIDE *was a tradition of the Minneapolis United Way campaign for three decades. Each day during the drive, the team with highest percentage of quota rode the fire truck. The group pictured were volunteers in the 1924 campaign.*

with costs estimated at 45%. The first Chest campaign raised $2,492,154 with 168,273 persons contributing. Five hundred thousand dollars were saved in overhead expenses!

In Rochester the Chest was becoming well known and respected and people began to turn to it directly for help, guidance, and direction. To answer their questions the Chest had found it necessary to create a Service Department which was the forerunner of the Council of Social Agencies organized in 1924. Jointly housed, sharing some equipment, and being in every way working partners, the Chest and Council were separate corporate entities. While all Chest participating agencies were members of the Council, not all Council member agencies were participants in the Chest.

Another method of handling community organization was employed in Louisville, Ky. Following establishment of the Community Chest in 1923, a three-headed planning body was brought into being, made up of the Health Council, Recreation Council, and Family and Child Welfare Council. They were to discharge the planning function of the Community Chest. Eventually (in 1935) the Family and Child Welfare Council and the Recreation Council combined to form the Council of Social Agencies, and in 1945 this organization united with the Health Council to form the Health and Welfare Council.

A new phenomenon was beginning to appear: the commercial fund raising organization. Three or four such groups were already in the business of directing Community Chest campaigns in smaller cities. The AACO had paid little attention, but now learned that one of the larger concerns was considering central office organization as well. It was realized that if this kind of service were given by private concerns, they would in effect be competing with AACO. It became the feeling that AACO must broaden its service to Community Chests so as to provide more concrete service than was being furnished. A committee studied the matter and its report led to later development of full-year training at Ohio State University in order to provide more trained personnel, and more extensive field work by AACO.

At this time the NIB and AACO helped win a court decision in a matter of vital importance to all charitable institutions, the question of deducting gifts to a social agency from a donor's federal income tax. The Bureau of Internal Revenue had raised the question whether, if gifts to social settlements, which are not "charitable" in the ordinary sense, are not deductible, gifts to Community Chests including them should be regarded as deductible. The AACO asked the NIB as its executive secretary to secure legal counsel and take all other steps to argue the matter before the solicitor general of the Internal Revenue Bureau, and to appeal any adverse decisions if necessary. The finance committee raised funds for this campaign and the arguments were successfully presented. Social settlements were ruled as charitable organizations within the meaning of the Revenue Act.

The growth of AACO membership and services was noted at a general session of the National Conference annual meeting held in Toronto in June of 1924. C. M. Bookman pointed out that "The social service infant whose birth was so deplored among social workers ten years ago, whose early years were so beset with dangers, and whose early actions were severely criticized,

has grown and developed until today it is a giant holding in his grasp the destiny of American social work for at least a decade to come. The two or three cities with federations 10 years ago have increased to nearly 200 . . . More and more cities are adopting the plan and nothing seems likely either to stop its growth or to hamper greatly its continued spread . . . No movement in the long history of social work has so quickly caught the popular fancy. Through Community Chest methods practically the entire populations of many cities have become interested in social work. Social problems and ways of solving them have become popular topics of conversations. Social work in these cities is recognized as one of the vital forces in the life of the people." [12]

Mr. Bookman also issued a warning. "An element

First President of the United States to give the United Way was Calvin Coolidge in 1929. Accepting his gift for the Community Chest of Washington is Robert V. Fleming, Chairman, Special Gifts Division. Other Chest officials present were (extreme left) Elwood Street, Executive Director; (extreme right) John Poole, Campaign Chairman; and Frederic A. Delano, President.

YOU SEND HER
Through All Seasons

During the cold days of November, December and January Visiting Nurses made 15,000 calls on Minneapolis sick.

When traffic was halted by sleet and snow Visiting Nurses continued their services to all sections of the city.

(To secure a nurse, call Main 7800)

(To secure a nurse, call Main 7800)

Braving storms and death-dealing temperatures — through all seasons goes the Visiting Nurse. She brings gentle skill, nursing efficiency, patience, sympathy and hope to Minneapolis homes. You are sending a nurse from the Visiting Nurse Association by supporting the

He Ain't Heavy, He's My Brother

Community Fund

65 Agencies Participating in the Community Fund

One of a series of service posters developed by the Minneapolis Community Fund in 1929.

of danger is that a Chest may take the position that it should be all-inclusive and that no social work should go on in the community save under its guidance. Community Chests, in order to be successful, must develop public opinion favorable to their work. There are, however, many social movements instigated by minorities which, though sound in their social point of view, are nevertheless militantly opposed. In their own interest, as well as in the interest of the Community Chest, these minorities should not entrust their programs to public opinion. Such agencies should not be members of the Community Chest." [13]

Speaking of another problem Mr. Bookman said, "Community Chests are experiencing difficulty in working out proper relationships that should exist between them and national agencies. The experience of the National Information Bureau shows one reason why this is so: more than 2000 national agencies apply for endorsement but only 150 receive it. There is overlapping and overlooking; militant groups are interested in legislation before educational processes convince the public that such legislation is desirable; agencies fight intolerance but become quite as intolerant as those they fight; agencies with carefully formed programs are mixed in the public mind with those with indefinite programs, and so on through the long list. Until some order is developed in national agency work, Community Chests will find great difficulty in contributing to national programs. Some methods of sound and sensible building up of national agency budgets must be devised." [14]

Further recognition of community organization was seen in the election of William J. Norton of Detroit as president of the National Conference of Social Work for the coming year. This was the first time a Chest-Council executive had been thus honored.

Corporate Contributions

During 1925 new concerns engaged the attention of the AACO. One was the question of the legality of corporation contributions to charitable causes. In one of AACO's newsletters, a New York banker was quoted as having told of a comptroller's opinion concerning contributions to charity. Since the Bureau of Internal Revenue had ruled that such contributions could not be deducted as business expenses, the bank had concluded that any such contributions by national banks were illegal. [15] It is small wonder that in 1925 corporation contributions to Community Chests were not impressive in number or amount. However, the subject was not closed and eventually dramatic and significant changes were made.

The AACO was squeaking along on its $23,000 share of NIB's $48,000 budget. During the previous year only 83 Chests out of 203 had supported the national association. Because of this financial handicap the association could do little toward working out a merger with the American Association of Social Service Exchanges other than send out information bulletins from time to time.

During the May meeting of the AACO executive committee, approval was given to the initiation of a novel project "for setting up registration areas of social statistics through which common measurements as to volume and rates of social service can be established and related to costs." This would be a joint activity of AACO and the Cleveland Welfare Federation (which wanted the data for its own comparative purposes). To finance the project, it was decided to ask federations equipped for research to cooperate in gathering data along uniform lines. Offers of cooperation came from Cleveland, Dayton, Detroit, Rochester, Philadelphia, and St. Louis. The study was begun and completed the following year. [16]

During 1925 regional conferences were held in Chapel Hill, N.C. and in Chicago. The success of these conferences led to the Southern Institute for Social Work Executives still held annually in Blue Ridge, N.C. Through the years several other annual and biennial conferences and institutes were established for both Chest and Council personnel and volunteers.

A momentous decision was made in 1925—that it was time for AACO to cut its ties to the NIB and to become an independent and self-operating organization. AACO would have its own staff and office, possibly in some Midwest Community Chest city. A budget of $50,000 was proposed, to be raised through the set membership fee previously established. The action would take effect January 1, 1926.

A study by AACO in Providence, R.I. was instrumental in formation of the Community Fund that year. Boston made its own study and found considerable opposition from social agencies. Spearheaded by the Chamber of Commerce, the Council of Social Agencies had sent a questionnaire to 307 of its agencies, asking their reaction to the Chamber recommendation for a Community Chest. Some 118 replied, showing hope-

The simple clarity of this Save a Life theme and illustration by Anton Otto Fischer in 1937 made this a distinctive United Way campaign appeal.

less division with strong anti-Chest feeling vociferously expressed. An opposition leader was Joseph Lee, a prominent and influential layman and philanthropist, active on several local and national agency boards. All the old suspicions and fears of federation were brought out, amplified, and broadcast: "Boston was doing very well without a Chest; Chests wouldn't support national causes; they destroyed the interest of givers; they almost destroyed the educational programs of agencies; they had too much power over agencies;" etc. etc. All the furor delayed federation in Boston for another 10 years.

New York City launched a "functional" federation, the result of work by a committee of social welfare leaders who began in 1922 to study the problems. This was the Welfare Council, forerunner of the present Community Council of Greater New York. The first communitywide financial federation was established in 1938 as the Greater New York Fund from which developed the present United Fund of Greater New York.

NOTES
Chapter 5

1. C. M. Bookman, "Plan for a Standard Legal Administrative Organization for a Community Federation," *Proceedings, National Conference of Social Work*, 1919, p. 710.

2. Aaron M. Lopez, "The Social Service Exchange," *Proceedings, National Conference of Social Work*, 1920, pp. 454-455.

3. Robert L. Frost, "Summary of Findings of Study of 1919 Money-Making Efforts and Post-War Attitude of Givers," *Proceedings, National onference of Social Work*, 1920, p. 424.

4. William J. Norton, "The Growing Demand for Coordination of National Social Work," *Proceedings, National Conference of Social Work*, 1920, pp. 27, 321-323.

5. Elwood Street, "Organizing and Financing Federations and Councils of Social Agencies," American Association for Community Organization (UCFCA), April 1921.

6. Guy T. Justis, *Twenty-Five Years of Social Welfare*, The Denver Community Chest, 1943, pp. 20-21.

7. H. P. Wareham, "Organization for a Community Chest Campaign," *Proceedings, National Conference of Social Work*, 1922, p. 410.

8. Ralph J. Reed, "Relation of National Agencies to the Local Community," *Proceedings, National Conference of Social Work*, 1922, pp. 426-427.

9. Sherman Conrad, "Direct Service Activities of the Federation," *Proceedings, National Conference of Social Work*, 1922, pp. 422-425.

10. Raymond Clapp, "Budget Making in a Federation," *Proceedings, National Conference of Social Work*, 1922, pp. 398-402.

11. Alice P. Williams, Buffalo, New York, letter to Elwood Street, August 14, 1962.

12. See note 7 (referred to in *Chapter III*), pp. 19-20.

13. Ibid., p. 26.

14. Ibid., pp. 27-28.

15. *Newsletter*, American Association for Community Organization (UCFCA) February 1, 1925, pp. 1, 2.

16. "Chronology of Federation," (MSS in UCFCA Library) p. 1.

GROWTH OF THE NATIONAL ASSOCIATION:1926-1930

January 1, 1926 was Independence Day for the American Association, for on that date it acquired its own staff, bank account, and office. Allen Burns became executive director of the forerunner of what is now known as United Way of America, while Pierce Williams continued as his assistant. A budget of $45,650 was allotted. One of the association's first activities was to establish a survey service to be paid for by Chests requesting it. Its purpose was to determine how well a local Chest was doing its job and to suggest improvements. In some cases the surveys would be made by a staff member and in others by an experienced executive doing a special assignment for the association.

In the spring the study of "Volume and Cost of Social Work" was completed and published. It had been organized under the leadership of Raymond Clapp, associate director of the Cleveland Welfare Federation. With 30 of the larger cities cooperating, the information showed the total expense of services usually financed through community funds in the fields of family welfare and relief, child care, hospitals and health promotion, recreation and character building. The expense of parallel government services financed from tax funds was likewise included. This information was secured in such a way that it was possible to compare not only the total expense of these services

for various cities but also to compare the cost of child care in hospitals, in dispensaries and by bedside nursing; the cost of character building through the settlements, young men's and women's associations, Scouting, etc. While comparison of financial figures would be of interest, it would be of comparatively little value without some indication of the volume and character of service rendered; therefore the information collected included the simplest possible statistics of service rendered.

The study revealed some startling facts not universally realized. For example: "The fact that public revenue or taxes exceeds in amount the sum of private support from contributions and endowments together, comes as a surprise to many. It shows the great importance of teamwork between public and private agencies." [1]

One of the most potent effects of this study was in showing need for considering the community's *total* service program including non-member as well as Chest agencies, and tax-supported agencies as well. Budgeting had to be done comparatively. This meant that joint planning was just as important as joint financing. To AACO this meant that service to Councils and promotion of their activities would have to become an important part of its program which had until then concentrated on Community Chests.

In gathering the information, Mr. Clapp discovered

that while getting financial facts was easy, obtaining figures on volume and character of services was difficult. He explained this difficulty to the AACO board which authorized a further study of volume and cost for 1926 with more cities included and improved report forms used. Thus was begun a statistical and research service which was developed through the years until the national organization became a leader in the collection of community social data and surveys.

A new idea came out of the AACO meeting during the 1926 National Conference in Cleveland, that of concentrating Chest campaigns at one time of year and fortifying them with area-wide campaign publicity. This suggestion took hold and spread until today, when the vast majority of federated campaigns are held between Labor Day and Thanksgiving, aided by a tremendous barrage of national publicity.

Allen Burns was now making relations between national agencies and Community Chests his chief responsibility, starting with the YMCA and working through a committee of laymen. Much staff time went into field service and correspondence and interviews with persons wanting information about organizing Chests which now numbered 308, with Winnipeg raising the number of Canadian Chests to four.

Meantime, Jewish federations were undergoing changes. "After several years of experience with Chests the Jewish federations learned that the Chest would not solve two basic problems facing the Jewish community: 1. They made no provision for raising capital funds for plant renewal and expansion, and 2. They did not undertake any financial obligation for national and overseas causes and for local services of a religious character . . . The answer in a number of Community Chest cities was the establishment of a Jewish Welfare Fund." [2]

From these beginnings, Jewish Welfare Funds have been organized in most of the larger American communities. They conduct their appeals for Jewish agencies not included in the local United Fund or Community Chest and their leaders participate in the overall community campaigns as well. In some communities Jewish Community Councils have been organized to coordinate activities of Jewish social, recreational, cultural, and educational agencies. A national organiaztion similar in nature to AACO was established in 1932 and includes more than two hundred local groups in the United States and Canada. This is now called The Council of Jewish Federations and Welfare Funds.

1927

By the dawn of 1927 a new problem was knocking on AACO's door, that of smaller communities wishing to launch their frail skiffs on the turbulent Community Chest flood waters. With a stream of inquiries coming to him, Allen Burns realized some plan must be worked out—such as countywide federations.

Speaking to the board of directors in January, Mr. Burns said the best way for AACO to promote Chest efficiency was to facilitate the exchange and interpretation of tested ideas, principles and methods. This would mean more than merely providing a clearinghouse of information, however. Since all the 300 Community Chests were interrelated in many ways, the failure of one Chest adversely affected the development of another. A large part of the AACO program during 1927 therefore would be focused on interesting Chest laymen in the national aspects of federation and encouraging Chests to do more research.

Social Service Exchanges now began to receive more attention from AACO and a larger place on conference programs. They were recognized as a generally essential factor in joint planning and it was not until much later that this position was challenged.

Up to this time the main concern of AACO had been with Community Chests rather than Welfare Councils. This was natural, for financial campaigns come back each year, and their success could be measured. The less obvious goals of joint planning were less readily marked for there were no timetables and success or failure was not easily recognized or publicized. To show its concern for both movements, the AACO board and membership concluded that the organization name should identify both, and changed it to Association of Community Chests and Councils (ACCC).

A national emergency struck during 1927 in the form of disastrous floods along the Mississippi. Secretary of Commerce Herbert Hoover appealed urgently to ACCC to spur its members to step up efforts to assist the Relief Fund Campaign and to cooperate fully with local Red Cross chapters. Prompt action was taken by ACCC in communicating these requests and Chests responded with pledges of hearty cooperation.

Two of the first public opinion polls regarding local Chest publicity were reported by Saginaw, Mich. and

President Hoover hands his United Way gift to Newbold Noyes, Chairman of Special Gifts for the Washington Community Chest. Others are (left) Elwood Street, Executive Director of Chest; (far right) John Poole, 1930 Campaign Chairman, and (to the right of President Hoover) Frederic A. Delano, Chest President.

Scranton, Pa. Results were both gratifying and thought-provoking. ACCC recommended that other cities conduct similar polls in order to determine the effectiveness of their publicity campaigns.

Community Trusts were being established in many communities, so when the Rochester Chest received a $50,000 memorial gift, officers decided to study the possibility of establishing a trust fund. Chaired by George Eastman, founder of the Eastman Kodak Company and president of the Chest, the committee recommended establishment of a Trust Committee within the Chest. An agreement was worked out with Rochester banks providing that each gift be placed in the trust department of the bank designated by the donor and given the same attention as if the trust were directly established with the bank. Thus the plan provided the flexibility of a community trust but control remained within the Community Chest board.

In September the ACCC moved from the quarters it had shared with NIB to offices of its own. The first bulletin from the new location announced that the Study of Volume and Cost of Social Work was proceeding on a larger scale. The plan was to create a permanent bureau to analyze and tabulate statistics, and by the year's end the University of Chicago agreed to establish a statistical office with a joint committee administering the statistical work. The cost of $18,000 would be equally shared. One of the changes made at this time was to gather statistics, not of the previous year, but as the events occurred. Monthly report forms were developed and used in 29 cities during the following year. At the end of 1928 an annual report was made and a similar report followed in 1929. On July 1, 1930 the entire project was transferred to the United States Children's Bureau in Washington where it remained until 1945 when the national office again assumed responsibility.

1928

In February of 1928 a long-awaited Citizen's Conference on Community Welfare for Chest laymen, sponsored by a National Citizens Committee was held in Washington. President Coolidge greeted delegates in the White House. Attendance numbered 245 laymen and 90 professionals. Herbert Hoover, Secretary of Commerce, spoke at a dinner meeting and told how Chests had increased community interest in charities, had eliminated misguided sentimentality, relieved officers of the time and anxiety in gathering funds, decreased overlaps, and protected against misrepresentation.

Following the conference, a committee of ACCC was established to study the problem of corporate giving, still hampered by laws forbidding the deduction of charitable gifts from corporate taxes.

That summer a new member joined the ACCC staff, a man who was to succeed Allen Burns as its executive director, and to steer its course through both troubled and serene waters. He was Ralph H. Blanchard, a 1917 graduate of Cornell University, a man with banking experience who for the past four years had managed the Chest in Niagara Falls, N. Y.

Assistant Director Pierce Williams took a leave of absence, to help Washington, D.C. organize a Chest. He conducted a study with the help of an organizing committee of nearly 100 men and women prominent in Washington. Through the committee's powers of interpretation and leadership, the whole Chest climate warmed and blossomed. After study and discussions, both contributors and social agencies agreed to the need for a Chest. Among the agencies signing up for membership was Catholic Charities, whose director had publicly opposed the Chest idea in 1926 but who was persuaded by his own laymen that in the national capital, of all places, all faiths should stand together in charity. Jewish charities also joined. By the time of the first campaign in January 1929, there were 57 member agencies. A goal of $1,343,349 was set; President Coolidge made the first gift ever made by a President of the United States to a Community Chest; and 112.8 percent of the goal was raised.

The addition of Washington and Pittsburgh, where the Welfare Fund had been chartered late in 1927, to the list of Chest communities meant that all the larger American communities except New York, Chicago and Boston had adopted federated financing of health and welfare services.

Margaret Culkin Banning, author and civic leader, has also been an active United Way volunteer leader both in her home community of Duluth and on the national scene. She served on the Women's Committee for the United Way, 1936 national Mobilization for Human Needs. She also was a member of the founding board of directors of the National Health and Welfare Retirement Association.

Chest campaigns that fall employed two new features. One was use of the red feather as a Community Chest symbol. Duluth and New Orleans both appear to have started the practice which spread over the country and in 1945 was adopted officially as the national symbol of the Community Chest movement. The second feature was that for the first time campaigns were permitted to quote the endorsement of a President of the United States, beginning a tradition of campaign endorsements by those in high office.

The Depression Approaches

Community Chests were among the first social agencies to hear and record the rumblings of the storm of the great depression which broke in 1929. Economists had already noticed the increasingly serious condition of American agriculture which soon resulted in loss of purchasing power and reduction in demand for industrial products. Men were laid off their factory jobs.

Gerard Swope (left), National Chairman of Mobilization for Human Needs, seeks support of Henry Ford for the 1935 United Way campaigns. Photograph, Detroit Free Press.

Gerard Swope, National Chairman, Mobilization for Human Needs, with Mrs. Harper Sibley, National Women's Committee Chairman, at 1936 Mobilization Conference, New York City. Photograph, Pictures, Inc.

Chests experienced rising difficulties. Relief expenditures mounted steadily and Chest appropriations to agencies giving relief increased. ACCC asked in a newsletter dated October 6, 1928, "What is the cause of this rise in relief expenditures? Can relief be budgeted? If not, what provision can the Chest make in its own finances that will put it in position to meet such a drain on its funds?"

Comments from Chest executives reflected their concern. "Our committees are wondering sometimes if the family welfare society is drifting away from its early ideals of reconstruction rather than relief . . . There is some danger that this unemployment is a permanent rather than a transient symptom due to the replacement of men by machinery. Chests cannot indefinitely increase the proportion of the total budget which goes to the family welfare and relief societies." [3]

These rumblings instigated studies by the ACCC and the American Association for Organizing Family Social Work and other agencies as well as government. Before they were finished, the whole program of social service, voluntary and governmental would be revolutionized.

In October 1928 a meeting of the ACCC committee to study corporate giving was held. Composed of bankers, industrialists, insurance men, and corporation officers from many parts of the country, it was an extremely influential group. At this meeting it was decided to initiate a fact-finding study to be carried out by an independent bureau of investigation. In addition, members agreed to study the facts of federation and to make personal visits to corporation officers in an effort to enlist their support.

In Cleveland the Community Fund had made its own study and concluded that an adequate, efficient program of social service provided through a Community Fund was an important factor in making a community a good place to conduct business. Therefore corporations did have a financial interest in maintaining these services. Also, corporations as employers had responsibilities for the welfare of their employees, and consequently an interest in making the community a good place to live. A further conclusion was that standards must be established in determining the amount to be asked of corporations so that the guide would not be simply "what the traffic will bear," or involve exploitation of a liberal corporation.

ACCC arranged for its study to be made by the National Bureau of Economic Research with Pierce Williams loaned to the Bureau to become study director.

Mr. Williams did not return to the ACCC staff, and his job was taken over by Homer W. Borst, former executive director of the Indianapolis Community Fund. Allen Burns now had two associate directors, both experienced in Community Chest work, Homer Borst and Ralph Blanchard.

In an attempt to cultivate understanding between national agencies and their locals with local Chests and Councils, ACCC and the YMCA had asked the National Social Work Council to gather data and make recommendations for action. In May of 1928, meetings had been held for representatives of 20 member organizations of the National Social Work Council and a dozen or more Community Chests. In them they tackled the thorny problem, long a subject of misunderstanding and irritation: namely, the budgets of national agencies and how they could best be presented to Chests. Among suggestions made were for national agencies to present both functional and administrative budgets, the former to show relations between expenditures and service and the latter for purposes of financial analysis; to approach Chests through local units; and for Chests to hold special budget hearings on the subject of appropriations to nationals. It was pointed out that Chest support for nationals might well be predicated not only on local service but on service to other communities.

To public relations personnel, one of the most useful sources of information through the years has been the publicity exchange which had its birth during 1929 Under the direction of chairman Arch Mandel, executive director of the Dayton Bureau of Community Service, the newly-formed Educational Publicity Committee set up a monthly exchange among 127 members whereby especially good examples of publicity materials were circulated and commented on.

At the Blue Ridge conference a committee was appointed to set standards for Chest executives. Their report listed various qualities for executives covering personality, ability, interest, and training.

As 1929 grew older, the world economic situation worsened. Unemployment spread while public and private debts mounted; speculation increased and credit was abused. On October 21, stock prices began to sag; on the 24th, more than 12 million shares changed hands; on the 29th, the crash came.

Community Chest campaigns, with their large relief allocations, did fairly well in the first year of the Great Depression. Campaigns increased from 331 to 353 and the amount raised increased from more than $73 million to nearly $76 million.

1930

The Depression was an economic disaster without parallel in United States history. By 1930 there were more than 3 million unemployed; by 1933 the number would rise to between 12 and 15 million. Eventually about one third of the population would be unemployed and receiving relief of one kind or another. President Hoover underestimated the seriousness of the depression from the start, feeling that a restoration of confidence would mean a return of prosperity. The administration was unwilling to grant direct relief, leaving that burden for local governments and private charity.

But while fear and despair stalked through the land, there rose against them men and women of compassion, courage, and determination who went into action. Prominent among them were agency leaders, lay and professional, who constituted a resource of experience, know-how, and compassion with which to help meet human distress. Their testimony, grounded in experience, contributed greatly to the national welfare legislation which finally evolved.

The first task of local Chests and Councils was to reorient both philosophy and goals of service. Chests added the problems of relief to their agenda, and allocated more funds for this purpose to agencies dispensing relief. They organized supplementary campaigns and formed committees to stabilize employment by appealing to employers and public authorities to open up job opportunities. Fortunately those who still had money were generous and top-flight citizens joined in planning and fund raising. Voluntary giving did much in the early days of the depression, though it would not hold up indefinitely.

No one really knew which agencies, voluntary or governmental, should administer relief funds. Local government relief agencies generally were inadequate and ineffective. Mass relief for able-bodied unemployed was foreign to the experience of family welfare agencies and they were too few to handle the swarms of needy.

He ain't heavy, he's my brother

This much copied United Way slogan and illustration originated in Minneapolis as the poster for the 1928, 1929 and 1930 Community Fund appeals. It was created by Mert Harrison, head of the Harrison and Guthrie advertising agency, which became the office of Batten, Barton, Durstine and Osborn. The poster was picked up by other United Way's throughout the country in the 1930's. Later it was used as the model for similiar posters by many other charities.

Furthermore nobody knew where the money would come from. Could voluntary contributions support it? Didn't the laws place responsibility on the local community for care of its poor? But suppose the community itself also was destitute, as in a one-industry town where that industry was closed and perhaps bankrupt: what did you do then?

The ACCC was in a quandary too, unable to counsel the 350 federated communities all varying in conditions and resources. And most important, Chest leaders wondered how to stimulate federal action when government continued to assume that a return to prosperity was just around the corner and that federal funds could not be used for relief purposes.

The struggle to raise more money was aided early in 1930 by an important legal decision allowing corporations to make tax deductible gifts to charitable institutions. This came about through the case of Corning Glass Works in New York which had contributed $25,000 to the local hospital with the idea that employees would be better taken care of at a hospital than by a company physician and dispensary. The Board of Tax Appeals disallowed the deduction and

the company appealed to the Court of Appeals of the District of Columbia which then decided that "business corporations may have authority to make donations of money or property to enterprises reasonably calculated to further their general business interests." The company's case was handled by Frederick R. Kellogg, volunteer legal advisor for ACCC, who later became its president. In Canada later that year the Federal Legislature passed an act permitting tax-deductible charitable contributions.

Many Chests had failures in 1930 and ACCC was called upon for assistance. In addition to this responsibility, the 38 existing Councils of Social Agencies now became a major concern of ACCC following the reorganization of the American Association for Organizing Family Social Work. This agency now became the Family Welfare Association of America and restricted its functions to family service. The staff of three and one-fourth members had to select carefully the services on which it should concentrate. The recruitment of students for the Chest training course at Ohio State was stepped up, and for the first time ACCC put staff time into helping the Blue Ridge Institute.

Florida was hard-hit by the depression and its Chests struggled to survive. Some tried supplementary financing in the form of benefits—card parties, balls, and the like—even though they were contrary to accepted practice. Yet member organizations preferred that Chests struggle along rather than give up.

Some ACCC rescue squads had encouraging results: Fort Dodge, Iowa raised $38,500 against a goal of $34,450; Memphis made its $528,529 goal with the help of Ralph Blanchard. Bradley Buell, director of the New Orleans Chest and Council, was dispatched to Atlanta where he helped resuscitate that Chest. The increased demands for field service, which so often brought remedies to faltering Chests, caused ACCC to realize the need for additional staff, and Mr. Buell was hired as a fifth member assigned to field service.

The long-awaited report on corporation contributions authorized by a special ACCC committee was released in the fall of 1930 by the National Bureau of Economic Research, after two years of preparation. It detailed past financial contributions, showing that amounts of less than $1000 to more than $1 million had been contributed to Community Chests in 1929. In 129 Chests studied, the total corporate contributions were 22 percent of the total funds raised. Evidence was uncovered that corporations based contributions on their estimate of the indirect benefit to stockholders which resulted from employee benefits. Plans got under way for use of the information gathered, and a national conference for corporation and community leaders was planned by the Board of Sponsors which had sponsored the National Bureau study. Facts gathered in this study, followed by intensive cultivation in the field and personal interpretation to corporations, resulted in substantial support for federation by corporations.

ACCC was very concerned about mounting relief needs and reported that most groups of givers were making smaller gifts, although big givers were increasing theirs. During fall campaigns, Chests were advised not to stress relief giving to the exclusion of other needs such as case work. "Our responsibility is for the development of the whole program, not just a part." [4] When the campaigns were over, it was found that giving had jumped almost $9 million.

This cartoon story was created by the Richmond, Va. Community Fund in 1938.

President Hoover asked Allen Burns how Chests might help in the crisis. He assured the President that Chests and Councils would do all in their power to mobilize the human and financial resources of their communities and to lessen, if possible, the spreading and deepening destitution.

Porter R. Lee, director of the New York School of Social Work, went to Washington at the request of the President's Emergency Committee on Employment to explain the resources of social work. ACCC was asked to supply the committee with information on community plans for meeting the situation. In preparation for this meeting, Mr. Burns visited several communities where substantial unemployment programs were being carried on.

Providence, R.I. cooperated in a drive by a municipal committee, which included all relief agencies whether in the Chest or not; St. Louis conducted a special $1 million drive for relief; Philadelphia had a $5 million supplementary drive. In New York an Emergency Employment Committee collected $8 million to pay for work done in public parks, sanitation projects, and noncompetitive institutions.

When the Roaring Twenties had closed, it was with a different sound than when it had begun—a wail of anguish at shattered hopes and increasing misery. Yet Chests and Councils and their national organization were becoming recognized as vital factors in America's social service structure. By 1930 the Chest movement reached the end of the period of rapid expansion which had begun around 1920. There were now Chests in 375 cities, all of them facing a crisis which nobody knew how to solve.

NOTES
Chapter 6

1. Raymond Clapp, "Study of Volume and Cost of Social Work," 1926, Introduction, p. 111, quoted from *Survey Midmonthly* article, March 15, 1926.

2. Harry L. Lurie, *The Heritage Affirmed* (Jewish Publication Society of America, 1961), pp. 104-105.

3. *News Bulletin,* Association of Community Chests and Councils (UCFCA), November 3, 1928.

4. Bulletin 52, ACCC (UCFCA), August 20, 1930, pp. 1-10.

7

CHESTS MOBILIZE TO FIGHT HUNGER AND WANT:1931-1939

As the depression grew during 1931, so did the war against it. When, early in the year, it became evident that the $75 million Red Cross campaign was in trouble, Red Cross officials and ACCC agreed to urge cooperation in communities where campaigns might compete. President Hoover was gratified and set a precedent by permitting the Washington, D. C. Chest to solicit federal employees. The local Red Cross chapter joined in that campaign which raised 103 percent of its goal. In other communities special emergency campaigns were conducted.

In May the President's Emergency Committee for Employment asked ACCC to assume responsibility for obtaining information on the status of relief needs and funds in cities of 25,000 population and greater; to obtain as many relief funds as possible; to promote organization for these purposes in non-Chest cities; and to develop understanding of the need for using all available resources to obtain relief funds.

Fred Croxton, vice chairman of the President's Emergency Committee for Employment, and former executive director of the Columbus Council and Community Fund, presented a plan developed by the committee and ACCC for a "welfare and relief mobilization." This plan would involve establishment of a national committee to enlist large corporations for sup-

port; a national educational and publicity campaign; and setting aside a specific campaign month. The intention was for nationwide support of local autonomous Chest appeals. This proposal was accepted by the board and membership of ACCC.

While the Welfare and Relief Mobilization was in progress, a significant public relations "first" took place. On October 10, 1931, in the studios of the Columbia Broadcasting System, the first televised philanthropic appeal took place. It was a report by Allen Burns on the progress of campaigns. "We realize," he reported later, "that in its present state of development television reaches a very limited audience and consequently can be of but little actual service, but it serves to give us a glimpse of the future when T.V. undoubtedly will play a great part, as radio is now doing, in education, philanthropy, and public service." [1]

Campaigns that year were generally successful. For the first time the total passed the one hundred million mark. Yet, one-fourth of the Chests failed by 10 percent or more, and Chest goals, rather than reflecting total needs, represented estimates of what could be raised. Badly depressed areas with no local charities and very little relief were, of course, unaffected by the campaigns. Despite these inadequacies, however, ACCC planned to repeat the Mobilization the following year and to establish a permanent publicity department.

1932

The problems which had begun in late 1928 continued to grow; more and more businesses shut their doors or reduced hours; more and more were unemployed; more and more savings were exhausted, and more and more applied for relief.

Many Chests were in serious difficulty. Typical perhaps was the Grand Rapids, Michigan Chest which had done well until 1930 when, in the face of declining returns, one agency was dropped and others were challenged. Chest leaders called in Harry Wareham of Rochester, who helped them raise $408,239 of the $459,566 goal. During 1931 ACCC's Ralph Blanchard was called in and changes were made. The cost of living had fallen drastically and it was felt that this could justify reduced budgets involving 25% reductions in staff salaries. Despite these and other changes, the 1932 campaign raised only $254,000. Even top-flight help from the national office was unable to bring success to destitute communities.

Allen Burns reported to the board that the number of families receiving relief was increasing more rapidly than the amount of money being spent for relief. Voluntary funds were harder to raise and at the same time relief money from tax sources had decreased from 75% in October 1931 to 62% in December. Local tax bodies, he felt, would have to vote more relief funds.

The problem was that sometimes local tax bodies could not do this because they didn't have any funds to vote. Some cities were paying employees in scrip; some had reached the limit of their bonded indebtedness and couldn't borrow more until their state legislatures raised their debt limits. It became increasingly clear that the Federal Government must help.

President Hoover resisted federal relief funds as long as he could, but in July 1932 he signed the Wagner Federal Relief Bill which authorized the Reconstruction Finance Corporation to lend the states a sum of $300 million for relief, not more than 15% going to any one state.

This was hailed as the beginning of a new era in the welfare and relief history of the United States and the loans did, indeed, prove helpful to many communities. In many states, however, the borrowing limits were soon reached and relief needs continued to plague many

(Left to Right) Dorothy Thompson and Newton D. Baker, speakers at 1936 Mobilization for Human Needs Conference.

communities. Later federal legislation cancelled the loans which were never repaid.

Newton D. Baker, former mayor of Cleveland and later Secretary of War during President Wilson's administration, accepted chairmanship of the 1932 National Citizens' Committee for the Mobilization, composed of 58 outstanding citizens. One of the committee's first acts was to call a citizens' conference of local social welfare leaders in Washington for September 15.

In describing the conference to *The New York Times,* Mr. Baker pointed out that private contributions still carried 40 percent of the relief load; that other indispensable social services must be supported; and that the Mobilization would attempt to reenforce all local efforts for relief and welfare purposes. An impressive array of speakers, including President Hoover, from government, business, and philanthropy focused national attention on the Mobilization and prepared the public for the campaigns soon to be launched. Under Mr. Baker's leadership 28 national organizations became co-sponsors of the Mobilization.

Despite a barrage of publicity, the campaigns did not produce the hoped-for results. Federal grants had dulled the edge of urgency, increased taxes had cut into income; and more givers were themselves out of jobs. In addition, Roosevelt's overwhelming victory over Hoover for the presidency with his promise to produce a New Deal for the "forgotten man" frightened many men of wealth into hanging onto what they had. The 401 campaigns that fall fell almost 16 percent short of their goals.

The failure of Chests in general to reach their goals did not, however, indicate that the Chest movement was a failure. It had raised funds for emergency relief which could have been raised no other way, and had done it at minimum cost. It had enlisted new citizen leaders in its activities and had saved the programs of many agencies which might otherwise have had to close shop. The Welfare and Relief Mobilization was given permanent national status.

With financial problems of its own, ACCC was helped by a $20,000 grant by the Carnegie Corporation for conducting field work among those Chests which had fallen the farthest short of their goals, enabling staff member Bradley Buell to devote six months of his time, and Charles C. Stillman three months to visit most of the Chests with large shortages and help find ways to reorganize for the next year's campaigns. The rest of the year Stillman served as Professor of Social Administration at Ohio State University. He was a former executive of the Grand Rapids Welfare Union.

1933

A few hours before Franklin Delano Roosevelt was inaugurated, every bank in America closed its doors to prevent economic collapse and out of fear of violence. The new President called for courageous action and declared, "We have nothing to fear but fear itself." He took swift action in presenting his Banking Bill which averted panic and gave the people hope for the future.

A sample of United Way campaign literature circa early 1930's.

67

Eleanor Roosevelt (center), Chairman of United Way Women's Committee's 1933 Mobilization for Human Needs, with committee members, Mesdames: 1, Lathrop, Alabama; 2, Paisl, YWCA: Sudler, Colorado; 4, Mrs. Mabolos Broady, Girl Scouts; 5, Eleanor Roosevelt; 6, Sloss, California; 7, Arkwright, Georgia; 8, Hopkins, Iowa; 9, Derborn, Maine; 10, Tucker, Public Health Nurses; 11, Noble, Washington; 12, Bullitt, Washington; 13, Murdock, Kansas; 14, Manning, New Hampshire; 15, Downey, Indiana; 16, Bowman, Business and Professional Women's Club; 17, McKessick, South Carolina; 18, Borg, National Council Jewish Women; 19, Ida M. Tarbell; 20, Mrs. John M. Glenn; 21, Cummer, Florida; 22, Goodwillie, Maryland; 23 Hawks, National Council of Catholic Women; 24, Sigmon, Arkansas; 25, Dalrymple, Minnesota; 26, Williams, North Carolina; 27, Phillips, Texas. Photo by Underwood & Underwood, Washington.

Under pressure of the depression, two new Canadian Chests were organized in Montreal and Ottawa. In Montreal it was the French Federation; in Ottawa, a federation of Protestant, Catholic, and non-sectarian organizations.

Chicago was in the process of developing a modified Chest, having started in 1931 with an Emergency Relief Fund. In the next year it was to become the Community Fund of Chicago. Member agencies reserved the right to solicit on their own, with the Community Fund restricting itself to solicitation of corporations and employee groups.

On April 20 Congress passed the Federal Emergency Relief Act and on May 20 President Roosevelt drafted Harry Hopkins to head the Federal Emergency Relief Administration (F.E.R.A. as it was called in the days of growing "alphabetical" agencies of the New Deal.) He was an experienced social worker who had served as executive director of the New York State Temporary Relief Administration. Hopkins was the first social worker to serve in a top government post, and was to influence the whole future of relief programs.

With federal relief assured, ACCC turned its attention to internal affairs, one of which was a change in name and purpose. "Community Chests and Councils" was chosen as more compact and descriptive, and the statement of purpose was broadened to stress the importance of cooperation with national agencies and with Canadian Chests and Councils as well as those in the United States.

Plans for the Mobilization were made, with a change in name to Mobilization for Human Needs instead of for "welfare and relief." A great deal of interpretation was needed because a large section of the public had been displeased by election returns and now said with bitter sarcasm, "Let Roosevelt do everything." Yet Roosevelt himself, at the time he signed the relief bill said, "The present Federal Relief Act would be a calamity if it resulted in a decreased sense of responsibility among private givers. Their support of the voluntary welfare services, so essential to our commonwealth, is required more than ever." [2]

A new element in the 1933 Mobilization was an active National Women's Committee, headed by Mrs. Eleanor Roosevelt. This was one of the first national responsibilities ever undertaken by a President's wife. The committee was most effective in organizing Women's Crusades throughout the nation, following the example of Cincinnati where the crusade idea had worked out remarkably well the year before.

In September a Mobilization Conference was held in Washington, with President Roosevelt giving his first Community Chest talk when he delivered a "Charge of Responsibility" to those assembled at the White House.

Despite the efforts made to counteract the difficulties, results of the 1933 Mobilization were discourag-

ing. The total raised was $70,609,000, more than $7 million less than during the previous year. The 399 campaigns reached only 91 percent of their lowered goals.

These results caused serious soul-searching among community organizations. A few wondered if Chests should be discontinued with the strongest though not necessarily the fittest agencies surviving on their own; others thought reorganization of programs and agencies might enable the maintenance of the most essential services. The National Committee of Volunteers which had been organized during the Annual Meeting of the National Conference of Social Work that year felt that volunteers could do much to supplement agency staffs while in no way attempting to substitute for professional social workers. (In 1943 this group became a committee of Community Chests and Councils.)

President Franklin D. Roosevelt addresses United Way volunteer leaders of the 1933 Mobilization for Human Needs on the White House grounds.

The Mobilization for Human Needs was organized by United Way at President Hoover's request in 1931. It was headed by Newton D. Baker from 1932 to 1934. President Roosevelt (above), speaking from the South Portico of the White House makes his "charge to citizens" at the launching of the 1935 Mobilization. F.D.R.'s opening of this United Way program in 1934 is shown at right.

REBUILD

Rev. Monsignor John O'Grady, Executive Director, 1919 to 1961, of National Conference of Catholic Charities, many local agencies of which participate in United Way funds. His successor Rev. Monsignor Lawrence J. Corcoran has served as a member of United Way's national Board of Directors. Blackstone Studios.

1934

During 1934 criticism mounted regarding many aspects of the government's program, and led to an end of the Civil Works Administration program which under Harry Hopkins had provided employment for more than four million persons. CWA was finished, with remaining parts of the program transferred to the Emergency Work Relief Program of FERA. Work relief continued in diminished form. The following year Hopkins was named to head the Works Progress Administration (WPA) which provided work for millions. It continued until 1943.

Community Chests and Councils, meantime, considered the possibility of a "new deal" in social services. CCC pointed out in a bulletin on Chest budgeting that "Any tendency which Community Chests may have had to accept the status quo received a rude shock when the depression brought about an acute shortage of funds for welfare services formerly accepted as essential. There is an increasing demand for reorganization and realignment of agencies to provide better services for less money. Communities are looking askance at services long accepted as a matter of course." [3] Many Chest cities conducted studies which resulted in mergers, elimination, or addition of agencies.

One of the most ambitious surveys made was that directed by CCC in Hartford, Connecticut which pointed out the changes in voluntary social service as a result of shared responsibility with public agencies.

As the national system of public assistance became accepted, voluntary agencies relinquished their role as a resource for relief funds, and concentrated on other service areas. New psychological theories began to take hold, and the idea that poverty and other social ills were congenital gave way. Effects were seen now in the fields of group work, guidance, and other areas of social service. Psychoanalysis was coming into its own, and social workers realized the interplay of family, group, and community influence on individual behavior.

The Mobilization swung into action in the fall of 1934 with larger citizen committees and even more highly organized publicity. Even so, the campaigns slumped to their lowest level since the campaigns of 1927-28 when there were fewer than 100 Chests in existence. With 409 campaigns, just $69,781,000 was raised. There was, however, faith that things would improve and the Board voted CCC its largest budget since 1931—$91,935.

1935

In February 1935 a community planning bulletin was produced, a summary of three papers presented at the New York State Conference of Social Work. One

David Dubinsky, President of the International Ladies Garment Workers Union (left), and John D. Rockefeller, Jr., talk it over at the opening meeting of the first annual campaign of the Greater New York Fund. New York Herald Tribune Photo, 1938.

of the most significant papers was that by CCC's field director, Bradley Buell, who stressed the importance of research and statistical data as a foundation for effective planning. "Community interest in social work is finally coming into its own," he said. "It wasn't so long ago that in most communities and in most fields of service the private agencies did what they happened to want to do, and the public agencies what some law happened to prescribe, and never the twain did meet. That situation has been changing rapidly during the past few years." [4]

That year Canada formed its own organization for Dominion-wide health and welfare planning, the Canadian Welfare Council, an outgrowth of an earlier group established in 1920 with emphasis on child protection. This had grown to include child and family welfare and now was encompassing community organization, leisure-time activities, public welfare administration and a very active French speaking division. Similarly affected by the depression, Canada had become all too familiar with unemployment, bread lines, and inadequate relief measures. During the 30's the Council took a leading role in meeting those needs, making surveys, calling conferences, making recommendations, and running Canada's first national publicity program for Community Chest campaigns.

In July, CCC president Frederick R. Kellogg, a prominent New York attorney, appeared before the House Ways and Means Committee, and in August, Newton D. Baker appeared before the Senate Finance Committee to plead the case of tax deductible corporate contributions to charitable agencies. With income taxes rising, including a new graduated corporation tax up to 15 percent of net income exceeding $40,000, welfare agencies were alarmed, for they depended on substantial corporation donations. They urged that corporations be granted the same kind of tax deduction for charitable gifts that had been granted individuals as early as 1917. Mr. Baker testified, "The need for character-building agencies in our cities is a part of the social structure of modern American industrial life . . . I deeply believe that the corporation has not only a right but a duty to be a good neighbor in the town in which its own employees live, and that there are obvious and direct benefits going to a corporation which makes a subscription to a fund of this sort, an incalculably valuable and direct benefit." [5] The Revenue Act, passed in August, included the desired provision, providing deductions for charitable contributions up to five percent of net income.

Another piece of legislation passed that year was the Social Security Bill signed on August 14 by President Roosevelt. For Community Chests and Councils the Social Security Act had two vital effects. First, it meant that the trend away from raising funds for relief was made permanent, with consequent program changes in many Chest agencies, particularly family service. Character building and leisure-time activities began to receive a major share of Chest allocations. Secondly, the act made it clear that public welfare was now a shared responsibility of federal, state, and local public agencies. This meant that joint planning on the federal, state, and local level must follow even more than before.

Prospects for the fall Mobilization were promising because of the tax allowance for charitable contributions, payroll deductions which were more widely used, and increased development of women's crusades. More of the population was employed, and while many did not like the New Deal, they felt they could at least plan and act with some degree of assurance. Though in some cases income from investment was down and taxes were heavy, the 429 campaigns raised more than $77 million, an increase of $8 million for 92 percent of goals.

Between Two Wars

Relief counts in 1936 at last began to go down while the relief granted became more adequate and better conducted. Benefits granted through the Social Security Act were aiding a great many people and helping to reduce the number who otherwise depended on relief. Resourceful people were finding work; voluntary agencies were adapting programs to the newly-accepted concepts of service; Councils were gaining new recognition and responsibility; and Community Chests felt hope stirring.

Boston, after 12 years of resisting federated financing, conducted its first Greater Boston Community Fund campaign with great success. There had been unemployment relief campaigns in previous years, all falling short of their goals. A strong citizens' movement for permanent federated financing had begun and a study commitee was organized by the Council. With a goal of $3,750,000 the January-February campaign raised $3,834,732.

American National Red Cross by 1936 had grown into a gigantic organization with 3,711 chapters, many of them offering a variety of services. They generally

REBUILD

In the depths of the Depression, United Way made a positive approach in its 1934 Campaign Appeal by this poster painted by Walter Beach Humphrey.

Painting by Haddon Sundblom for the 1939 campaign poster.

had won and kept impressive community leadership and enlisted large numbers of devoted volunteers.

Many chapters had been charter members of local Chests and Councils and had been good cooperators. Often leadership was the same in both organizations. Friction had developed in recent years, however, over such questions as the right to raise funds for disaster relief; the problem of determining Red Cross membership when its roll call was merged; the amount of funds to be sent to the national Red Cross; the amount and nature of local chapter budgets and the method for reduction in case the Chest did not meet its goal; and the degree and nature of control by the national. In 1929 the Annual Convention of American National Red Cross had adopted a resolution favoring withdrawal of chapters where it was believed Red Cross interests were jeopardized by Chest membership.

CCC now conducted an inquiry among Chests and

concluded from the answers that the somewhat turbulent local relationships with the Red Cross in various communities had their roots in the difficulties of reconciling the policies of an organization interested in a locally-proportioned program with those of one claiming priorities and preferred status because of a national program. A shortage of funds during the depression undoubtedly caused further questioning about national quotas for Red Cross. Serious attempts were made to accommodate Red Cross, such as giving special membership arrangements. While the inequities of granting such privileges were easy to overlook by other member agencies during periods of prosperity, it had proved more difficult during economic distress.

American National Red Cross and Community Chests and Councils represented two almost incompatible points of view: the control of Red Cross chapters from the top down vs. the control of CCC from the grass roots up. It was a long time before the two points of view were reasonably well reconciled. While an open break did not publicly come, some rather acrimonious points of view were expressed through the years. Red Cross chapters did continue to participate in Councils, however, as well as in Social Service Exchanges.

Social Service Exchanges were increasing in importance because of the establishment of permanent local welfare departments in accordance with requirements of the new Social Security Act. With development of the emergency relief organization, where emphasis was placed on the protection of the public from "chiselers," the Exchange became an instrument for accomplishing this end. As a result, the Exchange came to serve four purposes: one, as an index to case records for better service; two, as an index for the prevention of duplication in relief giving; three, to assist in giving information for determining legal responsibility; and four, to act as registration bureaus for emergency relief administrations until they could develop their own registration bureaus.

Corporate giving was one of the main topics at the Mobilization for Human Needs Conference preceding the fall 1936 campaigns, and many industrial, banking, and utilities leaders supported the idea of generous corporate giving. One-fourth of the money raised by Chests was then contributed by corporations.

For the first time in seven years, campaigns did not use a theme dependent on the depression. The public was satiated with the subject of relief, which was now accepted to be a governmental responsibility. "The concept that private agencies do what the government cannot do is trite and contains little positive interest," CCC advised its members. "Private services must this year justify themselves. The basis for their appeal must be stated in the positive terms of what they are doing that no one else can do as well." [6]

Since it was a presidential election year, campaigns were scheduled between the November election and Thanksgiving. With 452 campaigns, $81,707,787 was raised, or 94 percent of increased goals and $4,340,000 more than was raised the year before.

1937

With joint financing improving its position, the pendulum swung to the side of joint planning. In January, Allen Burns reported that, in the past year, local

communities had become less concerned about money raising and more concerned about the best use of money to secure programs adequate for human needs. This shift to greater service interest resulted in many of the most important national activities of the year, and was best illustrated in continued attention to intensive studies of community needs and organization. Seven studies were completed and it was the feeling that CCC would have to establish a regular field service. The Board voted to make this the next national development.

When the Social Security Act had been passed in 1935, employees of private charitable, religious and educational institutions and agencies were not covered by Old Age and Retirement Insurance or Unemployment Insurance. Many agencies had opposed the bill on the grounds that they could not afford to pay their share of the cost. Soon, however, they found they couldn't afford not to. Social workers and other employees of voluntary agencies grew old, like anyone else. They wanted economic security in their old age, and began to seek employment in the "covered" institutions of business and industry. Social agencies often found it difficult to fill vacated jobs, non-professional positions in particular.

(Left to right) Gerard Swope, 1936 National Chairman, Mobilization for Human Needs, with his successor, Charles P. Taft, newly appointed 1937 National Chairman.

"Thanks for the break, neighbor," was the 1935 campaign slogan used with this painting by Frederic Stanley.

This painting for the 1935 campaign was one of serveral painted by Haddon Sundblom for the United Way.

Aware of this trend, the Board of Directors of CCC on March 5, 1937 created a Committee on Social Security to study the problem and submit a plan of action. It also went on record as favoring participation in Social Security should the opportunity become available. The first action eventually led to organization of the National Health and Welfare Retirement Association in 1947 and the second to changes in the law permitting coverage under Social Security, but it took until 1950 to accomplish this.

The national economy had slipped into the Recession of 1937, brought about by a curtailment of government spending and a sharp reduction of relief rolls. The National Recovery Administration had been invalidated, removing federal control over hours and wages. There were 11 million unemployed and another 5½ million only partially employed. Wages declined and the stock market sagged. Interpretive activities became more important than ever and CCC provided national posters and printed matter for sale at cost.

While the recession was a handicap to campaigns, final results showed nearly $84 million raised, for 93.3 percent of goals, better than $2 million more than was raised the year before.

On December 17, the National Citizens' Committee, composed of about 175 national business, civic and social welfare leaders, met with the CCC board to discuss relief recommendations to the President and Congress. Their recommendations, in general, were for a direct relief appropriation as a grant-in-aid to the states and territories. Many of the proposals were enacted into federal law in 1938 or thereafter, establishing CCC in an important advisory role in federal health and welfare legislation.

1938

Prosperity was slow in coming. When Roosevelt took office in 1933, there were about 13 million unemployed. The total shrank to a low of 4½ million in the summer of 1937, but by March 1938 rose to 11 million, remaining about 10 million until March 1939. It would take American support of the Allies in the war in Europe and finally our own participation to put the economic machine into full gear.

In February, the Greater New York Fund was organized, following 10 years of study. From the beginning, the modus operandi of the Greater New York Fund was unique. The solicitation effort was organized so that the Fund would solicit publicly-held companies for a single annual gift in behalf of all participating agencies, and all employee groups at their place of work, whether it be a public or private business or a non-profit organization. The Fund and its agencies would jointly solicit private firms for company gifts to allow these firms to support the total effort as well as the individual sectarian agencies or federation they traditionally supported. Agencies would have exclusive responsibility for soliciting individuals, including the executive officers of public or privately-held firms. The first campaign in 1938 resulted in $3,790,558 for 380 participating agencies.

It was ironic that just when New York City, the presumed last citadel of independent financing, was accepting the federation principle, a new national agency was born, taking the position of go-it-alone rather than Chest participation. It was the National Foundation for Infantile Paralysis, established with the aid of President Roosevelt. While it is likely that no

one could anticipate the extent to which it would become a controversial organization, neither could anyone predict its spectacular success which would lead to formation of myriad of other national health organizations, many of them dedicated to going their own financial ways.

The twenty-fifth anniversary of the founding of the Cleveland Community Fund, generally acknowledged to have been the first modern Community Chest, was celebrated during the Community Mobilization for Human Needs conference in March, 1938. Looking back 25 years, Community Chests and Councils pointed out some of the accomplishments since then: more than $1,200,000,000 raised since the World War; 15 percent reduction in fund-raising costs or $180 million; 50 percent more money raised than by participating

The inimitable Professor "Charlie" C. E. Stillman (seated, center), Director of the School of Social Administration of Ohio State University, with his faculty in 1937. Left to right, standing, R. G. Paterson, Stockton Raymond, Virginia Hawley, Elsie U. Jones, William C. Batchelor, John A. Reimers. Left to right, seated, W. J. Blackburn, Carrol Day Tibbals, Charles C. Stillman, Mary Louise Mark, Merriss Cornell.
This school, which received United Way financial support, and the Boston College School of Social Work offered special graduate courses in United Way management, and from the 1930's into the 1960's were the principal professional training facilities for United Way executives.

agencies in individual efforts; a shrinkage of only 15 percent during the depression, less than any other form of philanthropy on record; a spread in the base of giving until one out of every five or six were givers, for a total of 9 million; givers freed from annoyance; interest spread to a broader view of community needs; stimulation of joint planning to prevent overlooking and overlapping; development of budget methods to take into account community needs; proving to be a unifying factor in 467 communities; and developing a national association with statistical information, experience, specialized literature, training courses and presenting a united front in the annual campaigns.

Newspaper coverage of the conference was overshadowed by news on March 12 that the German Army had pounded across the border and taken over Austria. From then on Chest publicity had to compete with news of the growing menace abroad.

Business continued to improve, nevertheless, and prospects for the fall campaigns looked better.

President Roosevelt opened the Mobilization with a radio address in which he said, "You may well ask . . . if the need for community action is as great as before, now that our government has provided a national program of social security. I would answer that the need is just as great as ever before, because government help was intended, and is intended, to improve the old conditions, and if local help and private help decrease today, we will nullify the improvement and return to just where we were before." [7]

Ominous events in Europe, however, shook the people's confidence and caused a bad case of war jitters. The stock market sagged and incomes slumped. At the Munich Conference near the end of September, Britain and France abandoned Czech Sudetenland to Germany. Winston Churchill said, "Britain and France had to choose between war and dishonor. They chose dishonor. They will have war." [8]

When all the campaign reports were tabulated, it was clear that war fears had hurt . . . The 523 campaigns raised only $82,771,362, more than a million dollars less than the year before, just 91 percent of their goals.

1939

At the midwest Chest-Council Conference in Chicago during February, C. M. Bookman, director of the Cincinnati Council, urged careful examination of private

Lillian Wald, innovative social worker and head of Henry Street Settlement in New York, was a member of the National Citizens Committee of the Welfare and Relief Mobilization in 1932. The Mobilization was organized by the Association of Community Chests and Councils at the request of President Hoover. (Photograph from Keystone View Co.)

programs to determine which of them logically should be supported by public funds. He pointed out "It is not desirable to turn work over to public agencies until there is a prospect that it will be reasonably well done, but there is need to work toward the development of public agencies capable of doing these things and doing them well. Private relief agencies doing little or no case work different from that which is being done by public agencies have little logical ground for existence at this time." [9] He also urged adequate public support for free hospital and clinic care and cited a group of miscellaneous agencies definitely public in character which ought to be publicly supported.

In June the Children's Bureau presented a report on its study of volume and cost of social services, based on data supplied through CCC in 29 large areas. This report showed their health and welfare cost in 1938 was $637 million, 72 percent going for family welfare, 3.6 percent for child care, 3.6 percent for leisure-time activities; 16.7 percent for hospital care, 3.7 percent for health services; and 0.4 percent for Chests and Councils, administration and campaign. Public general relief agencies had an average monthly case load of 234,000 while private agencies handled 62,000. The

Evangeline Booth, Commander-in-Chief of the Salvation Army in the United States, was an active United Way volunteer as a member of the National Women's Committee of the Mobilization for Human Needs in the 1930's.

federal government supplied nearly 50 percent of all funds expended for the welfare program, state governments 13 percent, local public administration 21 percent, and private sources 17 percent (9 percent of which was payments by beneficiaries). While Community Chests provided only 3.9 percent of the total expenditures, their agencies spent approximately $1 of every $10 for the total program, and $6 of every $10 spent by private agencies.[10]

As fall approached, Chest officials wondered about business prospects. Uppermost in all minds was the great imponderable: war. All talk about the future included the phrase, "Assuming no war." But Hitler had made his plans; war was to come. It was to change practically all of American life, including, of course, the program and activities of CCC and its members.

NOTES

Chapter 7

1. *News Bulletin,* ACCC (UCFCA), November 18, 1931, p. 1.

2. Newton D. Baker, "122,000,000 Partners of the Poor," *New York Herald Tribune Magazine,* July 23, 1933, p. 2.

3. "A Study of the Several Services Financed by the Hartford Community Chest, Inc., and Their Relationship to the Social and Health Program of the Community," CCC, 1934, as quoted by Ralph E. and Muriel W. Pumphrey, in *The Heritage of American Social Work* (New York: Columbia University Press, 1961), pp. 396-400.

4. Bradley Buell, "Content in Community Planning, Some Problems in Community Planning," *Bulletin No. 79,* CCC, February 1935, pp. 1-5.

5. Newton D. Baker, "Tax Exemption of Corporation Gifts to Community Chests," Testimony presented to the Finance Committee of the U. S. Senate, August 1, 1935.

6. "This Year's Campaign Strategy," News Bulletin, CCC, September 1936, pp. 5-6.

7. "Mobilization in Full Swing," *Community Chests and Councils,* November 1938, p. 35.

8. Samuel Eliot Morison and Henry Steele Commager, *The Growth of the American Republic* (New York: The Oxford University Press, 1950), Vol. 2, pp. 639-640.

9. "Midwest Conference, 1939," *Community Chests and Councils,* March 1939, pp. 97, 99.

10. Robert J. Myers, "Welfare Costs and Services," *Community Chests and Councils,* June 1939, p. 153.

THE STORM BREAKS -
WORLD WAR II: 1939-1942

On September 1, 1939 Germany attacked and overran Poland. A few days later, France and Britain declared war, and the United States entered the long and tortuous trail which led to its full entry into World War II two years later. As human needs intensified and multiplied, the United Way mobilized its resources nationwide to meet the social emergencies of the war.

The national association was quick to act on some of the war-born problems, and on September 2 Dr. George E. Vincent, CCC president, rushed to local Chest presidents a message which said, "What happens to 450 Chests in a brief, eight-week period when the world is in chaos will determine the private social work activities for 1940; may even decide the war-time future of the Community Chest movement." [1]

President Roosevelt, aware of the probability that war relief appeals would mushroom, issued a proclamation that all war relief organizations must secure certificates of registration from the Secretary of State before appealing for funds. Unequipped to make thorough investigations, the State Department proceeded to give the benefit of the doubt to applying organizations. Because of the inadequacy of this procedure and the need to review Chest plans in light of the war, Charles P. Taft, chairman of the 1939 Mobilization, called a conference of 50 Chest leaders for September 12.

One of the most pressing problems considered at the meeting was that of the Red Cross which already was receiving urgent requests for medical equipment. Although no emergency campaign was anticipated, Chest leaders concluded that they should begin immediately to plan for orderly and efficient coordination with local Red Cross chapters.

The second major problem tackled was that of foreign relief appeals, and a citizens' committee qualified to review requests for permits, and in other ways aid the State Department was authorized. In this quick and orderly way CCC began its long-continuing attack on the problem of rapidly multiplying war relief appeals.

Canada, meanwhile, was taking rapid and decisive steps toward control of war appeals and coordination of home front effort. Learning that the government intended to reenact the Canadian Patriotic Fund Bill and the War Charities Act, representatives of Chests, Councils and other interested organizations gathered to study the proposals and make suggestions for improving them. Because of their efforts, important changes were made, including conditions of agency efficiency and safeguards against duplications. Learning that the Canadian Red Cross was planning a national campaign preceding the Chest October campaigns, Canadian leaders conferred with the Red Cross which agreed to postpone its campaign until November 13.

The need was felt for a broad national Council representing all the cooperating war and civilian social services, since the revised legislation was to be administered by different governmental departments. In planning such an organization, need also was felt for a Central Committee of Chests and Councils in Canada. This was duly established with the 10 Chests then existing. The Canadian Welfare Council agreed to provide offices in its national headquarters.

In West Virginia a statewide Social Service Exchange was established to bring about a greater degree of efficiency and to prevent duplication of relief. Eventually statewide Exchanges were established in several states.

Despite the proliferation of competing war appeals and the worry of war in Europe, there was a rising index of business activity which augured well for Community Chest campaigns. With 561 campaigns, $86,217,068 was raised—about $3,600,000 more than the previous year. Councils of Social Agencies now numbered 332.

1940

Early in 1940, while Russia (having conquered Estonia, Latvia, and Lithuania) was endeavoring to subdue desperately-resisting Finland, the plight of the beleaguered Finnish people excited the sympathy of Americans. Since two appeals were being made for Finland, considerable confusion resulted. CCC's acting president George E. Vincent said, "It is the judgment of Community Chests and Councils, Inc. that there should be joint cooperative campaigns for foreign relief rather than competitive campaigns. We believe local coordinating committees should be formed." [2]

During the winter the new Canadian Chests and Councils Central Committee considered holding two campaigns, one for community services in the autumn and the other for war services in the spring. This idea did not appeal to Vancouver which was organizing the first united war and home welfare campaign of World War II. When in January announcement was made of three more national appeals impending for the three spring months, a Vancouver committee went into action and came out of negotiations with a United War Work Fund to be raised jointly during April.

Some 400 delegates attended the National Citizen Conference of the Mobilization for Human Needs in Detroit May 24 and 25. Announcements included the naming of a full-time CCC secretary in charge of personnel, and expectation that Congress would permit inclusion of non-profit employees in Social Security.

During the final session devoted to foreign relief appeals, a standing-room-only crowd heard the new CCC president, Robert Cutler, a Boston attorney who had been active in Boston civic and charitable work, say, "We feel that the Red Cross, a quasi-governmental agency in which we have confidence, and want to support, will tend to eliminate less worthy appeals by its success. We hope that the Red Cross will be a leader and we hope to strengthen its hand." [3]

Tom K. Smith (left), Chairman of 1941 Mobilization for Human Needs, and Dr. A. H. Giannini (right), Mobilization Vice Chairman, view the campaign poster with Edward G. Robinson, "Chairman of Big Town" Community Chest Campaign.

(Left to right) Charles Francis Adams, 1940 National Chairman, Mobilization for Human Needs, with Mrs. Adams, Judge Charles C. Cabot and Senator Leverett Saltonstall at opening of Boston's United Way campaign.

Eliot Wadsworth, a member of the Red Cross Central Committee, replied, however, "We're not going to do it all. Nobody can do it all . . . If relief appeals could be centralized, would money be saved in raising funds and waste in distributions be avoided? Is there power in this country—and if there is such a power do we want to exercise it—which could effect that central control? It isn't up to us to say, 'Stop, you shouldn't do that' to organizations raising and sending money direct." [4]

Gustavus D. Pope, chairman of the Detroit Red Cross chapter, described how the Detroit Community Fund, Red Cross, and nationality groups were working together on a United War Relief Drive. Leonard J.

(Left to right) Allen T. Burns, first national executive of the United Way, conferring in 1942 with volunteer leaders of the Dallas War Chest, Nathan Adams, Chairman of the Executive Council, and J. B. Adone, Jr., President. Dallas Times Herald photograph.

Mayor Maurice J. Tobin of Boston, Mass., speaker at the annual business meeting, and Robert Cutler, also of Boston, who was re-elected President of CC and C, Inc.

Cushing, representing NIB, stated that more than 400 appeals were already registered with the State Department.

A representative of the Finnish Relief Fund, Tracy S. Voorhees, speaking for it and several other funds, said, "We seek leadership and coordination from the Red Cross to avoid duplication, and we also want to cooperate with the Community Chests." [5]

C. M. Bookman, Cincinnati Chest executive, introduced a resolution which was unanimously adopted, calling for coordination of foreign relief appeals. American Red Cross would be asked to assume responsibility and leadership in working out such coordination, with local Chests and Funds assisting. The committee which was then appointed to carry out these ideas later presented the resolution to President Roosevelt who replied he was too busy to go into the problem and referred members to the Red Cross. On June 13 a meeting with American National Red Cross produced nothing but the repeated statement that the Red Cross could not undertake the task.

This marked the beginning of what might be called armed neutrality between CCC and the American National Red Cross, which felt it should be free to conduct whatever appeals for whatever amounts it thought necessary. Local chapters were forbidden to join Chests and those which belonged were encouraged and finally forced to withdraw. The impasse continued for many years.

The delegates to the Detroit conference had hardly returned to their homes, when the war situation grew worse. On June 4 the British Army completed its almost miraculous evacuation from Dunkirk and Hitler gazed across the Channel to England which he also hoped to conquer soon. Great Britain stood alone as the representative of the free world. On June 10 Mussolini brought Italy into the war as an ally of Germany. On June 15, Paris fell to Hitler's forces. Two days later the French government capitulated. Japan joined the Axis in the summer and stepped up its attacks on China. On July 10 Hitler began his assault by air, known as the Battle of Britain. The people of the United States at last realized their own potential danger and Congress and the President acted to meet the threat.

Canada, more directly involved in the war, established the Department of National War Services to promote, organize, and coordinate voluntary assistance.

In July the Canadian Central Committee of Community Chests and Councils met with the Canadian Welfare Council and national welfare agencies and developed suggestions for the new minister. They called for recognition of the importance of civilian health and welfare programs and the need for coordination and asked for extension of tax exemptions to cover them.

The first opportunity for American Chests and Councils to participate in program and campaign planning and the setting of local quotas for a nationwide campaign came during the summer from the U.S. Committee for the Care of European Children. Councils in 176 cities had taken the initiative in setting up information committees designed to disseminate information and to coordinate child care services which would become necessary if refugee children were to arrive in large numbers. Chests likewise were given the opportunity to determine local fund raising plans to help the cause.

The creation of this and other meritorious war service agencies, with their need for volunteer workers, stimulated the organization of Volunteer Bureaus. By the summer of 1940 there were about 25, most operated by Councils. Many had been established with the financial aid of local Junior Leagues as demonstrations. The Association of Junior Leagues of America was a leader in establishing programs for volunteers in the National Conference of Social Work, and urged local Leagues to stimulate and aid in establishment of Volunteer Bureaus. One of the purposes of the Volunteer Bureaus was to coordinate and clear local war relief and other volunteer activities because of the confusion likely to occur if it was not related to normal social work volunteer programs.

That summer Congress amended statutes to allow national banking associations to contribute to community funds. In New York, the State Insurance Department similarly ruled to permit mutual life insurance companies to make such donations, setting the pace for similar action in other states.

On September 16 the first peacetime conscription in our history was effected, calling for the induction of 700,000 draftees. As they and volunteers flooded into training camps, new recreation needs developed in camp communities. The relationship between civilian and military personnel was, however, unhappily complex. There was no national policy, and the Army and Navy began to operate their own programs, displacing the voluntary agencies which had rendered such services during World War I. After Paul V. McNutt was appointed Federal Security Administrator and Coordinator of Health, Welfare, and Recreation Activities in December, CCC urged close cooperation with him from voluntary agencies. Community Chests and Councils also favored a single unified administration of recreation activities through local administrators directly responsible to Mr. McNutt, plus federal financing which would enlist national agency cooperation. CCC also felt it was not advisable to conduct a nationwide campaign for funds by voluntarily-supported agencies.

Red Cross was given the responsibility of providing voluntary relief to servicemen as well as a home service committee in every chapter. When families were already being serviced by other agencies, they were usually to be left with them, Red Cross supplementing with its specialized services of communication, information, and medical social service. While cooperating with other agencies, Red Cross chapters were responsible for seeing that service and relief were provided.

The 1940 Community Mobilization for Human Needs was opened on October 13 by President Roosevelt and a week later in Canada by the Prime Minister and Her Royal Highness, Princess Alice, wife of the Governor General of Canada. Final returns showed that 598 campaigns raised $90,379,099, almost $4,100,000 more than the previous year. Chests reached 98 percent of their goals. Recovery from the depression had at last arrived with the increase in defense expenditures and armament orders from Great Britain.

With Recovery came increasing numbers of foreign relief agencies, plump purses among the public, and new need for the services of the National Information Bureau. Local Chests were urged to supply information and CCC allocated $2500 to NIB to help pay for enlarged services, an increase over its previous membership payment of $1250.

Simultaneously the 363 Councils of Social Agencies were expressing need for national information on joint planning. All needed advice concerning war-related problems such as relationships with local Defense Councils which were being set up in great numbers by the Council of National Defense. CCC's executive committee subsequently named a special subcommittee and employed a staff member to serve Councils.

In December the new Community Chests and Councils advisory committee on public information reported results of a questionnaire showing that 75% of the cities replying used campaign symbols, many of them

Norman Rockwell contributed his talent in this painting for Rochester, N.Y., Community and War Chest Campaign in 1946. Copyright Brown & Bigelow, St. Paul, Minn.

the red feather which had been initiated by Duluth and New Orleans some years before. Need was felt for a national symbol, but since agreement could not be reached, a subcommittee was appointed to study the matter.

1941

An article in the January issue of *Community,* the new name for the CCC magazine, told of the increasing value of Social Service Exchanges which were significantly aiding penal institutions, draft boards, and Defense Councils.

In February the Secretaries of War and the Navy plus the Federal Security Administrator issued a memorandum clarifying responsibilities for providing leisure-time activities for military and naval personnel. The War Department became responsible for all activities within army reservations and the Navy Department for all within naval reservations. The Federal Security Agency, together with local communities, was to be responsible for setting up and coordinating community-based programs. Commanding officers from each reservation would cooperate with community efforts, furnish military or naval police to supplement local police forces, and reserve the right to place objectionable operations off limits. Every effort would be made to stress the responsibility of local communities for carrying out the recreation program through local Defense Councils or other agencies.

Because no provision had been made for financing the program, pending advice of the President, the secretaries planned to urge Congress to provide funds for construction of facilities and to endorse a national fund-raising campaign for funds to operate the program.

CCC responded with a statement that the program should be financed by public funds with no national fund-raising campaign. But when the United Service Organizations was formed in February, and a fund-raising campaign was planned, Chests and Councils cooperated from the beginning. USO was established by six agencies; YMCA, YWCA, National Catholic Community Service, Salvation Army, Jewish Welfare Board and National Travelers Aid Association. President Roosevelt soon asked USO to take over operation of service huts or canteens. Walter Hoving of New York, president of USO, announced that a public campaign would be held and that Chest cooperation would be sought in the effort to raise around $10,500,000.

When Chests and Councils met at the Midwest Con-

Mobilization Chairman Tom K. Smith; CCC President Robert Cutler; St. Louis War Chest President Frank C. Rand in the Veiled Prophet's big parade for the United War Chest of Greater St. Louis.

ference in February, one of the speakers was Cincinnati's Charles Taft, three times chairman of the Community Mobilization for Human Needs, who had been appointed "Assistant Coordinator of Health, Medical Care, Family Security, Education, Recreation, and Related Activities in Connection with National Defense under the National Defense Council." (He later described this title as "a headache.") He called upon private agencies and state and local governments to cooperate dynamically in solving the problems in areas around army camps, naval stations, and defense industries.

A National Council of Defense had already been established and Defense Councils were being set up locally all over the United States. Mr. Taft reported the build-up of a competent Defense Council field staff which would eventually work toward complete community organization, and urged community organization executives to deal with recreational and other war-related problems in their communities. Many did this, and some Councils of Social Agencies were expanded to include the functions of Defense Councils. In some instances Council executives also served as Defense Council directors. Defense Councils, while publicly-sponsored and composed primarily of public agencies, in many cases added voluntary and private agencies as well.

The number of war appeals continued to plague many communities, and in Houston, Texas steps were taken to investigate campaigns. The Houston War Fund was organized and the city council passed an ordinance stating that no city permit would be granted to war relief organizations unless they were investigated and approved by the Fund. The Fund would also decide Houston's fair quota, try to raise the money in one combined campaign, and distribute it in amounts deemed justifiable and practical. Later, an all-embracing War Chest was formed.

On March 11, 1941 Congress passed the Lend Lease Bill making available 18 billion dollars worth of arms, food, and services to fighting democracies. Two days later the long-advocated proposal of CCC for control of war-related appeals was adopted, and a citizen's group, the President's Committee on Charitable Appeals, was named by President Roosevelt. The American Red Cross had been in the forefront in urging such a committee outside the State Department. It would have a broader scope and be responsible directly to the President. The following year foreign relief agencies raised more than $31 million.

On March 29, a CCC committee met with Red Cross in Washington and learned that no special Red Cross campaign was planned, and also that ARC anticipated no abrupt change in its policy against membership of local chapters in Chest campaigns. The Community Chests and Councils committee had developed a memorandum urging one war-time campaign in each community and had hoped that Red Cross would participate.

USO did agree to cooperate, having from the start worked with CCC and being itself a federated appeal. CCC sent out a memorandum in June urging each community to develop its own procedure for meeting its share of the USO goal. More than 50 added the local quota to the fall Chest campaign goal. In com-

1940 Campaign poster painting by Haddon Sundblom

munities where this was not done, USO conducted a June campaign, sometimes with Chest help in organizing the independent drives.

Minnesota set up a War Defense Fund; Seattle formed a Defense Chest including Chest agencies, USO, and a number of foreign relief appeals. Similar actions were taken in Boston, Pittsburgh, and Cincinnati. Sooner or later, practically all Chests joined the procession toward joint financing of Chest agencies, USO, and other war-related organizations. In Canada a War Services Fund drive was conducted in May, reaching a $5½ million objective in a fortnight.

When the Annual Conference of Community Chests and Councils was held May 30-June 1, immediately in advance of the annual meeting of the National Conference of Social Work, there was much discussion of financing war-related and all-time services. CCC President Robert Cutler of Boston said, referring to Red Cross, "The important thing is that there shall not appear and shall never be in the United States a conflict between the American National Red Cross and the Chests, the USO or any of these great agencies . . . The people back home are the people to decide when to give their money and how it is going to be raised, because they not only have to give it but they have to raise it." [6] A resolution was adopted during the CCC board meeting saying that in the case of war "it is the opinion of this Board that the United States will best be served . . . by the combination in a given local community in one annual campaign of the appeals for funds of the valid wartime, disaster, and all-time service agencies." The resolution went on to claim the right of local communities to determine how and when to raise the funds. "This right of the people back home to decide as to the raising and giving of charitable funds is fundamental to American freedom." [7]

On June 8 a letter from President Roosevelt to the American National Red Cross was released to the news media: "To assure the maximum strength of the entire nation, adequate support of the regular welfare and charitable services through Community Chests is even more important in time of national emergency than in normal times." He urged "adequate support of the regular welfare and charitable services through Community Chests" and the USO campaign then under way. He praised the work of Red Cross and said, "I therefore, heartily endorse the action of the Central Committee of the Red Cross in maintaining freedom to conduct a roll call for its annual membership and

President Roosevelt making the first presidential all-network radio broadcast in behalf of the 1938 United Way campaigns.

freedom to launch a campaign for funds . . . Plans for a national emergency should include a proper spacing of the three major campaigns, those for the Red Cross, the USO, and Community Chests." [8]

Chest leaders were pleased by the President's urging of adequate Chest support, but disturbed by his endorsement of separate campaigns. On June 26, however, the Board of CCC urged Chests to synchronize their efforts so that Chest campaigns would qualify as a single drive in the sense the President urged. October was suggested in order to avoid conflict with the Red Cross campaign beginning November 11, and with other campaigns.

Volunteer Bureaus were asked to help in the mobilization of volunteers to serve in defense-related activities, and it was suggested by the Office of Civilian Defense that they become an official arm of local Defense Councils. Soon after the war began, all Volunteer Bureaus did this, while Chests and Councils cooperated in establishing new volunteer offices in cities without them.

The 1941 Mobilization for Human Needs was opened October 3 with a radio broadcast by President Roosevelt and Wendell Willkie, his defeated opponent of 1940. When all the results were in, $104,575,890 had

been raised, $14 million more than the year before. Campaigns reached 99.6 percent of their goals, the highest percentage since record keeping was started in 1920. Success was attributed to many factors: willingness to help, the wartime mood of sacrifice, recovery from depression, more people working longer hours, growing emphasis on group solicitation, spreading acceptance of payroll deduction, and the interest of labor in doing its share.

On October 4 the President's Committee on War Relief Agencies recommended that all licenses issued by the State Department to foreign relief appeals be revoked and new licenses granted only when there was proof the aid would be dispensed and without duplication. The committee commended USO, Red Cross, and Community Chests for their cooperation, but felt the need for coordination of foreign relief appeals through a central advisory body.

All seemed to be going well or better than could be expected when on Sunday morning, December 7, Japanese planes launched their attack on the United States Pacific Fleet in Pearl Harbor. The next day Congress declared war on Japan. Three days later Germany and Italy declared war on the United States. Community

1946 Artwork by Batton, Barton, Durstine and Osborn.

Symbol introduced by national association of United Way in 1938 and used until national adoption of the Red Feather in 1946. The "Heart of the Community" symbol was used by some local communities but failed to "catch on".

for inclusion in those local united War Fund campaigns desiring it.

On June 25 newspapers across the country published the fact that "President Roosevelt has approved the combination of the usual November roll call of the Red Cross with its next War Fund appeal to be held in March 1943, and the previously announced policy of the Red Cross to 'maintain direct contact' with the people in preference to inclusion in War Chest campaigns." [10] While Chests were happy about the consolidation of Red Cross campaigns which would ease the fall competition, their hopes for further inclusion of Red Cross in War Chest campaigns were dashed.

On July 2 at a board meeting of CCC, Allen Burns, now 66, presented his resignation after twenty years of service to the organization as adviser, guide, consultant and executive. He was succeeded on January 1, 1943 by Ralph Blanchard, a staff member for 14 years, who was to serve for 18½ more years as executive director.

At this meeting the board also approved the establishment of the National Budget Committee on War Appeals and the National Quota Committee. The first was needed, Chest leaders felt, in order to subject national budgets to careful scrutiny because some of the budgets which had been submitted to local War Chests seemed sketchy or over-ambitious. The committee was composed of representatives from United War Relief, other war appeals, Community and War Chests, U.S. Chamber of Commerce, National Association of Manufacturers, AFL, CIO, National Information Bureau, and others. CCC provided staff, with research conducted by the NIB and financed by Community Chests and Councils plus foundation and individual gifts.

The Quota Committee was given $1,000 to employ a statistical corporation to provide data concerning the breakdown of goals into state quotas. The system devised was similar to that used by USO, using about 15 categories of national, social, and economic data from

which weighted averages were produced. The quota formula was soon found helpful, and while having undergone substantial revisions, was used as needed for many years thereafter. The committee was later that year enlarged to include representatives of the war-related agencies. Since it was too late to provide fair decisions for that fall's campaigns, it was suggested that NIB provide guidelines to communities including a quota plan and a general list of war appeals that Chests might wish to include.

Rapid progress was being made in the relationship between labor and federation. Two labor leaders had been elected to membership on the CCC board in 1941. They were D. J. McDonald, secretary of the Steel Workers Organizing Committee, CIO, Pittsburgh; and George Meany, secretary-treasurer of the American Federation of Labor. On August 17, a CCC bulletin announced agreement on cooperation by AFL and CIO with appeals approved by the National Budget Committee and the all-time local services in War Chests. It was suggested that local communities include union representation on Chest governing boards as well as campaign and allocation committees; that they incorporate the local U.N. Relief Committee of the AFL, and the National CIO Committee for American and Allied War Relief into the campaign; that they give union members separate credit for contributions and organize employee solicitation with employers and union working jointly. For its part, labor would endorse approved campaigns, promote organization among members and aid in solicitation.

Tentative recommendations for a national allotment for 11 foreign relief appeals were made at the end of August by the National Budget Committee, with a large unallocated reserve recommended for smaller appeals still to be heard. The committee cooperated with the War Relief Control Board which had been given authority to register and license war relief agencies, coordinate campaigns and establish solicitation methods. The total sum of $75,659,000 was set for the first national budget of war relief appeals. United Relief Inc. was not included because it was not an agency, but a federation of agencies.

Charles Taft, chairman of the newly organized War Relief Control Board which grew out of the President's Committee on War Relief Agencies, asked that national appeals for war relief be limited to one for Red Cross and one for all other appeals, including USO. Chest leaders were pleased by this anouncement, which preceded the Community Mobilization for Human Needs.

In the September issue of *Survey Midmonthly* Allen Burns discussed the rise of War Chests. "The War Chest is even more widely representative of the whole community than are many Community Chests . . . Chest leadership on the whole has recognized it as a patriotic duty to extend its well proved money raising techniques to the new appeals, foreign and domestic, which result from war."[11] There were then 300 War Chests.

In the same issue, CCC's Bradley Buell said, "Let no one think that the conversion to a war-time program of our complicated network of welfare, health, and recreation services is coming easily. For example, with family separations increasing, suitable homes for foster care of children are growing scarce. City after city reports a high turnover in public welfare staffs."[12]

At budget time for the CCC executive committee, a consensus was reached that war relief agencies should be asked to assume approximately one-half of the $60,000 special war budget for CCC to cover expenses in establishing fair share quotas for their use.

In the fall, Lyman Ford, who since January 1, 1942 had been secretary of the CCC Committee on Organization and Administration of Councils of Social Agencies, released a report showing that Chests, Councils or both existed in 675 cities of the world, 645 of them in the United States. In 57 percent, no Council existed. He also produced a manual on the organization and administration of a Council.

On November 5 officers of every war appeal agency approved by the National Information Bureau met with CCC and asked that the Quota Committee be enlarged to become a joint committee of Chests and war appeals, with functions increased and financing shared. The growing partnership was strengthened by favorable campaign reports which showed the first 265 cities reporting had increased the amounts raised by 71.4 percent, with goals exceeded by an average of 10.3 percent. Detroit led in money raised, with a total of $6,533,000, which was better than 153% more than its community fund had raised the previous year. St. Louis came in second, with $5,146,000 or 136% more than the 1942 Chest total. When results of the spring campaigns were tabulated, it was revealed that 649 campaigns had raised $162,334,486 or $57½ million more than the previous year.

On December 14 Winthrop Aldrich, who had led in formation of United Relief, Inc. met with five other men to set up a new organization for united war relief on a national basis, and planned what led to the National War Fund.

Just before Christmas it was announced that a State War Chest had been formed in Michigan. Leadership had been taken by Michigan Community Chests and Councils, an informal association organized in 1939 for discussion of common problems. The main purpose of the Chest was to cover local non-Chest areas.

At year's end, Ralph Blanchard, about to become CCC executive director, observed, "What we call 'our field' is so inextricably tangled with war and war-connected developments that its outlines and many of its basic procedures may become all but unrecognizable. Organization lines are shifting; War Chests have stretched our horizons as have also Councils of Defense. But the fundamentals of community organization remain the same. The way is pointed to a future in which Councils of Social Agencies will operate on a much broader scope than before the war. So too with Chests."[13]

NOTES

Chapter 8

1. George E. Vincent, "Message to Community Chests," September 2, 1939, quoted by Charles P. Taft in "Report of Conference of 50 Chest Leaders," September 12, 1939, CCC, mimeographed, p. 3.

2. George E. Vincent, "Looking Ahead in Foreign Relief," *Community Chests and Councils*, January 1940, pp. 66-70.

3. "The Red Cross and Foreign Relief Drives," *Community Chests and Councils*, June 1940, pp. 174-176.

4. *Ibid.*

5. *Ibid.*

6. "War Chests—Fer and Agin," *Community Chests and Councils*, June 1941, p. 153.

7. Resolution adopted by CCC Board of Directors, May 30, 1941, and ratified by membership, May 31, 1941, Minute Book, Vol. III, p. 377.

8. *Charitable Appeals in War-Time: A Look at the Record*, CCC booklet, June 8, 1942.

9. *Community* (formerly *Community Chests and Councils*), October 1942, pp. 28-29.

10. *On the Alert*, Communique No. 3, CCC, June 25, 1942, p. 1.

11. Allen T. Burns, "Rise of the War Chests," *Survey Midmonthly*, September 1942, pp. 228-229.

12. Bradley Buell, "Existing Agencies Tool Up," *Survey Midmonthly*, September 1942, p. 242.

13. *Community*, UCFCA, January 1943, pp. 66-74.

THROUGH WAR INTO PEACE: 1943-1945

Plans for the National War Fund which had grown out of United Relief, Inc. were developing rapidly as 1943 began. The organization was to be a philanthropic federation with three aims: to determine the nature and extent of war-related needs; to see that everybody had a chance to contribute; to channel the sums raised wherever help was most needed. No agency would be included until certified by the President's board and only one agency would be admitted for any given country or function. This resulted in many consolidations. The fund would associate its appeal with Community Chests or other like federations, or if none existed local leaders could establish a local War Fund by adding the National War Fund quota to other budgets for local purposes. Many towns did this, resulting in introduction of social services and later the creation of Community Chests.

Meeting in January, the CCC board recommended that the National Budget Committee on War Appeals and the National Quota Committee become part of the National War Fund. Publicity was geared to local program needs, with publicity materials provided by the joint efforts of National War Fund and CCC. Office space was provided by Community Chests and Councils. Later the staff services of Virgil Martin, who had recently been employed by CCC; Bent Taylor, now publicity director; and Allen Burns, retired, were added.

After the first year, Ralph Blanchard became secretary of the NWF board.

The National War Fund stimulated organization of new state War Chests which fell into several patterns: one where local Community Chests assumed leadership for establishing statewide corporations; another (as in West Virginia) where no formal state organization was established but where several Chest cities assumed responsibility for covering the state; and a third type in which the Chest assumed no expressed responsibility but the unorganized areas established the War Chest, as in Arizona. It was the general consensus that state War Chests should not be organized by elected public groups, and that the National War Fund should recommend quotas to states while permitting them to work out their county quotas. CCC suggested that every effort should be made to safeguard local autonomy as to quotas, beneficiaries and personnel. Organized labor gave its enthusiastic approval and cooperation.

Implications of statewide War Chests upon statewide health, welfare, and recreation services were discussed by the CCC Committee on Organization and Administration of Councils of Social Agencies. In March it reported that some of the regional committees organized by the Office of Defense, Health, and Welfare Services were beginning to function on a state basis, and that state War Chests should be urged to include planning functions. Reasonably competent and extensive planning did develop in many state War Chests and Defense Councils, leading to formation of statewide health and welfare planning organizations still active as well as to several continuing state Chests.

In February, CCC began a fully staffed personnel service designed for the "duration plus one year" but which has grown and continued in effectiveness and extent through the years. Public relations activities were stepped up at this same time, following recommendations of H. J. Heinz II of Pittsburgh, chairman of the National Committee on Public Information, who recommended that the 12-year-old Mobilization Program be replaced by a year-round program directed at the whole body of American public opinion. Fall campaign publicity would be handled by the National War Fund.

In April the Special Budget Committee of the War Appeals of All-Time National Social Agencies (a second budget committee appointed by CCC in September, 1942) made recommendations for financial support for six all-time agencies: Child Welfare League of America, Family Welfare Association, National Institute of Immigrant Welfare, National Organization for Public Health Nursing, National Urban League, and YWCA. The report was approved by the CCC board in May, and soon thereafter the agency budgets were approved and certified by the President's War Relief Control Board for approval and certification by the National War Fund. When the proposal was presented to NWF, however, lengthy deliberations took place about the advisability of including the war appeals of all-time agencies and it was decided they could not be included. The six all-time national agencies with wartime programs then proceeded to incorporate as American War Community Services. Its board of directors was headed by Henry Bruere, president of the Bowery Savings Bank, New York.

In April the CCC Board also agreed to take over management of the Committee on Volunteers in Community Service, which had been in existence for about 10 years. Mrs. Thomas Tolan, chairman, had made the request believing that its functions could best be performed when attached to the national organization of Chests and Councils. While most Volunteer Bureaus were then being run by Defense Councils, they would need a national organization to aid them after the war. Ultimately a department of Citizen Participation was established.

On July 1, 1943 a far-reaching event took place: the initiation of compulsory withholding of federal income and social security tax payments from employee pay. Since the machines set up for computing and deducting tax payments had room for additional deductions, it was not too difficult to persuade employers to authorize Chest deductions. Organized labor favored this practice because it became possible to know the numbers as well as the amounts of employee gifts and to give labor credit for its impressive and growing share of suport for united health and welfare services. The results of payroll deduction have been spectacular. Instead of a cash handout of a dollar or less, an employee might pledge 15 cents per week, "the price of a package of cigarettes," making a total gift of $7.80 for the year. The development of group solicitation and payroll deduction plans were two important aspects of increasingly cordial and effective voluntary cooperation between management and labor on behalf of United Way financing.

Three-fourths of the federated campaigns were scheduled for October, many of them including American War Community Services. But the AWCS was overwhelmed by the National War Fund and never did achieve the hoped-for success. Local Chests were generally apathetic about this tardily-presented claim and local branches of nationals didn't push the cause either, lest it vitiate the force of their local budget requests. There was no grass roots demand for inclusion of AWCS, and many felt it should have been included in the National War Fund. Thus it was that receipts were only $164,302 of the $742,945 approved by the Joint Budget Committee.

Despite continuing fulfillment of Winston Churchill's 1940 prophecy of "blood, toil, tears and sweat," the Allies were everywhere advancing and the Axis was everywhere retreating. Victory would, all America believed, come sooner or later and "the lights would go on again all over the world."

Chests and Councils began to think about post-war planning. Lyman Ford, who had been named head of the CCC health and welfare planning unit, brought the subject to the sphere of local community organization in a fall *Community article*. "It is evident that postwar planning which takes into consideration only economic problems, or only land use problems, or only health and welfare problems, or which excludes even one important element is unbalanced and off to a poor start . . .

Councils of Social Agencies and Chests have both an obligation and an opportunity in connection with post-war planning. The obligation is to see that health and welfare programs are given the attention they warrant in planning the community's future. The opportunity is to get action in situations which have too long awaited serious community consideration, and to strengthen existing planning machinery." [1] Mr. Ford thus forecast the broadening concern of local Councils in the overall planning for total community well-being which has been strikingly manifested in the years since the war.

That organized labor should be made an important participant in overall planning immediately and not merely after the war was proposed by a joint committee of organized labor and CCC which met during the summer of 1943 and issued a report on September 25. As a way to promote better knowledge and cooperation between labor and Councils, the committee proposed labor participation committees within Councils. Such committees would assist both groups by integrating the labor point of view into the health and welfare activity of communities. While labor groups would not engage in community health and welfare planning themselves, they would strengthen and work through the established local machinery for this purpose. A national labor program would also be established with a national advisory committee appointed to render counseling service, advise Councils regarding the aims and policies of labor and methods of developing participation, to check on local and national developments and keep the various committees informed; to publish bulletins; and to aid in training of community organization specialists with labor backgrounds and interests.

Many of these proposals had already been put into

Marking the opening of United Way campaigns in September 1948, H. J. Heinz II, C.I.O. President Philip Murray, Henry Ford II and William Green, head of the A.F. of L. (left to right), visited the day nursery of Friendship House in Washington, D.C. Mr. Ford was National Chairman of Community Chests of America; the others served as Vice Chairmen.

Gerard Swope, seated at center of table with volunteer members and staff of the National War Fund Budget Committee in 1946.

effect, as revealed by a questionnaire sent to Chests and Councils. War Chests had frequently employed labor staff members to serve in both financing and planning. CCC promptly set up a National Advisory Committee as proposed and put the suggestions into action.

As 1943 closed, CCC looked back on a year in which great achievements had been made. Most Chests had smoothly converted themselves into War Chests or had made other War Chest arrangements. The National War Fund, a national Chest, had been organized and operated successfully, with spectacular results. When all returns were in, it had raised more than $126 million on a $125 million goal, about 60 percent of it coming from organized Chest cities.

The New York Committee of the National War Fund collected more than $17 million, the largest amount yet reached by a Community or War Chest. Harold J. Seymour, general manager of the National War Fund later commented, "The Chest had the organization and the war agencies had the appeal. As long as the war lasted, it was a winning combination."

Stimulated by Ralph Blanchard, work toward establishment of a retirement plan had proceeded since formation of a CCC committee in July 1943. In November, 1944, the National Health and Welfare Retirement Association was incorporated with a plan whereby all benefits would be reinsured and guaranteed by the John Hancock Mutual Life Insurance Company. From the beginning the plan was designed to supplement and not compete with Social Security.

Gerard Swope, president of General Electric Company and former Mobilization chairman, became chairman of the board. The plan started operation in October, 1944 with 5,000 covered employees, more than 85 Chests and Councils participating along with agencies and institutions. Up to 1972, a total of $75 million had been paid out by NHWRA in benefits and its assets amounted to $381,849,000. There are now more than 83,000 individuals covered by its retirement and insurance plans.

Meeting in New York on February 4, the new CCC National Committe on Volunteer Service reported increased membership—29 members—who felt that central Volunteer Bureaus should be established in postwar years to aid in recruitment of volunteers wherever needed in the community. Such bureaus should be either directed by a widely representative board of its own or be tied in with the Council of Social Agencies.

Information and referral bureaus were developing at the same time, sometimes within industry, often within Chests and Councils. They were visualized as an opportunity for getting services to those who needed them, and had already been established on a year-round basis in Philadelphia, Denver, Detroit, Los Angeles, and Cleveland.

Servicemen's Centers also were putting in an appearance, designed to help servicemen returning to civilian life. Because of the multiplicity of agencies undertaking responsibility for such help, there was considerable confusion and waste, and most communities formed these centers, many connected with Councils, to help coordinate the efforts.

Anticipating the return of peace, the North Carolina State War Fund proposed changing to a state fund which would be not a super Community Chest for the state, but a federation of local organizations for their common service. One of its functions was to raise funds on a statewide basis for agencies dependent on statewide financing. Thomas L. Carroll, who had directed the state War Fund said, "To restrict our concern and our skills to the limited metropolitan area is short-sighted. Is it too much to believe that out of this

Recipient of the national Red Feather Award in 1954 was Thelma Shaw (Mrs. Victor), a President of the National Conference on Social Welfare. Her United Way volunteer service from the 1940's through the 1960's included Chairman of the Citizen Participation Committee and Vice President of the 3C's Board.

war will come a great new dimension in community organization, a spreading of its techniques, now tested and proved by experience, into the little cities, the towns and country neighborhoods from which come so much of the nation's strength?"[2]

The subject of statewide planning was discussed at a session during the annual CCC conference in May. There was agreement that a tremendous need existed for health and welfare planning on the state level. First steps were taken for establishment of a special subcommittee on statewide planning.

June 6 went down in history as D-Day, for on that date combined British, American and French forces landed on the Normandy beaches and the western wall of Hilter's "Festung Europa" began to crumble even as the eastern wall had already given way before the Russian advance.

On the United Way front, incorporation was completed in June for a new planning organization for agencies serving abroad. Led by Dr. Joseph P. Chamberlain, Professor of Public Service, Columbia University, and stimulated by the President's War Relief Control Board, 17 volunteer agencies had agreed to establishment of the American Council of Voluntary Agencies for Foreign Service, Inc. A chief purpose was to assure maximum effective use of contributions by the American people for assistance of people overseas. ACVAFS was financed for two years by National War Fund payments on behalf of its participating agencies, and by fees from non-War Fund agencies. Its first functional committee dealt with problems of displaced persons. The Council continued to grow until it numbered nearly 50 agencies, including such groups as CARE, Catholic Relief Service, American Jewish Joint Distribution Committee, International Rescue Committee, Lutheran World Relief, Salvation Army, Church World Service, and YWCA. Through the Council these agencies coordinated their plans and activities both at home and abroad, not only among themselves but also with non-member agencies and with governmental, intergovernmental, and international organizations. Thus, good community organization principles were applied again on the national scene.

In June the strengthened statistical department of CCC produced a bulletin on corporate contributions, revealing that 102 participating Chests had raised a total of $90,559,957 of which 32.8 percent was from corporate gifts, an increase since 1941 of 174.6 percent.

Douglas Crockwell, painter of the 1942 United Way poster, receives the Kerwin H. Fulton Award for the Advancement in Art in Outdoor Advertising. (Right) Arthur Blomquist of J. Walter Thompson Advertising Agency, which provided volunteer services to the United Way campaign.

A sign of prosperous times for Chests was found in a June bulletin devoted to Community Chest reserve funds. Over-subscribed goals had resulted, in many communities, in the accumulation of reserve funds. Some Chests had become increasingly concerned about the proper use and best methods of handling such money. CCC suggested that while the proper operating balance could only be determined by local Chests, as a general guide the amounts accumulated from previous years' operations and on hand at the end of the fiscal year might safely equal up to three months' average combined budgets of local Chest agencies.

Prospects for the fall campaigns were rosy, with

better cooperation expected between Chests and federal government bureaus. A plan for legislation to permit federal payroll deductions of contributions had been developed and it was felt that it might soon be put into effect. (Authorization for federal payroll deductions did not actually come until 1964.)

The subject of budget review of all-time national voluntary agencies was discussed at the September Community Chests and Councils board meeting. Several local Chests had asked for such reviews, and one national agency, the National Federation of Settlements, had asked to have its budget reviewed. The board agreed that since CCC had a special interest and obli-

"You Take Care of the Home Front" was the 1942 and 1943 campaign slogan used on this United Way poster painted by Douglas Crockwell.

Haddon Sundblom's painting for the 1936 United Way campaign poster.

gation for leadership regarding national budgeting, it would join with other national agencies to consider the problem. Subsequent discussions were to lead to continuance of the Joint Budget Committee of AWCS and CCC which would become the National Budget and Consultation Committee.

The November *Community* told of a new Council responsibility in the post-war period, that of helping to plan for sound and orderly home construction and community development. Suggestions for setting up a Committee on Social Aspects of Housing were made. Objectives would be to stimulate the development and execution of a long-range program to provide a good home in a wholesome neighborhood for all members of the community, especially for families of low income, and to help develop continuing and active citizen participation in housing and its related problems. The committees which resulted were early examples of the post-war Council expansion from the old "functional" fields of family and child welfare, health, and recreation to overall planning for the total welfare of the total community.

Early in December CCC's statistical director reported that campaign goals were slightly higher than the year

President Harry S. Truman is presented with a Red Feather from children representing Community Chest Red Feather services in 1945.

before and that more than half a million volunteers were participating in campaigns. When all the returns were in from 772 campaigns, they totalled more than $222 million, which was higher than even the most educated guesses. They raised 102 percent of their goals.

1945

On January 1, 1945 a West Coast Regional Office of Community Chests and Councils was opened with Guy Thompson, former executive secretary of the Tacoma Chest as the Pacific Coast representative. Most of his time was to be spent in the field, at the service of local Chests and Councils. This office continued in operation until 1955, when air travel made it possible for national office staff to serve the area more easily and more rapidly than in the past.

Citizen participation or volunteer service began to emerge as a major CCC concern, following liquidation of the Office of Civilian Defense and its volunteer office on December 31. Two CCC staff members were added on a project basis to provide field service in communities wishing to continue Volunteer Bureaus. Since CCC would be the only resource for sound advice on volunteer service, it was believed that volunteer offices would look to CCC for guidance.

The Joint Budget Committee reported on February 1 that it had voted to endorse the program of the National Federation of Settlements, and support its budget request of $33,400. Learning of this action the CCC executive committee approved and then voted "that in those instances where national agency budgets are approved by the CCC budget committee, such approval does not involve any responsibility for promotion of the campaign appeals of those agencies." This was an important statement, for it set a precedent in handling national agency budgets. [3]

Discussion followed concerning use of the present AWCS-CCC Joint Budget Committee for reviewing agency budgets other than those AWCS agencies. In consequence the executive committee authorized appointment of a National Budget Committee of which not less than 50 percent of the members would represent national agencies. Its function would be to review the budgets of national agencies only as requested by agencies, and to recommend action to the CCC board. Ten such agencies had already met and prepared draft proposals for such a procedure. They believed that such planning would aid local budget committees by providing a better basis for judging the merits of requests for support of related national agencies. The board approved, though Kenneth Sturges, executive director of the Cleveland Community Fund, felt that while the proposal had value as a first step, a second step was inevitable, namely, concern with expenditures and programs as well as income.

The CCC executive committee also considered draft proposals for transformation of the National Social Work Council into the National Social Welfare Assembly. Since 1920, eight national agencies for joint planning had been organized, several of them overlapping in function and membership. The new Assembly would be a national service and planning center for organizations, groups, and individuals engaged in, or interested in, health and welfare. The executive committee decided that the staff should proceed with study of the matter, bearing in mind its opposition to any move which would in effect remove from CCC the function of acting as the national organization for local Councils.

Another step of importance taken at this meeting was the final adoption of the Red Feather as the national campaign symbol. Since the last board meeting, there had been agreement on recommending the name Community Chest (already used by 79% of local federated fund raising organizations) to be used after the war. Use of the Red Feather, begun in 1928 in Duluth and New Orleans, had grown rapidly. More Chests now used the Red Feather than any other symbol except that of the National War Fund. Its use was continued with great effectiveness until well into the 1950's when growth of the United Fund movement and new local symbols brought about use of the "U" symbol nationally. This new symbol ("U" for United) continued for many years to be combined with the Red Feather in many communities.

In January, a gift of $10,000 had been made by *Parents Magazine* and the Book-of-the-Month Club to CCC for an education program aimed at school children. CCC asked the Bureau of Educational Research at Ohio State University to develop a program in cooperation with nearby Chests and Councils, working in cooperation with their school systems. Edgar Dale, professor of education at Ohio State University, directed the project which included units of instruction, a manual on come-and-see tours, a manual on showing services through pictures, film strips, exhibits, etc. and a bulletin on ways to develop student participation.

The Oasis was a traditional reception held by the Public Relations Clinic for all attendees of the United Way National Biennial Conference from the 1940's to the 1960's.

Because the U.S. Children's Bureau had failed to persuade congressional appropriation committees that the social statistics project was necessary to the war effort, it was due to be discontinued on June 30. CCC at its April 30 board meeting accordingly agreed to provide consultation, guidance and leadership to local communities in research and the collection and use of social statistics until they could find another federal agency or department to assume responsibility. In September, the advisory committee on statistics revealed that no such agency could be found, and the board consequently made an allocation to cover costs of the project which would be continued by the CCC statistical department.

The growing alliance between Chests and labor was graphically illustrated in a memorandum signed by the presidents of Community Chests and Councils and the National War Fund. It called attention to organized labor's significant contributions in support of Red Cross, Chest campaigns, and the National War Fund, but after the war it was expected that Chests might be asked to finance labor programs and they were advised to study this possibility. The board later urged Chests and Councils to consider the engaging of labor staff to integrate labor more effectively into the planning and financing of health and welfare services.

Following Germany's signing of unconditional surrender on May 7, a message from President Harry S. Truman was carried in the June *Community*. "Though we have won the military fight in Europe, we are virtually just beginning the fight on famine, pestilence, and general distress . . . May I, therefore, wish suc-

There Are Two Seas

A Parable by Bruce Barton

There are two seas in Palestine. One is fresh, and fish are in it. Splashes of green adorn its banks. Trees spread their branches over it, and stretch out their thirsty roots to dip of its healing water. Along its shore the children play.

The River Jordan makes this sea with sparkling water from the hills. So it laughs in the sunshine. And men build their houses near to it, and birds their nests; and every kind of life is happier because it is there.

The River Jordan flows on south into another sea. Here is no splash of fish, no fluttering leaf, no song of birds, no children's laughter. Travellers choose another route, unless on urgent business. The air hangs above its waters and neither man nor beast nor fowl will drink. What makes this mighty difference in these neighbor seas? Not the River Jordan. It empties the same good water into both. Not the soil in which they lie; not the country round about.

This is the difference. The Sea of Galilee receives but does not keep the Jordan. For every drop that flows into it another drop flows out. The giving and receiving go on in equal measure. The other sea is shrewder, hoarding its income jealously. It will not be tempted into any generous impulse. Every drop it gets, it keeps. The Sea of Galilee gives and lives. This other sea gives nothing. It is named the Dead.

There are two seas in Palestine.

There are two kinds of people in the world.

Which kind are we?

This challenging story has become a classic in the literature of unselfishness. It was written by Bruce Barton of Batten, Barton, Durstine and Osborn Advertising Agency and contributed by him to Community Chests and Councils of America in 1945.

cess to the National War Fund and all its associated state and community War Chests."[4]

A new task for local communities was now entering the picture. On January 2, 1946 the War Relocation Authority would close its centers and some 60,000 Japanese and Japanese-American evacuees would need to be placed within the time remaining. This required the assistance of many local and national groups, presenting a special challenge to local Chests and Councils.

On August 6, the first atomic bomb was dropped on Hiroshima, and on September 2 the Japanese surrendered unconditionally. World War II was over. In anticipation of the Japanese surrender, the National War Fund had decided on August 15 to make that fall's appeal the final one for the NWF, with a goal of $115 million. There were then 10,000 local units participating. Thus ended the most successful effort, even to this date, of federating agency appeals at other than the local level.

American War Community Services came to a halt when the National War Fund terminated, though the cooperative relationships among its agencies were maintained for about three more years, after which they were reshaped in the Field Service Committee of the National Social Welfare Assembly.

On December 7, the National Social Welfare Assembly adopted a new constitution and the next day the CCC board voted wholehearted participation. Three distinct advances were made in widening the circle of interest to include: government as well as voluntary national agencies; lay leaders as well as professional executives; and local community leaders as well as national. A total of 39 national agencies became affiliated. The National Health Council became an associate group.

In December, Community reported, "it is clear already that this is not to be a 'one hundred per cent' campaign year. One hundred and seventy campaigns reporting to date have raised . . . 89.4 percent of the amount raised last year. The story behind these figures . . . might be summarized in two phrases—post-war let-down and unfavorable conditions for industrial solicitations."[5] After all the returns were in, 89.9 percent of the goal was reached. The National War Fund did not come out as well, raising $89,703,934 (75.4%) of its $115 million goal.

At its December board meeting CCC approved new or enlarged services in campaign and finance, public relations, national budgeting, and statistics. Further, as the armed forces were being demobilized, price controls were abolished, and the cost of living increased sharply. CCC's budget accordingly reflected higher costs and totalled $403,916. The board voted to request an appropriation of one-third of one percent of the amounts raised by member Chests, compared with the dues of one-fourth of one percent then in effect.

Looking forward to 1946, Lyman Ford wrote in the December Community, "The function of health and welfare planning must be given its proper emphasis in the total community organization job throughout the next year. Planning must emerge, where it has not already done so, from a position as part of the overhead or administrative expense in connection with the annual fund raising campaign to a position of major emphasis." He called for competent staff to do this job.[6]

Thus joint planning and joint financing were shown as two sides of the same coin for teamwork in a better community.

NOTES

Chapter 9

1. *Community*, CCC, November 1943, p. 134.

2. *Community*, CCC, March 1944, pp. 107-8.

3. Minutes, Executive Committee, CCC, February 24, 1945, Minute Book, Vol. 5, p. 4.

4. *Community*, CCC, June 1945, p. 149.

5. *Community*, CCC, December 1945, pp. 66-67.

6. *Ibid.*

MULTIPLICITY OF CAMPAIGNS:1946-1949

The year 1946 began with reconversion, reconstruction, and reformation from war to peace. Surprisingly, there were fewer problems than anticipated, and the return of 12 million servicemen and women to civilian life presented less difficulty than half that number in 1919. There was neither depression nor runaway inflation, and prosperity continued.

"The Chest and Council movement is in a superb position to take leadership," Ralph Blanchard observed during the annual meeting and conference of CCC in February. "The public has trusted us and will continue to trust us if we continue to relate ourselves to forms of organization more inclusive than our own . . . It will be tragic indeed if national agencies are too individualistic or agency-minded; if local communities don't know how to use state and national agency resources properly or are so local-minded they won't use them. No national can really solve such questions; the answers have to come from the grass roots." [1]

Labor's role was explained to the conference by Phil Hanna of the Ohio State Federation of Labor who said, "Because we sincerely believe in promoting unity in American life, and because we are convinced that greater benefits and economy will result from the existing arrangements, we will work in the labor movement to strengthen the principles of federation." Another

speaker, H. L. R. Emmett, chairman of CCC's Labor Relations Committee, pointed to the growth of labor participation in planning and campaigning—from 125 AFL and CIO leaders on Chest and Council boards in 1941 to between four and five thousand in 1945, plus about 30 labor staff employed on a permanent basis and 20 part-time.

The April *Community* told how use of union counselors had helped in referring members to social agencies. Development of CCC's labor relations program continued, and Wilbur Maxwell was added to the staff to take charge of labor relations. In September, the board approved a $48,000 budget for development of a Labor Relations Department and voted to make the Advisory Committee on Labor-Employee Participation a standing committee of CCC. A higher budget was later requested and approved.

On March 11 the new and permanent National Budget Committee adopted a statement of principles and policies, describing its purpose "to provide national agencies with an orderly medium through which their budgets may be expressed and their requests for support channeled to local communities." [2] Only agencies which had received Chest support in the past and those which met NIB standards would be reviewed. By May, 18 agency budgets were reviewed.

Kate Smith sings the "Red Feather March" for President Harry S. Truman while Major George Howard, conductor of the U.S. Army Air Force Band and composer of the march, hums along. Photo Acme Newspictures, 1946.

Even though most of the State War Chests folded up along with the National War Fund, there were some substantial developments toward statewide planning and financing at this time. In Oregon the War Chest continued under the name Oregon Chest, Inc., but only included state agencies. In Ontario, the existing Community Welfare Council of Ontario became a social planning body on the provincial level. The former Ohio Institute for Public Efficiency (organized in 1913) reorganized as the Ohio Welfare Council, changing its name two years later to Ohio Citizen's Council for Health and Welfare.

All but a half dozen states had by then embarked upon some kind of program. There were four types of organization: state welfare conferences and associations of social workers; state citizens' associations; state Chests; and state associations of Chests and Councils. On May 10 the CCC board decided that such statewide organizations should be offered membership in CCC and that the finance committee should consider plans for experimental joint financing and planning with them. In an April memorandum, Lyman Ford indicated that such statewide programs seemed "destined to be one of the distinguishing features of the current period in community organization history." Actual development, however, has been considerably slower than this statement indicated.[3]

Also in May, CCC joined the National Health Council in considering the possibilities of federated fund raising by health agencies, and set up with them a joint

study committee. Dr. Reginald M. Atwater, director of the American Public Health Association, pointed out that following publication of the Gunn-Platt report the previous year, there had been strong general feeling that no logical relation existed between the extent of health needs or problems and the budgets of the various national health agencies.

This report of a three-year study financed by the Rockefeller Foundation had been published in 1945 under the auspices of the National Health Council. The study covered 18 national voluntary health agencies, 290 state or regionals, and 20,554 locals in 17 different fields. Among its findings were: the marked unevenness of the voluntary health movement; lack of central direction and planning; defective organization, poor leadership and technical direction; and a lag in adapting programs to changing needs of communities. Anticipating an increasing need for coordination at local, state, and national levels, the report had said more ways must be found to support the voluntary health program without competitive and confusing duplication of fund appeals. "Finally, there is great need for a strong central national agency representative of the varied interests in the health movement to give future leadership and direction . . . The National Health Council would be in a most advantageous position to carry out this task if it expanded its scope, increased its resources and found a new type of direction."[4]

The possibility of joint financing was also suggested in the Gunn-Platt report. "The war has taught us the common sense and effectiveness of the multiple war relief appeal. Have specialized health agencies nothing to learn from this?"[5]

The study committee formed in 1946 concluded in March 1948 that coordinated fund raising was impractical at that time (seven nationals had been willing to consider federation but five had opposed it) and that any steps toward federation would have to be initiated by the agencies themselves. As Dr. Louis I. Dublin of Metropolitan Life Insurance Co., who had directed the study, recalled in 1962, "Unfortunately the member organizations were reluctant to give up sovereignty and join in the building of a strong National Health Council. They have not changed very much since in that regard."[6]

Another abortive attempt to form a joint-financing organization was made that summer when members of the American Council of Voluntary Agencies for For-

Your ONE Fair Share pledge given the United Way is working MANY wonders like these, right now

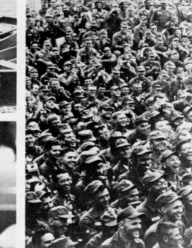

THANKS TO YOU and the 30 million other persons who pledge their Fair Share gift to their United Fund or Community Chest more than 25 million families benefit each year from child care, family service, youth guidance, health programs and services for the Armed Forces through 30,000 United Way health, welfare, recreation and other community-service agencies.

Your one gift works many wonders...all year round...THE UNITED WAY

This advertisement prepared by volunteer agency BBD&O was carried in contributed space by 210 magazines in 1964.

eign Service considered a united appeal for foreign relief. Herbert Hoover, who had gone abroad to study the food situation, suggested that strong backing might be obtained in support of a foreign relief campaign for child feeding and one or two other projects. In June the Council voted in favor of such an appeal, to be conducted nationally except in areas where Chests would include it. On August 1, James Brunot, secretary of the National Budget Committee and former director of the President's War Relief Control Board, reported the plans had not materialized. "Though virtually all of the agencies participating in discussions subscribed to the basic idea of federated action, the practical difficulties of working out plans to provide support in time to sustain ongoing programs in 1947 appeared too great." [7] The idea was taken up again a year later, but again failed to reach fulfillment.

Cessation of the war and demobilization brought about changing needs for USO. A year after the war ended, the armed forces had been reduced to 3 million and within another year to one and a half million, at which the number was stabilized. USO still was needed however, and a $19 million goal was set. At least 44 cities agreed to include USO and CCC urged further inclusion of war-related agencies.

The relationship between public agencies and local Councils was the subject of a CCC study with results published at the end of the year. The study set standards for public agency participation. Much of the governmental development of programs in social services, public recreation, health, probation, and schools "has been initiated, fostered, sponsored, and fought for through Community Welfare Councils which are working to expand and develop further public services . . . People now realize that community welfare needs are too great to be met entirely by private agencies . . . In 1944 public agencies accounted for 61.3 percent of the money spent for health and welfare services in our urban areas. It becomes apparent that public and private agencies each have a special role to play in the community and that through a Council they may work as partners rather than rivals." [8]

The fall campaign promotion was conducted under the name Community Chests of America, with the slogan Everybody Benefits, Everybody Gives which was to become a continuing theme. Results showed that most Chest cities had gone over the top and when all the figures were compiled, 96.6% of goals was reached.

The ten years since 1936 had been momentous in

Walter H. Wheeler, Jr. (left), Chairman of the Board, Pitney-Bowes Company and veteran United Way leader, with Spyros Skouras, President of Twentieth Century Fox (standing), and Harvey J. Firestone, Jr., National Chairman, 1954 United Community Campaigns of America.

the development of joint planning and financing. CCC prepared a study of those "Ten Eventful Years," pointing out such facts as the growth in Chests from 452 raising $81 million to 798 raising $197 million. Of even greater significance were philosophical changes such as the conviction that money raising could not and should not be divorced from social planning, a growing conviction that the Chest must continually grow in scope and membership, a new realization that gifts to a Chest are not "charity for the down and out" but community services for all the people; and a growing sense of national unity among Chests and Councils.

1947

There was considerable discussion about the value of federation during 1947. During the Annual Conference of Community Chests and Councils in March, Ralph Blanchard spoke of the local community's responsibility for support of national health and welfare services, and pointed out that "the public welfare is indivisible."

At the Pacific Coast Conference in April, Lynn D. Mowat, general manager of the Welfare Federation of Los Angeles, said it was time to make a choice between a greater degree of federation or becoming "just another campaign." Conference members adopted a resolution reaffirming belief in federation with an open door for participation which would become effective "when the supporters of federation provide adequate support of agency service programs which meet human needs and when federation provides a continuous program of public education about problems, amount, need, agency service programs and the advantages of federation." [9]

At the Southeast Conference in May a resolution was adopted urging extension of federation to include state and national health and welfare appeals, saying it was also essential for Councils to coordinate and bring into balance the national programs with local needs.

The weed-like growth of health or so-called "disease" organizations was a matter of growing concern. By 1947, 18 of the present-day national health organizations had been established. These groups usually were organized from the top down, and local chapters were granted charters which could be withdrawn if they did not follow national policies. Often the appeals were based on fear of the disease they were fighting, and sometimes unscrupulous methods were used by appeals which provided most benefit not to the victims of disease, but their own promoters. Because most local agencies were included in once-a-year Chest appeals, the rest of the year was free for the disease appeals, which often enlisted many enthusiastic volunteers. The new national agencies generally attempted to get all they could when and where the getting was good, and strongly opposed budgeting and other endeavors to relate dollars to human needs and agency programs.

Older nationals, such as the American Cancer Society and American Heart Association, which had started out seeking Chest support for their locals began to encourage or force their locals to withdraw from Chests and to prohibit others from joining.

The growing number of separate appeals began to give the impression to newer members of the givers' generation that the Chest was just one more appeal. The refusal of various agencies to relate budget, quotas, or programs to local needs was abhorrent to proponents of joint financing and planning. CCC meantime was promoting state Chests and Councils in an endeavor to assist in budget, quota, goal and program coordination of national agencies. It is small wonder that trouble was brewing.

Robert E. Bondy, director of the National Social Welfare Assembly, pointed out that national agency roots were in local soil and that "social welfare should fight only one fight—to achieve well-being for all the people. The fight can be won only through unity of all its forces." [10]

The indignation of Chest-Council people was roused by Basil J. O'Connor, chairman of the American National Red Cross and president of the National Foundation for Infantile Paralysis, who spoke at an NSWA meeting in May. On the first day of the meeting C. M. Bookman, then a volunteer in Cincinnati, had said, "The public is becoming very much confused and annoyed by the many ways in which they are being importuned to be helpful; for example, last year in Cincinnati we had more than 200 separate campaigns for funds . . . As I see it, national agencies must coordinate their programs and their financial needs at the national level if they, as well as local social agencies, are to progress soundly." [11]

Mr. O'Connor made his address the next day, explaining his belief in dramatizing and capitalizing on a cause in order to obtain support. "There is going to break out an open warfare between the school of federated financing and the school of independent financing . . . We are opposed and unequivocally opposed to joint fund raising . . . I have a very simple objection . . . that it is not the American way of life . . There is no more rhyme nor reason nor cause for the communization of our health and welfare activities or for the communization of our fund raising than there is for the communization of our insurance companies or our banks or our oil companies or our industry . . . I am not indicating . . . that those who favored federated fund raising or joint fund raising are communists in any sense of the word . . . I don't believe they realize the implications that would be involved . . .

"I have no hesitation in taking the position that the un-American way of handling health and welfare activity and fund raising in joint fund raising is unsound . . . Joint fund raising means the end of private activity in this country in health and welfare activities . . . I wish we could get away from childish talk about organizations having too much money . . . No organization could have too much money." [12]

The battle was now out in the open. CCC promptly sent copies of the Bookman and O'Connor speeches to member Chests and Councils. On May 20 the Board voted to develop a statement on federation for use by local Chests and CCC on public occasions rather than to reply directly. Such a statement was released in October.

The October *Atlantic Monthly* carried an open letter to Basil O'Connor by Robert Cutler, past president of CCC, who said, "The views which you have expressed are alien to me, and, upon serious reconsideration, appear to me unsound and misleading." He reviewed the growth of Chests and the advantages of federations saying, "The unification of local appeals in a single voluntary campaign, with its ever-widening participation in numbers of givers and workers, has made it possible more readily, more effectively, and with a finer spirit to raise the money necessary to carry on the local health, hospital, welfare, and social agencies which are vital to each community." He called Community Chests an expression of the American way.

"Liberty never says I will do it my way and everyone else in the neighborhood must take it and like it. No, in America we decide things in a town meeting . . . The validity of any Community Chest rests wholly upon the will of the people in that community." He called attention to the emotional appeals of some agencies compared with other social agencies "which are essential to decent and orderly living . . . There is all too little 'drama' in many of these necessary works of love and devotion. Yet it would be intolerable if, because of lack of glamour, they should be elbowed into the shadows of inadequate financial support, while the coffers of a more dramatic appeal were filled and overflowing." [13]

In July the United Health and Welfare Fund of Michigan was launched, erected upon the State War Chest framework. The president of Ford Motor Company, Henry Ford II, who had been active in the Fund's formation, said, "Both corporate managers and labor in our state practically demanded the establishment of such a federation and insisted that it be the all-inclusive fund-raising instrument operating alone. The state's largest industrial companies and many others are determined that they will make only one contribution a year and that their employees will be solicited only once a year in the future." [14] The next year and a half were spent organizing the first statewide campaign, which was conducted in February 1949, a campaign which led directly to the nation's first local United Fund campaign in Detroit that fall.

CCC sent out a questionnaire on local support of national agencies and published the results in June. In most of the 230 communities replying, the comment "everyone is against so many campaigns, but nobody knows what to do about it" was appropriate, but not

H. J. Heinz II, (left) 1947 National Chairman of Community Chests of America, receives Red Feather Award from Edward L. Ryerson, 3 C's President.

in all. In 48, an "open door" policy was established and in 71, special budgeting procedures were set up for national agencies. Six cities included a special fund for national agencies, and in 28 percent of the cities, a local appeals review board was established.

A new joint campaign by major foreign relief agencies and the International Children's Emergency Fund was organized that fall under the name American Overseas Aid. President Harry S. Truman promised support. Lee Marshall, chairman of the Board of Continental Baking Company, was chairman and C. M. Bookman, then retired, vice chairman. An allocations committee made a tentative recommendation for a campaign goal of $60 million for the 12 participating agencies. CCC offered its cooperation and asked for local assistance to the appeal. It was too late, however, to include AOA in that fall's campaigns.

On December 8, Red Cross reaffirmed its policy of nonparticipation in federation. "The American National Red Cross at one time yielded to pressure and became affiliated with some 400 federated fund-raising agencies although many persons questioned its right to do so. At first the arrangement seemed generally satisfactory. Shortly, however, a tendency developed for such agencies to become locally controlled and to become forced

Henry Ford II (right) accepts the leadership of the 1948 United Way Campaigns and the "Chairman's Schedule" from outgoing National Chairman H. J. Heinz II.

to disregard the national and international obligations of the Red Cross." [15]

In December, a Conference on District and Neighborhood Community Organization was held in Cleveland under the joint sponsorship of CCC and the National Federation of Settlements. Promoted as part of the civilian defense effort of World War I, and in the years following, neighborhood councils had been organized by a number of Councils of Social Agencies as well as by social settlements. Civilian defense problems during World War II accelerated their development and the post-war problems of housing and related subjects stimulated their further growth. Out of this conference came a report noting that 50 Councils were then offering full or part-time staff service to neighborhood organizations.

The CCC Board and National Social Welfare Assembly late in 1947 issued a joint statement of their common interest, distinctive functions, and working understandings. It recognized NSWA as the central national planning body for social welfare, while CCC was the national spokesman for state and local joint planning and federated support of social welfare services. The need for close cooperation was stressed, with three activities to be carried out under joint sponsorship: national budgeting and quota planning, citizen participation, and field service cooperation. NSWA would receive approximately 52 percent of its support from local Chests and Councils who were asked to make appropriations of one-twelfth of one percent of

the amount raised. The close bonds between the two organizations have continued with increasing benefits ever since.

During the board meeting on December 10, the first annual National Community Service Award for outstanding volunteer service was presented to Gerard Swope, honorary president of CCC and former Mobilization chairman, for his many contributions to the advancement of the United Way in community health and welfare services.

On December 12, 30 leading citizens from a dozen states met in Chicago to discuss the multiplicity of local campaigns by state and national agencies and to explore what could be done at the state level to bring about a more orderly approach to the problems of supporting them. The meeting was called by Edward L. Ryerson of Chicago, chairman of the board of Inland Steel Company and president of CCC. There was little evidence of an emotional revolt against support of outside appeals, but plenty of grim determination to find a more orderly method. The climax of the meeting was the unanimous adoption of a resolution expressing the feeling that there was merit in attempting to apply the principles of federated financing to all appeals: local, state, and national.

1948

The first National Conference and Citizens Workshop was held in Washington in January, during the National Social Welfare Assembly annual meeting. It was a project of the new Citizen Participation Department, jointly sponsored by Community Chests and Councils and NSWA. More than 300 attended the meetings which presented an inventory of the nation's health and welfare needs, and discussed ways to meet them in the good old American way—citizens, action on hometown soil.

An abortive attempt at joint financing in Japan was described in the March *Community*. Various reasons for failure were offered, among them: "The fact that the common man hasn't the slightest idea what Japan's first nationwide Community Chest drive is all about, or why it is necessary" and the different philosophy of people who traditionally had felt government should handle such matters and that one's own responsibility stopped with his family. In more recent years the Japan Chest has proved more successful. In 1961, it raised $5,891,426 on a goal of $5,537,218.

President Truman making the first all-network television broadcast in behalf of the 1948 United Way campaigns.

At the annual meeting during the March Conference of Community Chests and Councils, a change in name was approved because of confusion which often led people to think of CCC as a New York City organization. The name became Community Chests and Councils of America, though most people in the field continued to refer to it by its nickname, Three C's.

The status of state financing and planning bodies was reported in Chicago by Lyman Ford, CCC's Health and Welfare Planning director, at the Chest-Council Midwest Regional Conference. "National and local efforts to cope with the problem have reached a stalemate, with local people waiting for national action and national groups waiting for local pressure. It may be that state action is the intermediate step. Interested leaders in every state ought at least to meet and try to work out a plan." [16] The board in September arranged for Mr. Ford to spend a major portion of his

time during 1949 working with states in order to guide sound development of state organizations.

Late in June, a CCC bulletin reported, "A year ago general (local) Chest policy on the support of national agencies had not yet been defined, whereas this year's replies to a questionnaire indicate a general move toward crystallization of policy. More than 40% have officially adopted an 'open door' policy or are seriously considering such action. The number of cities which now report a definite policy of supporting only local services is limited." [17]

At the end of 1947 USO had announced it would dissolve, but early in July of 1948, Secretary of the Navy James Forrestal wrote to Community Chests and Councils president Edward L. Ryerson, asking for aid in reactivating the organization. The half-year of peacetime doldrums for the men in uniform had shown that the armed forces couldn't get along without USO.

At a conference called by CCC to consider USO inclusion, 54 cities agreed to add USO to their fall campaigns. By August, $2,276,000 of the $3,950,000 requests of Chests was accepted for inclusion in campaign goals.

At the end of the year, Ralph Blanchard discussed the challenges to federation and said, "These very charges only indicate the deep grass-roots strength of the federation idea . . . A Chest that insists it has no interests in life other than its own hometown, brings a charge of 'isolationist' down on the movement . . . A budget committee which appears to be more interested in making needs fit budgets than budgets fit needs tends to give all Chests a reputation of being more interested in wielding the pruning shears than in cultivating the good earth for federation and planting seeds of growth. But thank God the reverse is true too: when a Chest or Council takes a courageous stand, when it lifts its sights, when it opens its doors to democracy, then the whole movement gets a heartening lift, takes a new lease on life . . .

"The basic problem is unquestionably federation itself and that is why we see our basic job here in the national association this year and perhaps for many years to come as one of strengthening federation and reinterpreting it. This continuous pot-shotting and chipping away at federation sometimes makes me wonder whether this association will inevitably be forced by local and national pressure from all sides to take a more positive and aggressive stand than we have hitherto felt it our function to take. A new service might be sought and given—of leadership; a mobilization of our own local forces into a national spearhead that will carry this crusade for federation into every corner of these United States." [18] Mr. Blanchard's challenge of a "crusade for federation" represented a turning point in the 30-year history of the association.

1949—United Fund Movement

The first generally-inclusive, peacetime state Fund with quotas for both state and national agencies began operation in Michigan during January. Of the 24 national and state agencies invited to join, 19 had accepted. In all, $1,091,858 was raised among Michigan's 83 counties, each county reaching a little more than 80% of its goal. Despite problems, a great deal of new money was produced and local federated drives were able to present a more inclusive "package" and attract better volunteer leadership and contributor response. The State Fund raised practically no money directly,

concentrating its efforts instead on getting its quota included in local United drives and helping the smaller communities with their organizing and operating problems. Through the succeeding years the Michigan United Fund, as it is now called, has continued to grow both in inclusiveness and in money allocated.

Detroit Torch Drive

One of the most important successes was in Detroit, where widespread support of the idea of complete federation was obtained from community leaders. A pilot campaign held in January-February raised $804,996, more than the same agencies had raised from the same source by separate appeals. This confirmed the belief that the Detroit United Foundation's Torch Drive would be supported enthusiastically. The cry was soon taken up on all sides calling for unification of all drives in Detroit. The only agency holdouts were American Cancer Society, National Foundation for Infantile Paralysis, and American National Red Cross. The general manager of United Detroit Theatres stopped all canister solicitations for Infantile Paralysis, and Charles Wilson, President of General Motors and chairman of the Michigan Heart Association, insisted that this agency join. Negotiations with Red Cross resulted in their agreeing to participate in an in-plant solicitation. When news of this reached Basil O'Connor, he threatened the Wayne County Chapter with loss of its franchise. The Detroit Red Cross remained firm, however. Later that year, in the resultant furor, O'Connor resigned as Red Cross National Chairman and President Truman appointed General of the Army George C. Marshall in his place. When the American Cancer Society and the National Foundation for Infantile Paralysis refused to negotiate, the United Foundation said it would campaign in the name of the diseases they represented and turn over the funds to the Michigan Cancer Foundation and the Sister Elizabeth Kenny Foundation.

The first Torch Drive, with 143 appeals, opened on October 18 and raised $9,258,930 for 104% of the goal. This success made Detroit the model for the new United Fund movement. The outstanding public relations and advertising campaign which resulted in both local and national publicity and included pictures and articles in *Life, Newsweek,* and *Saturday Evening Post,* helped spread the story and bring about a nationwide revolution in federated financing.

One of the speakers at the Midwest Conference in February was Severino N. Luna, a young businessman from the Philippines, who had come to the U.S. to study federation. Having visited several cities with sponsoring help of CCC, his enthusiasm for federation inspired many at the conference. He returned to the Philippines in March and helped organize the Community Chest of Greater Manila, becoming its executive and campaign director. This Chest has continued through the years, and a Council has also been organized.

Ralph Blanchard also spoke on the "Future of Federation" calling attention to the voluntary spirit, characterized by full recognition of the right of local self-determination—hallmarks of democracy in action in America. He suggested improvements such as spreading the representation in financing and planning, developing better public education, and presenting a united front. He called on Chest and Council leaders to be flexible, unrestrictive, and progressive. He predicted the spread of federation to every community, and at the state and national levels.[19]

Recommendations for local and state action to bring about more orderly methods of raising and allocating funds for voluntary health and welfare agencies were adopted by the CCC board in April. Among the suggestions were formation of widely representative groups such as Community Appeals Planning Committees; meetings by key leaders on the state level; and services such as quota setting, budget reviews, study and research, development of agency "packages," and state Chests.

The National Foundation for Infantile Paralysis hired a consumer research organization, Charles C. Flarida, Jr. Inc. of New York to learn what the public and agencies thought about the red herring idea of a "Super Fund." A book entitled "Common Sense about Fund Raising" purportedly based on this data was published in 1949. CCC did not, of course, envisage such a Fund.

Analysis indicated that the questions and methods used by Mr. Flarida were not comparable with those used by recognized pollsters, and that the book was loaded against federated financing. The author, Robert Keith Leavitt, attacked the idea of this so-called Super Fund, and the National Information Bureau as well.

During the spring and summer a series of documents was issued by Red Cross with Basil O'Connor's authorization, calling for employee solicitation only in a separate and distinct drive, lest such cooperation lead to pressure to participate in joint fund raising on a

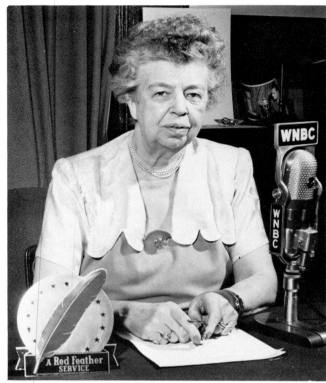

Eleanor Roosevelt making television-radio broadcast on behalf of 1949 United Way campaigns.

President Harry S. Truman is presented with Red Feather for his support of United Way campaigns by Evansville, Indiana, youngster as daughter Margaret and wife Bess stand by. The President was on his famous "Give 'em Hell Harry" train campaign for the 1948 election.

communitywide basis. They deplored "the threat of compulsory fund raising" by the Michigan United Health and Welfare Fund and the "agitation for federated fund raising" by CCC.[20] Shortly after Gen. Marshall took over, another bulletin was issued, repeating the basic fund-raising policy but going on to say, "In instances where an employer will permit no more than one annual in-plant solicitation of its employees . . .

the local chapter may participate in such payroll deduction plans" under certain specified conditions.[21] From then on, Red Cross chapters did participate increasingly in "in-plant" drives and United Funds. Compromises were effected, steps taken to maintain Red Cross identity, and relations between Red Cross and United Funds became increasingly cordial and mutually effective.

"Facts on Council Operations" were defined that summer in a CCC bulletin which described Council organization, delegate bodies, agency membership and relationships with Chests. A study revealed that civic and professional organizations were members of 132 out of 139 Councils reporting; Chests and Councils were combined in one operation in 20.4%; were separate with a shared executive in 41.6%; and completely separate in 33.8%. Almost all Councils participated in some way in the allocation of Chest funds to member agencies; more than half of them participated in the selection of budget committee members. Some form of participation in budgeting of governmental bodies was also reported by 35%.

A growing responsibility of Community Welfare Councils was that of services to the aging. "Caring for old people, planning with them and for them is one of the most challenging opportunities for Community Chests and Councils today," wrote Elizabeth Breckenridge, director of the Chicago Council's Project for the Aged, in the June Community. "There are many more old people in the average city than ever before. It is impractical to tackle problems separately. The community interested in its older people must turn to the formulation of a total program rather than a piecemeal approach." [22]

Early in the fall a new version of the spreading idea of state organization took place in New York State where Councils took the lead rather than Funds. Council executives had learned that the State Commissioner of Social Welfare would like a statewide Council organization in order to channel information to local health and welfare planning groups. In communities which had no planning agencies, Chests which performed planning functions were included. The State Charities Aid Association agreed to provide a secretariat and the new State Association of Councils of Social Agencies held its organizational meeting in November. One of its first projects was to study the New York State Youth Commission which was due to go out of existence the next year. Resulting legislation was generally in line with the Association's recommendations. The following year the Association changed its name to New York State Association of Councils and Chests and its objectives were redefined.

New Hampshire formed a similar Social Welfare Council for the purposes of studying state welfare problems and needs, stimulating joint planning and coordinating of effort, and conducting special demonstrations.

Concern about housing was growing. "Now that the Housing Act of 1949 has become Public Law 171 it has moved straight into the realm of local community planning . . . Community Welfare Councils can do much to create understanding of the provisions of the act and to stimulate community action," said an October Community article. The four programs included in the act were: slum clearance and community development, low-rent public housing, housing research, and farm housing.[23]

Throughout the country, industrial leaders were plagued by the increasing number of separate appeals, and many demanded the right to establish their own solicitations. Labor-management committees then agreed on making one appeal, which organizations to include, and what amounts to be sought for each. Plant committees conducted the campaigns, decided on apportionments, handled collections and made payments.

While Chests liked the increased amounts received, many raised skeptical eyebrows regarding the often unreasonable amounts allocated to a few of the new and glamorous non-participating organizations. There wasn't much they could do about these in-plant federations, however, as they often represented national policy of the great industrial corporations. Other Chests actively promoted their establishment. The real solution came when other communities followed Detroit's lead and set up United Funds which included state and national agencies. Then many industrial Chests became chapters of the United Fund and participated in an overall community approach to community budgeting.

Results of 1949 appeals were not heartening. A recession had begun, strikes were common, there was uncertainty about the future, the number of separate campaigns was increasing, and there was further competition from building funds. Final results showed that with 1318 campaigns, 93.1 percent of goals was reached.

The explosive decade of the 40's came to an end, with the promise of further tumult in the 50's.

NOTES

Chapter 10

1. *Community,* CCC, March 1946, pp. 124, 125, 132.

2. Progress Report, National Budget Committee, CCC, September 1946, pp. 3-5.

3. "Community Organization for Health and Welfare on a Statewide Basis," mimeographed memorandum, CCC, April 1, 1946, p. 24, and appendix, p. 1.

4. Selskar M. Gunn and Philip S. Platt, *Voluntary Health Agencies* (New York: The Ronald Press Co., 1945), pp. vii-viii.

5. *Ibid.,* pp. 221-222.

6. Louis I. Dublin, letter to Elwood Street, April 27, 1962.

7. *On the Alert,* CCC, August 1, 1946.

8. "Public Agency-Council Relationships," Health and Welfare Planning Department, CCC, December 1946, p. 22.

9. *Community,* CCC, June 1947, p. 196.

10. *Community,* CCC, May 1947, p. 168.

11. C. M. Bookman, "America's Stake in Social Welfare," Address before National Social Welfare Assembly, May 5, 1947, pp. 6-7.

12. Basil O'Connor, "Financing Social Welfare," Address before National Social Welfare Assembly, May 6, 1947, mimeographed, pp. 1, 2, 4-7.

13. *The Atlantic Monthly,* October 1947, pp. 48-50.

14. "A Red Feather Message from Henry Ford, II," CCC pamphlet, 1949, p. 11.

15. "Policy Regarding American Red Cross Fund Raising and Joint Fund Raising," American National Red Cross, Board of Governors, December 8, 1947, pp. 1-2.

16. *Community,* CCC, March 1948, p. 151.

17. *On the Alert,* CCC, June 29, 1948.

18. Ralph H. Blanchard, "The 1949 Program of the Association," presented to Board of Directors, CCC, December 8, 1948, pp. 1-15.

19. Ralph H. Blanchard, "The Future of Federation," CCC pamphlet, 1949, pp. 6-14.

20. "The Case for Freedom," American Red Cross, June 1949, p. 18.

21. Gen. George C. Marshall, president, American National Red Cross, Bulletin to Chapter Chairmen, November 18, 1949.

22. *Community,* CCC, June 1949, pp. 190-191.

23. *Community,* CCC, October 1949, p. 25.

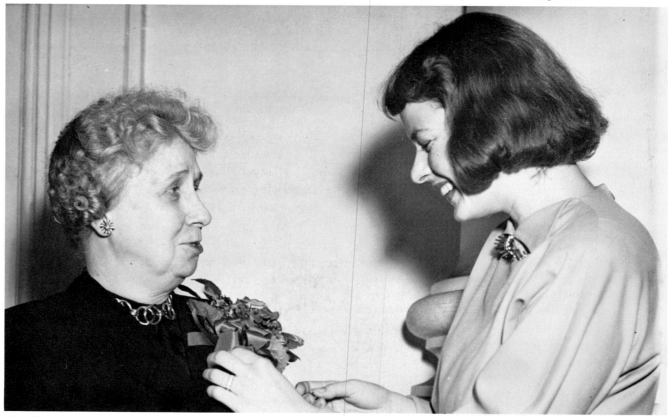

Ingrid Bergman pins a Red Feather on Mrs. Harry S. Truman for her help in the 1946 United Way campaign. Press Association, Inc. Photo.

11

THE RISE OF
UNITED FUNDS: 1950-1955

The turbulence of 1949 increased in various ways in the opening year of the 50's. The United Fund idea spread rapidly, encompassing more national agencies. The proponents of joint financing took the offensive in the battle with those who would go-it-alone, while an olive branch was offered to the American National Red Cross.

Early in 1950, fifty Chest executives meeting in Cincinnati at the call of CCC, approved the extension of federation to include national agencies in United Funds but questioned the advisability of any move toward a "package" of national agency budgets to be distributed on a quota basis to local Chests.

Reports of new local United Funds received close attention during the first Biennial Conference of Chests and Councils held in Cincinnati in February. (National Conferences would now be held biennially, with regionals during the off-years.) Flint, Mich. with a United Campaign, had reached 107 percent of its $594,000 goal (36% above the previous year's receipts). Rochester, N.Y. reported it had an open door policy for 32 years and already included all important agencies except Red Cross and the National Foundation for Infantile Paralysis. Chest President Joseph Goldstein said, "Our task is to make the Community Chest so strong and so highly regarded by the public that all

agencies will find it to their advantage to be included and associated with it." [1]

Thomas D. Carter, an attorney from Winston-Salem, N.C., described the success of the appeals review council which his community had set up independent of the Chest to deal with a rash of appeals which hit in 1946. It had succeeded in eliminating some nuisance campaigns, spread the principle of budgeting, set local goals for national appeals, prevented conflicts in campaign dates, and reduced costs. "It brings to citizens' minds the fact there is a limit to effective manpower in the community and thus it leads to the demand for coordinated planning." [2]

Retiring CCC President Ryerson said, "Chests have had to stand much sharp criticism from the public because they have seemed powerless to stem the tide of separate campaigns . . . A Chest is a voluntary association and it cannot compel any agency to become a member. State and national agencies have a solemn obligation to maintain policies which permit their local units to adjust to the moods and wishes of the communities in which they serve. To deny this right is to deny a first principle of democracy." [3]

USO found that its hopes of being included in a large number of Chest campaigns were not being fulfilled. It ran out of money and once again deactivated. Three of its former members—YMCA, National Catholic Community Services, and National Jewish Welfare Board—then formed a new organization with CCC help named Associated Services for the Armed Forces.

On June 25, forces of the Communist Democratic People's Republic of North Korea crossed the 38th parallel and invaded the Republic of South Korea. President Truman ordered United States air, sea, and ground forces into action. The Korean War was to continue until 1954, costing more American casualties than any previous war other than the Civil War and World War II.

This put more responsibility on the new Associated Services for the Armed Forces, and Community Chests were asked to include in their goals up to 5 percent for such services. Local Chests and Councils were soon asked to participate in civil defense plans also.

In September, Congress voted to amend the Social Security Act in ways important to both planning and financing. After more than 20 years of seeking coverage, employees of non-profit organizations would be covered by Old Age and Survivors Insurance. In addition, there would now be aid to the permanently and totally disabled, and federal expenditures for child welfare and maternal services would be doubled. "The major long-range effect of Old Age and Survivors Insurance will be to transfer more people to insurance coverage on a more adequate basis, with decreasing emphasis on public assistance to the aged and to surviving families," CCC reported.[4] By fall, community Chests and Councils had applied for Social Security coverage for its employees and had urged locals to do similarly. Most members of the National Health and Welfare Retirement Association decided to continue coverage as before, in addition to Social Security.

Gen. George C. Marshall, who was now Secretary of Defense as well as chairman of American National Red Cross, spoke to the Washington, D.C. Chest Federation that fall, citing the valuable contributions made by Red Feather agencies. He called the Chest "a very important unifying force in American life . . . The Community Chest campaigns give every American citizen an opportunity to strengthen the moral fibres of democracy at home."[5] A new era of goodwill between the United Way and American National Red Cross had begun.

Meeting in September, an NSWA-CCC Joint Committee on National Emergency Services took action

President Harry S. Truman announces his support of the newly-organized United Defense Fund for human care services related to the Korean conflict. Standing are (left) UDF President E. A. Roberts and Ralph H. Blanchard, Executive Director, Community Chests and Councils of America. Seated beside the President is Navy Secretary Francis Matthews, UDF Vice President.

with regard to the Korean War emergency, including affirmation of the need for Chest allocations for national emergency services; need for a single organization to serve the armed forces and another for emergency services to civilians; and organization of a national emergency fund. CCC then asked local Chests to do everything possible to help Red Cross, to urge its involvement in local Councils, and to work out local civilian defense plans. In November, the committee reported rapid progress toward establishment of a national defense fund to budget, raise and allocate funds for national welfare services made necessary by the defense effort.

The first board meeting of United Defense Fund was held November 29 with E. A. Roberts of Philadelphia, president of Fidelity Mutual Life Insurance Company, elected president and Ralph Blanchard, executive. Services to receive support fell into two groups, the first concerned with services to the armed forces, and the second to communities congested by the defense effort.

In December, the Fifth White House Conference on Children and Youth at Mid-Century was attended by many delegates who were active in Community Welfare Councils. These local planners stressed the importance of one overall community body concerned not only with children and youth but all aspects of community life. There was a feeling, however, that some Councils were

(Left to right) G. Warfield Hobbs, national United Way Treasurer, had a secret—a million dollars in cash in his pocket, the amount needed to keep USO operating for a month. Garry Moore, star of the television show "I've Got A Secret," presented a special appeal for the 1952 United Way campaigns.

too narrow in their scope and membership to make their influence felt as it should be. Educators, for example, were frequently not represented in Councils at that time.

In December, the CCC board was asked to sponsor the National Committee on Foundations and Trusts for Community Welfare. This committee had been formed during the 1949 annual meeting of the National Conference of Social Work and represented CCC, NSWA, and the leading community trusts of the nation. Since the first community trust was formed in Cleveland in 1914, a total of 114 community trusts had been organized. There were in addition an estimated 10,000 to 15,000 charitable foundations and trusts, the exact number known, it was said, only to God and the tax collector. The committee asked, "What will be the influence of such funds on community health and welfare services of the future? A good deal of confusion is already evident. Will serious losses and abuses arise?" [6] The committee's plan was to offer no cut-and-dried program, no whirlwind campaign, but to make available descriptions and plans of programs which had worked in some communities.

The board approved an expenditure of $1500 for the program but costs rose in 1954 when a part-time secretary was hired. In 1957, incorporated as the National Council on Community Foundations, Inc., a full-time operation was begun with a three-year, $45,000 Rockefeller Foundation grant to be matched by gifts from other sources.

There was great interest in the results of United Fund campaigns that year. They were still pioneering ventures. In Michigan, where the United Health and Welfare Fund was combined with nearly all Chests, the first eight "extended federations" campaigns reported reaching 101.4% of goals. In the total picture, 1498 Chest and United Fund campaigns raised $213 million, 95% of their goals, the largest sum since the War Fund campaign of 1944-45.

1951

New life was again pumped into the USO. On January 11, 1951 a joint announcement was made by the Associated Services for the Armed Forces and USO that they would consolidate their efforts and facilities and operate under the old familiar name of USO. USO became one branch of the United Defense Fund. The other, United Community Defense Services, served domestic areas. Rapid progress was made as prevailing sentiment held that this package of national services was what Chests were asking for. During the Midwest Conference, Robert Bondy, director of the National Social Welfare Assembly, said, "In this emergency the forces of social welfare are, for once, spectacularly prepared. Thanks to the Joint Committee on National Emergency Services set up last summer, we have an organized planning body, and through the United Defense Fund, a united financing body that makes sense." [7] The revived USO quickly set up 165 units and made plans for others in swamped communities.

United Community Defense Services, the second branch of UDF, was a revised version of American War Community Services and served many small communities, demonstrating ways they might mobilize their resources to serve themselves. In many of the "critical areas" as designated by the Office of Defense Mobilization, UCDS proved a range of services working closely with staffs of other interested agencies. It financed direct services to individuals and families such as public health nursing, casework, day care for children, leisure time programs, and also community planning and development. A representative of UCDS was stationed in each of five regions into which the country was divided. Louis B. Seltzer, editor of the Cleveland Press, and an outstanding leader in the Cleveland Welfare Federation, was named UCDS president.

In the June Community, Harold J. Seymour, former director of the National War Fund and then a consultant on institutional finance, said, "With higher

(Left to right) Bent Taylor, Executive Director, United Defense Fund, with General of the Army, Omar N. Bradley, 1954 National Campaign Chairman for UDF which was included in the United Way campaigns.

prices and higher payrolls, every Chest must face the choice between 'same money and less program' and 'same program and more money.' The UDF quota explains and justifies your increased goal in the easiest and simplest way possible . . . UDF will be the Chests' strongest argument for a sharp increase in corporate gifts. It looks to me like the very stuff the doctor ordered." [8]

On June 22 and 23 the first National Rally of Campaign Leaders was held at Sugar Camp in Dayton, Ohio, the recreation and conference center of National Cash Register Company. Stanley C. Allyn, CCC President, was also president of N.C.R. It was he who had extended the invitation to CCC. More than 200 Chest and United Fund presidents, campaign chairmen, and executives attended (executives were invited only if a volunteer campaign leader attended). It was such a success that the Campaign Leaders Conference became

an annual event. NCR continues as the host at the conference although in 1966 a plan of holding the meeting in different cities was adopted.

On July 10, negotiations for a truce between the United Nations forces and the communists were opened, but the fighting would go on for two years before an armistice was signed. UDF continued, of course, because of continuing needs of military personnel. Gen. H. Lawton Collins, chief of staff of the Army, said "We are going to have at least three-and-a-half million men under arms for some time to come . . . These men are going to be scattered all over the world and . . . they are going to need your help as much or more than they needed it in the past war." [9]

That summer, a unique organization was formed, the two-state Chest, Carolinas United Community Services. Federated campaigns in both North and South Carolina had been failing, with an increase in separate campaigns resulting. The general purpose of Carolinas United was to strengthen and extend federation. As it developed, it also provided services in community organization, agency financing, and statewide planning.

By May, United Defense Funds for Minnesota was in operation, one of the first such Funds. In all, seven statewide Chests were organized while UDF was active, the others being in Iowa, Wisconsin, Connecticut, West Virginia, and Kansas. In 1960 the Iowa UF disbanded because of feeling that fund raising could be accomplished better by local Chests and Funds. Of these seven, only the Carolinas Fund endured.

An important decision, reversing the trend of several years' duration, was made by the American National Red Cross on August 13 when the board voted to permit chapters to "cooperate with community or federated fund-raising agencies in joint or concurrent solicitations of industrial or business firms in which only one annual solicitation for a charitable contribution is

This Red Feather Award, a bronze medallion, was the first United Way award to be given for national voluntary service. It was used from 1947 to 1956.

permitted." [10] Previously, Red Cross policy did not permit chapters to enter into agreements for joint solicitation with federated fund-raising agencies, although they were free to make similar arrangements directly with the firms or industries involved.

When the fall campaigns were opened by President Truman in simultaneous radio and television broadcasts, every major Chest in the country had accepted the United Defense Fund, and more than 50 cities had organized some kind of United Fund. With 1500 campaigns, almost $241 million was raised.

In Detroit, relationships were clarified between the United Foundation (Torch Drive), the Chest, and Council after two years of study. The Chest-Council merged to form United Community Services of Metropolitan Detroit, while United Foundation assumed the fund-raising responsibility for UCS agencies, the Michigan United Fund and several other state and national participants. The arrangement served as a model for several other cities.

1952

Early in the year, a four-page leaflet titled, "Protect Your Freedom to Give," was widely distributed by the Roy Bernard Company, Inc., a New York public relations firm. "You are now in danger of losing your freedom of choice," it said, because of "well-intentioned men" who want to "control and dominate our social welfare agencies. They wish to combine all our welfare drives into a single federated fund. They would decide how your money is to be raised, who is to receive it, and how it should be spent. They would create a health trust more dangerous than any possible business or industrial trust. Compulsory joint fund-raising poses as a public good. But it can be used for evil ends . . . Now there is a trend toward national control of . . . local Community Chest campaigns. A national organization will seek to guide and dominate Community Chests and will make every effort to include all national welfare agencies in local fund drives . . . You have given your time, your money and your heart to America's welfare agencies. You must insist on your right to continue supporting them as you see fit. You must resist all efforts to destroy your freedom of choice." [11] CCC was unable to learn who was behind publication of the pamphlet, but decided to take no action since it probably would be given little attention by persons who knew federation's true aims.

During the biennial CCC conference in Milwaukee,

(Left to right) Stanley C. Allyn, Chairman of the Board of National Cash Register Company and host for the 1952 United Way Campaign Leaders Conference at Sugar Camp, Dayton, with two conference speakers, Dalton Feldstein, Pasadena, national United Way board member, and Robert F. Bondy, Executive Director of the National Social Welfare Assembly.

"Yardsticks for Corporate Giving" were presented by Kenneth Sturges, retired executive of the Cleveland Community Chest and then a CCC consultant. "There is no one best plan, though there are some principles which underlie any good yardstick plan. They include accounting for the community pattern of giving, adjusting to changes in the busines level, keeping in mind appropriate factors such as number of employees, net profits and the like . . . The yardstick plan should aim to win the confidence and cooperation of corporation donors by proving that it is equitable and practicable." [12]

Near the end of March, Three C's told of its interest in the development of state Chests and Councils. "A state Chest is not one big Community Chest for the whole state. It is a Chest which has as its participating agencies state and national organizations. It puts a package appeal together and attempts to raise the funds in a statewide campaign, seeking inclusion in the annual Community Chest campaign wherever possible . . . One of the difficulties in getting a state Chest organized is lack of staff service and a rallying point for citizen interest at the state level. Organization of the United Defense Fund appeal on a state basis may provide this in a number of states." [13] Most states, despite such encouragement, did not attempt to organize state Chests. In Pennsylvania, however, the need for such an organization was felt, and the Pennsylvania United Fund (first titled the Pennsylvania Health and Welfare Fund) was organized; it developed a "package" of state and national agencies, including: Pa. Welfare Forum, Pa. Citizens Association, USO, and others. In 1962, the Forum and the Association were consolidated to form the Pa. Citizens Council. Four years later, in 1966, PCC and PUF were disbanded and Community Services of Pennsylvania was organized.

The July issue of *Cosmopolitan* magazine carried a blistering attack on federation by free-lance writer Albert Q. Maisel. Titled, "Where Does Your Charity Dollar Go?" the article claimed that, "A tiny group of professional fund raisers is trying to take away your freedom to support specific causes. If they have their way, only one organization—a vast health and welfare trust, tightly controlled by a small board of directors—will be allowed to receive contributions . . . The monopoly scheme was originated about five years ago by a few top-level employees of an organization known as Community Chests and Councils, Inc. nicknamed the Triple-C. The Community Chests had developed over the previous quarter century as legitimate voluntary federations of local welfare agencies . . . But in recent years, although drives for cancer, heart, polio, and their specific causes have been extremely successful, the generalized appeal of the Community Chest Red Feather drives has often resulted in failure . . . Faced with this situation, a few ambitious leaders in the central organization . . . began to dream of a new kind of fund raising federation, a Super Chest." [14] Maisel went on with alleged instances of "coercion" of unnamed volunteers and givers, criticism of the Michigan and Detroit funds, charges of "fantastic expenses" and other alleged "abuses." The bitterness and extreme falsification used in these attacks were felt by Chest and Fund leaders to be a measure of the soundness and success of the United Fund idea.

In July, the CCC Committee on More Inclusive Fund Raising, made up of lay and professional representatives of expanded federations, met in Chicago and approved the policy of avoiding direct replies or acknowledgment of such attacks. Letters from local business, labor, and industry leaders to publishers were mentioned as being more persuasive and effective in turning the tables. Many such letters were sent, and many newspapers printed editorials showing the advantages of federation and correcting Maisel's errors.

So many letters were sent, in fact, that *Cosmopolitan*

MANAGEMENT AND LABOR talk campaign in the lee of a mammoth blast furnace at the Ford Rouge plant. (Left to right) E. J. Cote, Regional Director, United Auto Workers (CIO) and a Director of Detroit's United Foundation; Frank Martel, President of the Wayne County Federation of Labor (AFL) and a Vice-President of the Foundation and Henry Ford II, member of the board, and of Community Chests of America National Citizens Committee. Detroit, 1952.

soon announced it would carry a positive story on federation. This article came out in October, entitled "Charity's Civil War," written by Morton Sontheimer, an author of high repute. He said "the public alone should decide who should get its money." Advocates of federation were well pleased with the article.[15]

The entire episode was reviewed at the September CCC board meeting where the consensus was that the cause of federation had been helped more than hurt. James A. Linen, publisher of *Time* magazine, and chairman of public relations for CCC, said, "The Sontheimer article makes crystal clear the advantage of federated giving. In my opinion, a net gain for the Chest movement will have resulted." [16]

Reviewing the policies of national health agencies, CCC prepared a statement for the guidance of local Chests and Funds, and recommended that local campaigns negotiate with local agency citizen representatives rather than with the state or national headquarters. American Heart Association "regards with favor a cooperative fund-raising effort by health agencies limited to the solicitation of employee gifts . . . (and) for the general public, the usual communitywide campaign in February." The National Foundation forbade all joint solicitation, while American Cancer Society said, "The national policy allows for a considerable degree of local option." [17] In the fall, at least 341 cities in the United States and Canada conducted campaigns which included one or more of the "big six" national appeals.

Corporation Giving, a book by F. Emerson Andrews of the Russell Sage Foundation, was published that fall, the first extensive survey of the subject since 1930. "Corporations have risen to sudden prominence in the field of philanthropy," he wrote. "Their gifts and contributions as reported to the Bureau of Internal Revenue leaped from a level of $30 million in 1936 and $31 million in 1939 to a plateau of over $200 million in every year since 1944, with the probability that 1951 exceeded $300 million." [18]

H. J. Heinz II, President of the Community Chests of America and President of the food firm bearing his name, with E. C. Wood, General Chairman of Montreal's 1953 Red Feather campaign and President of the Imperial Tobacco Company of Canada.

1953

A new "first" in joint planning came with the new year: the first National Conference of Community Welfare Council Leaders, held in Cleveland January 8-9. This conference emphasized the fact that joint planning was perhaps the neglected half of joint planning and financing and should be considered as basic to all sound federated financial activity. H. J. Heinz II, who had been chairman of Community Chests of America in 1947, said, "We're going to discuss what can be done to strengthen the interest in planning so that it is recognized to be as dramatic and as dynamic as fund raising." [19]

Primarily a meeting of lay citizen leaders, the con-

ference used a round-table format to stimulate the exchange of experiences and techniques to help fortify community leaders in the conduct of planning activities in their home communities. Purposes of the Conference included giving recognition to the achievements and potentials of Councils as an essential part of our American system; to rally citizen leaders, and to emphasize the need for top citizen leadership. Louis B. Seltzer, president of United Community Defense Services, was chairman of the first conference.

In collaboration with United Defense Fund, CCC sponsored a two-day conference on state organization in St. Louis on January 18-19. Representatives from 12 states attended.

Although not represented at that meeting, Virginia formed the United Defense Fund of Virginia in 1953. Established by Community Chests and Councils of Virginia (which had been formed in 1945) it was incorporated to raise funds for UDF. Later, when UDF disbanded, the name was changed to United Fund of Virginia.

In March a new CCC bulletin on "Organizing a United Fund," pointed out that while Community Chests had a primary concern in organization of United Funds, they were not always in the best position to spearhead such action. On the other hand, unless Chest leadership took responsibility for some action, nothing was likely to happen. The bulletin pointed out that some causes were not subject to federation even though they were part of the multiple appeals problem, and that communities must decide if their problem was simply that of too many campaigns or if the difficulty was that the total given in all separate campaigns still left unmet needs and unsolved problems. "It's the giver who decides, finally. All sides must have their say, and the final decision as to whether or not a United Fund is to be formed must be based on a careful assessment of general community sentiment . . . Cooperation is the goal, and tight harness is almost worse than none when it comes to creating teamwork. If the organizing committee confines its efforts to dealing with the local boards and supporters of those agencies, and the latter in turn carry on the exchanges with the parent national bodies, ways can usually be found to solve problems, whatever they are. By the same token, if the local board of any agency does not agree to cooperate with a United Fund effort, it is probably not wise arbitrarily to include that cause in the campaign." [20]

A Code of the Chest and Council Movement was adopted by the CCC board in March, stating the basic concepts, objectives, and obligations of professional conduct by staff members.

Among the basic concepts are belief that: "Each individual has a responsibility to meet his own needs to the extent of his ability. People are interdependent, however, and the welfare of each affects the welfare of all. It is, therefore, desirable and necessary that people form organizations to work for their mutual benefit . . . Fundamental to community organization for social welfare is acceptance of change and development of health and welfare services and a firm belief in the value of preventive measures . . . The participation of citizens broadly representative of all community interests is a right which must be exercised if the Chest and Council movement is to realize fully its objectives."

Among its objectives were: seeking to "Promote preventive measures . . . Secure a balanced health and welfare program . . Foster cooperation . . . Encourage adequate support of an orderly, efficient, and humane system of essential voluntary and tax-supported services."

Obligations included: maintaining "high standards of personal and professional integrity . . . Respecting individual differences . . . Endeavoring to resolve differences in an atmosphere of mutual respect and confidence . . . Sharing knowledge . . . Disciplining the desire to seek personal recognition and acclaim." [21]

The code was printed and distributed to local organization members and it often appeared, neatly framed, on office walls.

President Eisenhower, who had taken office in January, broke precedent by accepting the honorary chairmanship of the United Defense Fund. He accepted the invitation "without any hesitation" saying, "It's a cause in which I am proud to serve."

Speaking before the National Budget Committee in April, CCC Executive Director Ralph Blanchard pointed out, "There is no joint or federated national fund-raising effort except that of the UDF . . . Community organization at the national level has always lagged behind local accomplishment . . . Only in recent times has the nation been generally recognized as a community with well-defined needs which must be met on a national basis. The great health agencies have rendered a great service in driving home that fundamental truth . . . Local communities must develop a clearer idea of national agencies and their role in the whole American scene. National agencies must develop more respect for local communities as the places where the people live who must be served. We must discover each other, not as antagonists, but as the natural partners we are and are meant to be, recognizing that our common aims can be achieved only through teamwork." [22]

A unique bit of pioneering in financing capital improvements in Norfolk, Va. was reported in the May *Community*. Between 1945 and 1952 the Chest had allocated a total of $1,116,327 from its capital improvement fund to provide new, modern facilities for agencies. This money came from separate capital account campaigns following the regular campaigns for three years and from Chest surpluses thereafter. Between 1945 and 1962, Norfolk distributed more than $20 million this way.

While the Norfolk plan was unique, Charlotte, N.C. had a somewhat similar plan. Other communities tried conducting joint appeals for current expenses and cap-

Alex F. Osborn, right, a founder of Batten, Barton, Durstine and Osborn advertising agency, receives the 1952 Red Feather Award from Stanley C. Allyn, UCFCA President, for distinguished volunteer service as United Way National Public Relations Chairman.

This painting by Stevan Dohanos used for the 1954 United Way campaigns, was the subject of a search by many local United Ways to find a "look alike" family which would appear at campaign rallies as a "live poster" holding the G-I-V-E cut out letters.

This "Happy Family" painting by Norman Rockwell was used for the 1953 Community Chests of America poster.

ital improvements in one campaign, with varying degrees of success. Some communities held separate capital account campaigns for member agencies singly or in groups, with Fund or Chest staff assistance.

On June 1, CCC moved into the new building of the Carnegie Endowment for International Peace across from the United Nations. In adjacent quarters were National Social Welfare Assembly, United Defense Fund and United Community Defense Services, all served by the same switchboard and mailing-room services.

At the annual meeting of the National Conference of Social Work much discussion was stimulated by a paper on "An Inquiry into the So-Called 'Chaos' in Fee Charging by Social Agencies." A surge of interest

had resulted from the bold and successful experimentation by a number of casework agencies which were feeling the effects of a budget squeeze, and who realized that a full-employment economy meant very few people were fully destitute. "Our generation has seen an increasing acceptance of the premise that because a person did not ask to be born he should be coddled through life. The fee-charging evolution represents a reversal in the trend . . . There is no justification for beneficiaries being 'given' social welfare services if their economic, physical, and psychological resources enable them to procure these services through their own effort in a well-organized community program . . .

"Chests and United Funds can cultivate better fee-charging practice in a constructive manner, if they will,

Beyond the Easel

Beyond the easel lies Norman Rockwell's world tions of Scouts to Be Prepared for little emer-
of truth and beauty in the everyday scenes of gencies and real disasters. Together, he and they
America. His calendars have inspired genera- have looked forward to tomorrow's challenge.

Throughout the years of his long career Norman Rockwell has freely contributed his rare talent to dramatizing United Way activities. He painted this portrait of himself at work surrounded by the thoughtful young critics in 1969. Reproduced with permission of the Boy Scouts of America and copyright by Brown and Bigelow, St. Paul, Minnesota.

through a simple change in budgeting philosophy. Rather than promote fees solely as a means of reducing the necessity for contributor support, Chests should also use the fee opportunity as incentive to those agencies that have legitimate channels of potential service expansion." [23]

These questions still are considered by budget committees. The consensus now seems to be that fees should be charged according to the cost of the service and the ability of the recipient to pay for them. Generally speaking, contributions to United Funds or Community Chests, and to their members, should be used for services to persons able to pay none or only part of the cost, or for services that benefit the total community and cannot be specifically allocated to any individual.

The first Workshop for District Community Council Leaders was held in June, sponsored by the Advisory Committee on Citizen Participation of CCC and the National Social Welfare Assembly. The following aspects of Community Council operation received special attention: organization, relation to federation of fund raising agencies, public relations, health, housing, recreation, youth participation, and work on legislation.

"A New Look at Federal and State Programs" was sent to CCC members in July, reviewing federal-state responsibilities in health and welfare. It reported that during the 1951 fiscal year federal funds constituted 22 percent of all expenditures for local and state public health programs, 66 percent of vocational rehabilitation expenses, and 57 percent of expenses for cate-

1951 poster design by Paulson symbolizing United Defense Fund.

gorical public assistance. Because no comprehensive planning would be possible without consideration of federal programs, Council responsibility for digging out facts and assisting in formulation of public policy was emphasized.

Encouraging progress was reported in relationships with Red Cross. More than 160 chapters had participated in the fall campaigns with better results than when they had last campaigned separately. During 1953, more than 200 participated, and 97% of all goals was reached.

Another problem of the times, that of the rising tide of Puerto Rican migrants, was described in the October *Community.* Many agencies and Councils were cited as already working on ways to provide language training, housing, employment and education.

1954

During the Biennial Conference in February, there was considerable talk about the possibility of a recession. After the Korean War ended the previous July, prices increased, defense spending was reduced, and unemployment began to rise. James Linen, CCC board member and publisher of *Time,* declared, however, "In my opinion, our economy will continue to grow despite the hand-wringing of the pessimists." Taking into account factors of growth, expanding economy, growing population, and the broadening of federation, he foresaw greatly increasing Chest and Fund goals.[24]

Several guides for dealing with the uncertainties of the future were presented by Ralph Blanchard. "We must not be guilty of talking ourselves into a depression, for we can be sure there will be no depression in human needs. If our leadership does not hold its sights high, the public cannot be expected to do so. Federation should never be sold short; it is the best device yet developed to build and support sound programs of health and welfare." [25]

Another speaker, John J. Corson, management consultant, economist, and former high official in the Federal Social Security program, pointed out a 25% increase in unemployment, and listed five forces which had brought about an increase in health and welfare expenditures: the emergence of an urban civilization; growth of a money economy in which security lies not in land or herds but in cash wages; decline of the family as a unit; population changes bringing more aged, more children, more working mothers and greater mobility; the complexity of modern life with its strains and stresses showing up in increased illegitimate births, divorce rates, juvenile delinquency, crime, and suicide.[26]

Three-quarters of a century after the first social service exchanges were put into operation, their validity

Washington, D.C.... February 10, 1954. President Dwight D. Eisenhower is shown with Michael T. Kelleher, (left) Boston, Mass., President of the United Defense Fund, and Lt. General James Doolittle, New York, N.Y., National Campaign Chairman of the Defense Fund. President Eisenhower met with representatives of more than 30 Community Chests to discuss the relationship between the national defense effort and the United Way Korean-related health and welfare services.

Speaker at the 1952 National United Way Conference in Milwaukee was veteran volunteer leader, C. Virgil Martin, former 3C's Vice President and President of Carson Pirie Scott Company, Chicago.

was now being questioned. Several had actually closed. About 10 years before, the values and ethics involved in using exchanges began to be challenged because of heightened awareness of the client as a person and growing conviction that he should be the prime source of information about himself. There was also a growing belief by many caseworkers that clearance through the exchange violated the confidential relationship between worker and client and hence was unethical and incompatible with the democratic base of social work itself. A special committee was appointed by CCC to explore the present-day value of exchanges. In June, a bulletin on minimum standards for exchanges was printed by CCC in which the exchange was described as an effective means of integrating community services and seeing that agencies worked together. The desirability of financial support from all participating was emphasized. "Paying one's own way in the Exchange is one of the firmest assurances that it will be widely used, and carefully nurtured and developed." [27]

A change in policy of the American Cancer Society was announced in April. No unit that had not been approved for federation in 1953 would be permitted to participate in a federated campaign in 1954, and any unit participating in 1953 and desiring to participate again in 1954 would have to obtain the approval of both the division and national organization. The ACS bulletin announcing this change was accompanied by a series of charts purporting to show that federated areas fell behind non-federated areas in money raised. As

CCC pointed out, however, these figures were based on just 64 federated units, although Cancer was included in 321 local campaigns.

Soon thereafter CCC released a report showing that in cities conducting their first United Fund campaign, 21% more money was raised than in separate drives the year before. For United Funds which had been in existence two years or more, the median percent of goal achieved was 100 percent, and of aggregate goals, 98 percent. [28]

In May, there were signs that increased unemployment was causing uneasiness in private casework agencies. Local Travelers Aid Associations were exhausting their relief budgets because of the movement of unemployed people who, as nonresidents, often were not eligible for relief by public agencies.

During the May 20-21 Campaign Leaders Conference at Sugar Camp, Alfred H. Williams, president of the Philadelphia Federal Reserve Bank, presented charts and figures to support his prediction of a favorable economic climate during what the British referred to as our "prosperous depression." "A Chest or Fund campaign is an annual resurgency of the sense of civic and personal responsibility; it is an antidote against centralism, an experience in self-government, a conscious sharing of the experience of human fellowship. Every man can serve God in every effort that any of us makes to raise the quality of human life. The spiritual climate of your community is in your hands. It depends on that quality we call leadership. As John Stuart Mill said, 'One person with a belief is a force equal to ninety-nine who have only an interest.' " [29]

During the second annual National Workshop of Community Leaders in June, a manual, prepared by the National Advisory Committee to District Community Councils of CCC, was distributed, defining the role of district councils. "Often city planning cannot effectively handle neighborhood problems. District councils were aware of the difficulties of daily life, of how hard it is to be heard outside one's community and of the trials and tribulations facing the 'little guys.' In true American fashion, neighborhood councils are dedicated to Lincoln's proposition of government of the people, by the people, for the people." [30] District councils then were active in 100 communities and in nearly 50, Community Welfare Councils were connected with them, involving either full or part-time staff. Later in the year a CCC policy statement affirmed the importance of neighborhood councils and the desirability of Community Welfare Council interest and participation.

State lines were crossed in Missouri and Kansas where the two Kansas Cities joined forces in the 1954 Heart of America United Campaign. The combined service and solicitation area covered 88 communities in five counties. The same principle was being worked out in the Cincinnati area where three northern Kentucky counties joined the city in the United Appeals Community Chest, actually a United Fund which included Red Cross, four of the big national health agencies and United Defense Fund.

Albert Q. Maisel in his *Cosmopolitan* article of the previous year had made charges of extravagant costs in United Funds. Evidence to refute these charges was carried in a fall bulletin showing that costs of campaigning, planning, and all other central activities, averaged 10.8 percent of totals raised.

1955

To meet the pressures for leadership which the growing United Fund movement had been voicing in the preceding months, the board took action in February to revamp the whole CCC program, increasing staff, and expanding and intensifying all services, particularly in the areas of campaign, research and public relations. With an estimated $100,000 added to the budget, CCC could now embark upon dynamic interpretation of the United Fund movement to national corporations, national health and welfare agencies, and others; would provide consultation services and a confidential executive newsletter, and would adopt a new name and background symbol on which local symbols could be superimposed. The United "U" was chosen.

On February 24, the United Defense Fund voted not to make an appeal for 1955, since USO had withdrawn and was making its own plans for financial support. Since its organization in 1950, UDF had received more than $37 million from federated campaigns.

A new device to counteract the separate appeals of national health agencies was announced in Durham, N.C. on March 23: a statewide United Medical Research Foundation to "formulate a research program for polio, tuberculosis, heart disease, cancer, diseases which cripple children and adults, and other diseases, and to receive and disburse monies for these purposes." [31] The deans of three medical schools attended

Richard C. Borden, National Public Relations Chairman for United Way, discusses 1951 promotion program with Advisory Committee member, Mrs. Leroy H. Newmyer of Toledo Community Chest.

the organization meeting and expressed approval. Concurrently the Durham United Fund founded the Durham Better Health Foundation for health education and direct patient services for victims of these diseases.

This action met with interest in other communities, many of which developed similar programs. Eventually it led to a national vehicle, United Health Foundations, Inc. This was a "grass roots" movement which grew out of the irritation of local community leaders at the multiplicity of appeals but whose real aim was improvement of voluntary health programs.

The growing amity and understanding between CCC and American National Red Cross led to an important announcement on April 5 when Red Cross Chairman E. Roland Harriman, who had replaced Gen. George C. Marshall, announced a new fund-raising policy which would give local chapters greater flexibility in determining how to raise funds. They could now participate in local federated campaigns, provided: they retained control of their own budgets and goals; retained the right to conduct a roll call for members during Red Cross month; retained the right to conduct emergency campaigns in case of disaster; and that each person contributing $1.00 or more would receive a Red Cross identification card. This quickly led to increased participation until in 1967 a total of 1,685 chapters were included in United Way campaigns.

At its April meeting, the Community Chests and Councils board voted that partnership relationships between CCC and state organizations be developed on a state-by-state basis with organizations that offered supplementary community organization service to small communities. Later in the year, CCC joined with the National Conference of Social Work and the National Social Welfare Assembly in forming a committee on state organization to study the role of the state as a unit in organizing for health and welfare.

In December, a Consultation on Problems of State Community Organization sponsored by CCC, the National Conference of Social Work, and National Social Welfare Assembly adopted a four-point resolution: "1. There is a real need for state community organization; 2. As unified an approach as possible to the problems in this area is desirable; 3. A more adequate and more unified national consultation service would aid state community organization materially in strengthening their services; and 4. A continuation committee will seek to develop a plan for a more adequate and unified national service." [32]

Social Service Exchanges had long advocated special staff for exchange matters, a request never granted. By now the function of exchanges was being questioned and many had closed. [33] Dissident exchanges asked that CCC discontinue its service to exchanges and finance a new agency to serve as the clearinghouse in this field. A special study committee later rejected this proposal, recommending that CCC appoint an ad hoc committee to consider the broader issues of communication between agencies and the place of exchanges in modern social work practice. The committee also adopted a statement, later approved by the CCC board that "We are supporting the exchange idea and doing what we can within budget limitations to assist exchanges to improve their services. We are continuing to support this community organization service until and unless it becomes clear that the service is no longer necessary under present conditions of social work practice . . . We will be guided by research findings, whether they point to extension and strengthening the exchange or to the discontinuance of the service. We would not wish to perpetuate an institution should valid research indicate that it has outgrown its usefulness." [34]

The first national Conference on the Churches and Social Welfare was held in Cleveland in November under the auspices of the Social Welfare Department of the National Council of the Churches of Christ in the U.S.A. Chairman Leonard Mayo, director of the Association for the Aid of Crippled Children, called for a closer working partnership between churches and

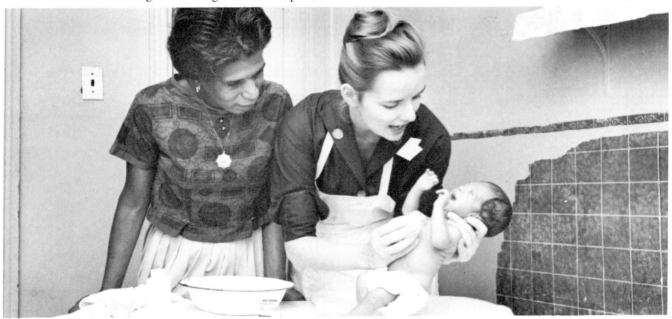

This Lady in Blue is instructing mother in proper infant care. Visiting nurses provide one of the familiar United Way services. Photo by Richard Keller, Philadelphia.

the social work profession. The session devoted to relationships with Chests, Funds, and Councils emphasized the needs for improved standards of Protestant agencies, cooperation among Protestant agencies, support of federated fund raising, and support by Chests and Funds of the Protestant social services.

On December 5, upon the merger of the AFL and CIO into a single giant labor organization, the AFL-CIO Community Services Committee was established.

Joseph A. Beirne, AFL-CIO vice president, became chairman and Leo Perlis, the committee's director. Both had long been active in CCC affairs. Among the committee's objectives were: to encourage equitable labor representation in agencies; to interpret agency programs to union members; to coordinate fund-raising drives; and to participate in all efforts to improve social work standards and practices. All affiliates were urged to establish community service departments or committees.

NOTES

Chapter 11

1. *Community,* CCC, March 1950, p. 128.

2. *Ibid.,* p. 129.

3. *The United Way in Planning and Financing Health and Welfare Services,* CCC, 1950, pp. 13-14.

4. "Social Security Act Amendments of 1950," *On the Alert,* CCC, September 13, 1950, pp. 1-3.

5. *Community,* CCC, November 1950, pp. 47-48.

6. *Community,* CCC, January 1951, p. 96.

7. *Community,* CCC, March 1951, p. 130.

8. *Community,* CCC, June 1951, pp. 189-190.

9. *Community,* CCC, September 1951, pp. 3-4.

10. "Summary Statement on Revision of Fund Raising Procedures," Adopted at Special Meeting of Red Cross Board of Governors, August 13, 1951, pp. 1-3.

11. *Protect Your Freedom to Give* (New York: The Roy Bernard Company, pamphlet, 1952), pp. 1-4.

12. *Community,* CCC, April 1952, p. 153.

13. "State Chests," *On the Alert,* CCC, March 24, 1952.

14. Albert Q. Maisel, "Where Does Your Charity Money Go?" *Cosmopolitan Magazine,* June 1952.

15. Morton Sontheimer, "Charity's Civil War," *Cosmopolitan Magazine,* October 1952.

16. *On the Alert,* CCC, September 1952.

17. *On the Alert,* CCC, July 1952.

18. F. Emerson Andrews, *Corporate Giving* (New York: Russell Sage Foundation, 1952), p. 15.

19. *Community,* CCC, March 1953, p. 123.

20. "Organizing a United Fund," CCC, March 1953, *Bulletin 165,* p. 3.

21. "Code of the Chest and Council Movement," CCC, March 1953.

22. *Community,* CCC, May 1953, pp. 175-176.

23. *Community,* CCC, January 1954, pp. 87-89, 98.

24. *Community,* CCC, March 1954, p. 123.

25. Minutes, Annual Meeting, CCC, January 29, 1954, pp. 1-2.

26. *Community,* CCC, March 1954, pp. 131-132, 140.

27. "Minimum Standards for Operation of a Social Service Exchange," SSE Bulletin No. 57, CCC, June 1954, foreword and pp. 1, 5-6.

28. "Experience in United Funds and Extended Federation Campaigns," CCC, 1954, pp. 1, 3.

29. *Community,* CCC, June 1954, p. 187.

30. *District Community Councils: A Way to United Community Action,* CCC, 1954, pp. 30-32.

31. *Community,* CCC, April 1955, Newsletter Section, p. 2.

32. *Executive Newsletter,* CCC, December 12, 1955, p. 2.

33. Minutes, Executive Committee, CCC, April 22, 1955, Vol. VIII, Exhibit C, p. 403.

34. "Statement of Position Adopted by Advisory Committee on Social Service Exchanges," CCC, November 30, 1955.

12

HEALTH AGENCIES WITHDRAW: 1956-1958

Operating independently since United Defense Fund was dissolved, United Community Defense Services in 1956 found that local Funds and Chests could enlist very little popular support for the UCDS program of financing the field-service endeavors of 15 national agencies in small, defense-impacted communities. UCDS funds were barely enough to finance the limited 1956 service program and several proposals were made for obtaining outside help. None of them worked out and by the end of the year UCDS became inactive. In January 1960 it was dissolved.

During the 1956 Biennial Conference in Detroit, Chest-Council membership approved a change in the national organization named to United Community Funds and Councils of America, Inc., reflecting the growth and importance of United Funds. Use of the name United Fund by many federations to indicate inclusion of state and national organizations had now become predominant in the field of joint financing.

The increasing amity between Red Cross and federation was stressed by a conference speaker, W. Croft Jennings of the Red Cross board of Governors. Referring to the relationship as a "marriage" he said, "We have but to deny ourselves the incalculably costly luxury of friction among ourselves; we have but to unite our efforts in a common undertaking to carry the great-

est good to the greatest number." [1] Later that year when Red Cross undertook an emergency campaign for $5 million to assist Hungarians who had conducted an abortive revolt against Communist rule, local Funds and Chests cooperated in various ways, from providing their quotas out of reserves to launching public appeals without direct solicitation.

A look to the future was presented by Hugh R. Jackson, former social worker, president of the Better Business Bureau, and chairman of the National Social Welfare Assembly's Administrative Committee, who told of new needs for leisure-time activities, day nurseries, and services to the aged. "We raise far more money than we did a decade ago, but these amounts will be pitifully inadequate in the decade ahead of us . . . We must make sure that we are setting our sights to meet the needs of the people as they are, rather than the convenience or tradition of some people or some part of the community. Reducing irritation because of multiplicity of campaigns is an important objective, but meeting basic needs is even more important." [2]

The now-famous St. Paul project was described to conferees by its Chest-Council executive director Charles Birt. With a $90,000 grant from the Hill Family Foundation, the study involved 140 families selected from the six percent seriously disorganized (or "hard core") families in the city. Each of the families worked with but one caseworker who coordinated all services to the family. After a year and a half, 50% of the families showed positive change. The experiment indicated, the seven cooperating agencies concluded, that in the future they should seek more source material from "six percent groups" and do more planning from the bottom up. "Maybe the result will eventually permit Chests and United Funds to reallocate present funds for more preventive services; governmental services to reduce expense and to become more flexible under their statutory obligations; and Councils to develop a better coordinated pattern of community welfare services." [3]

Bradley Buell, a member of the CCC staff from 1930-1943, wrote a book based in large part on the study which was completed in 1949. Titled *Community Planning for Community Services*, it was described by Arthur Dunham, a leading professor of community organization for many years, as "one of the most creative, provocative, and valuable contributions to community organization thinking and literature within the past 30 years." [4]

A *Look* magazine article in 1962 also described the project and its results. "In a six-month period, a sixth of the families were able to get off relief, a sixth were greatly improved, and a third showed improvement. This has been encouraging enough to warrant switching the entire county public welfare system over to the new method by the end of the year. And St. Paul is now trying to work out ways whereby its private social services can also use the new techniques . . . They may solve a national problem." [5]

Metropolitan area planning was the subject of a round-table discussion at the spring 1956 National Social Welfare Assembly meeting in April. Hugh R. Pomeroy, planning director for Westchester County, N.Y., said health and welfare Councils should join with governmental planning agencies in overall planning for total metropolitan development and redevelopment, including transportation, housing, education, recreation, health and welfare. [6]

The following year, Joe R. Hoffer, executive secretary of the National Conference on Social Welfare (the new name of the National Conference of Social Work), speaking during a social work meeting in Arizona, pointed out that, "Services must be located where peo-

"WELL DONE, ALBERT!" rang out as the unanimous voice of the United Way Biennial Conference in Detroit, when retiring President Albert J. Nesbitt, left, became the recipient of the Red Feather Award for 1956 at the hands of newly-elected President James A. Linen.

ple can use them and must be adequate to meet the needs. Most suburbs cannot finance the many different services available in large communities. Therefore more generalized services are needed." [7]

The trend toward urbanization of the population was expected to continue, it was pointed out during the third national Workshop for District Community Council Leaders, along with the physical problems of eliminating blight and those of inter-group relations. Dr. Philip M. Hauser, director of Chicago's Population Research Center, called for concerted citizen action through district councils as the most effective means of dealing successfully with these problems. [8]

Organization on the state level continued in various ways. In Oregon, a "state affiliation" plan was launched, whereby the Oregon Chest would provide affiliation with UCFCA for the very small federated groups without executives which were raising less than $25,000 annually.

In Texas, which had organized a statewide agency in 1951 to support USO, a reorganization in 1956 had brought about the Texas United Defense Fund which not only provided for joint financing of statewide appeals, but gave service to local United Funds and Chests. In 1958, it became Texas United Fund, with 130 Funds "buying" the TUF package. In 1962 when TUF voted to accept the Medical Research Foundation of Texas into membership, 146 of the 186 Texas United Funds supported TUF.

Yet organization of statewide United Funds was more difficult than had been anticipated. Lyman Ford, UCFCA associate executive director, pointed out the difficulties of organization including the time needed for local communities to accept the idea of taking a fair share of a package put together at the state level, plus the problems of national health agency anti-federation policies. By 1965, when Texas United Fund voted to discontinue fund raising, only Oregon, Michigan, and Carolinas United remained as state fund-raising organizations.

Statewide planning organizations met with greater success than statewide financial federations, despite considerable difficulties. As Joe Hoffer told the Michigan Welfare League, "State community organization is a weak link in the overall pattern of organization in social welfare. It often suffers from underfinancing and lack of leadership." [9]

On the local level, new United Funds were organized in Canada's largest city, Toronto, and in Pittsburgh. The Toronto United Fund included 89 agencies, and its goal of $7,200,000 was oversubscribed that fall. Other Canadian cities followed Toronto's example, and by 1962 a total of 68 of 122 Canadian federations were United Funds. Pittsburgh's first United Fund campaign with provision for allocations to health causes reached 109% of goal.

Relations with national health agencies were causing considerable concern. In January 1956, UCFCA had met with American Heart Association and American Cancer Society in an effort to discuss mutual problems. Agreement was reached that neither UCFCA, Heart, nor Cancer would make detrimental statements about the other. It was specifically suggested that ACS withdraw its film, which contained anti-federation statements by ACS board chairman Governor Walter Kohler of Wisconsin.

In April, Ray R. Eppert, of Detroit, chairman of the USFCA United Fund Advisory Committee, reported however, "The attacks on federation have continued . . . Cancer is definitely aggressive in its anti-federation attack. Heart continues its position but has toned down some of its statements. It has revised its statistics to make them accurate in terms of actual digits, although the statistical basis still remains misleading . . . Cancer, Heart, and Polio are teaming up apparently in their attack in local communities, particularly in those places where a United Fund 'is imminent,' as a Cancer house organ phrases it.

"Our staff has been asked to help refute the statistics and statements made, but they have not done so because of the time-honored traditional approach of UCFCA to any kind of statement concerning another organization. These have always been temperate and have often been cleared with other organizations before issuance." The UCFCA board then authorized communications to be sent to Cancer and Heart calling attention to these continued attacks and suggested that the staff stimulate magazine articles on the positive side of federation and mobilize both local and national lay leaders to visit individual board members of national agencies. A statement was then developed stressing the values of federation and noting the ironic fact that "If federation should fall, or if the trend in federation should be reversed and fewer causes were included, the national health campaigns would find the going increasingly difficult." [10]

Later, UCFCA's Public Relations Advisory Committee adopted a position statement on ways federation should react when under attack. A positive and educational year-round public relations program would be undertaken, with materials helpful to local communities under attack provided by UCFCA. In the event of national attacks, the decisions on how or whether to reply would be left to the discretion of the staff and national lay leadership.

Lorain, Ohio's found a solution to the problem of non-cooperating health agencies by forming the United Health Association to administer the health funds raised through the United Appeal which, for any reason, the local chapter of a national health agency refused to accept.

On June 27, a long-awaited announcement came from the White House regarding solicitation of federal employees at their places of employment. The new policy would limit the number of health and welfare campaigns within federal agencies and departments, to those for: local community needs such as Community Chests; national welfare and emergency relief such as Red Cross; national health agencies; and international volunteer agencies such as Care. "In cases where communities have a United Fund serving all recognized agencies, only one solicitation will be necessary." [11]

Chest and Fund leaders, after studying the provisions of the policy, found that there were several unsatisfactory provisions including the implication that "true voluntary giving" and traditional person-to-person solicitations were incompatible; the fact that sealed-envelope provisions for "privacy" made impractical the use of fair-share guides and installment pledges; the bypassing of local autonomy and the rights of local communities to determine which health and welfare causes should be included; and the fact that a voluntary payroll deduction plan was not provided.

On August 2, more than 40 lay and professional Chest, Fund and participating agency representatives met with Philip Young, Presidential Adviser on Personnel Management, and his staff. Their primary request was that implementation of the policy be delayed beyond that fall's campaigns to permit reexamination and further study in light of local experience and reactions. Mr. Young said, however, that the policy had been in effect since released by President Eisenhower on June 27. The greatest threat to successful campaigns, the committee felt, was the envelope system whereby gifts would be made in sealed envelopes with no accountability for pledges.

One of the provisions of the federal plan was for solicitation of military and civilian personnel overseas. Seven national agencies united for an overseas campaign, but UCFCA did not feel it wise to join in such an effort. Operating under the name of Federal Services Overseas Fund Campaign, it included USO, CARE, Crusade for Freedom, International Social Service, National Recreation Association, American Social Hygiene Association, and United Seamen's Service.

President Eisenhower's new policy provided for a spring 1957 campaign by national health agencies willing to unite their appeals. Announcement was made in late fall that eight major national health agencies, Polio excepted, would campaign jointly.

In Omaha, Nebraska a new method for raising capital funds was developed during 1956. After a special committee had analyzed five-year agency building needs, it learned that more than $2 million would be required. These needs were explained to a group of business and labor leaders at a meeting called by the Chamber of Commerce, and a united building fund drive was endorsed for inclusion with the United Red Feather–Red Cross Campaign. The budget was then readjusted and a fair share plan worked out. After the five-year period of payment to the original fund was completed, a second combined campaign was held.

The next year, Charlotte, N.C. initiated a plan whereby capital funds would be raised in a special campaign to start, and as part of regular United Appeals

campaigns thereafter. Not all capital needs of the agencies were financed this way but the plan proved helpful.

At the December 1956 UCFCA board meeting, "new status" was given to the community planning program of UCFCA when the three advisory committees relating to health and welfare planning were merged into one inclusive body made up chiefly of laymen and renamed the Advisory Committee on Health and Welfare Planning. The three predecessor groups were the Advisory Committee on Health and Welfare Planning, Citizen Participation Committee, and Social Service Exchange Committee. Health and Welfare Planning became a division of UCFCA, joining Campaign and Public Relations.

Social Service Exchanges continued to dwindle. Earlier in the year, a round-up revealed that while 219 remained in operation, more than 50 exchanges had closed. Among them were those in Houston, Hartford, New Orleans, and Los Angeles.

During 1956, the first meetings of the new AFL-CIO Community Services Committee were held, along with a conference attended by 150 local labor staff. In December, the UCFCA board approved a new Labor Participation Project integrating UCFCA staff with that of the Community Services Committee.

For the first time, UCFCA's expanded services called for a central budget which broke the $1 million mark.

1957

The Federal Solicitation Plan evoked considerable discussion during the winter. While some campaigns reported happy experiences, others told of diminished amounts and pledges because of the sealed-envelope system. A special UCFCA committee sent a list of proposed changes to Presidential Adviser Philip Young who replied, "The plan has not yet had a fair trial." [12] In March, President Eisenhower signed a message stressing the principle of "true voluntary giving," but permitting local federated campaigns and Red Cross (but not the national health agencies) to ask for pledges with dollar goals and quotas. Assignment of dollar quotas to individuals, however, was expressly prohibited. [13]

In April, President Eisenhower named Harris Ellsworth, Chairman of the U.S. Civil Service Commission and Chief Adviser to the President on Personnel Man-

Grandma Moses (Mrs. Anna Mary
Robertson Moses) with her painting
THE RED FEATHER which she
made and contributed to the
United Way in 1948. She is shown
at the Troy, N.Y., 1955 Community
Chest kickoff where she was guest
of honor at age 93. (Left to right)
H. J. Marshall, Campaign
Chairman; J. I. Millet, President,
Community Chest and A. W.
Hennessey, Chest Manager.

agement, to take the place recently vacated by Philip Young. Many letters were sent to Mr. Ellsworth, and meetings were held with him to explain the Chest-Fund position. Mr. Ellsworth said he thought the plan could be made to work and that the envelope was but an alternative which the employee could either use or not use. In June, the White House issued fund-raising bulletins further explaining and clarifying the policies and announced the Federal Service Overseas Fund Committee.

While the effect of the "new policy" on the fall campaigns was hard to ascertain, a UCFCA study showed that the total amount raised in major federal establishments was $4,115,929 or 13.9% less than had been raised the year before. The percentage of employees' giving dropped from 90.6% to 75.8%. Miami reported that the sealed-envelope system resulted in "a great collection of washers, Confederate money, and baking powder coupons." The two factors causing most difficulty were the envelope system and the fact that payroll deduction was not permitted.

A recommendation for a National Health Fund was made by the AFL-CIO Community Services Committee "for the purpose of fund raising, budgeting, and program coordination." In a resolution which was widely distributed, the committee said, "The raising of funds in a United Way, through the Community Funds or Chests wherever possible, the allocation of funds on the basis of relative needs, and greater coordination in basic medical research will strengthen our voluntary health agencies and help improve the total health of the whole person." [14] Of special interest in the statement were the words, "basic medical research" and "total health of the whole person"—concepts soon to be emphasized throughout the country.

In September it was announced that the Medical Foundation of Metropolitan Boston had been established to support medical research which would not be limited to any specific categorical disease and to conduct a program of health information and education. It had come about when organizers of the United Fund observed that with local chapters of Heart, Cancer, and Polio staying out, there were two missing parts in the UF: medical research and health education. The Foundation was a participating agency of the United Fund, and in its first year was allocated $450,000.

Neighboring Quincy soon followed Boston's example, and despite a letter distributed by the local National

Elwood Street receives commendation from United Way National Executive, Ralph H. Blanchard for 42 years of dedicated professional United Way service at his retirement dinner in Bridgeport, January 19, 1956. Mr. Street began his career in the first campaign of the Cleveland United Way in 1913. In 1961 he was retained by United Community Funds & Councils of America to research the early history of the United Way.

Foundation for Infantile Paralysis calling the United Fund unethical and undemocratic, the "polio attack" was not harmful and the campaign went over the top with 103% of goal.

Paul Dietrich of Los Angeles, president of the National Society for Crippled Children and Adults, announced on November 11 that Easter Seals Societies might no longer participate in federated fund raising and that all local groups then affiliated must withdraw. This action was matched by the American Cancer Society which said further that money so raised for the cause of cancer must not be accepted. Several local units later refused substantial donations from United Funds because of this ruling and many others withdrew from the national society.

Red Cross continued its ever-closer partnership with federation, joining United Funds in Cleveland and Chicago, bringing to almost 1000 the number of local United Funds including Red Cross.

Indianapolis was host that year to the National Workshop on Community Research Personnel. Out of this meeting came recommendations for development of more qualified leadership in community welfare re-

Edward L. Ryerson, President of Community Chests and Councils, Inc. (1947-1950), receives pat on the back from President Eisenhower for his voluntary leadership in the United Defense Fund at a meeting of that organization in Washington in 1953.

Ike and Mamie present their 1956 United Way pledge to James H. Lemon, Chairman of the National Capital Area, United Givers Fund.

search. There were then close to 100 research positions in Councils, with perhaps a dozen unfilled. Over the next 10 years it was expected that 100 additional positions would open up. Proposals were made for curriculum improvements in schools of social work.

In 1957, Fund and Council Training Scholarships (FACTS), a program of scholarship aid, was established for persons preparing for a professional career in United Funds or Community Health and Welfare Councils. Funds are contributed by local United Funds and Councils and by their professional staff to assist in attracting highly qualified persons to the community organization field. Scholarship recipients agree to accept employment in United Way organizations following their graduation. By 1973, grants totaling $195,000 had been made to 103 students.

A Council concern of increasing significance was pointed out during the Biennial Conference of Council Leaders by Dr. Philip Hauser, professor of sociology at the University of Chicago: "Mass migration of Negroes is another major health and welfare problem with which social agencies will have to cope more and more." [15] His prophecy was to prove most true.

1958

This was to be another turbulent year in the area of financing health services. The long-continued cold war between several of the go-it-alone national health agencies and federation flared into a hot war, and there were many withdrawals of local health-agency chapters from United Funds as well as cases of stubborn insistence on staying in them. This sometimes involved the creation of local agencies independent of the nationals. Despite the turmoil, United Funds increased in number, and more of them included health "causes," or else organized health foundations.

Early in the year a special committee of 15 United Fund leaders met with eight national officials and laymen of American Cancer Society and asked for a change or modification of ACS policy against participation in United Funds. ACS refused.

In Pittsburgh the Health, Research and Services Foundation was formed to "mobilize the citizenship for united effort in the promotion of research, education, and services in the field of health needs for the total man." It would receive funds from the United Fund, and would not conduct a separate general public campaign.

Artist Stevan Dohanos at work on the 1956 United Way campaign poster. He also painted the 1954 United Way poster.

The Foundation's establishment followed recommendations of the Pennsylvania Economy League, which had conducted a study of health needs in the area. The Foundation would permit givers to make once-a-year gifts to battle diseases on a more objective basis than the amount of emotional appeal the disease might have. The total amount of contributed funds would be spent for the specific diseases mentioned in the solicitation. All administrative and organization expenses would be borne by the United Fund.

"This new direction in the health field is not an answer to the problem of 'too many campaigns for too many national health agencies.' Only the giver has the answer to that problem. The foundation which will be formed is not a substitute for the unwillingness of national health agencies to participate in a federated campaign, but is a premium-quality, much-needed research, education, and service organization to which the community will be able to point with pride." [16]

In March Dr. Robert M. Wilkins, president of the American Heart Association, signed a statement which was distributed nationally saying, "If United Funds are permitted to continue to undermine the efforts of the voluntary health agencies, research will dwindle and the conquest of disease inevitably will be delayed." [17]

Because of the increase in the "disease-of-the-month"

approach to funding medical research, there was growing uneasiness among medical men. A special committee of the American Medical Association had been appointed to study the implications. UCFCA President James A. Linen and Vice President Ray R. Eppert headed a UCFCA committee to present federation's story to the AMA.

In consequence, the United Fund Advisory Council adopted an 8 Point Program. When this was unanimously adopted by the Board in February, President Linen declared, "This is war!" The program called for a special committee to explore possibilities of a national vehicle for contributed funds for health research, service and education, based upon needs as related to the whole man. Local United Funds were urged to continue friendly, positive relationships with local persons representing the specific national health interests. In view of prohibitive policies of certain national health organizations, however, local communities were urged to consider development of their own alternative plans.

The 8 Point Program was put into effect immediately, providing a platform for much of UCFCA's future activities relative to national health agencies.

UCFCA's Special Committee to Explore a Possible Medical Research Foundation met with the National Fund for Medical Education and in July NFME announced it would establish a Medical Research Program "to provide a specific channel whereby contributors could help to develop a coordinated advance in scientific knowledge." [18] NFME had been organized in 1949 to seek funds for the teaching budgets of the nation's accredited medical schools. UCFCA pointed out that MRP could attract new funds for non-categorical and unrestricted research which was at the time receiving minimal support, thus complementing research efforts then being undertaken.

When United Way campaigns began that fall, the Medical Research Program was included in many communities.

The American Heart Association, in a paper circulated during United Way campaigns, refuted the need for basic research and said that those who participated in sponsoring medical research projects outside health agencies were incompetent to allocate the funds properly and that local health foundations would duplicate their efforts. At its annual meeting, AMA clarified its policy regarding participation of local chapters, refusing, however, to set a specific date by which affiliates must withdraw from United Fund drives. Chapters not members before October 1955 were forbidden to join. Chapters participating before that date would be permitted to continue if they received what they demanded. When goals were not reached, local chapters would be expected to conduct independent campaigns.

American Cancer Society prepared a statement to be signed by voluntary health agencies, UCFCA, and the National Fund for Medical Education, acknowledging the need for continuing medical research and training of competent research workers, and welcoming the supplemental aid of NFME. It also stated that "the participation of the National Fund should not be used as a basis to attempt to divert contributions from the national health agencies in any manner." [19] While UCFCA's executive committee recommended approval of this statement, local United Funds voiced objection, and UCFCA's board concluded that the statement was unnecessary at the time.

The American Medical Association, apparently prevailed upon to take a position, passed a resolution saying it "neither approves nor disapproves the inclusion of voluntary health agencies in United Fund drives" and requested its board of trustees to arrange a top-level conference with voluntary health agencies and United Funds with a view toward resolving misinterpretations. [20]

A startling change took place in one of the major health agencies when Basil O'Connor announced that the National Foundation for Infantile Paralysis would henceforth solicit funds to fight arthritis and congenital defects. The incidence of polio had dropped dramatically since the famous Salk and Sabin vaccines had been put to wide use, and contributions had also dropped. The organization would now be known as The National Foundation.

UCFCA observed that there were already numerous agencies engaged in these areas and that National Foundation fund-raising costs had been 12% of funds raised, compared with United Way costs of approximately 4½%. There was widespread discussion throughout the country, including considerable opposition, since the Arthritis and Rheumatism Foundation had rejected a proposed merger with The National Foundation and asked the polio group to keep out of the arthritis field for one year to permit further study. In answer, The National Foundation declared, "Individual diseases are not the personal property of individual organizations." [21] In 1964, however, The National Foundation did withdraw from the field of arthritis because of lack of funds.

Many Council concerns also were in the limelight

Edgar B. Stern, Jr. (right), UCFCA Vice President and National Public Relations Chairman, introduces Fred Stashower, Cleveland advertising executive, at the 1957 annual United Way rally in Dayton. Mr. Stern innovated many United Way communications programs through his active personal leadership and financial assistance. Through the Stern Family Fund, grants were made to start the United Way Film Fund, the annual United Way Photo Contest and a Research-Reporter Project. He initiated the series of the United Way "Hands" campaign posters of the 1950's.

This 1965 poster painting by Walter Bomar gave recognition to the proud United Way contributors.

during 1958. As John A. Greene, chairman of the board, Ohio Bell Telephone Co., and chairman of the UCFCA Advisory Committee on Community Planning, said during the Biennial Chest-Council Conference in Cleveland, "Today as never before we live by planning . . . For any community, an effective Council is the best protection against stagnation in the social welfare program." Traditional Council structure was being questioned he said, but "Structure is simply a means to an end." [22]

Three solutions to the questions raised were provided by Columbus, Ohio, Pittsburgh, and New York City, where reorganizations took place during 1956-57. "Agency-centered" approaches were replaced with those which were "community-centered," and there was increased emphasis on development of long-range plans and community policies.

Walt Disney contributed his character JIMINY CRICKET as a United Way campaign volunteer in 1967. JIMINY appeared on posters, campaign buttons, in magazines and films for several years.

142

"Courageous Defiance That Stands To Win" was what the Detroit Free Press *called the decision of the Southeastern Michigan Division—American Cancer Society to continue in Detroit's United Foundation. Sealing the agreement at the 1958 UF Annual Meeting with a four-way handclasp are, L to R, Ray R. Eppert, president of the Burroughs Corporation and chairman of the UF Board; Charles F. Arnold, chief engineer of the Cadillac Company and board member of the Cancer Society division; Dr. James E. Lofstrom, president of the division; and Henry Ford II, UF board member.*

Widely publicized, these reorganizations stimulated other Councils to reorganize. They emphasized widened citizen participation and policy making, diminishing the dominance of participating agencies and their executives, and breaking up the old formula of functional divisions by substitution of ad hoc committees and task forces on a priority basis. Both structures are used today, with the trend toward temporary study-action committees increasing.

With various structures employed successfully, Council leaders point out that structure is a means and not an end in itself. It is significant and important only to the degree that it facilitates or hinders sound community planning.

The spreading disease of unemployment was again becoming a problem to Councils because of its effect on member agencies. Many were faced with the old confusions in the public mind as to the roles of public and voluntary services in cases of financial distress. A report of the National Social Welfare Assembly that winter restated these roles. Voluntary agencies have a responsibility "first to give active leadership in strengthening the hand of the public agencies to do their job. Next is to make their own services of casework, health

143

and medical services, recreation and leisure time programs available as far as possible to the ranks of the unemployed." [23]

Council participation was also needed "in efforts to get rid of slum housing, and through neighborhood rehabilitation to prevent new slums from springing up . . . If the renewal of a neighborhood is limited to the brick and mortar aspects of the program," Albert G. Rosenberg of the Baltimore Urban Renewal and Housing Agency pointed out in the March *Community,* "it is safe to say that the fullest dividend of the enormous public investment will not be reaped. The responsibility of local Councils to take the initiative and offer leadership in planning for the human aspects of renewal would seem to be clear-cut." [24]

Another report was issued at the end of the year by the Committee to Study Social Service Exchanges. Many exchanges had experienced a decline in use, the report showed, and many had gone out of business. Responsibility for financial assistance had been centralized in public welfare departments, and thus the problem of preventing duplication of relief was simplified. Conclusions reached were that exchanges were useful in a very small proportion of cases; that use of the exchange did not influence relationships between worker and client either favorably or unfavorably; that use

of the exchange did not lead to joint efforts with other agencies; that for family service agencies, use of the exchange provided valuable information in less than 3% of the cases; and use of the exchange did not have a vital influence on case outcome.[25]

Increasingly popular in the United Way campaigns that fall was the use of "loaned executives" from local corporations and businesses—junior executives or other employees loaned to the fund-raising organization for periods of several weeks or months to assist in campaign organization, solicitation, or other phases of the campaign.

A new campaign technique was also employed, that of pilot campaigns. Initiated in South Bend, Indiana, the idea of pilot campaigns quickly caught on in other communities. Through them, below-average executive and employee contributions were brought up to the fair-share mark by bringing the full resources of the campaign organization to bear on a few selected business organizations prior to the actual campaign. Their successful conclusion, even before the campaign began, developed great prestige for the companies, their employees, and organized labor, whose wholehearted cooperation was generally obtained, and built up a bandwagon spirit for fair-share giving.

NOTES

Chapter 12

1. *Community,* CCC, March 1956, p. 125.

2. *Ibid.,* p. 126.

3. *Ibid,* p. 131.

4. *Community,* CCC, October 1951, pp. 23-24.

5. Jack Star, "A Way Out of Our Welfare Dead End," *Look,* May 8, 1962, pp. 29-31.

6. *Executive Newsletter,* CCC, March 26, 1956, p. 2.

7. Joe R. Hoffer, "The Changing Concept of Social Welfare," presented during Arizona State Conference of Social Welfare, meeting of Phoenix and Tucson Chapters of NASW, March 26, 1958, pp. 7-14.

8. "Working Together to Build Good Neighborhoods," *Proceedings, District Council Workshop,* June 9-10, 1956.

9. Joe R. Hoffer, "State Community Organization in Social Welfare—A Weak Link," presented to Michigan Welfare League, November 28, 1956, pp. 194, 197-200, 205.

10. Report of the Chairman of the United Fund Advisory Committee to the Executive Committee of UCFCA, April 5, 1956, Minute Book, Vol. IX, p. 45.

11. *Executive Newsletter,* UCFCA, July 2, 1956, p. 1.

12. *Executive Newsletter,* UCFCA, March 11, 1957, p. 1.

13. *How the New Fund-Raising Policy and Program for the Federal Service Affects You* (Washington, D.C.: Government Printing Office, March 21, 1957), pp. 1-4.

14. *Executive Newsletter,* UCFCA, February 11, 1957, p. 2.

15. *Community,* UCFCA, March 1957, pp. 119-220.

16. *Executive Newsletter,* UCFCA, March 31, 1958, pp. 3-4.

17. *Executive Newsletter,* UCFCA, March 24, 1958, p. 1.

18. "Questions and Answers Regarding the Medical Research Program of the National Fund for Medical Education," UCFCA, July 21, 1958, pp. 1-5.

19. Draft of Proposed Joint Statement to be Signed by Major Voluntary Health Agencies, UCFCA, and National Fund for Medical Education, October 7, 1958, pp. 1-2.

20. *Executive Newsletter,* UCFCA, December 22, 1958, p. 2.

21. *New York Times,* July 17, 1958, reprint attached to *Executive Newsletter,* UCFCA, July 21, 1958.

22. *Community,* UCFCA, April 1958, pp. 123-124.

23. *Community,* UCFCA, March 1958, p. 111.

24. *Ibid.,* pp. 103-104.

25. "Summary Report of Research on the Social Service Exchange," UCFCA, November 1958, pp. 2, 3, 19, 20.

MUTINY OF THE BOUNTIFUL: 1959-1961

The heat of the attack of joint financing continued during 1959 while United Funds sharpened their defenses and set alternative plans into motion. At the same time Community Welfare Councils were engaged in soul-searching as they, too, faced new challenges.

Mounting problems in central cities and suburbs were described during the CCC Conference of Council Leaders in Chicago, when Alfred G. Williams, retired president of the Federal Reserve Bank, Philadelphia, said that "a demand for social services is outrunning resources, and a set of hodge podge, catch-as-catch-can community policies which lack design exists . . . There is an enormous amount of planning and research going on, but most of it is being done by planning commissions, traffic boards, redevelopment authorities—all being directed to the physical and economic aspects. How does one explain this dominating emphasis on engineering and economics to the neglect of the human, social and moral values?"[1]

G. Horace Duling, executive director of the Lilly Endowment, pointed out that where foundation monies were being placed locally they were used primarily for physical planning and agency developmental program. "Only small amounts were being used for research and planning." To help remedy such deficiencies, the Lilly Endowment made a tentative grant not to exceed

$150,000 "for the support of graduate training programs in community welfare research sponsored jointly by selected universities and Community Welfare Councils."[2]

Leonard Mayo, director of the Association for the Aid of Crippled Children, was emphatic. "It is time for Councils to aim at something higher than a mere balancing of community needs and resources. Council planning should reach out to include groups outside the health and welfare field. Get aggressive. Don't stand and wait for the ball to come to you; run up and grab it. We have waited too long, for instance, to find a solution to the gigantic problem presented by the multiplicity of national health agencies . . . We must eventually join with other groups in such tasks as the rebuilding of impoverished areas, housing and urban development, the restoration and reclaiming of unproductive land, reforestation and flood control, and the resettlement of large numbers of people."[3]

The Federal government had been making more grants for special research and demonstration projects in recent years, but most often the federal agencies recommended new programs or changes in existing services without consulting Councils or Funds. Often the Council found it was not the leader, but only a participant in a new kind of overall planning. This was presenting a great new challenge to Councils. In Providence, R.I., however, the Council was awarded a $46,000 three-year matching grant by the U.S. Public Health Service to set up a pilot demonstration for an information and consultation service geared particularly to the aging and chronically ill.

In New Haven, Conn., local foundation grants enabled the Council to undertake an anti-deliquency program. The Neighborhood Improvement Project began in February 1959 with a $20,000 grant from the New Haven Foundation plus $75,585 from the National Institute of Mental Health. Results of the project were so convincing that in 1962 the Council received a two-year extension of NIMH support with an additional $124,000 grant, plus an additional $27,500 from the New Haven Foundation.

Another New Haven Council project received NIMH support in 1960, the Community Project for Cooperative Care of Mental Hospital Patients. This project was intended to assure a high level of continuous service for patients and their families from the time the patient entered the state hospital until he was restored to full function as a useful member of society. Later grants raised the five-year total to $354,260.

The cause of health and welfare planning was further enhanced by publication in January 1959 of a Public Affairs Pamphlet entitled, "Good Neighbors—the Rise of Community Welfare Councils." Written by Elizabeth Ogg, who had spent several months studying Councils, the result was a briskly-written piece that took an objective view of Councils.

Another publication created a stir in the already troubled federation-health agency waters. It was the abridged version of Marion K. Sanders' December *Harper's* article, "Mutiny of the Bountiful," in the February *Reader's Digest*. Mrs. Sanders discussed the great number of campaigns and noted, "Protests are, at present, about money and ways of raising it. They are being observed, however, by experts in public health and philanthropy who have long held that splintering up the human body into competing sovereignties is a poor way to fight disease or to promote habits of health . . . It is generally agreed that, within the organizations' chosen fields, the money has been wisely spent . . . The problem is that in these crusades, built largely on pity and terror, and ballyhoo, basic statistics have been ignored . . . The creation of preferred classes of patients highlights the fact that the disease agencies

LABOR—MANAGEMENT TALK at Campaign Leaders National Conference, 1959. (Left to right) Charles M. Torongo, President of Local 4108, Communications Workers of America, and a conference speaker; Conference Chairman, Hugh A. Duffield and John A. Greene, President of Ohio Bell Telephone Company, and Board President, United Community Funds and Councils of America.

need not worry about the overall growing tug of war between local and national interests . . . The Heart and Cancer Societies along with the March of Dimes have actually spurned a million dollars or more that was collected for their diseases rather than their organizations!" [4]

The article's impact was quick and impressive. Newspapers all over America quoted Mrs. Sanders' material and editorialized on it. Probably no article ever published in the long struggle between the forces of federation and of separate solicitation ever received so much attention.

The National Foundation reacted with a memo sent to its field staff commenting, "We regret that this unfair, unbalanced and unthinking article is being given such widespread circulation . . . The only 'mutiny' among our volunteers and the only 'givers revolt' are those stirred up in some places by the pressures, intimidations and misrepresentations used by the United Funds in their efforts to force all separate solicitations into one drive." [5]

In Baltimore, the Mayor's Coordinating Council for Fund-Raising Campaigns said it would not approve solicitations by individual health agencies after January 1960. A Commerce and Industry Combined Health Appeal (CICHA) was organized to include Cancer, Crippled Children, Mental Health, Muscular Dystrophy, Arthritis and Rheumatism, Cerebral Palsy, Multiple Sclerosis, Mentally Retarded Children, and Kidney Disease. When the March of Dimes refused to cooperate, its drive was not endorsed. Basil O'Connor at once termed the Mayor's Council a "self-constituted group of individuals who have set themselves up to pass on organizations they don't know much about." [6]

Later the AFL-CIO refused to endorse the drive until changes were made to increase board membership to include general community representation, to incorporate budgeting procedures, and to abolish individual campaigns by the appeal's member agencies. When the national health agencies asked for time to consider these conditions, the AFL-CIO agreed to go along with the first year's campaign. Despite this and some broadening of representation, however, the first campaign did not do well. After the health agencies failed to make the suggested changes the AFL-CIO refused to support or endorse further campaigns.

For a number of years two separate campaigns existed in Baltimore and both prospered. At the urging of community leadership, CICHA re-affiliated with the United Fund of Central Maryland in the mid-seventies.

National health agencies provided a major topic during the Annual Forum of the National Conference on Social Welfare in May. Lyman Ford, UCFCA's associate executive director, said, "It is a great tragedy that full advantage has not yet been taken of the co-operative procedures and facilities which exist in our local communities today in relation to problems in the voluntary health field . . . National voluntary health agencies must recognize the inherent right of a community to develop its own health and welfare program in line with its own special needs and its own de-

sires . . . More state and national joint planning and action is the crying need in the voluntary health field today." [7]

During the Midwest Conference for Funds and Councils in Chicago, Basil O'Connor made an eloquent plea in defense of The National Foundation's 20-year record with which he identified himself. As president of the organization, he expressed his long-held belief in the value of competition among agencies and restated his strong opposition to United Funds. He called the voluntary health and welfare agencies "the last bastion" of free voluntary association and predicted that the end result of United Funds would be "so much power in so few hands that the government would take us over." [8]

In brief rebuttal, Walter Laidlaw, executive vice president of the Detroit United Foundation, said that belief in the competitive free enterprise system is basic to federation; that federation's only purpose is to serve all the people, and its only concern is to achieve a better product.

United Cerebral Palsy Associations in October ruled that no UCP affiliate could become a member of federation without national office approval, and that effective October 1, 1960, all such affiliates must pay 25%

Richard R. Deupree, (standing) National Chairman, United Community Campaigns of America, presents the 1959 United Way program to television networks and Advertising Council representatives in the Plaza Hotel in New York.

147

President Dwight D. Eisenhower discusses the 1959 United Way campaigns with National Chairman Richard R. Deupree.

of all income to the national organization. Furthermore, the national office would explore ways of additional fund raising to supplement Fund allotments. In October 1964, UCPA declared a moratorium on joining United Funds, though it was then receiving 43.7% of its total income from local United Funds. In 1967, this policy was reversed and local affiliates again were permitted to participate in United Way campaigns.

In Cleveland, there had been a "Women's Revolt" the year before, in which volunteer solicitors told 15 health campaigns they would solicit only once a year for all health agencies. Upon the recommendation of the Chamber of Commerce, a Health Fund was established in 1959, raising $402,000 in its first community-wide campaign.

Health Foundations were finding increasing support in many communities. During the first National Conference on Local Health Foundations in January, Benson Ford, president of Detroit's United Foundation, said that "if the United Fund is to continue to appeal through the program it offers, then its programs must have a continually adjusted balance designed to care for the whole man." [9] Conference Chairman J. Stanley Purnell later told the UCFCA board of the need for a national coordinating body. The board then approved a recommendation of the United Fund Advisory Council for a Committee on Local Health Foundations. Still interested in promoting the Medical Research Program of the National Fund for Medical Education, the board also approved the addition of a field staff person to work on this program and help communities understand it.

A report of the first year's operations of the Medical Research Program was made during the September board meeting at which it was announced that the following communities were including MRP that fall: Detroit, Philadelphia, Cincinnati, Houston, Toledo, Kansas City Heart of America Campaign, Tacoma, Springfield, Ill., Canton, Ohio, Chattanooga, Galveston, Indianapolis, Northern Westchester, N.Y., Norfolk, San Bernardino and Stockton, Cal., and Syracuse, N.Y. MRP was also being included in statewide appeals. Approximately $840,000 was allocated by United Funds during the program's first year.

In early autumn, the President's Committee on Fund Raising Within the Federal Service announced that United Fund solicitors would no longer be required to distribute envelopes to federal employees. If individual employees wished, however, they could use any envelope they wished.

Earlier in the year, the National Tuberculosis Association, which had participated in the coordinated health drive of the Federal Employee Solicitation Plan, withdrew from the plan. One of the reasons was the feeling that such participation left the agency open to the charge of engaging in one form of federated fund raising while refusing to participate in another.

Changes in the National Budget Committee were made in May, following recommendations of a UCFCA–National Social Welfare Assembly committee. NBC effectiveness had been limited by the fact that many large agencies such as Red Cross, YMCA, YWCA, Girl Scouts, Boy Scouts, and many national health agencies did not submit their budgets and programs to the budget committee. The appraisal committee concluded that not only was the budget process valid, but NBC should be broadened to: include an information and consultation service related to the programs of 50 national agencies, about 30 of which used NBC services; provide basic quota data; give service to local budgeting and allocation programs; and make efforts to increase agency and contributor respect for its procedures and findings.

Problems of the aging received increased Council attention during the 1950's. The National Social Welfare Assembly's National Committee on the Aging undertook production of five films and sponsored a conference of national organizations concerned with aging. In 1960, the Committee became independent of NSWA and organized the National Council on the Aging, with membership from many groups concerned with older persons, including business and industry, labor, government, the health professions, clergy and local communities.

The special UCFCA committee studying social service exchanges reached a conclusion in 1959 that exchanges were declining in use and effectiveness. Chairman Elmer Tropman, director of the Health and Welfare Association of Allegheny County (Pittsburgh), reported, "It is to be hoped these findings will not develop defensiveness on the part of many people identified with the Exchange, but that instead they will face a challenge. Such a challenge could stimulate every community to evaluate its Social Service Exchange to determine if it is the best instrument for its community at this time . . . It took courage and leadership to launch the SSE movement. It is hoped that similar courage and leadership will now further improve our machinery and methods for achieving the much needed coordination in the health and social welfare fields." [10]

A further report was issued in January 1961 presenting arguments for and against continuation of exchanges. To most persons responsible for health and welfare planning, the arguments against continuation prevailed, and exchanges declined in number until in 1968 there were only 103.

At the December UCFCA Board meeting, the subject of Executive Director Ralph Blanchard's retirement the following July came up for action, and following the unanimous recommendations of a screening committee, Associate Director Lyman Ford was appointed, effective July 1, 1960. Henry Weber was named Associate Executive Director with responsibility for volunteer development and public relations and was appointed to succeed Ralph Blanchard as Director of United Community Campaigns of America.

1960

Turbulence continued in the national health agency scene during 1960. In Toledo, Ohio, a revolt was taking place following Chamber of Commerce disapproval of the Cancer Crusade on the basis of Chamber policy against organizations withdrawing from the Community Chest for the purpose of conducting a separate campaign. The time had arrived, the Chamber felt, to demonstrate to national organizations that they could not dictate to local communities how to give their money for charity, health, and welfare purposes.

Throughout the country, American Cancer Society was experiencing fund-raising difficulties in communities where it had dropped out of United Funds. UCFA's research division compiled a report in 1960 based on 63 such communities, showing a 47.2% decrease. Total

Designation of United Community Campaigns of America as winner of the Silver Anvil Award of the Public Relations Society of America for conducting the best public service effort of its kind in 1961 brings smiles to (left to right) Henry Weber, Campaign Director; John Hayes, President United Community Funds and Councils of America; Benson Ford, National Campaign Chairman; and John Millis, Public Relations Director, Mercury Division, Ford Motor Company.

funds in these communities dropped from $2,865,740 to $1,514,240.

So many local chapters had withdrawn from the national organization because of this ruling that a conference of autonomous cancer societies was held in September, and a committee formed to advise on methods of allocating research funds received from United Funds.

In October ACS revealed that it had raised $2 million less than in 1959, and for the first time in 16 years would be unable to make all its research grants. The New York *Herald Tribune* reported that ACS had spent about $6 million for fund raising and administration during 1959, while raising a total of $28,400,000, and that its withdrawal from United Funds was responsible for most of its decline. In areas where the local chapters had broken with Funds, they had raised about half of what they had received from United Funds. [11]

The Boston *Herald* commented editorially on October 16, "The theme song of the giant independents has always been that this is a free country, that anyone has a right to stake out a charity claim in America. It is a song more and more new health agencies are singing, and if it sounds rather sour to the established giants, perhaps they will want to consider the advisability of joint fund raising. We hope so, for joint fund raising is, beyond any doubt, the only way to bring the greatest benefits to the greatest number of Americans." [12]

In its annual report the following spring, ACS said that while "firmly committed to the premise that independent fund raising is in the best interest of a truly effective national cancer and medical research program, the ACS favors the practice of joint solicitation in industry." [13] This was a reflection of the increasing difficulty health agencies were having with door-to-door solicitations and the increasing success of United Funds with employee campaigns.

Because of these differences, the growth of new agencies, programs, methods of fund raising and levels of giving, many questions were being raised in the public mind. Are so many agencies needed? Is there unnecessary duplication? Are so many solicitations necessary? Because of these and other questions the Rockefeller Foundation had formed an ad hoc committee of distinguished civic leaders to determine whether the role and responsibilities of voluntary agencies could be clarified. A preliminary report stated, "The American tradition of voluntarism, as reflected in its private health and welfare agencies, now faces at least three formidable challenges: the increasing demands of an expanding population for additional services; the growth of the public's sense of social responsibility; the adjustments required by the expansion of government and its assumption of many functions formerly performed largely by voluntary agencies. It is important that public confidence in the voluntary way not be undermined." [14]

Guidelines for local health programs were drawn up by a special UCFCA Committee and accepted by the board in September. "A local health program," the document stated, "may assume whatever particular structure or form the community chooses. Many communities have developed a new communitywide structure known as a health foundation." The paper described basic concepts of such foundations including their acceptance of United Way budgeting and allocations. "Health fund-raising drives which bring several national health appeals together solely for fund-raising purposes lack these factors." [15]

The frequently-asked question, "What is the cost of health and welfare services?" was answered in a UCFCA bulletin detailing expenditures in 23 cities. In these areas, more than $1.9 billion was spent for an average per capita in-area expenditure of $90.80. [16]

While voluntarism was massive, with philanthropic contributions rising from $4 billion in 1950 to $7.8 billion in 1959, Robert Bondy, director of the National Social Welfare Assembly, pointed out that glaring inadequacies of service and coverage remained. Quoted in a Bulletin of the American Association of Fund-

Nancy Anne Fleming, 1961 Miss America, brightened up United Way campaign meetings in a dozen communities in a cross-country speaking tour.

Raising Counsel, he said the increasing specialization of voluntary agencies called for balancing and unifying efforts. The Association, an organization formed in 1935 to serve member professional fund-raising counselling firms, estimated that 47 million volunteers were then serving all nonprofit organizations. [17]

In addition to the tremendous contributions of voluntary agencies, there were increasing governmental expenditures for public assistance. Frank H. Woods, chairman of the Advisory Council on Community Planning, told the UCFCA board that such current governmental expenditures totalled about 3 billion dollars. Although initiated by the federal government, the programs were administered by state and local communities. "Today, gaps have developed in public assistance, chiefly because of the mobility of population and stringency of laws in some states which forbid the giving of assistance to families until they have lived in the state a year or more. This has caused hardships to many families and has created in some areas a drain on the funds of local voluntary agencies. Chests and Funds last year spent some $12 million for emergency assistance, which they are no longer set up to give." [18]

The board then approved a position statement that public assistance is the responsibility of government, and that "public assistance programs without arbitrary restrictions such as residence or place of birth should be available in all parts of the country on the basis of need. The federal government should take leadership in studying and seeking, with the several states and voluntary social welfare interests, an equitable and common solution to this problem." [19]

In another governmental-federation relationship, the UCFCA board approved a memorandum of understanding with the Social Security Administration's Bureau of Public Assistance regarding emergency welfare services. The "U-2 Incident" in which an American reconnaissance plane was shot down over Russia, had helped to intensify the cold war with Russia and Communist East Germany. If the United States were to suffer a nuclear attack, the people would look to social welfare agencies, public and voluntary, for leadership in meeting emergency welfare needs. Community Welfare Councils would become valuable resources in bringing about cooperation and support of voluntary agencies, and accordingly were advised to gain knowledge of civil defense in general and of the emergency welfare services in particular.

Another Council concern, services for the aging, resulted in five grants from the Ford Foundation to Funds, Chests, and Councils and two to local welfare departments for "a series of community organization experiments to improve or develop new programs for older persons." [20]

Changes in structure and philosophy for Community Welfare Councils brought about the need for more national support for community planning. These needs, including advice on urban renewal, chronic illness, juvenile delinquency, and public relations, were referred to the UCFCA Program Study Committee which made proposals for seven vitally-needed extensions of national organization services. They included additional staff for corporation cultivation, public relations for planning, community planning, campaign research, and field service. The board approved these recommendations along with creation of the position of Associate Executive Director for Community Planning filled by Rudolph N. Evjen.

At the same time the Institute of Community Studies was established. Its functions would include consultation to communities on surveys, special research and experimentation, and studies of central services; sponsorship of basic special studies nationally stimulated and specially financed, plus assessment of research and experimentation pertinent to community planning and federated financing. Most often, staff would be recruited from outside sources and employed on a contract basis.

With needs and services growing in every community, more and more Councils had experimented with plans for setting up service priorities on a standardized, orderly and objective basis. Some had attempted to establish a numerical weighting system, but most had concluded that this was not practicable. UCFCA studied the various plans and reported on them and suggested criteria in a booklet, "Priorities in Community Services."

When fall campaigns opened, top volunteer leaders appeared in a closed circuit telecast received in 200 cities. President Eisenhower gave his annual kickoff address on September 15, reminding Americans that "our spiritual heritage includes a deep sense of responsibility for our fellowman." [21]

During the presidential campaigning, Senator John F. Kennedy revealed that he, too, had been a United Way volunteer. "For three months in 1946 I was assistant chairman of the Community Fund drive in Boston." [22] Despite the distractions of the political campaign, United Way campaigns hit a new high by raising $470 million, an increase of $12 million over the previous year.

1961

Although American Cancer Society and other national organizations had begun to feel the adverse effects of their independence, the attacks on federation continued. A new book was published in 1961, *The Gentle Legions,* by Richard Carter, a New York writer. The title referred to women volunteers for national health agencies. Such agencies were praised and even visualized as the model for planning organizations. The book's final chapter consisted chiefly of criticism of federation including "case stories" of the alleged costs of United Fund campaigns, and their "pressure" on givers and agencies. The appendix listed names of all members of all medical advisory committees assisting The National Foundation since 1938, and perhaps supplied a clue as to the special interests behind the book's publication.

UCFCA quickly compiled a six-page memorandum on "points of omission and error" in the book, followed by news that the General Federation of Women's Clubs was providing a 33% discount on the book through an arrangement with the American Cancer Society, American Heart Association, and National Foundation. ACS then sent complimentary copies to the Contributors' Executives Group of the National Industrial Conference Board. Another UCFCA memo noted, "Carter sees United Funds primarily as an effort on the part of business to escape paying its fair share of the nation's health and welfare costs. This interpretation finds no place for mention of the enthusiastic, firm, and continually increasing support of organized labor for the United Way. Despite the fact that the author devotes an entire chapter to Red Cross as a national health agency, it does not mention the fact that the major share of Red Cross financing today is done through United Campaigns. No mention is given to the fact that smaller health agencies raise major portions of their funds the United Way. In view of the major stress that Carter places on fund raising, these omissions could only have been deliberate." [23]

The UCFCA board, following advice of John S. Hayes, chairman of *The Washington Post* executive committee and chairman of the UCFCA Public Relations Advisory Committee, decided to leave the book alone, and to keep pointing up the positive aspects of federation. Later, the staff prepared statements pointing out advantages of federation such as flexibility to meet changing conditions and the strength inherent in federation. They emphasized that many health agencies were unable to raise increased amounts, and some found receipts dropping sharply. Principles necessary for "keeping federation on the move" were listed.

Because of the flow of published material on social welfare subjects during the year, the National Information Bureau in a program report said, "As this awareness increased, the flow of warning articles and dramatizations addressed to prospective contributors increased . . . More contributors, too, evidenced awareness of the need for answers to such questions and to the suggestions that they seek advice as an aid to wise giving. There are some very real problems such as the growing numbers of philanthropic agencies that ask for contributions; the topsy-turvy structure of much of our philanthropy; and need for improved tools for appraisal of philanthropic organizations and programs." [24]

Such problems had been recognized and were being studied by the ad hoc committee of the Rockefeller Foundation which released a report of its two-year study of voluntary agencies. While recognizing the "unique and priceless contribution (of these agencies), the proliferation of agencies and the expansion of their activities have not always paralleled the public need or interest." Two steps were recommended: appointment of a National Commission of Voluntary Health and Welfare Agencies, and development of uniform accounting and financial reporting. The Commission could stand as a court of appeals for the contributing public as well as for the agencies themselves. The Commission was never established, but a uniform accounting system finally was developed.

Commenting on the rising influence of governmental expenditures on health and welfare, the committee said, "It is important for voluntary agencies and government to recognize more clearly that they are allies, not competitors, in providing the health and welfare services needed by the American people." [25]

The report stirred up a great deal of public comment. UCFCA President Irving A. Duffy said, "UCFCA has always favored this kind of constructive action to focus attention on important problems in today's complex health and welfare field," [26] and labor wrote to the committee chairman expressing hearty appreciation and full concurrence with the major recommendations. Representatives of the American Cancer Society, National Foundation, and National Tuberculosis Association commented sharply on the report to the New York press. Spokesmen for both ACS and NTA criticised it for "lumping together" all health and welfare agencies as though they were similar. NF president Basil O'Connor denounced the recommendations and called the report "another in a long series of attempts to undermine public confidence in voluntary activities in the nation." [27] Leo Perlis, Director of the AFL-CIO Community Services Activities Committee, voiced labor's approval of the report.

Stung by the criticism, committee chairman Lindsley Kimball said, "The American people will have the final say on how money will be raised for health and welfare purposes. The report is based upon solid documentation available in the files of the committee. It is not an expression of mere opinion." [28]

The New York Times, in an editorial on August 2, said, "The recommendations . . . should go a long way, if put into effect, toward increasing the confidence of the public in the 100,000 such organizations to which it gives no less than $1,500,000,000 a year. Its two major proposals should be promptly carried out." [29]

Harvey S. Firestone, Jr. (right), 1954 National Chairman, United Community Campaigns of America, congratulates Benson Ford, 1961 National Chairman, for the record breaking United Way campaigns which passed the half-billion dollar mark in 1961.

Irving A. Duffy (left), immediate past President of UCFCA, presents United Way National Community Service medallions to (left to right): Joseph A. Beirne, President of the Communications Workers of America; Oliver G. Willits, former Chairman of the Board, Campbell Soup Company; and Edgar B. Stern, Jr., President of WDSU Broadcasting Corporation, New Orleans. Presentation was at 1963 annual meeting in Chicago.

J. Edgar Hoover, Director of the Federal Bureau of Investigation, makes "Kickoff Address" for the Washington 1962 United Way campaign to 5,000 government workers in Constitution Hall.

Later, Robert M. Hamlin of Harvard University, director of the study, said, "Several of the major independent national voluntary health agencies, who preach cooperation but practice a 'let me alone—you have no right to know what I am doing' attitude, are strongly opposing the recommendations. This opposition is mostly behind the scenes, and is, I am sorry to say, highly organized and well financed, largely by contributors' dollars given for other purposes." [30]

United Health Foundations, Inc., was organized during 1961, growing out of recommendations of the UCFCA Committee on Local Health Programs. It was an association of organizations seeking to provide a nationally coordinated medical research program both on a categorical and unrestricted basis. It would have no national goal and would not conduct a national fund-raising campaign nor would it organize local chapters. It would conduct a limited national promotion effort directed primarily at assisting members to conduct their own local public information programs, and would issue an annual report listing all medical research under its auspices. Medical Research Program leaders of the National Fund for Medical Education had worked closely with federation leaders in developing the association and an orderly transition was worked out. Later that year, S. Sloan Colt, president of the National Fund for Medical Education, confirmed the arrangements and announced that MRP would be terminated as of December 31, 1961, after three years of operation. "We are most pleased to learn that you have now organized the United Health Foundations Inc.," he wrote, "and that this group is in a position to continue the work which the MRP pioneered." [31] UHF was chartered on February 5, 1962.

While relationships with national health agencies continued to be a problem, improved cooperation with Red Cross led to a statement of understanding between UCFCA and American National Red Cross. For the first time, real review of the local portion of the Red Cross budget was agreed to.

A conference on National Agency–Local United Fund Cooperation, the first of its kind, was held in March under sponsorship of the National Social Welfare Assembly. UCFCA's executive director, Lyman Ford, spoke on agency responsibility for financing within the context of federation. Those who attended agreed that the conference was helpful in establishing mutual acquaintance and understanding of each other's problems and common concerns. In June, representa-

Paintings by August Bleser

154

August Bleser with the winsome model, Loretta Frawley, for his 1957 United Way poster. He created the art development of the United Way "helping hand" and painted the themes for three more campaign posters following his 1957 work. Community Cover, March 1957.

Herbert West, United Way National Advertising Chairman and Vice President of BBDO, displays graphic theme for 1959 campaign to Oliver G. Willits, Chairman of the Board, Campbell Soup Company (center) and Theodore S. Repplier, President of The Advertising Council.

tives of 12 national agencies with affiliates traditionally participating in federation met with members of the UCFCA board and staff to discuss mutual concerns.

The values of federation were commonly recognized by corporation executives, a UCFCA brochure pointed out. Most corporation executives felt that federation is the most intelligent way to support health and welfare services because it applies businesslike methods to financing community services; it encourages member agencies to increase earnings and payments for services where it can be accomplished; and it substitutes communitywide planning and coordination for an otherwise haphazard development of services. Through communitywide budgeting, needs are related to financial resources. In this way a balanced community program is developed in much the same way that a corporation maintains a balance between its sundry operations. Corporate philanthropy then totalled nearly half a billion dollars per year. [32]

But providing individualized services in the suburbs

was increasingly difficult, as leaders in the voluntary health and welfare field well recognized. In an effort to assist in the modifications and changes being made by urban agencies as metropolitan areas changed, UCFCA issued a manual, "United Funds, Chests and Councils Go Areawide," which brought together some of the practical considerations involved in areawide organization, as worked out by local Funds and Councils across the country, and offered some guidelines. A workshop sponsored by The Assembly in January also developed many practical suggestions for effective areawide operation in both fund raising and planning.

Services to the aging received nationwide attention during the first White House Conference on the Aging. More than 100 local Council members attended and heard confirmation of the need for more planning for the well-being of the aged, planning which should include active participation of aging persons themselves. In late August UCFCA joined six national organizations in sponsoring a seminar on Community Organization for the Aging. The addresses and a summary of discussions were published the following year.

The change in the federal administration with the inauguration of President Kennedy in January brought with it a recommendation from the outgoing President's Committee on Fund Raising Within the Federal Service that payroll deduction for federal employees was not feasible. While this action was not binding on the

(Right to left) President Kennedy meets with Benson Ford, 1961 National Chairman and Vice-President, Ford Motor Company, and his United Way Campaign Cabinet in the White House: Oliver G. Willits, United Way Vice Chairman and Chairman, Campbell Soup Company; George Meany, United Way Vice Chairman and President, AFL-CIO; Irving A. Duffy, President, United Community Funds and Councils of America and Vice President, Ford Motor Company; (standing) Lansing B. Lindquist, United Way Television-Radio Chairman and Vice President, Ketchum, MacLeod and Grove, Inc.

new administration, it was felt unlikely that the finding would be reversed. In mid-March President Kennedy ordered termination of 17 departmental committees, including the committee on fund raising, with responsibility for future coordination given to the chairman of the Civil Service Commission.

In June, President Kennedy issued a memorandum to heads of departments and general agencies, stressing support of local campaigns. Later he participated in the closed-circuit television show for campaign workers, and opened the campaigns with an address carried by all television and radio networks.

Chapter 13

NOTES

1. *Community*, UCFCA, February 1959, pp. 83, 85, 91, 92.

2. *Ibid.*, p. 82.

3. *Ibid.*, pp. 83, 85, 91, 92.

4. Marion K. Sanders, "Munity of the Bountiful," reprint from *Reader's Digest*, February 1959, summarized from *Harper's Magazine*, December 1958, pp. 1-6.

5. Joseph F. Nee, Memorandum to National Foundation Field Staff, The National Foundation for Infantile Paralysis, January 20, 1959.

6. *Executive Newsletter*, UCFCA, January 9, 1961, p. 2.

7. Lyman S. Ford, "Better Planning for Better Health," presented before National Conference on Social Welfare, May 27, 1959, printed as pamphlet by UCFCA, 1959, pp. 6-9, 15-16.

8. *Community*, UCFCA, April 1959, p. 119.

9. *Community*, UCFCA, March 1959, p. 103.

10. *Community*, UCFCA, June 1959, p. 176.

11. *Executive Newsletter*, UCFCA, October 31, 1960, p. 3.

12. *Ibid.*

13. *Executive Newsletter*, UCFCA, March 20, 1961, p. 1.

14. *Voluntary Health and Welfare Agencies in the United States* (New York: The Rockefeller Foundation, May 1960), pp. 3-9.

15. *Guidelines for a Local Health Program*, No. 12 (revised) of the series "How to Develop a Balanced Health Program the United Way," UCFCA, October 1960, pp. 2-4.

16. "Summary Report, Expenditures, UCFCA, 1960," Bulletin No. 221.

17. *The Bulletin*, American Association of Fund-Raising Counsel, Inc., December 1960.

18. Minutes, Board of Directors, UCFCA, May 6, 1960, Vol. 12, p. 230.

19. *Executive Newsletter*, UCFCA, May 16, 1960, "Position Statement on Public Assistance."

20. *Executive Newsletter*, UCFCA, Jan. 25, 1960, "Ford Foundation Program to Study Community Organization for the Elderly."

21. *Community*, UCFCA, October 1960, p. 5.

22. *Community*, UCFCA, December 1960, p. 18.

23. *Executive Newsletter*, UCFCA, May 15, 1961, p. 2.

24. "Safeguard We Must the Contributor's Trust," National Information Bureau, 1961, pp. 8-10.

25. *Executive Newsletter*, UCFCA, July 1961, Press Release, pp. 1-3.

26. *Executive Newsletter*, UCFCA, August 7, 1961, pp. 1-2.

27. *Ibid.*

28. *Ibid.*

29. *Ibid.*

30. *The Changing Role of American Corporate Philanthropy*, Report of 1961 Midwest Public Relations Conference, October 10, 1961 (Madison, Wisconsin: The University of Wisconsin, 1962), pp. 3, 29.

31. S. Sloan Colt, letter to George B. Plain, M.D., December 14, 1961, in UCFCA files, pp. 1-2.

32. *Corporations in a Changing America*, UCFCA, 1961.

WAR ON POVERTY: 1962-1964

Winds of change were blowing across the social welfare scene as 1962 began, bringing about new needs and new methods of meeting them. The nation's growing population had become more mobile, suburbs had grown while the inner core of cities was decaying, foundations and government were granting more funds for experimental programs, local health foundations were increasing in size and number, incomes had risen for all but the very poor, the rising tide of unrest in the ghettos could be noted.

"Community Councils are facing today the biggest test of their six decades of history," a UCFCA publication, *Essentials for Effective Planning,* pointed out. Another booklet, *The Challenge of the Sixties,* said, "Few at the moment can foresee how local communities will attack these changing conditions, but only as we experiment with new and different ways of doing so, will we successfully meet the challenge."

Robert H. MacRae, associate executive director of the Chicago Community Trust, said, "Planning grants from the federal government and from foundations are making social planning a reality for almost the first time. This change is threatening Community Welfare Councils. Government officials have tended to identify Councils entirely with voluntary agencies and as a result are not likely to turn to Councils for help with the

new problems arising out of urban renewal or public concern about juvenile delinquency. As urban renewal programs develop, social planning will become a city function . . .

"The interest of large national foundations in urban problems has also presented Councils with problems. There have been occasions when these foundations have bypassed Councils and dealt directly with large voluntary agencies or the local government . . . In spite of these somber observations, I believe that there are new dimensions of planning that are within the competence and the reach of Welfare Councils. We are at a significant crossroad in the history of the Community Welfare Council movement." [1]

The problem was reiterated by Sanford L. Solender, executive vice president of the National Jewish Welfare Board, at the annual meeting of the National Social Welfare Assembly. "There has developed a tendency to create new instruments rather than work through the established ones . . . The time is at hand for an honest query as to why this is happening." [2]

This relationship of Councils to grant-making activities of federal agencies and national foundations was examined by the UCFCA Planning Advisory Council which concluded that the UCFCA staff should work more intensively with both local Councils and grant-making bodies in order to improve the Council image. As a result of the committee's efforts, the President's Committee on Juvenile Delinquency, which had by-passed Councils previously, agreed to maintain closer working relations with them in the future.

The UCFCA board in 1962 approved a *Guidelines for Action* statement which for the first time put the national association in the position of saying that these are the things which ought to be done to keep up to date: "The basic approach of the Fund and Council movement is to develop an overall community point of view and to promote unity of action among citizen leaders and operating agencies. This is its distinctive and most important contribution." [3]

In February, it was announced that Councils in five large urban communities would participate in a national study in the field of aging to be conducted by Western Reserve University under a $267,000 Ford Foundation grant. The three-year program, involving Councils in Harrisburg, Pa., Houston, Indianapolis, Los Angeles, and Milwaukee, would study ways that communities determine and implement health and welfare priorities in the field of aging. A four-year follow-up to test selected findings would be made under an additional $62,100 Ford grant.

Other significant grants made during 1962 were those by the Federal Department of Health, Education, and Welfare to the Minneapolis Council "to prepare a comprehensive and coordinated Demonstration Project for the reduction and prevention of juvenile delinquency in two areas of high social need in Minnesota;" [4] and a Ford Foundation grant of $2.5 million to New Haven, Conn., to improve, expand, and modify educational, vocational, health, welfare, recreation and related services aimed at eliminating factors that impede an individual's ability to acquire an adequate education, to secure suitable employment and to find decent housing. The Council's job was to give direction and stimulate leadership in social welfare planning.

Standards for admission into United Health Foundations, Inc., were described during the UCFCA Biennial Conference in San Francisco by Dr. George Plain, vice president of UHF. He had served as chairman of the UCFCA Committee on Local Health Programs which had brought about organization of UHF a year before. "One major contribution that UHF will make is to help prevent the birth of new and duplicating specialized agencies . . . Through UHF the know-how gained in

(Left) Lee H. Bristol, 1962 United Way National Campaign Chairman, tells Clarence Francis, 1953 Campaign Chairman that he will raise more than $500 million in the 1962 campaign. Amount raised was $533 million.

Charles H. Brower, Chairman of the Board, Batten, Barton, Durstine & Osborn, Inc., receives citation for 20 years volunteer service by his advertising firm to United Way, January, 1962.

Leo Perlis, left, Director, AFL-CIO Community Services, receives citation from John S. Hayes, President, United Community Funds and Councils of America, for AFL-CIO support of United Way Campaigns.

TURNING OUT IN SUPPORT—At the Government Division Kickoff of the 1962 United Givers Fund of the National Capital Area on September 18 are left to right: John Duncan, Commissioner, District of Columbia; Postmaster General J. Edward Day; Anthony J. Celebrezze, Secretary of Health, Education and Welfare; George C. McGhee, Under Secretary of State for Political Affairs; and Fred Korth, Secretary of the Navy.

cities like Boston and Pittsburgh can be shared with United Way communities in every state." By the end of 1962, with a membership of 200 local health foundations in 36 states, UHF, Inc., had received $1,800,000 to dispense for health research. [5]

Regarding national health agencies, the UCFCA board approved a memorandum stressing positive, constructive action. It suggested that local communities do more than maintain open-door policies by taking the initiative in seeking health agency participation; that they experiment with cooperative health programs particularly in the area of common administrative services; that they be advised of the danger of letting national health agencies gain access to corporate and employee giving without the contributors and community getting the protection and benefits of federation. [6]

Implications for community planning of financing health agency programs were discussed by Lyman Ford during the Annual Forum of the National Conference on Social Welfare. "Cooperative financing of voluntary health agency programs in some form eventually will be the key that unlocks the community health-planning door." The speech, printed as a UCFCA pamphlet titled, "Better Planning for Better Health," had wide distribution.

Even though the Citizens Commission proposed by the Rockefeller-financed study had not been set up, the National Health Council undertook a project on uniform accounting. When its book on accounting procedures was published in 1962, UCFCA's *Executive Newsletter* commented. "Some of the recommendations run counter to methods of voluntary agency accounting which United Funds have long considered to be sound and are geared particularly to health agencies that raise funds separately from the United Fund. It tends to promote the idea of non-federated fund raising. The system makes it possible for a health agency to minimize its reporting of fund-raising costs." [7]

A second project aimed at delineating uniform reporting and accounting procedures was also begun that year, when Rockefeller and Avalon Foundation grants were awarded to the National Social Welfare Assembly and National Health Council. The UCFCA board agreed to cooperate because of the need for a single system for all agencies. When results were published in 1965, UCFCA fully endorsed the recommended standards and urged local federated units to adopt them since they had incorporated corrections of the weaknesses of the previous study.

159

In Kansas City, the local Association for Mental Health decided to rejoin the Heart of America United Campaign rather than hold a separate drive. In the four years it had conducted separate appeals, it had "seen more and more volunteer time devoted to raising money and preparing for the fund-raising drive instead of developing our service program." Also it had found that campaign costs lessened the amount available for their program.

The Kansas City *Times* editorialized, "The door to the United Campaign has always been kept open to those health appeals which, at least temporarily, have decided to go it alone. The Mental Health Association is the first to return. It may now be hoped that others will follow suit." [8]

In Los Angeles, federation expanded into "United Way," a consolidation of 38 Chests and Funds in Los Angeles County. With Red Cross included, the goal for 1963 needs was $16 million. Although not the biggest United Fund in dollars (Detroit had raised more than $20 million in its 1962 campaign), it was the biggest in other respects, and was a graphic example of the trend toward mergers of Funds within urban areas.

Another California development was the organization of United Community Funds and Councils of California. While the idea of such an organization had been considered following the conclusion of World War II, it had not borne fruit until 1958 when a concerted move for a statewide, staffed association was started. As work progressed, it became clear that the organization's objectives, methods, and activities would closely parallel those of UCFCA.

UCFCA accordingly entered into negotiations with the new organization in order to integrate the two associations; agreeable arrangements were worked out in time for a financial appeal in June, 1962. UCFC of California had a board of 36, an annual budget of $30,000, and one full-time staff person. He had the status of a full-fledged staff member of UCFCA, though based in California and responsible for executing the program adopted by the board of UCFC of California. Local United Funds and Community Chests in the state paid dues only once to UCFCA, which in turn paid the costs of the new association.

On the national level, a new organization long promoted came into being, the National Association of Statewide Health and Welfare Conference and Planning Organizations. Its organization had come about through efforts of a special committee named during the 1961 Annual Forum of the National Conference on Social Welfare, which agreed to serve as its secretariat. Within a year the organization produced a newsletter and directory, held a full day of meetings during the Annual Forum of NCSW, and co-sponsored a study on statewide planning as proposed by Brandeis University. In 1967 the organization's name was changed to National Association for Statewide Health and Welfare. By 1968 its membership totaled 59.

When President Kennedy made the film for his United Community Campaigns of America all-network simulcast, UCFCA President John S. Hayes mentioned the matter of payroll deduction for federal employees, pointing out that 20 states then provided this service. President Kennedy replied that he would like to hear more about it at another time. UCFCA named Louis B. Seltzer, editor of *The Cleveland Press*, to serve as chairman of a Citizens Committee to Promote Payroll Deductions. Later in the year, this committee reported that there was great feeling within the federal establishment for one annual campaign, though not for the type of single effort which United Funds preferred.

National recognition was given the UCCA program in 1962 when the Silver Anvil Award of the Public Relations Society of America was presented to its Director, Henry Weber, "for outstanding public relations performed in the field of community organization and fund raising." The PR program was later described in the PRSA *Journal*: "Behind last year's results are countless hours of planning, research, brainstorming, ideas and designs developed, discarded, and redeveloped . . . A partial listing of final results shows 212 full-page advertisements by national magazines, 1.7 billion contributed network television home impressions, a total of more than $15 million of contributed time and space by national media." [9]

As the Cleveland Welfare Federation was preparing to celebrate its half-century of work in January 1963, it concluded its first major reorganization in 25 years—the development of a new central planning board with augmented planning and research staff. The Federation would maintain its basic organizational structure with the five functional Councils: case work, children's, group work, health, and hospital. The principal objective of the change was to preserve the strengths of the Councils and at the same time equip the Federation with the research and planning manpower needed to work on the community's massive long-range problems.

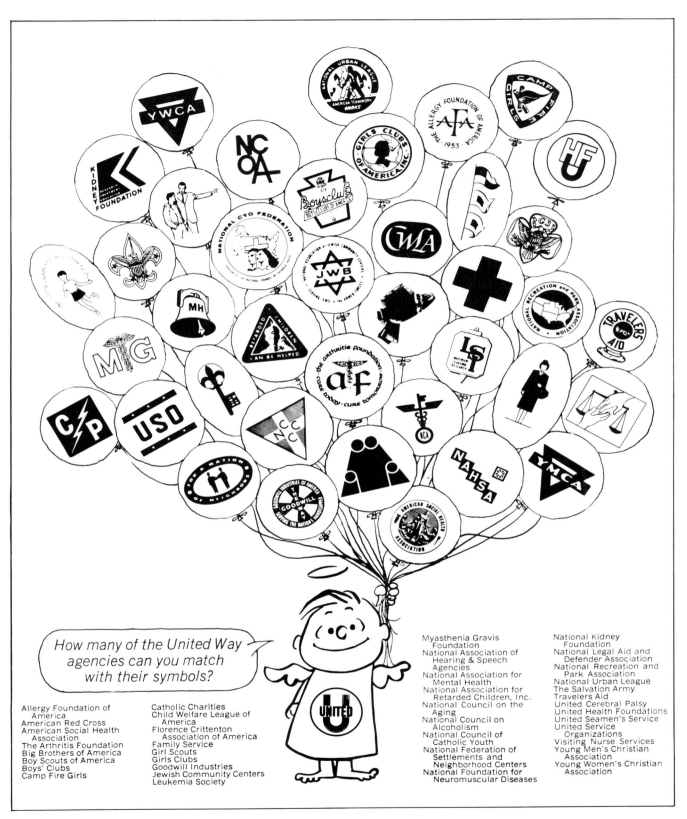

How many of the United Way agencies can you match with their symbols?

Allergy Foundation of America
American Red Cross
American Social Health Association
The Arthritis Foundation
Big Brothers of America
Boy Scouts of America
Boys' Clubs
Camp Fire Girls

Catholic Charities
Child Welfare League of America
Florence Crittenton Association of America
Family Service
Girl Scouts
Girls Clubs
Goodwill Industries
Jewish Community Centers
Leukemia Society

Myasthenia Gravis Foundation
National Association of Hearing & Speech Agencies
National Association for Mental Health
National Association for Retarded Children, Inc.
National Council on the Aging
National Council on Alcoholism
National Council of Catholic Youth
National Federation of Settlements and Neighborhood Centers
National Foundation for Neuromuscular Diseases

National Kidney Foundation
National Legal Aid and Defender Association
National Recreation and Park Association
National Urban League
The Salvation Army
Travelers Aid
United Cerebral Palsy
United Health Foundations
United Seamen's Service
United Service Organizations
Visiting Nurse Services
Young Men's Christian Association
Young Women's Christian Association

The "Little Good Guy" created for the United Way by cartoonist Charles M. Schulz was used in United Way campaigns during the mid 1960's.

161

Changes were also in store for USO. Because USO support was rapidly declining, the National Budget and Consultation Committee had urged a study of services under voluntary auspices to the armed forces. The ad hoc committee reported in December, making 19 recommendations, among them that national USO management of operations in the USA should be terminated and transferred to local USO boards, with local autonomy and responsibility for local financing. This would not apply overseas or in the militarily-impacted areas within the country. The prime source of funds for USO services overseas would continue to be United Funds and Community Chests, with the National Budget and Consultation Committee establishing an approved budget and setting fair-share quotas. USO adopted most of the recommendations in March 1963. Many questions later arose concerning local programs and financing, requiring the establishment in many communities of special study groups.

1963

During the Citizen's Conference on Community Planning in January, UCFCA President John S. Hayes asked, "How can Councils measure up to the job?" He spoke of the growing criticism of Councils, their being bypassed by federal grants, and the implication that Councils lacked the capacity, resources, and power structure to carry on a total community planning job. While listening to the objections, he said, "Councils must not sell themselves short." He cited the general know-how developed over the years, the grass-roots participation of local citizens, and the long list of Council accomplishments. "Councils are generally under-financed," he said. "United Funds need to think through more realistically the amount of money it takes to carry on effective community planning activity . . . A Council's budget should be measured in terms of total health and welfare expenditures in the community, and not in terms of a per cent of the annual amount raised by the United Fund." [10]

In an annual review published in April, UCFCA executive director Lyman Ford said "The expanding and ever-more-complicated society in which we live demands two things of the United Way. They are: continuing effectiveness and growing efficiency in financing health and welfare services; and continuing and growing concern with devising new methods and revising old ones to meet the needs of men, women, and children . . .

IN ST. LOUIS—Sister Gilda of the Society of the Helpers of the Holy Souls, a United Fund agency in St. Louis, delivers a 1963 campaign talk to the professional football Cardinals prior to their solicitation. A tireless United Fund Ambassador, she makes innumerable talks as a member of that year-round speakers group. Sister Gilda stole the show in the locker room meeting with the remark: "Your Eminences—that is what I always call a Cardinal."

AT SAN DIEGO—The U.S.S. Kitty Hawk steams into San Diego Bay the day before the early September kickoff of the 1963 United Community Services Fund there. More than 1,000 sailors stood at attention in the formation spelling out UCS, symbolizing the consistently high support given the county-wide United Way drive by the U.S. Naval Forces in San Diego.

"In the future there must be enhancement of what Adolph Berle called 'The Transcendental Margin' which is the extra effort put forth—with no private gain in mind—by citizens for the improvement of their society. It is this margin which separates successful and prosperous nations from those which crumble and decay." [11]

The vastness and rapidity of social change taking place in America was resulting in solutions requiring the united effort of national, state, and local forces. Consequently the need was now recognized for clarification of the planning efforts of UCFCA, the National Social Welfare Assembly, and local Councils. Accordingly, the Statement of Understanding between UCFCA and NSWA was revised and expanded in order to bring the full forces of their leadership to bear on national issues and the concerns of local Councils, to avoid

Reminiscing about their long association are, left to right: Joseph A. Beirne, President, Communication Workers of America, AFL-CIO, and UCFCA Vice President; Walter M. Upchurch, Jr., Senior Vice President, Shell Companies Foundation, and UCFCA Treasurer, George Meany, President, AFL-CIO; and Hess T. Sears, Secretary of Equitable of Iowa and Chairman of UCFCA's Executive Committee. Mr. Sears presented Mr. Meany with a portrait in token of his role in furthering relations between labor and the United Way, at a testimonial dinner, September 21, 1965, in recognition of two decades of Labor—United Way productive relationships.

duplication of effort, and to encourage further cooperation. Both agreed that national planning should be more closely related to local communities and that they, in turn, should be more intimately involved in national planning. The statement, which described divisions of work, areas of joint activity, channels of communication, and organization structure, was given final approval in 1964. It strengthened the NSWA role but in no way changed the relationship of UCFCA with local Councils.

The Federal Government, becoming more and more involved in local community planning, issued a report in February on *Goals for Community Service,* intended primarily for use of personnel in state and local welfare departments. Prepared by the Department of Health, Education, and Welfare, it said, "Active participation of citizens in services and planning at the community level is sorely needed . . . Voluntary agencies are involved at all levels of planning for service . . . An organized planning and coordinating group is needed in every community with a population of 25,000 or more." [12]

Another publication was issued by the Department of HEW on *The Voluntary Agencies' Role in the Nation's Program of Civil Defense Emergency Welfare Service.* It embodied "memoranda of understanding" between the newly-established Welfare Administration Bureau of Family Services of the Department of HEW and sixteen national voluntary welfare organizations including UCFCA. [13]

Attorney General Robert F. Kennedy asked UCFCA for an opinion concerning the feasibility of a National Service Corps for domestic purposes, similar to the Peace Corps which had been organized in 1961 to aid underdeveloped nations. A special committee studied the proposal and concluded that the objective of promoting wide-scale volunteer service was too broad; that there was possibility of confusion between truly volunteer work and partially compensated full-time service as envisioned for the corps; and that it failed to recognize the large volume of volunteer service already being rendered. They recommended approval, however, without much change except use of the word "corpsman" instead of volunteer for those thus enlisted. [14] These governmental efforts resulted in establishment of Volunteers In Service To America (VISTA) in 1965.

The endeavor to arrange for payroll deduction of United Way pledges among federal employees continued. Federal representatives were developing the idea of a single campaign for all approved groups, production of campaign materials by federal personnel with reimbursement by participating groups, and distribution by donor designation. United Funds and Community Chests were vehemently opposed, feeling that the plan was contrary to United Way principles.

President Kennedy asked John Macy of the Civil Service Commission to study methods by which costs for payroll deduction could be assumed by the benefitting organizations, and Mr. Macy later announced a plan whereby a type of in-plant federation for all agencies would be tried on an experimental basis in nine communities selected by the Commission in the fall of 1964.

With racial discrimination and methods for fighting it becoming a topic of widespread importance, UCFCA's board reaffirmed its long-standing policy of non-discrimination during 1963. "Services of the United Community Funds and Councils of America are rendered without discrimination or segregation because of race, creed, color or national origin. It is the policy and practice of the Association that its Board of Directors and its Advisory Councils are open to representatives from all segments of the public." [15]

During the year, UCFCA took major steps in four areas cited in 1960 as critical: both the National Corporation Participation Program and personnel recruitment and training services were expanded and strengthened; a public relations program for Councils was insti-

United Way agencies at work...these award winning photos were made in United Way agencies.

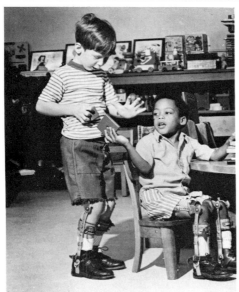

tuted; and through the generosity of the Stern Family Fund a special public relations project was initiated to emphasize the human side of the United Way.

In other activities, the National Budget and Consultation Committee published *Standards for National Voluntary Health, Welfare, and Recreation Agencies,* a definitive work which drew immediate praise and response from many leading corporation executives, agencies, and media for its value in assessing the relative worth and efficiency of national voluntary health and welfare organizations.

The result of an important UCFCA research staff project was also published in 1963, the Master Guide Plan for long-range comprehensive community planning, evaluating services both in and outside federation.

A 1963 report of the National Council on Community Foundations, incorporated in 1957 and now fully financially independent, showed that its membership had grown from 51 to 176 in the five-year period—indicative of the desire of community foundations to exchange information. In the summer of 1964, the organization's name was changed to Council on Foundations to reflect its broadening direction and membership: 77 community foundations; 115 family-or-company sponsored, and other foundations; plus one individual foundation. In 1967, a further expansion of program was made to include field consultation services, regional meetings, workshops and institutes, and additional publications.

1964

Though the government's role in health and welfare had been growing through recent years, it took a tremendous leap forward during 1964 when Congress passed civil rights legislation, broadened Social Security benefits, and established the Office of Economic Opportunity and its War Against Poverty. Federal grants-in-aid rose to $10 billion in 1964. The implications for voluntary philanthropy were many and great, causing considerable soul-searching, reevaluation, and redirection.

"The President's War on Poverty presents a challenge—and an opportunity," Bayard Ewing, chairman of the United Fund Advisory Council, commented. "Our traditional methods may no longer suffice as private and public agencies begin to operate more closely side by side in many sectors of the health and welfare field." [16]

The increasing demands on the administrative staff

of UCFCA resulting from these rapid changes in government programs led the board to appoint a fourth Associate Executive Director at this time—Charles X. Sampson, long-time staff member. His duties included the administrative aspects of the association.

By June, more than 45 Councils were designated as the official Community Action organizations for local Economic Opportunity Title II programs. Another 150 were heavily involved in creation and operation of the projects.

UCFCA and the National Social Welfare Assembly sponsored Workshops on the War on Poverty in San Francisco, Pittsburgh, Atlanta, and Chicago in order to help voluntary agencies assess their roles in the program. In October, UCFCA cooperated with the Department of Health, Education, and Welfare, NSWA, and American Public Welfare Association in sponsoring a workshop on Public Welfare Agency–Council relationships.

NSWA prepared a position statement regarding HR-10443, the Economic Opportunity bill. While concurring on the purposes and principles of the bill, the Assembly recognized that many other measures would ultimately become necessary because "in fact, poverty is a composite of many problems and requires many programs for its eventual solution . . . It is seen as a limited but important step in combating poverty and the public must not be led to expect that its measures will reach all poor people or that it will solve the problem of poverty . . . The Assembly believes that any attack on poverty will require a total and comprehensive mobilization of Federal-State-local and public voluntary effort." [17]

UCFCA in September distributed "Notes on the Poverty Program" explaining the importance of Council participation, what goes into the program, sponsorship needed, and what Councils should do. It pointed out that while Councils should play a large role in development of local programs, their participation must be earned individually. While administrators of the Title II program seemed to favor separate incorporated organizations, some Councils felt they should operate them.

"It must be admitted," the notes said, "that the idea of setting up an organization separate from the Council to apply for and receive funds, and to operate and coordinate programs is not without merit, since: the Council can thus avoid getting into direct service program

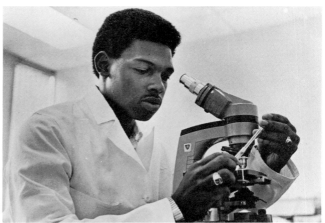

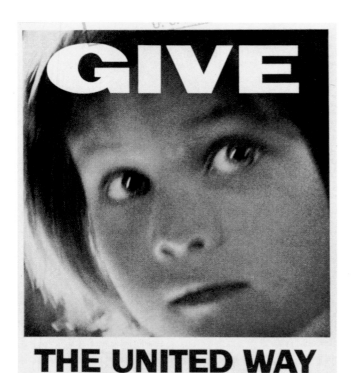

1961 Photograph by Szasz

operation; the Council is still free to operate experimental and demonstration projects as part of the community's coordinated program; the Council is free to evaluate the poverty program itself."

Sargent Shriver, director of the Office of Economic Opportunity (OEO), announced a list of local projects in November which showed that in practically every instance the Council was actively involved in planning and would be participating in carrying out the program in some way.

Passage of Civil Rights legislation focused attention on the need for desegregation, and United Funds in a few communities found themselves the objects of attack because of their positions. In some cities, the problem stemmed from the feeling of certain groups that the United Fund or its agencies were not moving fast enough in desegregating services, facilities, employment, or volunteer participation. Conversely, some were attacked for supporting agencies and services favorable to integration.

Most United Funds thus attacked were unprepared to cope with the problems, for often they were caught by surprise (perhaps on the eve of their campaign), and the attacks took place in strategic quarters. Sometimes they took the form of "hate literature" passed out at plant gates or put in employee cars. The most

widely-used piece was a leaflet attacking Funds for supporting Urban League. Through the years, a few Funds yielded to local pressure and dropped Urban League from membership, but experience showed that those which had stood firm in the face of such pressure had continued as strong as those who had given in. In many of the latter, plans were now afoot to return Urban League to membership.

UCFCA prepared a memo on the subject, pointing out that "This is a damned-if-you-do, damned-if-you-don't situation in which it is impossible to please everybody. Therefore the United Fund should do what it thinks is right and move in the direction of what it considers to be the long-term trend. One of its jobs is to bring reason into play in the support of community services . . . Experience tends to show that when a United Fund wilts in the face of an unjustified attack, it becomes more vulnerable to further attacks." Several helpful suggestions were made, and it was pointed out that there was just one legal position, which all citizens have an obligation to support.

The memo also called attention to further policies which would take effect on July 1, 1965, requiring all United Funds and their agencies to follow racially non-discriminatory policies and practices as a condition for solicitation of Federal employees.[18]

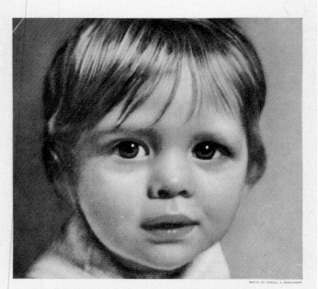

1964 Photograph by Daniel J. Ransohoff

President John F. Kennedy questions Henry Weber, Director, United Community Campaigns of America, about the broadcast he is about to make on behalf of the 1963 United Way Campaigns, from the Cabinet Room in the White House. Present for the occasion are (left) Donald S. Frost, National Media Chairman, and John C. Hodnette, National Campaign Chairman, September 22, 1963.

In Dayton, Ohio, a Human Relations Commission had been formed in 1962, and a Council committee had effected a non-discrimination policy within agencies. The HRC promoted a merit employment program which began in the fall of 1963 by asking 2300 employers to accept merit employment as personnel policy. A total of 95% supported the policy.[19] As non-discrimination became a timely topic, more and more communities followed suit with similar policies and programs.

Federal solicitation continued to be a major UCFCA concern during 1964. By February, 4,000 letters were sent to Congressmen, Senators, the Civil Service Commission, and the White House protesting the new federal plan which would be tried out in selected cities. Philadelphia felt strongly that it could not take part since a precedent would be established which would undermine the whole united-giving approach. Chicago was then substituted. As in Philadelphia, the Fort

Worth, Minneapolis, and St. Paul Funds declined to participate. United Funds finally participating were those in Washington, D.C.; Chicago; San Antonio; Macon, Ga.; Bremerton, Wash.; and Morristown, N.J.

Objections to the plan stemmed from feelings that, even though payroll deduction was now permitted, campaigning was being taken out of United Fund hands; the example for in-plant federation was set; contributor designations were substituted for communitywide budgeting and allocations; and United Fund agencies were discriminated against in favor of go-it-alone agencies by making the United Fund "just another drive." Further, a charge was instituted for payroll deduction, and the plan provided no immunity to contributors from separate house-to-house drives by national health agencies. In March, the USO Board of Governors adopted a resolution opposing the plan because it didn't conform to the time-tested and proved principles of federated fund raising. Family Service

1962 Poster. Photograph by Batten, Barton, Durstine & Osborn

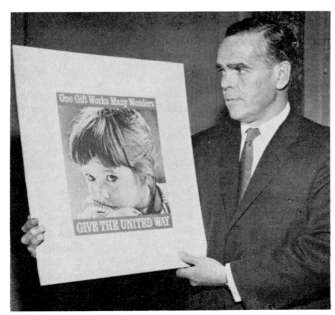

Mark W. Cresap, Jr., United Way National Campaign Chairman, displays the 1963 poster at Campaign Leaders Conference in Dayton.

Association of America and American Red Cross soon added their opposition.

Following the campaigns, results were carefully analyzed in participating cities. As expected, more money was raised from federal employees than the previous year because payroll deductions were permitted. Yet, the use of contributor designations resulted in United Funds realizing a smaller proportion of the total than in former years; there was a deterioration in public relations benefits; and heavy processing expense resulted from designations. In addition, the plan rejected the principle of community planning and budgeting on the basis of relative need.

The UCFCA board, therefore, adopted a resolution to oppose the plan and established a committee to make a personal presentation to President Johnson, voicing such opposition.

While the Federal Plan was resulting in increased competition for the contributor dollar, there was similar competition in another quarter. A. A. Paradis, secretary of the American Airlines contributions committee, wrote in the May-June *Community*, "The day has gone when most corporations discharged their civic obligations by giving solely to the United Fund or Community Chest. Today, United campaigns must compete for the corporate dollar with education, separate health organizations, civic and cultural organiza-

tions, and a variety of other enterprises which look upon the corporate treasury as a potential source of funds." Five percent of every corporate contribution dollar was then going to cultural organizations—further indication of the increased competition United Funds were facing.

In conducting their campaigns that fall, local United Funds were aided by the first national solicitor training film, "Moment of Truth," conceived by William Kaufman, executive director of the Mobile United Fund. A total of 2207 United Way communities conducted campaigns, raising $580 million, an increase of $30 million. This was the first time since World War II that campaigns exceeded the total of their goals.

As millions of volunteers planned to work in United Way campaigns and to take part in the new programs and activities throughout the nation, they assumed a "New Look," as described during the Volunteer Bureau Workshop in May by David F. DeMarche, of the San Francisco United Community Fund. He pointed out new volunteer jobs: school volunteers, vocational retraining, public welfare assistance, relocation, and easing racial tensions. Volunteers were coming increasingly from the ranks of the aged, professional workers, teen-agers, and men.[20]

"The most imminent change in the agency board of the future," predicted Mrs. Charles Balfanz, a director of the Welfare Council of Metropolitan Chicago, in a speech presented in Chicago, "will be that recipients of the agency's service will be represented on the board and will be involved in policy making." [21]

Because of the need for more and better service to local budgeting committees, UCFCA designated a new "Budgeting and Agency Relations" unit, only one duty of which was to serve as secretariat for the National Budget and Consultation Committee. As Hess T. Sears, chairman of the Executive Committee, noted, "Even a casual look beneath the current threats to sound federation reveals that it is the survival of the budgeting principles that is really at stake . . . Federation without budgeting is pseudo-federation." [22]

The problem of Fund-Council relationship was tackled in many communities where it was found that neither organization, alone, was able to turn out top-quality performance or to cooperate effectively. Studies made with UCFCA help often indicated that merger was necessary. This resulted in formation of United Community Services, directed by citizens answerable to the whole community, not just to donors and agencies. UCS was usually organized along functional lines, with planning, fund raising, allocations, affiliations, and public interpretation carried out through standing committees.

Another kind of local problem was successfully handled in South Bend, Ind. when the Studebaker Plant closed, putting thousands out of work. Yet, eight months later, the city was bustling. Why? Because of the efforts of Project Able (Ability Based on Long Experience) designed to assist the unemployed worker past 50. Instituted jointly by the United Community Services of St. Joseph County and the National Council on the Aging, and financed by the Office of Manpower, Automation and Training of the Department of Health, Education, and Welfare, the program was administered and coordinated by United Community Services which worked closely with local union counselors.

Just as organized labor was taking an important part in tackling South Bend's unemployment problem, it was also participating in fund-raising and planning activities throughout the nation. To evaluate labor's involvement in federated fund raising after 20 years, the Community Service Activities Department of AFL-CIO conducted a study of giving patterns, attitudes, knowledge, agency use, and opinions. Conclusions reached were that union members in general held favorable attitudes toward United Fund campaigns; that they had good knowledge of what agencies were thus supported (except for recreation agencies); that nearly half had contact with agencies; nearly four-fifths had signed pledge cards; 78 percent of the rank and file did not feel there was pressure to give while 55 percent did not like suggested standards of giving. [23]

Because of the undeclared war by go-it-alone agencies against federation, fund raising had occupied the limelight during the 1950's. By 1964, however, it was clear that the major emphasis during the 60's would have to be on the role of planning in a changing society.

During the Biennial Conference in January, outgoing UCFCA President John S. Hayes had said, "The United Fund must accept responsibility for seeing that good health and welfare planning takes place . . . When there are two separate organizations, the United Fund shouldn't dominate the Council. A fate far worse than domination, however, is for a Council to be ignored by the United Fund . . . When voluntary effort doesn't or can't or won't do a health and welfare job, government moves in . . . There is a further compelling reason for increased attention to further planning in the United Way. This is the need for recognition of the political, social, economic, and education needs of American Negroes." [24]

Elliott L. Richardson, Boston attorney then-vice president of the United Fund, and subsequently the Secretary of Health, Education and Welfare, writing in the May-June 1964 issue of *Community,* compared the amounts raised by voluntary contributions with vast governmental expenditures. "We can't go back. But we could encourage government to absorb an even greater share of health and welfare expenditures. Why not, after all, let government take over? One answer—an obvious one—is this: a fair-share gift is voluntary; tax increases are not . . . In supplementing governmental services and performing functions that government cannot perform, voluntary agencies make an indispensable contribution to our society's total capacity to cope with its human problems." [25]

New Haven's United Fund president, Daniel W. Kops, president of radio station WAVZ, observed in the September-October issue of *Community,* "The plain fact is that Federal investment in local social services is already a substantial one and the trend is up, not down. It is my belief that local community leaders should realistically come to terms with this fact and recognize that officials of federal, state, and local governments are very much involved in how the needs of local citizens are to be met . . . The real challenge is for local citizen leadership to play an active role and not leave it to government. Anti-poverty programs cannot be fully effective unless the voluntary as well as the public social welfare system is fully engaged in the attack." [26]

Because Councils were facing the biggest tests in their four-decade history as they rallied forces to meet the impact of social change, a special UCFCA committee prepared a position paper on the Council role. It showed the great number and variety of Council projects related to juvenile delinquency, school dropouts, urban renewal, public housing, multiple-problem families, hard-to-reach youth, relocation, etc. Effective liaison with governmental agencies was stated as a prime objective of Council efforts, though it was pointed out that Councils could not realistically be expected to move immediately into the wider areas being opened up through governmental programs. "As

School principals study a United Fund agency that provides the handicapped with both vocational training and work.

Attorneys, members of a United Fund campaign committee, visit an agency that helps youth, the aged and the needy.

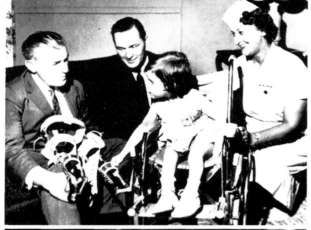

Union leaders chat with a child being helped by rehabilitation, nursing and other United Fund services.

Your Fair Share Gift is insured

When you contribute your fair share to your local United Fund or Community Chest campaign, you can be certain that your gift will be handled in a business like manner.

Business, labor and the professions are strongly represented among the volunteer community leaders who visit participating agencies before each campaign to study their programs, performance and value to the community.

To these volunteers, a United Way dollar looks like one of their own, to be budgeted, allocated and spent where it will accomplish the most good. Their active interest in both the humanitarian and business side of United Way operations is your assurance that your United Way gift will truly work many wonders.

An industrialist inspects an agency that provides a ''day camp'' for children of working mothers.

 Your Fair Share Gift
is working
many wonders
THE UNITED WAY

25 million families benefit by child care, family service, youth guidance, health programs, disaster relief and services for the Armed Forces from 30,000 United Way agencies.

Bank presidents call on a family whose three children were adopted through an agency of the United Fund.

This picture-story of community surveillance of United Way allocations and services was carried as a public service message by 37 national magazines in 1967.

Councils move into broader responsibility, they should keep their activities within the bounds of what they can do well and effectively . . . Council relationships to Federal programs should be positive and complementary . . ."[27]

Further, because of the questions raised concerning the role of both Funds and Councils in light of new government programs, civil rights developments, and other changes on the local and national scene, the UCFCA board in December moved to conduct a study on the role of federation and why voluntary activity was still needed. This was called the Voluntarism Study.

NOTES

Chapter 14

1. Robert H. MacRae, "The Challenge of Change to Community Welfare Councils," *Family Service Highlights,* May 1963, pp. 105-111, 130, reprinted from National Social Welfare Assembly *Newsletter,* October 1962.

2. *The Assembly Letter,* No. 110, National Social Welfare Assembly, January 1963, pp. 1-3.

3. *Guidelines for Action, the United Way to: Better Planning, Better Financing, Better Communities,* UCFCA, 1962, pp. 4-6.

4. "Youth Development Planning Grant Process and Minneapolis Youth Development Planning Project," Community Health and Welfare Council of Hennepin County, Minnesota, June 23, 1962.

5. George B. Plain, M.D., *Moving Ahead in Health,* UCFCA, April 1962, pp. 5-7.

6. "General Policy, Strategy, and Approach to National Voluntary Health Agency Situation," Minutes, Board of Directors, UCFCA, May 25, 1962, Exhibit C, pp. 1-3.

7. *Accounting and Financial Reporting Procedures for Voluntary Health Agencies,* National Health Agencies, National Health Council, 1962, review enclosed with *Executive Newsletter,* UCFCA, November 26, 1962.

8. *Executive Newsletter,* UCFCA, March 26, 1962, p. 2.

9. *Community,* UCFCA, July-August 1962, p. 96.

10. John S. Hayes, "How Can Councils Measure Up to the Job," address before 1963 Citizens Conference on Community Planning, printed as pamphlet by UCFCA.

11. *Community, UCFCA,* March-April 1963, pp. 4-5.

12. *Goals for Community Services,* Planning for Community Needs in Health, Education, and Welfare (Washington, D. C., U. S. Department of Health, Education, and Welfare, August 1963), pp. 11-13, 18.

13. *The Voluntary Agencies' Role in the Nation's Program of Civil Defense Emergency Welfare Service* (Washington, D. C.: U. S. Department of Health, Education, and Welfare, leaflet, February 1, 1963).

14. Minutes, Board of Directors, UCFCA, February 15, 1963.

15. "Successes in 1963," *Community,* UCFCA, March-April 1964, p. 14.

16. Bayard Ewing, "Fund Raising," *Community,* UCFCA, January-February 1965, pp. 10-12.

17. "Position Statement on H. R. 10443," National Social Welfare Assembly, April 10, 1964.

18. "United Fund Campaigns and the Civil Rights Controversy," UCFCA, August 7, 1964.

19. Mrs. John B. Greene, "Dayton's Progress in Human Relations," *Community,* UCFCA, September-October 1965, pp. 5-7.

20. *Proceedings, Volunteer Bureau Workshop,* May 26-28, 1964, pp. 20-24.

21. Mrs. Charles Balfanz, "The Voluntary Board of the Future," *Community,* UCFCA, March-April 1965, pp. 18-19.

22. Hess T. Sears, "1965 and Beyond—Budgeting," *Community,* UCFCA, January-February 1965, pp. 8-10.

23. "A Report on Labor Participation in Federated Fund-Raising Campaigns," AFL-CIO Department of Community Services, October 1964.

24. "1963 . . . Eventful Year for the United Way Movement," *Community,* UCFCA, March-April 1964, pp. 9-10.

25. Elliott L. Richardson, "Default: A Threat to the United Way," *Community,* UCFCA, May-June 1964, pp. 13-14.

26. Daniel W. Kops, "Ivy League Prototype for the Attack on Poverty," *Community,* UCFCA, September-October, 1964, pp. 3-6.

27. "The Role of Community Health and Welfare Councils," UCFCA Bulletin, February 1965.

CHAPTER 5

GOVERNMENT AND THE VOLUNTARY SECTOR

The United Way faced more challenges during the 1960's than ever before: integration with gigantic governmental programs, combined health drives, in-plant federations, and increased competition for the contributors' dollars from educational and cultural organizations. Despite these and other challenges, United Way campaigns in 1965, reflecting the rising national prosperity, again surpassed their goals.

The relationship of voluntary agencies to government programs continued to be a major United Way concern, along with finding a way to make the Combined Federal Campaign conform more closely to United Way principles. Of 100 cities invited to participate in the 1965 governmental combined campaign experiment, only 33 accepted. Under the leadership of President John Hayes, UCFCA had induced the government to establish Combined Federal Campaigns only if the United Fund agreed to participate. After results of these 33 campaigns were analyzed, UCFCA President Ralph Lazarus, president of Federated Department Stores, Inc., met with John Macy, Jr., chairman of the Civil Service Commission, and presented several recommendations: that option of a local United Fund to participate be continued and those not participating be allowed to conduct their usual campaigns in federal establishments with payroll deduction; "designations off the top" should be discontinued and funds

allocated according to pre-campaign percentage distribution; fair-share giving guides should be determined locally and be compatible with those for other employee groups; new employees should be solicited at the time of employment in order to offset the loss in collections because of employee mobility; the federal government should bear the cost of payroll deductions. In 1967, for the first time local communities were permitted to divide CFC proceeds in a way which minimized the harmful effects of designations.

Anti-Poverty Programs authorized by Congress the year before were rapidly going into action, with both UCFCA and the National Social Welfare Assembly making regular contacts with federal officials in order to keep up-to-date on developments. UCFCA began publication of a monthly newsletter, *Newer Federal Programs: Local Developments in the War Against Poverty,* made many field visits to communities with active programs, and included the War on Poverty in conference sessions.

Despite these efforts, the UCFCA Committee of Planning Executives felt that in many cities there was lack of coordination between Councils and their health and welfare agencies on the one hand, and the Anti-Poverty programs on the other. UCFCA President Ralph Lazarus and Executive Director Lyman Ford met with Sargent Shriver, director of the Office of Eco-

Ralph Lazarus, President of United Community Funds and Councils of America, shows the 1965 United Way campaign poster to newly-elected member of the UCFCA Board of Directors, Inez Robb, newspaper columnist.

R. Sargent Shriver, (left) Director of the Office of Economic Opportunity, and Joseph A. Beirne, UCFCA President meet the press on September 27, 1966 in Washington following the signing of the Statement of Consensus on Government and the Volunteer Sector in Health and Welfare.

nomic Opportunity, in June to discuss mutual concerns. At this time Mr. Shriver said that local Community Action projects would result in greater demand for services of United Fund agencies, not less. "We hope that the poverty program will stimulate self-analysis by voluntary agencies and the development of new and imaginative methods of operation and delivery of services to the people," Shriver said. "Any reduction of effort (by United Fund agencies) would be unthinkable." [1]

Vice President Hubert H. Humphrey, in a press conference during the summer, said, "If I thought the antipoverty program was going to do away with private philanthropic work, I would lead the fight against the program. I do not want to have an America in which all the needs of the people are taken care of through public authorities." [2]

In May, UCFCA listed 270 Community Action organizations, with 40 Councils designated as the official agency. [3] In Philadelphia, a dozen certified poor persons were elected to membership on the Antipoverty Action Committee, chaired by C. F. McNeil, executive director of the Health and Welfare Council, who said, "This election system is one of the greatest social experiments of our time." [4] The experiment received national recognition, and since then such membership has become a requirement of all Community Action Programs.

A group of nationally recognized public relations counselors joined UCFCA in a study of government activity in health and welfare, and recommended that the United Way work closely and creatively with government in these programs. They also suggested that a simplified public policy statement defining the United Way's basic role be written, that special effort be made to develop and strengthen citizen management leadership to oversee the spending of all funds for health and welfare both public and private; and that the United Way perform a positive role in searching out new and better ways to meet the human needs of urbanization.

That Councils were becoming more involved in government programs could be seen in the increase of Council support from public funds. In 1960 less than 5% of their income came from public funds; in 1965, however, that figure had risen to 28.6%. Most of this money was expended on special projects and research.

UCFCA also kept abreast of another governmental development: federal tax policies. Two proposals that year, if passed, would have jeopardized voluntary contributions. Representatives of major tax-exempt groups —churches, private schools and colleges, health and welfare agencies, museums, and others—met to discuss mutual concerns. They agreed to convene from time to time and take joint action when necessary on matters affecting tax exemptions or deductibility of charitable contributions. UCFCA produced a leaflet, *How the Tax Laws Help You to Help Others,* and played a leading role in the National Social Welfare Assembly's Tax Policy Committee.

Because of the increasing number of pertinent federal developments, the UCFCA board considered employment of a Washington, D.C. representative. In 1967 the proposal was approved, with provision to be made in the 1969 budget for a Washington office.

The many new federal programs, with their impact on the local scene, resulted in an increasing demand for community surveys. Several dozen communities called on UCFCA's Institute of Community Studies for assistance during the year. On the national level also, several studies were undertaken: the Voluntarism Project as proposed in the December 1964 board meeting, and a comprehensive undertaking entitled the Urban Living Project. The latter was an effort to chart directions for community policies and programs to provide full opportunity for people in urban areas to attain a satisfactory level of living. The Voluntarism Project, with funds from Sears Roebuck Foundation, would include a study of a group of cities selected for intensive work in order to help Funds be sure they were geared in with today's problems and were flexible in adjusting to rapidly changing conditions. In January 1968, the two studies were combined.

Results of a study concerning involvement of Negro leadership in positions of responsibility in Funds and Councils showed that all 58 organizations in the 42 cities responding had Negro board representation. Twenty-seven United Funds reported 120; 26 Councils had 121 and five United Community Services listed 16.

When a revised version of the non-discrimination requirement for federal employee fund raising was issued in July, local United Funds moved swiftly and positively. So far as UCFCA could determine, only nine United Funds failed to comply. In 30 communities where some member agencies had not yet complied, a few of the agencies withdrew from federation; others agreed to comply. These United Funds campaigned in the federal establishment only for complying agencies.

The extent of Negro support and participation in United Fund campaigns that fall was later reported at the Campaign Leaders Conference by Henry A. Spears, Negro administrator of Alabama State College. During this campaign, he said, "Negroes became full and equal partners in the campaign and standing committees, speaking to employee groups, etc. . . . (The) 1965 campaign proved conclusively that there was undeveloped and unsuspected potential of support within the community. The potential is there—the purchasing power of the Negro is an economic fact which is becoming recognized." [5]

During the 1965 Citizen's Conference on Community Planning, the first recipient of the Newton D. Baker Award was named. The award was established to honor the memory of the late Newton D. Baker II, former mayor of Cleveland and a founder of its Welfare Federation, Secretary of War in President Wilson's cabinet, and chairman of the National Mobilizations from 1932 to 1934. The award honors an active citizen volunteer demonstrating outstanding leadership for a local Council project leading to concrete action and accomplishments.

Four major areas of concern received attention during the Citizens' Conference: poverty, health, urban planning, and formulation of community policy. One speaker, the Rev. Dr. Henry Balsey Clark II, made a suggestion that has since received considerable attention—a guaranteed annual income. The idea had been proposed now and then since the mid 50's but not given much serious consideration until then. The same proposal was made the next month by the Delegate Assembly of the National Association of Social Workers.

While the social welfare scene was undergoing changes, there was change in another area as well: the national economy. Corporate mergers and acquisitions resulted in larger national corporations and it soon became apparent that United Way support from these national organizations was not keeping pace with that of the smaller, locally-owned concerns. UCFCA's National Corporations Participation Committee reported that while corporate support in the past 10 years had increased from $120 million to $190 million, its proportion of the total support for the United Way had decreased from 40 to 30.5 percent. Corporate giving for all purposes averaged around one percent of company net income before taxes as it does today.

In January 1965, UHF sponsored a national confer-

Beverly Hills meeting of UCFCA's West Coast Media Committee on October 28, 1966. Left to right: Cornwell Jackson, Paisano Productions; Samuel Thurm, Chairman, UCFCA National Television-Radio Committee; Mrs. Cornwell Jackson (Gail Patrick); Milton C. Mumford, National United Way Campaign Chairman; Herminio Traviesas, Vice President of Batten, Barton, Durstine and Osborn, Hollywood; and Lorne Green, who donated his services as star of the United Way campaign film.

ence in Detroit, involving management, labor, government, medicine, and United Funds. The conferees agreed that United Funds must take the initiative in bringing order into the chaotic voluntary health organization situation; that greater emphasis must be placed on health planning both locally and nationally, and that more support must be obtained from national leaders. During the previous year UHF Inc. had distributed some $200,000 in 23 grants.

One of the health agencies which during the 50's had adopted a policy of non-participation in federation, underwent sweeping changes during the year. One change approved by the National Society for Crippled Children and Adults (Easter Seals) was to permit federation under certain conditions. By 1968, a total of 157 local societies participated.

Studying the part that Councils could play in health planning, Council executives agreed that Councils must assume increased responsibility for affecting comprehensive community health planning by strengthening their relationship with the health interests at all levels.

Not only health services, but also many new welfare services, were now competing for the voluntary dollar. The subject of agency self-support was therefore of timely interest. Following an extensive survey, UCFCA produced *Agency Self-Support, a Guide for United Funds and Participating Agencies,* which proved so valuable that it was reprinted five times in six months. Not all national agencies agreed on those parts of the guide which discussed self-support for parts of their programs, particularly the Girl Scouts, Boy Scouts, and Salvation Army, but most found the guide very useful in opening new channels of support.

Abroad, the stepped-up war in Vietnam placed new demands for service upon United Way agencies. Al-

though some 40 American agencies supported programs in Vietnam, the majority were under religious or other voluntary auspices. Red Cross tripled its staff in Southeast Asia during the second quarter of 1965, but no need was felt for increased appropriations. By 1966, however, its needs had grown and 100 American Red Cross staff members were assigned to Vietnam.

International Social Service established formal operations in Vietnam, opening an office in Saigon. With a large part of the ISS program devoted to children, and with the number of war orphans and racially-mixed children born out of wedlock increasing, supplementary funds were sought from campaign coverages or reserves. There were then 10,000 children being cared for in 63 Vietnamese orphanages.[6]

USO embarked on an expansion program, enabling it to operate on "full wartime footing" and on August 30 USO representatives met with the National Budget and Consultation Committee to request a 1966 budget increase. Similarly, United Seamen's Service, with a stepped-up program, also sought increased allocations from NBCC.

1966

The need for a communitywide approach to problems of the day was emphasized in many ways during 1966, and the scope of United Way activities ranged from participation in programs to prevent racial rioting, to efforts to reach accord with uncooperative health agencies.

Labor's important role in the United Way was dramatized in a significant manner when Joseph A. Beirne was elected UCFCA president during the annual meeting at the February Biennial Conference in Toronto, Canada. Beirne, president of the Communi-

..."a common task to reach a common goal"

"I'm glad to give"

*"I'm glad to give. The Community Chest is a fine idea."
(Mr. Coolidge was one of the first Presidents to endorse the United Way of voluntary support of community health, welfare and recreation services while in office.)*

"Stands for spiritual growth"

"The true hope of progress is in the spiritual field, and these are the helpful actions in the world and the worthwhile things in the community. The Community Chest stands for this spiritual growth. It occupies a position that must constantly be built stronger if we would build the spiritual side of American life..."

"They must not be forgotten"

"Care of the aged, service to demoralized families, hospitalization of the needy sick, home nursing, settlements, guidance of youth, care of the children without a chance —these and hundreds of other services are in the hands of your local welfare organization . . . they must not be forgotten . . ."

"Our help will really count"

"The Community Chest gives us a chance to make sure our help will really count. When we give to the Chest, we can be sure that we are helping our neighbors and our neighborhood in the right way. And when we do that, we are making our country a better place to live in for ourselves and our children."

"A splendid opportunity"

"We can't possibly know about all our neighbors in need. Somebody must show us the way to help them. This is the purpose of these United Campaigns in over two thousand communities across the land. They provide us with a splendid opportunity to express the traditional neighborly concern of America."

"I hope that you will join"

"I hope that you will join in this great national effort, this great national crusade through the United Way, and give. It will make your community a happier place; it will make you a happier person, and in the real sense that your community is your country—it will make our country a finer place in which to live. United, there is little we cannot do..."

"A proud record"

"One of our enduring American traditions has been the voluntary contribution of time and money to strengthen our country's many communities. Nowhere else in the world do people give so generously toward this end. Millions of Americans perform both a public service and an act of human compassion by their participation in and generosity to their United Fund or Community Chest. In doing so, they express a common desire to help their community assist the young and old, the sick and distressed."

One gift works many wonders/Give the United Way

cation Workers of America, AFL-CIO, thus became the first representative of organized labor to hold this office. He had served UCFCA in various capacities since 1956. Many national leaders including President Johnson expressed personal pleasure at his election, which was cited as a milestone in voluntary fund raising on the editorial pages of both the *New York Times* and the *Herald Tribune.*

Concern over the changing relationship between voluntary agencies and government led to development of a position statement on the United Way and Voluntarism. "The mission of the United Way is to work for a healthful, happy, useful life for everyone in the community, regardless of race, creed, or economic status." In pursuing this objective the United Way must, it continued, work constructively with government, probe to find new ways of meeting social needs and to initiate fresh designs and new dimensions; proclaim and demonstrate the benefits of balanced health and welfare programs, exercise responsibility for positive leadership. "The temper of the times tingles with action . . . Public attention is high on health and welfare; Great Society programs have revived lay leader interest in preserving and strengthening voluntary agency programs . . .

"The United Way is the 'best buy' for the philanthropic dollar. It saves contributors' money. It makes the best use of volunteers' time. For each dollar contributed to the United Fund, the agencies provide three dollars worth of services. It stretches each gift to help more people and enrich more lives. Voluntary agencies are an example of the free enterprise system at work in the health and welfare field." [7]

The intensification of urban problems and the steady growth of federal activity was causing the voluntary sector to reassess its contributions and role. UCFCA, as spokesman for the largest voluntary effort, was especially aware of the need for viability in governmental-voluntary relations. Out of this concern, a *Statement of Consensus on Government and the Voluntary Sector in Health and Welfare* was developed to formalize the complementary, rather than competitive, nature of health and welfare efforts. It called for a total mobilization of our society and noted that "there is a place for everyone" in such efforts. The Statement, released on September 27, predicted an expanding role for voluntary organizations and their leaders, and urged close liaison between the federal government and such agencies as the National Social Welfare Assembly, National Health Council, and UCFCA.

The leadership role which the voluntary sector could play in "mounting a joint attack by governmental and voluntary agencies on the basic social disorders" was stressed, and government was reminded of the need to consider the "strengths of existing programs of voluntary agencies."

Four Cabinet members and the head of OEO sub-

In this pastoral setting more than 16,000 Volunteer Campaign Leaders gained knowledge and inspiration for their responsibilities as United Way campaign chairmen in annual spring conferences from 1951 to 1966 at Sugar Camp, Dayton, Ohio, as guests of the National Cash Register Company. The spring "cram sessions" were started by NCR Board Chairman Stanley C. Allyn when he was President of United Community Funds and Councils of America.

178

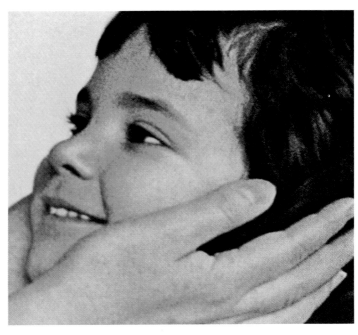

This photograph by Jack Fleming of Portland, Oregon, was used to illustrate the national poster of 1965.

This prize-winning Cleveland Community Chest photograph by Donato Leo was the 1966 national poster.

scribed to the statement: John T. Connor, Secretary of Commerce; W. Willard Wirtz, Secretary of Labor; John W. Gardner, Secretary of Health, Education, and Welfare; Robert C. Weaver, Secretary of Housing and Urban Development; and R. Sargent Shriver, director of the Office of Economic Opportunity. UCFCA President Joseph A. Beirne called it, "not just a treaty between bureaucrats; it is a solemn pledge among men of responsibility in government, business and labor to work together collectively and individually, on America's most important social welfare problems."

Vice President Hubert H. Humphrey again stressed the importance of voluntary activity when he addressed the opening campaign meeting in Allentown, Pa. "I never have seen any basic conflict between the work a government seeks to do and the work that needs to be done by individuals. Government at its best is impersonal; it has to be. Government even at its best is burdened with a degree of overlapping and bureaucracy because of the very nature of our work. There is no way to escape it. But in a voluntary program such as this, you get so much out of each dollar of giving for those who need the gift, but more importantly you get something for yourselves." [8]

In Congress, the Demonstration Cities Act squeaked through the 89th Congress. Designed to cure or eradicate urban blight, it provided for incentive grants to encourage comprehensive metropolitan health planning, rent supplements, and funding to improve housing conditions for low-income families, and to expand job opportunities, thereby reducing dependence on welfare payments. At the same time a bill to extend unemployment compensation to employees of charitable organizations failed to pass, because House and Senate conferees could not agree on adoption of federal standards. UCFCA produced a manual for members, *Guidelines for the Model Neighborhoods Program*, showing ways local Councils could become involved in model neighborhood planning.

Passed during 1965, the Older Americans Act resulted in 26 state grants during 1966, four of them sponsored by Councils or affiliated Volunteer Bureaus. Whereas Councils had often been by-passed in previous years when grants were made, they were now receiving a greater share. The San Francisco Bay Area Council received so many grants that it adopted a policy statement in the fall of 1966 defining criteria for acceptance of planning grants. During the past four years it had received grants valued at $4,262,069, and was then

Twenty years of voluntary advertising service to the United Way by Batten, Barton, Durstine & Osborn, Inc., was lauded by The Advertising Council in 1966 as its President Robert P. Keim (right) presents award to Chairman of the Board of BBDO, Charles H. Brower (center), and 1969 United Way National Campaign Chairman, as Harold W. Olsen, BBDO Vice President and Art Director shows his gratification.

at work on 33 grant-financed projects.

While the government was expanding its support of welfare activities throughout the nation, it was also increasing its support for health research and related health needs, growing from an estimated $27 million in 1947 to $1,364 million in 1966, according to the National Information Bureau. In the voluntary health field, UCFCA continued its efforts to reach an understanding with two national agencies—American Heart Association and American Cancer Society—regarding United Way participation. While they agreed to the desirability of fewer separate specialized campaigns, both organizations continued to prefer separate drives.

Recognizing the need for coordination of health services on the community level, a new private corporation, the National Commission on Community Health Services, was established under sponsorship of the American Public Health Association and the National Health Council. The Commission's report, made after an intensive four-year nationwide study, recommended "that communities by deliberate planning develop patterns of comprehensive health services of optimum quality and assure their availability, accessibility, and acceptability to all." Marion B. Folson, former Secretary of Health, Education, and Welfare, was chairman of the 32-member citizen group. [9]

A fund-raising analysis of total funds raised by United Way campaigns during the past 13 years was released in 1966, showing that the total had increased from $241.7 million in 1953 to $503 million for 1966. This corresponded to an increase in disposable personal income from $238.7 billion to $465.3 billion. Disposable personal income is defined by the U.S. Department of Commerce as including wage and salary disbursements, other labor income, proprietors' income, rental income of persons, dividends, personal interest income, and transfer payments (OASI, Unemployment Compensation, Veterans Benefits, and other) less deductions for personal tax and non-tax payments to general government.

Further analysis revealed that the amount raised by all United Community Campaigns increased at a faster rate than did disposable personal income up to about 1960. This was primarily the result of inclusion of new agencies in the campaigns, especially Red Cross.

Between 1960 and 1966, amounts raised by all federated campaigns increased at about the same rate as campaigns not including Red Cross, and at about the same rate as disposable personal income.

Analysis of firm gift performance to United Community Campaigns revealed that prior to 1956 firm gifts accounted for approximately 40% of the total raised by United Campaigns. Since 1955 that percentage decreased to 31.2% of the total raised, while the amounts received increased by $74,363,000 or 61.6%.

Non-firm gifts closely followed changes in disposable personal income. The percentage received increased from 60% of the total raised in 1955 to 68.8% in 1966. In dollars this amounted to an increase of $249,064,619.

Compiled in a booklet entitled *Trends in Giving 1966,* the information also included detailed summaries of campaign performance in various cities, as well as a summary of trade group contributions, showing the number of firms in each group, number of employees, and percent of employees contributing.

The public relations program of UCFCA had received national recognition before, but in 1966 it earned yet another honor when the Institute of Outdoor Advertising selected the 1966 United Way poster as a winner. The development of national posters over the years has been the result of preference polls among members, and the contribution of Batten, Barton, Durstine and Osborn, Inc., the advertising agency which had been volunteering its expert services to UCFCA for the past 20 years. The commercial value of time and space contributed nationally by network radio, T.V., and magazines during the 1966 campaigns rose to $16 million.

During the "long hot summer" riots broke out in many cities throughout the nation. Omaha, Nebraska was not unprepared. A month prior to the Fourth of July weekend when racial rioting and looting took place, United Community Services initiated a crash program of summer neighborhood services. The UCS board allocated $17,500 as seed money for a program which involved member agencies and representatives of the Parks and Recreation Department, State Employment Service, Urban League, and other interested groups. Among the projects undertaken were employment of a "blue ribbon" committee to study long-range needs of the inner-city area; special neighborhood employment service (by August 5 more than 300 had been placed); establishment of an extension Volunteer Bureau office; initiation of basketball clinics, dances, and other recreational activities. UCS Director Joseph E. Klug said, "We're not fooling ourselves that these things are going to solve the basic problems, but they should give us some valuable experience as well as vital communication with both the leadership and young people on the Near North Side upon which more fundamental long-range programs can be developed." [10]

Sweeping changes were brought about in the National Social Welfare Assembly when, during the December annual meeting, its membership approved recommendations of a study which had been authorized in 1964 and begun in 1965. Because of the pervasive problems of society then being recognized in both the voluntary and governmental sectors, the Assembly had felt there was great need for a revitalized, more incisive, and broader-based attack on critical social issues. Though the Assembly had undertaken reevaluations before, this was the most comprehensive ever attempted. The study committee of eighteen outstanding citizen leaders was aided by a well-qualified management consultant firm.

Changes brought about as a result of the study included a broadening of purpose and scope to encompass other fields in addition to those of social welfare; changing the corporate membership to consist of 300 individuals serving in their own right (compared with membership composed of 3/5 representatives of national governmental and voluntary organizations and two-fifths citizens at large); opening associate status to state, regional, and local planning bodies and to all governmental and voluntary organizations concerned with the preservation and development of human resources.

The proposed relationship of the new Assembly to UCFCA was described by Mrs. H. M. Rozendaal, vice chairman of the study committee, as "very much as the present with one exception. As this new organization moves more widely into planning, UCFCA may concentrate more on the techniques of fund raising, planning, and strengthening organizational work . . . National planning involving wider fields that are not necessarily so technical and not involved in actual procedural matters would be done by the reorganized Assembly. I see no conflict whatsoever between the two." [11]

C. F. McNeil, former executive director of the Health and Welfare Council of Philadelphia, who had become director of the Assembly earlier that year said, "There is no question as to the overriding need in this land of ours today for a national voluntary instrument devoted to social policy, a central point of strategy, of intelligence, and action. And there is no question as to the need for increased citizen involvement and participation." [12]

The following year the organization's name was changed to National Assembly for Social Policy and Development, reflecting the Assembly's concern with national social policy as well as with the organization and operation of social programs.

1967

With a new awareness of the serious health and welfare problems facing a large segment of the American population, the nation mobilized for its expanded war against social ills and poverty. Many ramifications were felt in the voluntary sector, and the United Way, which had begun an extensive study of voluntarism and urban living in 1966, continued to assess its role in the community and the nation.

"A combination of many community forces is needed to raise the quality of life in urban America—particularly in the ghettos," UCFCA President Joseph Beirne pointed out. "No single organization can do it all. United Funds and Community Councils should and must, however, give leadership to all community efforts to bring the disadvantaged into the mainstream of American life . . .

"A major challenge to the United Way is to increase

C. W. "Tex" Cook, Chairman and Chief Executive of General Foods Corporation and United Way National Campaign Chairman, entertains Danny Thomas with a United Way story at 1967 Beverly Hills meeting of West Coast Communications Committee.

the amount of voluntary funds available and the productivity of the services supported . . . A second major challenge for our movement is to keep Funds and Councils properly related and pertinent to the problems of the day . . . The third pressing and always somewhat vexing problem is how to keep the initiative in the solution of the multiple appeals problem with the United Fund . . . Local action rather than national level negotiation will provide the answer to this problem . . . Our fourth challenge is to preserve the principles of community budgeting and efficiency in fund raising . . . The final challenge faced by the United Way is to find the appropriate role for our Community Health and Welfare Councils." [13]

Councils must take a more aggressive part in community planning, it was emphasized during the "Million and Over" Conference in St. Charles, Illinois. Owen R. Davison, executive director of the Philadelphia Health and Welfare Council, said that Councils had not been sufficiently involved in controversial issues, or willing to take some of the risks and to face the criticism which is inevitable when one takes sides aggressively on sharply drawn issues. He cited recent instances in which Councils in large cities had taken such positions and "lived to tell about them."

With the creation of separate planning organizations directed toward resolution of specific problems or needs and stress on non-social service systems for planning to meet health and welfare needs, local Councils "have had to cope with the problem of fractionated community planning, reassess their role, and come to grips with what should constitute their community overview planning function" said UCFCA Vice President Harry T. Sealy of Cleveland, chairman of the Community Planning Advisory Council.[14]

Many local communities were undertaking voluntarism studies of their own, as in Philadelphia where the United Fund approved a statement that "Voluntarism may become obsolete unless it spells out its mission in a definite way and takes appropriate action to implement that mission." [15]

In Westchester County, N.Y. an extensive study was made, including a consumer survey, to learn what contributors felt was the appropriate role of voluntary agencies. In Saskatchewan, Canada, the Council studied voluntary-municipal responsibilities for social welfare, and in Wilmington, Delaware the United Community

Fund defined UCF responsibilities. Detroit's UCS produced a position statement clarifying the constitutional right of citizens to organize, to petition on behalf of their needs, to freely choose services. It described the need for voluntary services in those areas where the government gave inadequate attention, and pointed out that all governmental health and welfare services had developed out of the initial efforts of the voluntary community.

While the implications of government programs were being felt on the local level, there was growing emphasis on the state's part as well. In many instances the state now served as liaison between the federal government and the community. Applications of many sections of the Economic Opportunity Act were determined at the state level. The need for better citizen planning at the state level now became acute, and several statewide planning organizations became more active. UCFCA, through a state planning subcommittee of the Community Planning Advisory Council, provided supporting services for state groups.

A policy statement of the Michigan Welfare League said, "In the last analysis, voluntary planning may well be the most vital aspect of the entire voluntary sector, since we find public programs assuming an increasing

Walter H. Wheeler, Jr., (left), Chairman of the Board, Pitney-Bowes Company, and C. W. Cook (right), National Chairman, United Community Campaigns of America, tell the United Way story to Albert L. Cole, Readers Digest, *at meeting of national magazine publishers in New York, April 13, 1967.*

proportion of those direct services traditionally provided by the private agencies. We must look to voluntary planning not because of its resources, which cannot match those of the public, but because of its comparative freedom, its potential for creativity, and its ability to pose alternatives for the public sector to consider." [16]

Because many misunderstandings had developed between Councils and local Community Action programs, local Council and CAP executives met in June to review War on Poverty experiences. Councils said they felt planning, coordination and development could be better carried out if administration of direct services was not done by the planning organization. They admitted trouble relating to CAP groups which "raise hell with community leaders one day, then invite them to sit around the table the next and do constructive planning."

CAP groups, on the other hand, doubted Councils could be part of social change because they often rigidly maintained traditional services. Some agencies refused OEO projects and were afraid to take risks to help the poor. Several CAPs said they "would be glad to use Councils but when we are confronted with a problem we can't wait for Councils to do long-range planning."

Agreement was reached, however, that local planning should replace federal initiatives, that there was need for good communication, pooling of data, and more long-range and less crash planning.[17]

Several workshops, jointly sponsored by UCFCA, OEO and the new National Association of Community Development (whose membership was primarily CAP staff), were held during 1967, and a special subcommittee was appointed to work out a Statement of Consensus. UCFCA received a $75,502 grant from OEO for a joint training effort to review War on Poverty experiences. Its overall goal was to bring about more effective working relationships between Community Action Programs and local Funds and Councils in accomplishing a task to which they were mutually committed: better and more effective planning and delivery of services to the poor. Seven institutes were held during the following year, with 444 CAP, Fund and Council executives from 199 cities across the country attending. Of the 100 largest cities, 73 were represented.

Workshops were also held to keep local Council staff abreast of developments in the Model Cities pro-

National Campaign Chairman C. W. Cook (left) shows 1967 Publishers Kit to C. E. Wilson, 1950 National Campaign Chairman.

gram. By May 1, applications from 194 cities for Model Cities planning grants were received by the U.S. Department of Housing and Urban Development. Of the 63 chosen, Councils in 54 had assisted in preparing applications. In December, UCFCA co-sponsored a meeting for Council executives in participating cities.

Council involvement in newer governmental activities such as the Poverty Program, Model Cities program, comprehensive health planning, Medicare, and other extensions of Social Security were now estimated to require approximately 50% of staff time.

While new programs were being put into effect, there was growing questioning of public assistance programs. Speaking during the 10th annual meeting of the Harrisburg, Pa. Council, Rita D. Kaunitz, Ph.D., an affiliate of the American Institute of Planners, said much of the $5 billion spent each year in public assistance is not used wisely. In New York, she pointed out, $7 million per year was spent on 600,000 relief clients, 80% of whom were mothers and children lacking a father. Many of the mothers could, and wanted to, go to work but could not because of the lack of day care centers.[18]

A *New York Times* article reported a welfare study which revealed that the commonly held notion that "many millions" on welfare are loafers capable of working was dispelled by showing that "less than one percent of the 7.3 million Americans on public welfare are capable of getting off the relief rolls and going to work." [19]

Joseph A. Beirne (right), national United Way president, with Dr. George B. Plain, South Bend, Ind., surgeon and national United Way board member. Dr. Plain led the volunteer effort in the formation of local and national United Way health policies and programs throughout the 1960's.

Tulsa, Oklahoma: UCFCA Board Member Samuel P. Goddard, Jr., a former governor of Arizona, is made an honorary chief of the Acoma Indian tribe, in recognition of his interest in and support of the United Way. In making the presentation of the symbolic Indian headdress at the Southwest Regional Conference, Chief Wolf Robe praised Governor Goddard for his "Heap Big Job," and explained that his Indian name may be translated as "Chief U Tell 'em." A warrior of the Acoma tribe (right) witnessed the ceremony and presented native dances at the Conference.

Radical revision of public assistance programs was recommended by a federally appointed Advisory Council on Public Welfare. To review these recommendations, UCFCA appointed a Committee on Public Welfare Policy. This committee was charged with looking at alternate plans of income maintenance, such as guaranteed annual income, reverse income tax, guaranteed employment by the federal government, and others.

As summer riots spread across the nation, bringing death, destruction, fear and turmoil, dozens of United Way agencies sprang into action. In all communities struck by riots, the Red Cross and Salvation Army went to work, providing food, clothing and shelter. In Detroit, an emergency blood donor program was set up, along with special services by the YMCA, Urban League, and Neighborhood Service Organization. United Community Services established "Operation Find," a telephone registry for locating displaced persons. The Detroit United Foundation established a $1 million fund for agencies to cover emergency expenditures. In Cincinnati, a $15,000 campership fund was established for ghetto youngsters, and the Council took part in employment planning. During its annual campaign the United Bay Area Crusade in San Francisco set aside $100,000 for serving slum youth, and an Ad Hoc Committee on Community Preparedness recommended 38 projects in 22 agencies including day camps, arts and crafts classes, tutoring and job training. It was estimated that 16,000 children from 8 to 20 years of age would be served. Throughout the nation, one million unemployed youths found summer jobs through the President's Council on Youth Opportunity. In many cases, local Councils aided in finding these jobs.

While the old familiar health agency dilemma continued as before, more communities, such as Philadelphia, Dayton, and Beaumont, Texas, were finding a solution to the go-it-alone health appeals which would not agree to united fund raising. These cities created local health foundations. Some 215 communities were members and program participants of United Health Foundations Inc., and the number of local health foundations grew to 38 during 1967. Since 1962, UHF on its own raised and allocated more than $1 million for medical and health research. The total raised and allocated for this purpose during the same period by UHF and local communities combined was approximately $14 million. Of the total $11,675,000,000 expended

(Left to right) James M. Roche, President, General Motors Corporation; Arjay R. Miller, President, Ford Motor Company; Walter C. Laidlaw, Executive Vice President, United Foundation of Metropolitan Detroit; and Virgil A. Boyd, President of Chrysler Corporation meet to make plans for the year-round Detroit United Way program in 1967.

during 1967 for health by voluntary philanthropy and government, 87.5% was spent by government.

The National Information Bureau compared 1967 and 1963 campaign income for several national health agencies. Among the agencies listed, the following were of special interest:

Organization	1967 Campaign Income	Compared With 1963		% for Research in 1967
American Cancer Society	$41,071,000	up	24%	36% est.
American Heart Association	29,904,000	up	22%	31%
Arthritis Foundation	5,300,000	up	37%	23% est.
National Foundation	22,193,000	down	3%	10%
Planned Parenthood Federation	11,250,000	up	153%	6% est.
United Cerebral Palsy	12,400,000	up	18%	6%* est.

*National headquarters only

The total for 13 national health agencies was $200,-652,000 raised, an increase of 17% over 1963. Local United Way campaigns in 1966 raised $656,000,000 for 1967, an increase of 34%.[20]

A report *Voluntary Health Programs—The Case for Change* was published during 1967 following a year-long study by a special UCFCA committee. It urged local United Funds and Councils to initiate and support local community efforts to merge and consolidate voluntary health agencies, to promote a comprehensive health agency to carry out broad-scale community programs, to extend local autonomy, and to speed up development of new and pioneering services. It pointed out that "the present organizational pattern is no longer consistent either with current needs or the future role of voluntary health agencies. Substantial reorganization and consolidation of voluntary health agencies and programs should take place both locally and nationally. United Funds and Health and Welfare Councils should initiate and actively promote this reorganization . . . National programs should stem from local needs that can be met only through national activity. National agencies should be so organized that they can function effectively at the community level when a local program in their field is needed . . . The total voluntary health program should be organized so that it can develop services to meet new needs and opportunities in the health field. It should be able to shift quickly as new problems arise, while providing adequately for maintenance and growth of existing services." [21]

American Cancer Society and the National Foundation continued to prohibit their local units from participating in United Funds and the number of American Heart Association chapters participating leveled off at 262. Rather sizeable increases occurred in the number of other specialized disease agencies joining United Funds, however, for example:

	1958	1967
National Association for Mental Health	428	754
National Association for Retarded Children	186	610
United Cerebral Palsy Association	268	509
Arthritis and Rheumatism Foundation	234	459

United Way statistics showed that in 1967 the United Way helped a total of 27,500,000 families; 8½ million volunteers were at work; 32,800,000 contributed to the United Way; and 31,300 agencies were members. Expenditures of United Way dollars were as follows:

Administration	3.3%
Campaign	4.3
Health & Welfare Planning	3.1
Special needs (studies)	3.0
Red Cross	13.4
Health	15.2
Youth and Recreation	28.7
Family and Child Care	29.0

United Way campaigns during 1967 resulted in more than $700,000,000 raised despite problems of civil disturbance, work stoppages, and general unrest. The UCFCA public relations program resulted in ads worth $829,463 in 481 magazines, with total circula-

New York Governor, Nelson Rockefeller, speaker at the first United Way Annual Trustees Meeting, November 30, 1967, with (right) Joseph A. Beirne, President, United Community Funds and Councils of America, and Mrs. Rockefeller.

tion of 440 million. TV spots resulted in 2.3 billion home impressions worth $13.3 million at commercial rates. Only the National Safety Council and U.S. Savings Bonds, both year-round appeals, were given more free time.

Twenty-five years of labor participation in the United Way were marked during 1967. Beginning during World War II, organized labor and UCFCA had cooperated in the National War Fund and the CIO War Relief Committee. By 1965, local United Funds and Community Chests employed 130 labor staff representatives, and in 1967, AFL-CIO leaders estimated that some 75,000 representatives of organized labor were serving on boards of Funds, Councils and member agencies.

One of the major activities of UCFCA throughout its history had been sponsorship of conferences at which both professionals and volunteers could exchange information and discuss topics of mutual concern. As the number of specialized and regional conferences grew, UCFCA staff found itself devoting more and more of its time and income to these conferences. At the same time, questions were being raised as to whether they were meeting needs in the most satisfactory manner. A special committee accordingly was formed in 1966 to study the situation and make recommendations. Its proposals were accepted in 1967.

Under the new arrangement, which took effect immediately, UCFCA would hold an Annual Meeting of one day's duration with official participants, consisting of one volunteer from each Fund and Council, to be known as Trustees; plus one professional to be known as a UCFCA Associate. Trustees were the voting representatives, though Associates were invited to all annual and special meetings of the Trustees. The first such meeting was held on November 30, 1967 in New York City. Two Advisory Councils were established among the Trustees and Associates, the United Fund Advisory Council and Community Planning Advisory Council.

An effort had been made to cover the special interest of both professionals and volunteers at Biennial Conferences in the past. The new plan called for each conference to focus on one or the other. For volunteers: Annual Campaign Leaders Conference; Citizens Conference on Community Planning; and the Budget Leaders Conference. In addition UCFCA encouraged state associations to hold conferences for small communities in their areas.

For the professionals there were now a biennial United Way Staff Training Conference in the even-numbered years, plus four regional conferences in odd-numbered years.

In preparation for the first meeting of UCFCA Trustees and Associates, a review of the present state and potential future of the United Way movement, entitled *Backdrop and Breakthrough* was compiled and distributed to each member Fund and Council or United Community Service.

During this meeting, the Trustees discussed and took action on a total of six resolutions. The first urged national agencies and local members to comply with the Accounting and Financial Reporting standards produced by the National Health Council and National Social Welfare Assembly. The second urged local Funds and Councils to strive for greater public recognition and support, and to search for more effective methods of intercommunication. The third urged reorganization of the voluntary health field to include mergers and consolidation of agencies, promotion of local comprehensive health services, development of efficient administration and avoidance of duplication and competition, extension of local autonomy, and development of new and pioneering services.

The fourth resolution placed UCFCA on record as not approving the Combined Federal Campaign program as then constituted, urging local option and reaffirming the importance of sound budgeting and allocation of funds. During 1967, 137 local communities participated in the CFC program.

The fifth resolution pointed up the need for a full mobilization of all resources to fight growing social ills with need for concerned and enlightened participation of local citizen leaders, and the challenge to and obligation of Councils to provide leadership and direction in application of federal resources.

The sixth and final resolution stressed the need for a strong, well-organized citizen voice in the field of health and welfare at the national level and in each state, with clear channels of collaboration between local Councils and both national and state associations.

Accelerated change in almost every aspect of life was being recognized throughout the nation. For United Funds such change meant looking ahead and appraising their future direction. UCFCA accordingly took a look ahead, and during 1967 published *Projections for*

Quebec City, Canada: The annual Quebec Winter Carnival ended this year on the opening day of the 1967 National Biennial Conference of Community Funds and Councils of Canada, so Bonhomme Carnaval, who symbolizes the spirit of the festival, stayed on and joined the receiving line at a city hall reception. L. to r.: Marcel Fortier, President, Conseil des oeuvres et du Bienetre de Quebec; Herbert R. Balls, Chairman, Community Funds and Councils of Canada; Hon. Mr. Justice Paul Lesage (Chairman of the Conference) and Mrs. Lesage; Bonhomme Carnaval; Mrs. Balls; and His Worship Mayor Gilles Lamontagne of Quebec.

Toronto, Ontario: Speakers at a United Appeal Inter-Faith Women's Rally held in spring, 1967: Mrs. Frank Taylor, Chairman-Elect of the Inter-Faith Women's Committee, who introduced Sister Mary Andrew Hartmann, a member of the Grey Sisters of the Immaculate Conception, and an Associate Professor of Psychology at the University of Ottawa; and 1967 Campaign Chairman H. A. (Hank) Brundage, Vice President-Finance, The Goodyear Tire and Rubber Co. of Canada. The 1,000 women in the audience, representing 12 different faiths, were asked to be goodwill ambassadors, working for the community as "people helping people" in the $10.5 million campaign, which opened September 27.

the Seventies, a portrait of the American economy in 1975 and the new challenges and promises for united fund raising. Among the topics covered were population and other census predictions; employment, productivity, gross national product, and other economic factors; a look at business in public affairs; the prospects of more areawide United Funds; management ingredients for effective agency performance; and basic local leadership decisions affecting future campaigns.

"In summary, what may we expect of United Funds by the year 1975? A minimum of $1.06 billion raised

President Johnson autographs the 1968 United Way campaign poster for National Campaign Chairman, Orville Beal.

in the United Fund campaigns; corporate giving of $335 million and individual giving of $725 million; twenty-five areawide United Funds each raising $10 million or more in the largest metropolitan areas; merger of separate funds into single areawide or regional structures in most marketing areas; more sophisticated fund raising, directed at a richer and better educated public; the transfer of those programs which are properly the responsibility of tax-supported agencies; more use of scientific and systematic analysis in determining needs and priorities for services; more functional budgeting; consolidation of services for greater efficiency and flexibility; higher quality and more individualized services to all segments of the community; more public funds being spent through the medium of United Fund agencies; local programs to strengthen United Funds by greater inclusiveness, by closing the "needs gap," and by providing uncommitted funds to meet new needs; leadership of health and welfare services in the private sector and ombudsman for the public sector." [22]

The publication was one of the most popular ever produced by UCFCA.

NOTES

Chapter 15

1. "Shriver Stresses Importance of United Way in War on Poverty," *Community,* UCFCA, July-August 1965, p. 19.

2. "Vice Presidential Praise for the Role of Voluntary Agencies," *Community,* UCFCA, September-October 1965, p. 19.

3. *Local Developments,* Vol. 1, No. 3, UCFCA, May 1965.

4. *Executive Newsletter,* UCFCA, May 17, 1965.

5. Henry A. Spears, "Making Everyone Equal Partners in the Campaign," *Community,* UCFCA, July-August 1966, pp. 8-9.

6. Paul R. Cherney, "The Abandoned Children of Asia," *Community,* UCFCA, September-October, 1965, pp. 12-14.

7. "The 1966 United Way Campaigns and the Great Society," UCFCA, July 19, 1966.

8. Vice President Hubert H. Humphrey, "The Promise of America," *Community,* UCFCA, November-December, 1966, pp. 5-7.

9. Harold A. James, "Comprehensive Personal Health Services," *Community,* UCFCA, July-August 1967, p. 4.

10. *Citizen Planning,* UCFCA, August 1966.

11. *Proceedings, 1966 Annual Meeting,* National Social Welfare Assembly, pp. 17-19.

12. *Ibid.,* pp. 20-22.

13. Joseph A. Beirne, "The State of the United Way," *Community,* UCFCA, January-February 1968, pp. 3-6.

14. Harry T. Sealy, "Community Planning Activities of UCFCA," *Community,* UCFCA, January-February 1968, pp. 17-18.

15. "Focus: Voluntarism Project," No. 2, UCFCA, April 1967.

16. *Citizen Planning,* UCFCA, April 1967.

17. *Newer Federal Programs,* UCFCA, July 1967.

18. Rita D. Kaunitz, "The Challenges to the Urban Professions," *Community,* UCFCA, September-October 1967, pp. 15-18.

19. *Newer Federal Programs,* UCFCA, July 1967.

20. "Tabulation V," National Information Bureau, February 1968.

21. *Voluntary Health Programs — The Case for Change,* UCFCA, January 1967, pp. 7-8.

22. *Projections for the Seventies,* UCFCA, November 1967.

16

WHICH WAY...
UNITED WAY :1968-1969

The closing years of the turbulent sixties found the United Way confronted with critical problems of prime magnitude.

Originally designed to reduce annoyance and waste among competing charitable drives, the United Way was finding its traditional function becoming more complex. Through the years it had promoted citizen budget committees to study and approve agency budgets, had reduced fund-raising costs, and had effected economies in agency operations. Now a new dimension was to be added. Gigantic government expenditures in health and welfare during recent years had caused voluntary agencies to question their programs and support, and there was growing pressure for change in community allocations.

Such pressure might require United Funds to move in two directions, UCFCA predicted. One, to develop a more problem-oriented budgeting process placing greater emphasis on agency responsiveness to changing community problems and less weight on allocations of previous years. The second, to include in United Fund goals, over and above the amounts allocated to established agency programs, uncommitted funds for innovative programs, experimentation, local matching of federal project funds, and ultimate community pick-up of successful government demonstrations. In whatever direction budgeting should move, it would of course continue to uphold its long-time principles of economy and coordination.[1]

To examine the role of voluntarism on this issue, more than 160 United Way volunteers and professionals participated in the First Biennial Budget Leaders Conference in Miami Beach, January 9-11, 1968. Keynote speaker Senator Abraham Ribicoff of Connecticut said, "No organization, regardless of its size, can survive as an important community agency if it does not address itself to the major public business . . . We can no longer fall back upon ignorance of urban problems; we are unwilling to act upon the information we already have. We prefer to devise elaborate theories of urban behavior and develop techniques of systems analysis, as if stating the plans were equal to solving the problems. We engage in national debates about what caused riots when we have mountains of evidence in our central cities about severe unemployment, the low quality of the public schools, the number of substandard housing units, the high crime rates, and the poor health care." [2]

In the closing general session, UCFCA Vice President Samuel P. Goddard, Jr., a former governor of Arizona, said, "We must find ways to extend our services to make them more available, to increase quantity without sacrificing quality. It becomes of extreme importance that the story of community service be told to open the heart and pocketbooks of our local communities in the name of volunteer service." [3]

Kenneth L. Block, a vice president of A. T. Kearney and Company, pointed out that "the challenge is to assure the adequacy of future community support for voluntary welfare programs . . . In the past, social

Eliot Batchelder

planning has not been able to reconcile its advocacy for directive policy with its faith in the vitality of an undirected, individualistic, market-oriented society." [4]

While obtaining adequate financial support for new and innovative community programs was presenting a challenge to the United Way, some observers felt that the very future of voluntary effort itself was being challenged. Two years before, UCFCA had begun a Voluntarism Project to determine the proper role for United Way voluntary agencies. Early in January, 1968, an interim report was published.

The real issue confronting voluntary agencies, the report declared, was the effective application of voluntary effort. Among the factors impeding voluntary agencies were fragmentation of efforts, too many specialized agencies, removal of volunteers from direct participation, lack of innovation, and lack of voluntary agency response to the opportunity for identifying weak spots in the social welfare system and advancing proposals for remedial action. Suggestions were made for ways agencies could achieve their full potential and implement their ideas.

Governmental and voluntary agencies, with common concerns and objectives, must become working partners while voluntary agencies are permitted to function as constructive critics of government. The report also concluded that the realistic issue is not *whether* but

Walter H. Wheeler, Jr., President, United Community Funds and Councils of America, seeks support for United Way in 1968 from both sides of the Senate.(Left)Republican Senator Jacob K. Javits, New York,and (right) Democratic Connecticut Senator Abraham Ribicoff.

192

Philadelphia: To kick off the United Fund Torch Drive, a 30-foot torch was lighted in front of Independence Hall by representatives of two UF agencies—Earl Harris (left, front row), of the West Philadelphia Boys' Club, and Ronald Miraflor (right, front row), from the Big Brother Boys' Club. Also at the ceremony were Mayor James H. J. Tate (left, rear), General Chairman G. Stockton Strawbridge and Elaine Hemighaus, Miss United Fund Torch. The Torch, used first by Detroit in 1949 was a popular symbol used by some 50 United Way campaigns in the late 1950's and through the 1960's.

under what conditions federal funding can be used without neutralizing the independence of voluntary agencies, and without committing the voluntary sector to filling gaps, when and if federal support is curtailed.

United Funds were urged to refine their budgeting operations, support research and development, and give high priority to planning and action programs. The United Way has a stewardship responsibility, the report declared, and any agency supported by the community is accountable to that community. Enlightened leadership in both agencies and the Fund is necessary, along with a willingness to forego individual agency identification. "The United Fund must be more than a col-

lection device to preserve the status quo . . . It must be a spokesman for social goals and take initiative in making cooperation with government a reality. Voluntarism has the vitality and capacity to grow to new proportions and dimensions." [5]

While the Voluntarism Project interim report thus defined the role of voluntarism, the importance of united fund-raising was stressed by UCFCA Executive Director Lyman Ford. Speaking to representatives from 35 national agencies with local units participating in local United Funds, he pointed out the way united fund-raising mobilizes citizens to meet community needs through voluntary agencies. In meeting needs, the United Way must adequately finance a system of voluntary services, plan a coordinated community program, make judgments as to priorities and relative needs, and pay attention to collective as well as individual agency efficiency and effectiveness, he said. [6]

President Johnson spoke to Congress in March on "Health and America," and pointed out many of the nation's health needs and called for a budget increase to help meet these needs. He also pointed out, "In our drive toward a healthier America, Federal programs and Federal dollars have an important role to play. But they cannot do the job alone. An even larger role belongs to state and local government, and to the private enterprise system of our nation." He called upon various health organizations, voluntary civic associations, charities, and church groups to join this effort, and presented suggestions for a 12-point volunteer effort to build a healthier America. [7]

Guichard Parris and Mary Hobbs Fry, retiring Public Relations Directors of the National Urban League and National Travelers Aid Association respectively, were honored at the June 1968 meeting of UCFCA's Public Relations Advisory Council of which they were members.

This bronze medallion, Community Service Award was presented to volunteers for "distinguished national service" as the highest honor of the national association from 1958 to 1968.

George Romney, Secretary of HUD, (left), shown chatting with Bayard Ewing, then Chairman of the Executive Committee of UCFCA, was speaker at the 1969 Annual Meeting of Trustees, UCFCA, in New York.

Walter H. Wheeler, Jr., President, United Community Funds and Councils of America, pins United Way button on President Richard M. Nixon's lapel on occasion of the 1969 annual United Way Presidential Broadcast.

The health efforts of local consolidated health agencies were the major topic during the Second United Way Health Conference in February 1968 sponsored by UCFCA, United Health Foundations, Inc. and the National Sponsors' Committee for the United Way in Health. The first conference had been held in 1964 when the UHF National Leadership Program and National Sponsors' Committee were established. Since then, 12 regional conferences have been held.

Irving A. Duffy, chairman emeritus of the Board of UHF, said voluntary agencies should not attempt to compete with government programs or pretend to be partners because of their differences in size. They should rather assume the purposes of: existence as an independent and objective voice in the health and welfare system; stimulator and innovator of new and needed concepts; and setting an example of personal involvement and dedication.[8]

194

One separate health agency, the National Foundation, was having difficulties with several of its local March of Dimes drives. In St. Petersburg, Florida the Chamber of Commerce disapproved its drive, following a report that the National Foundation spent 40% on fund raising, administration, and other expenses. It also pointed out that the national board hadn't met together for several years. This action was duplicated by Chambers in Fort Worth, Toledo, and Rochester, New York and by the Appeals Review Board of Chemung County, New York.

The National Information Bureau reported that the avalanche of appeals for contributions continued during 1968. One national agency mailed about 10 million letters, enclosing a small piece of merchandise. It exaggerated its accomplishments and falsified its financial report to hide the cost of fund raising, which was 40 cents for each $1.00 contributed. Another national agency which mailed 40 million appeal letters enclosing a small personalized item, spent approximately 80 cents of each dollar for fund raising.[9]

The need for comprehensive health planning, as pointed out during the first national United Way Staff Training Conference at French Lick, Indiana in April[10] was also discussed at the Midwest Regional Workshop on State Planning, co-sponsored by UCFCA, the National Assembly for Social Policy and Development, and the National Association for Statewide Health and Welfare.

Community organization, a branch of social work long associated with the United Way, had been a subject for study in schools of social work for many years. More recently the growing demands for social workers had resulted in rapidly rising enrollments and an even more rapid rise in the percentage of students concentrating on community organization. In 1965 the Council on Social Work Education began a Community Organization Curriculum Development Project under a federal grant. The project was completed in the fall of 1968 and a major document on community organization practice produced, along with a general report and curriculum recommendations.

In September, President Johnson made his fifth and final broadcast launching the United Way campaigns. He was responded to by National Chairman, Orville E. Beal.

The campaigns raised a total of $766,870,879 for 106.6% of the previous year.

National Campaign Chairman Gavin MacBain shows United Way Facts folder to comedian Buddy Hackett who shows his amazement that 36,000 health, welfare and community service agencies share in the funds collected each year in the United Way campaigns. Looking on (left) is J. Neil Reagan, National Media, West Coast Chairman, and (right) William Kirk, member, United Way National Citizens Committee.

Because of changing needs, a study of United Community Funds and Councils of America was authorized during 1968. Three phases of the study, to be conducted during 1969, would be: 1. delineation and agreement on the objectives and role of UCFCA; 2. assessment of the program and activities of UCFCA in the light of the objectives and role determined in the study; 3. review of the organizational, administrative, and financial aspects of UCFCA in view of the findings. A 25-member committee of volunteers and professionals in the United Way movement was named to oversee the study. Bayard Ewing, of Providence, R. I., was chairman.[11]

In December 1968 the Phase I report of the now-designated Voluntarism and Urban Life Project was issued. Merrill Krughoff was director of the project and Irving A. Duffy chairman of the Citizens Committee. By this time a number of other foundations and corporations had joined the Sears Roebuck Foundation in helping finance the operation.

The report was the first product of the program suggested by Ralph Lazarus in his closing address as UCFCA President. The overall purpose of this undertaking was to provide the community leader with practical guidelines to help him apply his time, effort and money in support of health and welfare programs relevant to the needs of the day, and to stimulate action. It sought a fresh appraisal avoiding, insofar as possible, the artificial influence of traditions and habit patterns.

The approach was uncommon in that it started with the needs of people, the reverse of starting with existing agency services and attempting to justify them. The

This picture taken at the 1970 National Urban League Conference shows that Urban League leaders also serve as United Way leaders. James A. Linen (right), President of the Urban League and former national United Way President; Ramon S. Scruggs, (center), Senior Vice President, Urban League and former United Way Board Member; and Whitney M. Young, Jr., Urban League Executive Director and United Way of America Board Member.

procedure was to identify obstacles which prevent attainment of human goals in the urban community and assess programs for their effectiveness and practicality in removing or offsetting these obstacles. The final report, scheduled for publication early in 1971, would be a series of "Community Strategy Outlines" then in the process of being tested with a number of cooperating communities.

In 1969 an intensive effort was made by the national association to stimulate all local United Funds to follow the example of a number of communities that had taken fairly dramatic steps to institute and support new and innovative services related to the so-called domestic crisis. The effort was called the United Voluntary Mobilization. The objectives were stated in a landmark resolution adopted by the UCFCA board in May, before the campaigns and reaffirmed by the membership at the annual meeting in December.[12]

Peat, Marwick, Mitchell and Company were retained by the UCFCA Study Committee and much time and attention of the national association and the field was focused on this project during 1969. The United Way along with all other community institutions was being challenged as to its relevancy and its ability to adjust to rapidly changing conditions. It was most timely to have this searching inquiry in process—the United Way could truthfully say that it was examining itself even as local budget committees and boards were insisting that participating agencies do likewise.

In May, UCFCA Executive Director Lyman Ford anounced his intention to retire not later than June 30, 1970.

Walter H. Wheeler, Jr., Board Chairman of Pitney-Bowes, Inc., gave dynamic national leadership to the movement during 1968 and 1969. He had formerly served as Chairman of United Community Campaigns of America and of the national Corporations Participation Program. His efforts were highly productive in establishing useful working relationships for the United Way Office of Washington Affairs opened in 1969 with Henry Weber as Director.[13]

During 1969 Councils were extremely busy with the near-chaotic conditions which prevailed in many communities. One of the fast-emerging issues was how to bring about the total coalition of community effort which was obviously necessary to the solution of any of the major social problems.

Related to this issue was the UCFCA Coalition Planning Project, partially financed by an OEO grant. Its aim was to discover if any guidelines or principles for overall coalition planning in a local community could be identified out of experience to date.

Lyman S. Ford, Executive Director, United Community Funds and Councils of America, catches a crystal fish as a rewarding recognition of more than a quarter-century of professional service to the national United Way organization. The award was presented at the 1969 Annual Meeting of United Way Trustees.

Five National Chairmen of United Community Campaigns of America meet in reunion at United Way Volunteers Luncheon January 22, 1970 in New York. (Left to right) Walter H. Wheeler, Jr., 1965; Charles E. Wilson, 1950; Gavin MacBain, 1969; Milton C. Mumford, 1966; and Oliver G. Willits, 1960. Carl Rosen Photo.

Pick one to die.
Pick one for jail.
Pick one to waste away.
Pick three for happiness.

Some youngsters find happiness easily. Others need the help and guidance only a trained person can provide, medical attention they cannot afford, love they have been denied. When you decide to give to your United Way, you may change a life. (Magazines carried this United Way message in 1968.)

1967 Photograph by Daniel J. Ransohoff

Daniel J. Ransohoff is inspecting results of one of his photographic shooting sessions, "sometimes I take only 6 or 8 shots to get what I want, other times I take up to 200," he explained. Social worker and teacher as well as photographer his pictures were used for the 1964 and 1967 United Way posters. He is the author of two books, Pictures Tell Your Story and How Cincinnati Helps. He is Special Services Director of the Community Chest and Council, Cincinnati Area.

1969 Poster Photograph by Phoebe Dunn

1968 Poster Photograph by Harold Halma

Mrs. Gerald Schmidt of Worcester, Mass., shows her gratification for being made the recipient of the NEWTON D. BAKER AWARD. Daniel W. Kops, Chairman, National United Way Committee on Community Planning, made the presentation in New York City, December 1969.

United Funds also were feeling the effects of confrontations, polarization of attitudes and community strife. The whole idea of social services operated by the "haves" generally for the benefit of the "have nots" was being questioned. Militant minority and Welfare Rights groups asked for a major voice in allocation and administration of United Way funds and insisted the regular agencies were irrelevant to their needs. On the other hand blue collar workers, the backbone of support in many United Fund communities, threatened boycott if funds were given to some of the new and controversial causes and agencies.

These problems and the higher goals resulted in an aggregate goal achievement of 97.3% in the fall of 1969, one percent less than the year before. However $50,000,000 in additional funds were raised, a larger dollar increase over the previous year than was achieved in 1968.

During August, as the time of the annual national campaign kickoff approached, President Nixon, after repeated requests, declined to make the traditional Presidential Broadcast. Finally, Walter H. Wheeler, Jr., UCCA President, went to the White House at San Clemente, where he refused to leave until the President recorded the annual broadcast, which he did on Labor Day.

The main item of business at the December 1969 annual meeting of UCFCA was a review of the report

Mrs. Charles W. Engelhard, member of the National Women's Committee, United Community Campaigns of America, addresses a meeting of United Way volunteers in New York, January 22, 1970.

Governor Ronald Reagan visits the United Bay Area Crusade 1967 campaign headquarters in San Francisco and pledges his support of the United Way to Loaned Executive William J. Noonan of IBM, on three-month's loan to the campaign, as other loaned executives look on.

of the PMM&Co. consultants and discussion of the issues involved in the Study. The Study Committee, as planned, then took the consultants' report and the record of the annual meeting discussions and prepared the official Study Report. This was approved with minor revisions at a special meeting of the UCFCA Board on January 30, 1970.

While the recommendations of the Study were largely related to the organization and operation of the national association, they reflected the status and future of the entire United Way movement. The report in part had this to say about the "movement":

"The Study Committee recommends that the movement reaffirm its belief in the united voluntary way; in its future role as a viable partner and sometime critic of government; as a spokesman stressing local responsibility and local decision-making as a counterweight to pressures for national centralization; and as the voice of citizens' concern for human beings who are victims of developments keyed to masses rather than individuals. In short, to give national leadership and strength to local operations through initiative and influence and by formulating policies and procedures in areas where a common thrust is wise and practicable.

Nancy Reagan (Mrs. Ronald) served as National Chairman of the Women's Committee, United Community Campaigns of America, from 1969 to 1971.

"Within the framework of local autonomy, more unity of thought and action can and must be developed nationally." [14]

Later in the report six areas of leadership for the national association were identified, which in effect constituted a statement of the major problems facing the movement at this time. They included:

1. The promotion of improved management skills and effectiveness in local Funds, Councils and operating health, welfare and character-building agencies.

2. The further development of techniques for the evaluation of agency effectiveness and the development of priority systems.

3. By research, consensus statement, agency program reviews and better communication and participation, the promotion of more unity and greater discretion in the allocation of local United Way funds.

4. Resolution of relationship problems with national voluntary agencies, national corporations, national and international labor bodies, the Federal Government and other national institutions.

5. In carefully-selected instances, and after a considerable degree of unity has been developed, positions should be taken on issues related to social welfare services, both public and private.

6. The promotion of a more rational pattern of national health and welfare agencies and services. [15]

As the rebellious Sixties drew to a close, the high priority problems facing the United Way were coming into sharp focus.

- It needed a new, comprehensive program of action and services.
- It needed to establish itself as a significant force in the national community.
- It needed a national spokesman for the United Way on issues of common concern.
- It needed superior executive direction.
- It needed volunteer leadership of the highest calibre.

Such a cluster of critical challenges was unprecedented in United Way history. Many wondered, "could the United Way surmount them?"

The attack began with the search for a new chief executive by a Selection Committee headed by board member Harry T. Sealy.

NOTES

Chapter 16

1. Evjen, Rudolph, foreword to article by Roger Thibaudeau, "UGN's Development and Demonstration Fund," *Community,* UCFCA, March-April 1968, p. 3.

2. "The First Biennial Budget Leaders Conference," *Community,* UCFCA, March-April 1968, p. 17.

3. *Ibid.,* p. 18.

4. *Ibid.,* p. 17.

5. "The Voluntarism Project: An Interim Report," *Community,* UCFCA, March-April 1968, p. 16.

6. "Opening Presentation by Lyman S. Ford," National Agency Executives Meeting, March 14, 1968, UCFCA.

7. *New York Times,* March 5, 1968, p. 22.

8. "The Second United Way Health Conference," *Community,* UCFCA, March-April 1968, p. 11.

9. *Wise Giving Bulletin,* National Information Bureau, Spring 1968.

10. *Executive Newsletter,* UCFCA, April 15, 1968.

11. *Executive Newsletter,* UCFCA, September 23, 1968.

12. Minutes, Board of Directors, UCFCA, May 23, 1969.

13. *Executive Newsletter,* December 21, 1968; UCFCA Board of Directors Meeting, December 13, 1968.

14. Organization and Management Study, Report of the Study Committee, 1970, UCFCA, p. 3.

15. *Ibid.,* pp. 4-5.

REBIRTH AND RENEWAL: 1970-1972

Four months of exploration and evaluation, both within and without the social welfare field for a United Way national professional leader, culminated in the recommendation from a group of 75 of a candidate for that position by the Selection Committee to the UCFCA Board of Directors on April 3, 1970, and on that date the appointment of William Aramony was approved, effective as of May 15.

The new National Executive's educational background [1] was broad, with degrees in business administration as well as in social work and community organization. In addition, he had demonstrated his competence in a variety of skills through experience which included work in a family business, social service officer in the Army, surveys for the Federal Government, and executive management of both community planning and united fund raising in several communities. But key to his capability was the dynamic drive and systematic attack with which he moved against the challenges of the job.

In the first two-hundred days of William Aramony's administration, a Rebirth and Renewal process was activated which produced innovation and accomplishment of a scope and depth never before known in United Way history. [2]

Action was taken on each of the 27 recommendations made in the PMM & Co. study.

Prestigious volunteer leadership, newly enrolled, was making United Way policy determination through an improved governance structure.

An effulgent, thirteen-faceted program was launched and in operation.

United Way was emerging as a significant social power in the national community.

The reaction of local communities to the first half-year of the new United Way's performance (as recorded in Chapter 1) was evidenced by their joining in unprecedented support of the national association.

Ground was broken for the new national headquarters of United Way of America at 801 North Fairfax Street in Alexandria, Virginia on April 7, 1971. Presiding at the ceremony for the first building ever to be owned by the national association was the Board of Governors Chairman, Bayard Ewing.

Speakers included Virginia's Lieutenant Governor, J. Sargeant Reynolds; Flaxie M. Pinkett, member, United Way of America Board of Governors; Alexandria's Mayor Charles E. Beatley, Jr.; the Reverend Monsignor Lawrence J. Corcoran, Secretary of the National Conference of Catholic Charities; and William Aramony, National Executive. Among those present were representatives of business, labor and national health and welfare organizations.

Demonstrating that it is good for unity to begin at home, some 900 volunteer leaders met in Chicago from May fourth to the sixth in the first United Way national conference ever to bring together volunteers dealing with all three major United Way functions of planning, campaigning and budgeting.[3]

Secretary of Health, Education and Welfare, and former campaign chairman for the United Way in Boston, Elliot L. Richardson, in commenting on the combining of what had previously been three separate conferences, said "You are to be congratulated for again acting as the knife edge in the social service areas . . . for greater coordination of planning and delivery of needed services is one of this country's most pressing needs.

"The United Way is proof that the spirit of giving, of helping each other, still guides the conscience of this land. And it is that very spirit of compassion and goodwill," he declared, "that will help us meet the challenge of integrating our social services—and close the gap between promise and performance."

In a speech of key significance, penetrating questions were directed toward long-standing policies and procedures of Funds' and Councils' planning and allocating, by Donald S. MacNaughton, Chairman and Chief Executive Officer of Prudential Insurance Company of America. Mr. MacNaughton pointed out that in the face of "tighter dollars, but greater demands . . . old methods may not suffice for the new problems. If we can think of new ways . . . let's experiment with them."

He suggested that, as a new system for allocating funds, local United Ways consider providing to an agency its core cost for administrative and basic services on an annual basis for three to five years, in lieu of annual budget hearings. The agency could supplement its base United Way support through government contracts, fees for services, membership dues, foundation grants, etc. as long as the integrity of the one general community campaign concept was maintained, especially as it affects corporate and employee giving.

Essential to this allocations approach, Mr. MacNaughton said, "There must be . . . a method for determining results (and) evaluating performance."

Such a system would free funds for United Way to purchase specific necessary services from any organization or group in the community, old or new.

Keynote speaker for the 1971 Volunteer Leaders Conference in Chicago was Secretary of Health, Education and Welfare, Elliot L. Richardson and former Chairman of the Greater Boston United Fund Campaign.

Mr. MacNaughton said this approach "enables the agency to reach as far as its imagination, resources and demonstrated effectiveness can take it."

"It makes it possible to multiply voluntary dollars through matching arrangements with government.

"It translates community judgment as to priorities of need into programs.

"Finally," he said, "it imposes on the United Way the responsibility of leadership."

Mr. MacNaughton stated that two kinds of planning in United Way were necessary:

One, for United Way allocations for agency "core costs," and also for selection of "services to be purchased."

"The other kind," he said, "is overall community planning . . . "covering a large number of service delivery systems, many without direct connection with United Way, such as schools, courts, legislatures, etc.

"Overall planning is . . . difficult. It requires community-wide participation—(including) top decision-makers . . . considerable research capacity . . . and authority to implement plans. The group that does this kind of planning would be in the nature of a consulting firm, available to the entire community, and with community leaders standing back of the planning designs it produces.

"I believe the United Fund should provide base support for such a planning group," he declared, "but (it) should be independent."

In setting the stage for a battery of Round Table

discussions, Budget Session Chairman, Laurence D. Bolling, owner, L. D. Bolling & Sons, told conferees that "the real strength of the United Way in the seventies will stem not only from its proven ability to raise increased amounts of dollars, but increasingly upon the effectiveness of its budgeting and planning functions."

The provocative planning and allocations concepts presented were designed more to stimulate a variety of cognitive and innovative experimentation in local communities than to induce implementation of any particular plan.

The new United Way leadership—volunteer and professional—recognized the responsibility of United Way as the most comprehensive and influential force in voluntarism to give leadership and encourage initiative for development of a coordinated system of services . . . accountable for results . . . and involving the total community of funders, suppliers and users.

Indication of United Way concern on this complex question was demonstrated in subsequent examination and discussion at a Conference on the Future of Independent Planning Councils in Detroit, April 6-7, 1972; a two-day symposium of 200 volunteers and professionals on Pressing Issues in Planning and Allocations at the Volunteer Leaders Conference in Washington, May 1-2, 1972; and the presentation of three thoughtful papers representing differing views of professional leaders in United Way planning at the National Biennial Staff Conference of United Way of America in Los Angeles, March 4, 1974.

Fifteen sessions were held on Campaign and Public Relations. Robert E. Brooker, Chairman, Executive Committee of Marcor & Montgomery Ward, made the Campaign Keynote speech. His community, Chicago, had in the previous week made the largest United Way of America membership dues pledge to date of $90,000, an increase of $40,000.

John B. Andersen, Vice President, Sales and Services of Eastern Airlines, and National Public Relations Chairman for United Way of America, presented the 1971 campaign promotion and communications program. A campaign film for the hourly wage earner was shown featuring Loretta Lynn and marking the beginning of the annual production of highly-successful employee solicitation tools.

"We are working toward a national statement," Mr. Andersen said, "that will supersede the multiplicity of

Medallion struck to commemorate dedication of Alexandria National Headquarters Building of United Way of America.

images that fragment our effort and diminish our strength. We need a national voice that speaks for each and all through consistent local and national use."

The Newton D. Baker Award was presented at the conference to Mrs. A. W. Graessle for her *Child and Youth Care Study* which brought major changes in services to children in Jacksonville, Florida. President Nixon wired congratulations.

Four biennial Regional Conferences for volunteers and staff from local United Ways were held in the spring of 1971: Northeast, March 21-23, New York City; Mid-America, March 28-31, Dallas; Southeast, April 18-21, Asheville; and Western, May 24-25, Phoenix, Arizona.

In a speech delivered at all of the Regional Conferences, National Executive William Aramony spoke on the role of voluntarism in maintaining a free society and the part the United Way could play.

"The ability of the voluntary health and welfare system to survive meaningfully will depend on our capacity to understand the nature of social change, to embrace that change as our own, and to rethink and restructure our way of operating so that we enhance the capacity of the voluntary system in health and welfare to contribute to social problem-solving—rather than being a part of the problem," he said.

"The segmented nature of our lives and the loss of confidence in the system coupled together are the greatest danger to our society. The United Way has a great opportunity to work toward offsetting these twin perils.

"The heart of our business is people—the giver and the receiver. We must again believe in one another . . . we must open up all the doors to everyone . . . to give them full access to every institution and organization . . . so that there is no 'we/they'—we become one.

"The demands of the emerging groups to be included in the system must be heard. To duplicate the system by creating their own mechanisms will be wasteful and unsuccessful. We are one society, not two or more. We need to open up our hearts and our doors. There is room for all—this is the only way we can preserve a democratic society.

"We are one another's keeper—we must reject divisive ideology. We must whip off the labels that we put on one another (Catholic, Protestant and Jew—white, black, brown—labor and management—suburbanite and urbanite).

"Our goal is to make modern man whole again—by giving him the opportunity to relate to others," Mr. Aramony declared, "to give and to receive—by paying homage to the unity of the individual and the unity of our communities in every program we undertake, in every organization and in every United Way activity."

James R. Kerr, President and Chief Executive Officer of AVCO Corporation, served as National Chairman of United Community Campaigns in 1970 and 1971. He participated in the United Way all-network simulcast September 9, 1970 with Miss Tricia Nixon and the President.[4] The following year Mrs. Nixon joined the President in the kickoff broadcast. At a luncheon on November 9, 1971 honoring J. Neil Reagan, West Coast Media Chairman, for 25 years of United Way volunteer service, Mr. Kerr reported that over $42 million of national advertising space and time had been donated in 1971.[5]

The following week, Batten, Barton, Durstine & Osborn was also honored at a luncheon in New York for 25 years of volunteer service to the United Way. BBDO was presented with the Red Feather Award, the only time this medallion had been given other than to an individual for national United Way volunteer service.

Edward N. Cole, President, General Motors Corporation and member of the Board of Governors, United Way of America, was keynote speaker at the 1971 Annual Meeting of the United Way National Congress.

Whitney M. Young Jr., Executive Director of the National Urban League, whose death at age 49 cut off a brilliant career.

Tricia Nixon speaks on behalf of the 1970 United Way campaigns over all broadcast networks. James R. Kerr(left), United Way National Campaign Chairman, participated in the program.

In the keynote speech of the Annual Meeting of the National Congress of United Way of America December 2, 1971 in New York, Edward Cole, President of General Motors Corporation and member of the United Way Board of Governors, told attendees that "to achieve the full potential of our national program for voluntarism, we need local leadership with a national vision.

"We must provide real solutions to social problems. We must innovate. And we must reject the appeal of partisan interests at the sacrifice of the good of the whole," he declared.

"It means, among other things, that we must employ minority members on our staffs and have minority representatives at all levels in meaningful roles. It means submitting programming—traditionally an agency prerogative—to tough communitywide study in order to evaluate urgency and determine priorities. It means using management-by-objective. It means the use of the systems approach. It means fewer agency administrative units and very likely the consolidation and coordination of local United Way organizations. We need strong administrative units capable of utilizing modern management technique and dedicated to serving the people.

"With a clear statement of purpose, reasonable objectives and effective programs, the United Way movement can help to shape the forward progress of America," Mr. Cole concluded.

A progress report on the Thirteen Point Program along with objectives for 1972 was given by the National Executive. He noted that staff efforts in 1971 were based on direct observation and personal contact with local United Way volunteers and staff. Mr. Aramony's travel in this task was over 175,000 miles in 1971. He said that action had been taken on all Thirteen Points, adding that another program for a new Communications Division had been added.

Program Point One was for the establishment of a *United Way Systems Institute.* First an Advisory Committee was formed and a Systems Institute Master Plan developed. Next a top systems staff was recruited from business. Then four projects were initiated during 1971:

a) Inhouse systems were developed to improve the national association's capability in Membership Services, Accounting, Manpower, Research and Communications, Orders, Sales and Materials Inventory.

b) Technical Subcommittees composed of local EDP staffs were formed and Workshops held.

c) Direct Services were given to local United Ways, including consultation and assistance in systems development.

d) Standardized Computer Based Accounting System was created for local members.

For Program Point Two, *The United Way Census Project,* a Committee was organized and several meetings held with U.S. Census officials. A Guidebook for local United Way members was published. This was cited by the Census Bureau and the Department of Commerce as "the best private effort on census data use."

Point Three was concerned with *Foundation Grantsmanship.* Contacts were made with major foundations to update them on new United Way programs and needs and consultation with local members was given to assist them with information on obtaining grants. A grant of $25,000 was made by the Rockefeller Foundation to United Way of America for assistance on implementation of Standards of Accounting and Financial Reporting for Voluntary Health and Welfare Organizations.

Government Relations was the focus of the Fourth Program.

a) To establish credibility, national volunteers and staff had meetings with key federal officials including Secretary Richardson, Secretary Romney, Presidential Counselor Robert Finch, Representative Wilbur Mills, and many others.

b) In-depth relationships were developed with HEW's Social and Rehabilitation Administration. Major accomplishments were made by becoming involved in planning of legislation affecting voluntary sector and preparation of Guidelines for carrying out social welfare programs, thus giving local communities a voice in federal decision-making. Liaison persons were assigned to United Way by HEW at each of the Federal Regional Offices. (Similar action was later taken by HUD).

c) Three publications were produced: 1) a guide on how local United Ways could tie into the 1967 Social Security Amendments, *Expanding Local Service Programs Through Government Purchase of Service;* 2) another, *Guide on Government Grants and Contracts,* to assist local members and their participating agencies, and 3) also produced was a directory of *Regional HEW Personnel.*

d) Finally, among many meetings held on Government Relations, the most significant was in Chicago attended by 130 communities' representatives. HEW staff were present to discuss United Way participation in programs funded through Title IVa. Within a year, over 50 million dollars were made available to voluntary agencies as a result of this program and continuing follow-up with Federal Departments and Agencies.

Allocating Systems was the subject of Point Five. The objective of this program was the development of allocating systems, including a standard service classification system, a standard accounting system to be computerized, and setting up and testing usable techniques for measuring effectiveness of agencies' services.

United Way Service Identification System (UWASIS) was developed in 1971. This publication (released in January 1972) was a major breakthrough in setting human service programs in proper perspective. The Guidelines issued for its use included a caveat that UWASIS was merely a beginning and that it would be subject to changes, refinements and revisions as its shape and strength were tested through use. However, it was intended to be a "keystone" in the arch of comprehensively developing proper directions in needs-delineating, priorities-planning, problem-solving, and service-delivering. UWASIS is a compendium of 256 titles woven into an interdependent and interrelated system of 6 broad human goals, 22 services systems, 57 services and 171 human care programs. UWASIS provides a conceptual framework for identifying, classifying, describing, and wherever feasible, defining most current human endeavors for dealing with human problems and aspirations. In the first few months following publication, 7,000 copies had been requested by voluntary and governmental health and welfare organizations.

Point Six covered *Information/Referral Services and Volunteer Bureaus.*

a) A full national study of Information and Referral Services was launched. A committee studied and clarified the role of United Way of America in programming for I/R Services. Recommenda-

The United Way

Saul Bass, recipient of scores of awards and honors, and creator of the new United Way symbol, speaking at the 1972 United Way Leaders Conference. He said that "the sun-like rainbow growing out of the hand...is a positive symbol. It helps signal a new United Way...vibrant, exciting, colorful, positive and changing.

This "Celebrity Poster" attracted attention in 1972.

HEW Secretary Elliot L. Richardson (left) congratulates actor Edward G. Robinson for Award given to him at 1970 Volunteer Leaders Conference in Chicago for more than a quarter century of volunteer service to United Way. (Center) Mario Pellegrini. Vice President, Communications, United Way of America.

tions were made on the needed steps to provide more effective services in this area. Finally, in February, 1973, a document, *National Standards for Information and Referral Services,* was published by United Way of America with developmental assistance from some thirty voluntary and government agencies.

b) Continuing cooperation was given to the Association of Volunteer Bureaus and the National Center for Voluntary Action to determine how United Way of America could most effectively assist communities in volunteer recruitment and placement.

Representation of Local Interests with National Voluntary Agencies, which was the Seventh Program, was the center of much activity in 1971. The position of United Way of America, speaking for itself and for the interests of its local United Way members, was that "the Agencies and United Way . . . need one another . . . and the nation needs both; that a cooperative relationship based on mutual responsibility and dependency is essential."

a) A volunteer United Way committee headed by Arthur M. Wood, President of Sears Roebuck, met with volunteer leadership of American Na-

tional Red Cross to review and discuss relationships not only in an effort to solve mutual problems, but also to strengthen the partnership. As a result, a *Joint Statement* was adopted by the Boards of both organizations and distributed nationally in May, 1972. In addition, at both volunteer and staff levels United Way representatives met on numerous occasions, attending national, regional and local meetings of Boy Scouts, Girl Scouts, Boys Clubs, Camp Fire Girls, Urban League, Salvation Army, YMCA and YWCA.

b) United Way supported Traveler's Aid Association and International Social Service in connection with negotiations in 1971 for a merger of the two agencies which took place in January 1972 with the formation of TAISSA.

c) Finally, for the first time, the national chief executive officers of the seventeen largest United Way participating agencies came together at the invitation of the United Way National Executive in June 1972 for a highly-productive meeting. Not all problem issues vanished, but real progress was made in identifying areas of common concern and the meetings were continued.

Planning and Delivery Systems comprised Program Eight.

a) Two informal sessions were held with local executives in 1971 to discuss the issue of Fund-Council relationships.

b) A trial balloon for defining the role of Planning Councils was presented at the Volunteer Leaders Conference in May by Donald MacNaughton, stimulating considerable dialogue.

c) Fund and Council structures were specifically dealt with in several reorganization studies, including Seattle, Baltimore and Cleveland.

National Corporation Cultivation was Point Nine. Although no major changes were made in programming this function, several service improvements were made.

a) Better data on national corporations' campaign performance was provided, via print-outs on the new United Way of America computer.

b) Consultation with national companies was provided on their United Way programs, i.e., General Electric Company, Sybron Corporation, etc.

One of the most significant of the Thirteen Points was number Ten, namely, *Voluntary Accreditation Standards.* Exploration got underway on this question in 1971 with the possibility of developing a model for what a local United Way should be. The best features of standards and accreditation policies of other organizations were reviewed. Hidden in this probing process was a sleeping giant which later arose as the *Standards of Excellence,* a major breakthrough with great potential for improving the United Way in communities everywhere.

United Way Project on Opportunity for Youth, Minority and Other Groups was Point Eleven. Activities included:

a) Recruitment of minority groups to national staff was accomplished.

b) Formation of a Committee on People Relations headed by the Honorable Samuel P. Goddard, Jr., former Governor of Arizona. Meetings were held with Spanish-speaking groups.

c) Relationships were strengthened with Urban League, Black leadership, and Black United Appeals.

d) Development of the Affirmative Action Program for the national association by a representative employee group was completed and approved by the Executive Committee in September 1972.

e) The Mesbic experiment. The Minority Business Enterprise Project was staffed by people from the United Fund of Dade County, Florida. Capital was provided by local businessmen. Objective was to determine whether United Way voluntary leadership would be effective in developing successful free enterprise experiments for minorities.

Measuring Public Opinion was Twelfth.

a) In 1971 John F. Maloney, Vice-President, Readers Digest Foundation and Chairman of Communications Division's Research Committee consisting of nine public opinion professionals, evaluated studies in eight local communities in a report, *The Public Looks at the United Way.*

b) In November 1973 an analysis of more than 50 Public Opinion studies made by United Ways was compiled in a report for presentation at the National Biennial Staff Conference in Los Angeles in March, 1974.[6]

The last of the original Thirteen Points, the *National Academy for Voluntarism* program opened a new era in upgrading the quality of United Way leadership.

a) The mission of the National Academy for Voluntarism is to provide opportunities for volunteers and professionals to update knowledge and skills and to deal more effectively with constantly-changing conditions. The educational goals of the Academy include skills but more importantly the teaching of initiative and innovation in accomplishing goals. Its objective is to increase the productivity of voluntary-managed resources.

b) The main training center for the National Academy for Voluntarism has been established at the United Way of America headquarters in Alexandria, Virginia. Additional classes are conducted at several locations across the nation to facilitate participation by a maximum number of local United Way organizations and agencies.

The National Academy for Voluntarism focused originally on upgrading the skills and knowledge of United Way professionals and has developed a certificate program for participants that complete a prescribed course sequence. Certificates are awarded for career specialties and broad based career development. Additionally a management

1971 Artwork by Batten, Barton, Durstine & Osborn.

First two Chairmen of the Board of Governors and the National Executive of the new United Way of America at meeting of the board in New York, April 27, 1973. (left to right) Bayard Ewing, William Aramony and James R. Kerr.

certificate is awarded for completion of a three week long management skills unit.

c) Faculty for the National Academy for Voluntarism courses are selected from local United Way organizations, industry, universities, consulting firms and United Way of America staff. Curriculum are designed to meet specific course objectives and are evaluated continuously to assure quality control.

Course tuition is paid for each participant by the sponsoring organization. Starting in 1974 United Way professional staff tuition has been prepaid by those local United Way organizations participating in the Personnel Development Program which gave a major thrust to continued professional career development.

In 1971 a fresh promotional thrust was given to United Way visibility through the new *Communications Program.*

Three films were produced and used by local campaigns in recorded quantities, paced by the Loretta Lynn film with 2,000 prints ordered by 400 communities. For the first time, a full line of materials including a film was created by United Way for the Combined Federal Campaign.

New volunteer communications leadership was recruited and Campbell Ewald Company became the volunteer advertising agency.

In a unique national promotion program, 1,000 boys and girls served by United Way agencies from major communities were flown to Disneyworld November 16 for a holiday of free rides, special parades, gifts, entertainment and meals. Organized by United Way of America, all services and costs of the project were contributed by commercial suppliers.

United Way in Canada

In Canada, the first years of the Seventies in the United Way movement were accented by self-evalua-

Executive and administrative staff of Canadian Welfare Council, 1951. Back row: Elizabeth Govan, Henry Stubbins, Marie Hamel (Lanctot), Marion Murphy (standing). Second row: Gladys Dickson, Patricia Godfrey, Bessie Touzel, Phyllis Burns (standing). Front row: W. T. McGrath, Marjorie King, Jack Anguish, Doris Roy. Remaining two men standing on right side: R. B. G. Davis, Executive Director (rear) and David Crawley (front). Capital Press Service.

Dominion Headquarters for what is now the United Way of Canada and the Canadian Council on Social Development was opened in Ottowa May 4, 1956 by His Excellency The Right Honourable Vincent Massey, C.H.

214

tion and research, changes in structure and program, and outreach into new areas of role and leadership.

One of the major undertakings of Community Funds and Councils of Canada in 1971 was the National Consultation on identification of Issues and Strategies for Action. A study was commissioned through the research firm of Henley and Walden Associates, and carried out in ten cities. The study identified five major issues affecting Funds and Councils in Canada. As a second step, a National Consultation involving 54 representatives of Funds and Councils in 27 local communities was held in January 1972 in Toronto to consider the report and to test views and reactions about these and other issues. A National Implementation Committee was set up (1972) to provide guidelines. It published *Meeting the Issues* for use by local communities.

Significant for their impact on new directions for the United Way movement in Canada were the results of an intensive three-year reexamination by the United Community Fund of Greater Toronto released in 1971. Highlights of the many recommendations included:

- the former concept of the Fund as a givers' organization to be replaced by a voluntary coalition of givers, agencies and recipients of service;

- the Fund to provide domestic planning services for its own agencies (Toronto Council to become more "global");

- the Fund to create a special priorities development committee;

- more flexible financing of agencies along with supplementary fund raising for programs outside areas of United Fund support;

- newly identified needs to be immediately supported for interim financing on a "Trusteeship" arrangement with member agencies;

- special committee of the board to deal with government on behalf of the Fund and its agencies;

- Campaign Goal Committee to serve year round;

- pre-campaign budgeting instead of post-campaign budgeting with numerous structural changes in budget committees, staff and procedures, agency agreements and review;

- development of Community Data Bank on services;

- special funds to enable studies of management-services aspects of agency operations.[7]

A functional budgeting manual developed in Vancouver was endorsed by CFCC in 1972 for use by local Funds and recommended to government agencies.

Another study led to the decision to replace the former Councils Committee of CFCC with a Planning Committee. The conclusion was that it is essential that "planning" be formulated as part of the total concept of the United Way method not only for Councils but also for Funds and Agencies. It was felt that a momentum must be created on planning issues. "The work of the Committee now centers on the provision of a Social Planning Support Program for local Funds and Councils. It is to collect, analyze and disseminate information and data related to planning needs."[8]

Two major studies were launched in 1973 in which CFCC cooperated extensively. The first was a study on the fund-raising experience of campaign leaders by Dr. Samuel Martin of the University of Western Ontario, School of Business Administration. In addition, CFCC collaborated with the Canadian Council on Social Development to obtain a Federal Government grant to probe the issues of voluntary support for nongovernmental agencies. This study sought new clues on attitudes and concepts of giving.

A thrust toward the development of a Centre for Voluntary Action was given when the CFCC gave leadership in the preparation of a paper on the whole concept of voluntarism in Canada.

The Funds and Councils movement in Canada became a separate entity from the Canadian Council on Social Development (formerly, Canadian Welfare Council) when it was incorporated in 1972 as the Community Funds and Councils of Canada.

Henry E. Stegmayer became Executive Director of CFCC in 1972 succeeding Henry Stubbins who had held that position since 1966.

"United Way" identification was increasingly adopted by more communities to better describe the method through which planning, fund-raising and allocation of resources is carried out.

In May 1974 the CFCC membership at its annual meeting in Toronto approved changing the corporate name of its national association to United Way of Canada.

Regional Offices

Throughout the Fifties and Sixties, UCFCA had op-

Elliot J. "Swede" Jensen, retired Campaign Director of the United Appeal of Greater Cleveland and Community Fund General Manager, was honored with two awards for his 26 years of service in the community. One, presented on behalf of the United Way of America by Harry T. Sealy (left), Vice Chairman of the Board and Chairman of the Executive Committee, and the other presented by Mr. Jensen's successor, Calvin E. Green, on behalf of the Fund.

erated a field service program from its New York headquarters, and professional staff there were assigned to regional desks: Western, Southeast, Midwest, etc.

In line with United Way of America's objective of achieving closer contact with, and providing more personalized service to local communities, a new membership services program was designed. Headed by a Vice President for Field Services, four Regional Offices were to be located in New York, Atlanta, Chicago and San Francisco. The United Way regional boundaries were drawn so as to be compatible with those of the newly-established ten Federal Regions.

One of the final actions of 1971 was the initial step in the regional program; the appointment of a Task Group Chairman for each of the four United Way of America Regions. They were: for Mid-America, Louis Martin, Chicago; Northeast, Glenn E. Watts, Washing-

ton; Southeast, John H. Halliburton, Miami; and Western, Charles I. Stone, Seattle. All were members of the National Board of Governors.

First of the Regional programs to be activated was the Northeast with its office in New York City in January 1972.

With the closing of the Office of Washington Affairs at year's end and transfer of its program to the new Headquarters staff in Alexandria, Henry Weber was assigned to establish the Northeast Regional Office as well as a New York Office as a base for carrying out national United Way of America activities with national media, advertising agencies, national corporations and national social agencies headquartered there.

In mid-December 1971, the entire United Way of America staff packed up and left the offices at 345 East 46 Street in New York, where the national headquarters had been maintained since 1952, for their first owned home at 801 North Fairfax Street in Alexandria, Virginia. The doors of the new building were opened for all United Way business on January 3, 1972.

NOTES

Chapter 17

1. *Minutes, UCFCA Board of Directors Meeting,* April 3, 1970.

2. *Proceedings, Annual Meeting of Trustees, United Way of America, Rebirth and Renewal,* December 3, 1970.

3. *Community,* UWA, Summer, 1971.

4. *Community,* UWA, September-October, 1970.

5. *Community,* UWA, September-October, 1971.

6. Henry Weber, *United Way Opinion Research Analysis, November, 1973.* Unpublished Report.

7. *Report of Self Study,* United Community Fund of Greater Toronto, 1971.

8. *Report to CFCC,* July 12, 1974, by M. A. MacLean.

THE UNITED WAY TODAY: 1972-1976

The advent of the new year was a watershed in United Way history. With a gratifying number of Rebirth and Renewal Programs coming into place, the new United Way was ready to direct its attention to additional projects in line with its objectives.

The first new national service to be announced in 1972 was the creation of the United Way of America Information Center and appointment of its Director. The aim of the Center, in addition to providing central reference and library service, was to systemize the collection, storage and retrieval of information; the abstracting of selected documents; the development of topical loan folders; and the periodic distribution of special educational materials to the field.

New United Way Symbol

Coincidental with United Way's emergence as a movement of rising national significance was the creation in 1972 of a new ideogram by Saul Bass—a helping hand, under a rainbow, with symbolized humanity at the center.

As the rainbow, in a fusing of nature's elements, achieves unity from variety . . . so does the United Way, in a blending of human diversity, create harmony and unity of purpose.

The 1972 Campaign Theme "Thanks to You, It's

Working" was illustrated with the new Saul Bass logo. Presentation of the new graphic theme was made in dozens of cities and at United Way conferences to induce local adoption for the fall drives. A continuing marketing campaign by the Communications Division succeeded by 1976 in gaining acceptance and use of the slogan, the helping hand logo and the "United Way" name by some 904 communities. A campaign film, *God's Children,* starring singer Johnny Cash was offered to the field for preview. Widely used by United Ways, the film won the First Prize Gold Medal in the Public Service Category of the 1972 International Film and Television Festival of New York.
York.

New National Headquarters

The largest gathering of United Way leaders ever to convene took place April 30 to May 4, 1972, when over 1,200 volunteers and professionals took part in the dedication ceremonies of the new National Headquarters building in Alexandria and attended the Conferences in a hotel in Washington.[1]

Beginning with Housewarming Tours at noon on Sunday, April 30, a meeting of the Board of Governors was followed by commissioning of the building at which Bayard Ewing presided. A time capsule containing United Way film and documents was buried in a cement

Largest gathering of United Way volunteers and professionals was held in Washington, D.C., April 30 to May 3. More than 1200 attended the conference which included the dedication and housewarming of the new United Way National Headquarters building in Alexandria.

M. M. Brisco, Director and President, Standard Oil Company of New Jersey, and member, Board of Governors, United Way of America, places "Times Capsule" in underground vault. The sealed capsule containing United Way documents is to be opened in the year 2072.

encasement in front of the building. At the opening dinner of the Volunteer Leaders Conference, Charles F. Adams, Chairman of the Board, Raytheon Company, President of the Massachusetts Bay United Fund, and member of the United Way of America Board of Governors, was keynote speaker.

"If we can reaffirm in our own communities people's innate desire to help each other," Mr. Adams said, "then perhaps by this simple act of faith, we can bring together once more the now harshly divided elements in this nation. To all of you who believe in the United Way, I venture to suggest that we have today a broader mission than merely caring for the unfortunate in our communities—we have the mission of reaching into the hearts and minds of people to join them once more in a common cause and thus commence to rebuild Americans' faith and trust in each other which our ancestors fought so hard to create. We must not falter or retreat before this greater challenge. It could turn out to be United Way's 'Finest Hour,' " he concluded.

Simultaneous conferences were held for Volunteer Campaign Leaders chaired by Mr. Adams and Planning and Allocations Volunteer Leaders, chaired by Laurence D. Bolling.

Mrs. Richard M. Nixon was honored at a dinner for all Conference attendees. In addition to being awarded a scroll naming her "First Volunteer" for her many volunteer activities she was presented with a Waterford crystal bowl as a personal gift.

Congressmen were invited to the dinner. Among them was Congressman Gerald R. Ford at a table with United Way leaders from Michigan. Two years later the then President Ford was to give the annual United Way campaign kickoff broadcast, one of the warmest and most perceptive of all the traditional Presidential appeals.

A joint all-Conference luncheon marked the end of the Volunteers' sessions and the beginning of two days of meetings for local United Way professionals in the National Biennial Staff Conference. The luncheon speaker was The Reverend Leon Howard Sullivan, Pastor, Zion Baptist Church of Philadelphia and Founder of the Opportunities Industrialization Centers and member of the United Way Board of Governors.

Affirmative Action

The National Executive made a strong plea to the United Way professionals for Affirmative Action. "We must have staffs and boards that reflect our communities, mix. It is our own moral imperative to act . . . not because someone is demanding it, but because it is right," William Aramony declared.

A presentation of the national campaign materials for 1972 was given and special workshops were held on communications.

Ralph H. Blanchard, who had planned to attend the Conferences, died May 13 at his home in Bronxville, New York, from a cerebral hemorrhage at age 76. He was the second Executive Director of the national association which he served from 1928 to 1960. In 1948-49 he held the presidency of the National Conference on Social Welfare. He was the creator, and in his later years President, of the National Health and Welfare Retirement Association.[2]

1972 Campaigns

The National Campaign Chairman in 1972 was C. Peter McColough, Chairman of the Board and Chief Executive Officer of Xerox Corporation.

The annual campaign kickoff broadcast included, in addition to Mr. McColough, Saul Bass, designer of the new United Way symbol; Anthony G. DeLorenzo, Vice President of General Motors Corporation and National Media Chairman for United Way; Johnny Cash, star of the United Way film, *God's Children;* and Julie Nixon Eisenhower, who spoke from the White House. An estimated 200 million viewed the simulcast which represented a $400,000 contribution of time by the networks. During the entire campaign period, a record

four billion TV network home impressions, and six billion radio impressions, were made.

Final 1972 campaign reports were to show an increase of 5.7% over the previous year for a total of $914,622,000.

At the behest of several national groups, including religious, educational, cultural, the arts and foundations, United Way of America sponsored a meeting in New York on September 21, 1972, to develop a coordinated program to arouse a renewed awareness of the significance of voluntary initiative in American society. James R. Kerr, as Chairman of the United Way of America Leadership Task Force, served as Organizing Chairman and host for the luncheon session. It planned to remain an informal, unincorporated group without staff or budget. Subsequently, it became known as "Coalition for the Public Good Through Voluntary Initiative." Bayard Ewing was elected permanent Chairman and United Way of America provided staff services.

Standards of Excellence

On December 2, 1971, at the Annual Meeting of the National Congress of United Way of America, a one-year program was announced for the building of a "Model" for local United Way organizations. One year, less two days, later, November 30, 1972, the United Way National Congress approved adoption of *Standards of Excellence for Local United Way Organizations,* the sought-for "Model."

What happened between those two dates is an example of how the winds of pride and fear, which so often storm around the towered defenses of community autonomy, can be tempered and directed to productive use for the benefit of the community. In this case, intensive and united effort by hundreds of committed volunteers and professionals, coupled with a painstaking process to "include everybody," brought breakthrough and success where the strong pillars of local determination have too frequently blocked useful progress, rather than supporting it.

Responsibility for guiding the project to successful completion rested with an indefatigable National Steering Committee, co-chaired by Harry T. Sealy and Laurence Bolling, which met at Carmel, California, in early June to review a first draft which had been developed from a questionnaire sent to local United Ways asking them what they thought "a United Way Ought to Be."[3]

An executive committee of the group met in Alex-

*Pat Nixon displays Waterford crystal bowl
presented to her by the Board of Governors,
United Way of America, in recognition
of her volunteer service.*

andria on a hot Saturday in July to incorporate revisions made at the initial meeting. The resulting draft then went to each of the four United Way of America Regions' Volunteer Task Groups and their Professional Advisory Committees which met between August 7 and 11 in San Francisco, Chicago, Atlanta and Alexandria.

Mailings were also made to national organizations, consumer groups, labor, management and others for comment. Also, the professionals present at the committee meetings were asked to present drafts to their local boards and advisory committees.

Then, the full Steering Committee met September 12 and 13 to reconcile and consolidate the accumulated comments, recommendations and suggested changes. The proposed Model was considered also at a meeting October 12 and 13 in San Francisco of the United Way of America Corporate Associates, comprised of executives from major corporations. Next step was the preparation of a draft for consideration by the National Congress of United Way of America in New York November 30. There, in an open meeting of several hundred representatives of local United Ways, the "Standards" document was subjected to serious scrutiny, with changes and amendments being proposed from the floor on a line-by-line basis. Eventually it was approved.

As it emerged in its final form it had three sections. Part I was designed to give an overview of mission and goals. Part II went into implementation of the Standards in depth. Part III set forth basic guidelines for United Way organizations to regard as the minimum in operating performance.

Standards of Excellence uses the format of "management by objectives." It contains goals, programs, and elements. It is a check list for United Ways to measure their roles and effectiveness.

Also approved by the Congress was a separate document, *Eligibility for Organizational Membership* in United Way of America.

Standards of Excellence
for Local United Way Organizations
Mission:

North Americans share a unique tradition of voluntary assumption of responsibility for the conduct of community affairs. Concerned people have always banded together to cope with human problems. To deal with such problems through joint action, the modern social agency, and more recently, the United Way evolved. It is the mission of the social agency to unite people with a common interest in a more effective attack on particular problems. It is the mission of United Way organizations to unite the diverse elements of entire communities through one or more flexible and reasoned vehicles to contribute to the evolution of the nation toward a more satisfying life for all.

Goal:

The primary interest of the United Way is people. The strength of the United Way is people. The goal of United Way organizations is to provide a means by which a cross section of citizens and agencies, governmental and voluntary, may join in a community-wide effort to deliver efficient human service programs effectively related to its current needs.

Objectives:

To fulfill the United Way mission and goal, local United Way organizations should involve contributors, taxpayers, users, agencies and government in a continuing program to:

Assess on a continuing basis the need for human service programs; seek solutions to human problems; assist in the development of new or the expansion or modification of existing human service programs; promote preventive activities, and foster cooperation among local, state and national agencies serving the community.

Develop as fully as possible the financial resources, both governmental and voluntary, needed to meet the human service needs of the community and reduce the number of appeals for financial support for services.

Deploy United Way financial support so as to maximize the resources available to agencies for services aimed at the most urgent current needs of the community, including those supplied by organizations not now receiving United Way financing.

Muster community support and commitment for the entire United Way enterprise through a systematic communications program which both speaks and listens to the community.

Manage United Way operations effectively, and offer assistance to agencies wishing to improve their management skills.

E. Roland Harriman receiving a United Way Award Medallion, April 26, 1973, for more than a quarter of a century of volunteer service as Chairman of the American National Red Cross. Members of the Board of Governors of United Way of America, congratulating the recipient are (left to right) Arthur M. Wood, Chairman of the Board, Sears, Roebuck & Co.; John D. deButts, Chairman of the Board, American Telephone and Telegraph Company; A. W. Clausen, Vice Chairman of the Board, United Way of America, and President, Bank of America Corporation & Bank of America NT&SA; E. Roland Harriman; James R. Kerr, Chairman of the Board, United Way of America and President and Chief Executive Officer, AVCO Corporation; C. Peter McColough, Chairman of the Board and Chief Executive Officer, Xerox Corporation.

Within six months of the release of the *Standards of Excellence*, 128 communities reported having already put them to use in general appraisal of structure and operations, for selecting local objectives, for setting long-range goals, for implementing selected programs, and in other ways to improve the quality of their local United Way organization. The National Steering Committee and the four Regional Task Groups will continuously review the "Standards" as they are put to work by local United Ways and will seek amendments to keep their usefulness current.

Appointments and Elections

With the announcement November 20, 1972, that Vice Admiral Fred G. Bennett, U. S. Navy, would be joining United Way of America as Vice President for Finance and Administration, recruitment of the new cadre national staff was completed. Other Divisional Vice Presidents were: Mario Pellegrini, Communications; John H. Yerger, Field Services; George A. Shea, Manpower and Labor; William A. Wynn, Voluntarism; Paul Akana, Systems, Planning and Allocations; Oral Suer, Fund Raising; and Hamp Coley, National Agencies Division.

James R. Kerr was elected Chairman of the Board of Governors and Laurence D. Bolling, Vice Chairman and Chairman of the Executive Committee at a meeting of the national United Way Board in New York, December 1, 1972.[4]

A member of the United Way Board since 1970 and former National Campaign Chairman, Mr. Kerr, in addition to being President and Chief Executive Officer of AVCO Corporation, was also Chairman of the Board of the Paul Revere Life Insurance Company, AVCO Broadcasting Corporation and Carte Blanche Corporation. Mr. Bolling, first elected to the Board in 1970, had served during the past year as Chairman of the Planning and Allocations Task Force and as Co-Chairman of the National Steering Committee for the Standards of Excellence project. President of L. D. Bolling and Son in Oakland, he is an active civic, social welfare and church leader in the San Francisco Bay Area.

Volunteer Leaders Conference

John D. deButts, Chairman of the Board, American Telephone and Telegraph Company, and Member of the Board of Governors, United Way of America, was the opening speaker April 8, 1973, in Chicago at the annual national conference for 750 local United Way volunteer leaders. "Theme for my remarks tonight," Mr. deButts said, "is the matter of a community's responsibility for meeting its own needs . . . there is a whole lot more at issue in the campaign on which you will embark this year than your ability simply to meet a stated dollar goal. At issue, . . . is the very character of our society and the directions in which it is evolving.

"More than 130 years ago, a very astute Frenchman

wrote a very perceptive book about American institutions and the American character. In his *Democracy in America*, Alexis de Tocqueville notes that one of the most remarkable attributes of our democracy is 'the extreme skill with which the inhabitants of the United States succeed in proposing a common object for the exertions of a great many men and inducing them voluntarily to pursue it.'

"It is the continued vitality of that principle of voluntary association that seems to me to be at stake in your current exertions. There is to my mind no single issue with a greater bearing on the future of our democracy than this one: the degree to which we are ready—voluntarily—to apply hometown talents and hometown resources to hometown problems. That is what United Way is all about." [5]

In a dissertation on the future of voluntarism, Samuel J. Silberman, President, Gulf & Western Industries Foundation, and Chairman, Planning and Allocations Task Group, United Way of America, said that "de-

Happy occasion at 1973 Volunteer Leaders Conference in Chicago. Cliff Robertson accepts Award from James R. Kerr, Chairman, Board of Governors, United Way of America for his contribution of time and talent as the star in the 1973 United Way campaign film, **The Turning Point.**

mocracy is not an inherited form of society. Each generation must re-create its own. Voluntarism must do likewise. Voluntarism is a unique, American concept; it is the social underpinning of our democratic system. Whether or not voluntarism survives will depend upon vigor and the basis upon which it is defended. Voluntarism represents the vehicle through which the quality of national life in the United States is enhanced and safeguarded. In addition, we must never forget the objectives of voluntarism to undertake tasks and responsibilities for the benefit of others." [6]

Cliff Robertson, star of the United Way campaign film, *The Turning Point,* was on hand for its preview at the Volunteer Leaders Conference. He received a special citation for his contribution of time and talent.

Bob Hope became the first recipient of the Alexis de Tocqueville Award in recognition of his outstanding service to the nation as a volunteer. The award, a free-form star of sculptured crystal, was presented by James R. Kerr, as President of the Alexis de Tocqueville Society, a Virginia corporation created by United Way of America to honor persons deemed to have rendered distinguished volunteer service.

The Reverend Theodore M. Hesburgh, President, University of Notre Dame, told the conferees that in this age of discontent and pessimism, the United Way takes on ever greater importance because it brings people together as human beings. "There is one thing that unites all of us" he said, "and that is our humanity." [7]

While affirming organized labor's support of the United Way, William C. Marshall, President, Michigan State AFL-CIO, and Vice President of the Michigan United Way, raised several questions in regard to labor's United Way relationships. Stating labor's agreement with United Way's *Standards of Excellence,* Mr. Marshall asked, "What part will organized labor play in this development?" [8]

"We believe that the closer we work together on mutual concerns, the better the results . . . for our communities." He said that for each yearly campaign a potential contributor should have the opportunity of reviewing his previous contributions.

Calling for more inclusion of labor units in campaign meetings and reports, he declared that while contributions through payroll deduction had increased, corporate contributions had remained the same.

This 1974 poster, painted by Gil Meekins, shows givers as well as receivers of United Way services.

"I believe that the United Way program will improve as the United Way leadership, executive employees and volunteers accept organized labor for its rightful and earned place of leadership and responsibility."

Regional Organization

Several programs, in developing stages since their beginnings in 1970, came on line in 1973. One of these was the Field Services program which centered upon the launching of four satellite United Way Regional Offices in Atlanta, Chicago, New York and San Francisco. By early 1973 they were fully manned by Regional Directors together with government relations and labor staff. One fundamental function of the Regional facility was to bring the services of the national association through direct personal contact to the local United Way. This included consultation on local problems in campaigning, planning, allocating, etc. The other function was to provide a two-way channel for the flow of information and recommendations between the national office and the local community, and more particularly between national volunteer leaders and local volunteer leaders as well as between national professionals and their local counterparts. To accomplish this, Regional Volunteer Task Groups were formed, comprising both local and national representatives, along with Professional Advisory Groups made up from local United Way executives. This made possible the more rapid adoption of nationally developed services and programs, i.e., Standards of Excellence, new name, symbol and campaign theme. It also provided for speedier and more effective input of local ideas, and recommendations to the national board and staff for development of needed projects and programs.

One of the major United Way of America objectives given momentum in 1973 was to encourage and assist local United Ways in forming areawide United Way organizations in natural socio-economic areas to achieve more effective and efficient ways of producing more dollars and improving the quality of human care. Aided by the Regional Offices, the already existing trend toward areawide United Way structures was accelerated, and a review and analysis of local experience resulted in the publication in 1974 of *Guidelines for Areawide United Way Organization.*

MACSI

Another new national service, the Management and Community Studies Institute (MACSI), made studies and surveys of local United Way operations and their internal management as well as evaluation of agencies and programs supported by United Ways. Since its beginning in 1972 over 35 studies have been conducted in major cities throughout the United States.[9]

United Way . . . World Wide

Canadian United Way volunteers and professionals joined with their colleagues in the United States, Thailand, Korea, Singapore, Hong Kong and Japan in the First International Conference on United Fund Raising for Social Work Services in Tokyo, Japan, in 1973. The second such Conference, hosted by United Way of America took place with fifty delegates attending in Honolulu in 1974,[10] and the third conference took place in Hong Kong in 1976. Vancouver, British Columbia, Canada, is scheduled for the site of the fourth conference May 1 to 5, 1977.

An International Council was established in 1974, with Bayard Ewing, veteran United Way of America volunteer leader, being elected President, and William Aramony, Secretary General.

In addition to the more than 2,360 United Way organizations for fund raising, allocating and planning throughout the United States and Canada, the United Way idea has spread around the world.

United Way organizations are now operating in Australia, Brazil, Belgium, Hong Kong, South Africa, Thailand, Japan, Panama, Puerto Rico, the Philippines and Taiwan.

General Douglas MacArthur introduced the United Way to Japan during the American Occupation in the late 1940's.

The Central Community Chest of Japan and the National Council of Social Welfare, both in Tokyo, are the headquarters associations for United Way fund raising, allocating and planning. A highly organized network of 94 member United Ways is now operating in 46 prefectures.

United Way came to the Philippines also at the close of World War II with the establishment of the Community Chest Foundation of Greater Manila. The national association, Community Chests and Councils of the Philippines, Inc., now has local United Way members in 74 communities throughout the islands, most of which have been organized in recent years.

The first meeting of the Board of Directors of another newly formed organization, United Way International, was held in Alexandria, Virginia, on November 21, 1974. Officers are: Rafael Fábregas, Puerto Rico, Chairman; John A. Scott, Hawaii, Vice Chairman; Bernardo Benes, Miami Beach, Florida, Secretary; and Glenn E. Watts, Treasurer.

Current directors are: Gale Bennett, Laurence D. Bolling, Mrs. Ernestine Carmichael, Bayard Ewing, O. Stanley Smith, Jr., Louis E. Martin, Francis A. Coy, Don Shoemaker, and Charles I. Stone. William Aramony is President.

Requests for assistance from a number of nations for the development of new United Way fund raising campaigns and for consultation with those already established were considered. A broad program to explore service options and priorities for future activities was endorsed at the meeting.

Government Relations

In the five years following the establishment of the United Way Office of Washington Affairs in 1969, a dramatic turnabout in United Way relations with government was effected. Prior to 1970, federal agencies and the Congress were largely unaware of the national significance and importance of the United Way. By 1974, United Way had become a recognized leader for the planning, support and delivery of voluntary social services, with its counsel being sought by government.

In one instance, when HEW was proposing regulations for new Social Security amendments, considered regressive by United Way supporters, professionals, workers and consumers of health and welfare services, a record 80 thousand letters of reaction received by HEW were reflected in changes made in the regulations when issued in final form.[11]

A comprehensive and continuing communications program, including legislative analysis, now enables local United Ways to maintain a high level of knowledgeability on pertinent federal programs, plans and proposals.

In addition, the United Way Regional Offices have worked with and assisted both local and state United Way organizations to develop effective relationships with the federal regional agencies as well as with state, county and municipal governments.

In many local communities there has been a corresponding increase in viable and productive United Way relationships with governmental bodies at all levels. United Ways and member agencies have participated in "purchase of services" and "matching funds" programs involving hundreds of millions of dollars. These programs have provided benefits in a range extending from child care services to programs for the aging.

At the initiation of the national association, the General Counsel of HEW ruled on March 10, 1975, that United Way dollars could be used as match money for financing Health Systems Agencies under the National Health Planning and Resources Development Act of 1974. A special effort was undertaken in 1975 to insure voluntary agency involvement in the implementation of the Title XX of the Social Security Act.

Federal Grants and Contracts

Federal grants and contracts to states and local communities ranged from $27,000 in Atlanta for service to the aging, to amounts exceeding a million dollars in Minneapolis to combat juvenile delinquency; for anti-drug programs in Miami and in New York for anti-poverty projects.

Other cities in which United Way organizations played an active role in government-volunteer partnership programs included Chicago, Seattle, Louisville, York, Pa., Columbia, S.C., Baltimore, Elizabeth, N. J., Grand Rapids, St. Paul, Memphis, and many others including states with United Way organizations such as Pennsylvania, South Carolina, North Carolina, California, Michigan, Ohio, Minnesota, New York, Oregon, Texas, Virginia, Washington and Wisconsin.

Revenue Sharing

With a windfall total of $30.2 billion suddenly offered to state and local governments over a five-year period beginning in 1972, local United Ways' hopes were raised that sizeable amounts of the Revenue Sharing funds would become available for many pressing local social needs. However, by 1974 it was evident that only a miniscule portion of the Federal bonanza of the funds was used for children's programs; only 0.3 percent was authorized for aid to the handicapped; and only 0.2 percent was spent on programs for the elderly. With the bulk of the money being used by states to pay bills, lower or hold down taxes, balance budgets, or to avoid borrowing money; and with counties and municipalities using a sizeable proportion to substitute for funds which could be obtained from other sources, the outlook was dim for any substantial amount ever being applied for human care needs—unless mandated by future Congressional legislative action.[12]

Unity of Effort

Time was when government and voluntary social agencies operated in isolation and conducted activities, largely unilaterally. Today, it is generally recognized that America's health and welfare problems require the combined attention of the nation's total resources.

The beginnings of cooperative planning, financing, and delivery of human care services by government, business/industry, and the voluntary sector is currently in evidence, but in hardly more than an experimental stage. This embryo development represents a broader application of the underlying principle of the United Way. As William Aramony has stated, "The United Way goal is no less than to help make modern man whole again—by giving him an opportunity to relate to others; to give, serve and receive; by paying homage to the unity of the individual man and the unity of communities—in every program we undertake, and in every organizational activity."[13]

Rev. Leon Sullivan, Board Member, and William Aramony, United Way of America National Executive, discuss the Opportunities Industrialization Center. Reverend Sullivan is Executive Director of the Center.

Personnel Development Program

When William Aramony outlined his 13-Point Program for Rebirth and Renewal of the United Way in 1970, he called for a National Academy of Voluntarism to provide for the continuing education of United Way professional staff. By 1973 the Academy was well established, and meeting its objectives. Under the leadership of a volunteer Advisory Board, chaired by Samuel Goddard, Jr., and an able staff, the Academy after one year of operation reported these results:

... 29 courses and seminars
... 500 United Way participants
... 85 agency participants
... 30 local government participants
... A major pilot effort in developing community leadership.

However, even as the Academy thrived, and as other parts of the 13-Point Program proceeded toward their goals, and as United Way passed the billion-dollar mark in fund raising, it became apparent to Mr. Aramony that the original concept of "personnel development" as contained in the aim of the Academy needed some stretching to meet an increasing need to attract and maintain an interested, aggressive and achieving voluntary leadership. He also knew that the key to mobilizing and helping to make this volunteer leadership truly effective is the *local professional staff*.

Realizing that any plan adequate to meeting this urgent personnel gap was beyond the existing capacity of the National Academy for Voluntarism, he drew up a proposal for a three-part plan which would bring new staff to the United Way movement, which would reinforce good current staff. The plan would be financed on a 50/50 basis, with local United Ways securing their half from the local community and the national association raising its share from outside sources, e.g., foundations, individuals, and corporations.

Reaction of the field to the proposal was mixed, with some feeling that recruitment and training of staff should be done exclusively by the local United Way. Questions were raised on cost. However, there was little disagreement that the purpose of the idea was highly meritorious.

On April 26, 1973, Louis E. Martin, Vice President and Editorial Director of the *Chicago Daily Defender* and a member of the Board of Governors of United Way of America, introduced to the Board discussion of the proposed Personal Renewal and Development Program and asked Mr. Aramony to give highlights of the proposal. The National Executive stressed that this was a proposal and not a set plan; that suggestions for changing it were welcome; that it is futile to create tools and systems for doing the local United Way job better if there are not enough trained people to use them, and that the program should be undertaken with the guidance of a national committee involving the majority participation of representative local United Way leaders—volunteer and professional.

As a result, a committee [14] of volunteer leaders from 15 different communities was appointed with John W. Hanley, Chairman of the Board and President, Monsanto Company, as Chairman. Following a whirlwind around-the-nation program of discussions that included input from four regional meetings and hundreds of letter responses, a revision of the earlier proposal was presented by Mr. Hanley to the Board of Governors on November 29, 1973, and approved.

Praising Mr. Hanley and his committee for the outstanding performance, Mr. Aramony said, "He made it a matter of personal commitment, and he never lets himself or anybody else down."

"I'm a salesman by trade," Mr. Hanley told the United Way Board of Governors, "and I'm convinced we've built a product that will sell!"

Among the revisions made by the Committee were the elimination of an early retirement plan, the placing of major emphasis on the overall program of training, reduction in costs, joint local-national recruitment of interns, and the addition of correspondence courses.

The program met with widespread support and enthusiasm.

Augustus H. Sterne, President, Trust Company of Georgia and Mrs. Ernestine Carmichael, of South Bend, Indiana, headed a special committee charged with raising funds from corporations and foundations. By February 1976 they were able to report that the national share of the $4.2 million program was fully funded and that local United Ways were close to subscribing their share.

PDP INTERN PROGRAM IN FULL SWING. This was the headline in the newsletter, *Focus—United Way Personnel* which reported, "On July 1, 1974, six young men and women arrived at United Way of America headquarters in Alexandria to begin their year of internship in the newly-developed Personnel Development Program." Thus began a program which, in

Contribution Campaign Pins used by Rochester, New York from 1918 through 1974.

addition to recruitment of four interns per year, will provide one thousand scholarships at $400 a year for four years at the National Academy for Voluntarism.

In 1944, the long-time labors of **Ralph H. Blanchard**, Executive Director of CCC, as architect of a pension plan for United Way professionals, were realized with the founding of the National Health and Welfare Retirement Association. Twenty years later, a breakthrough was made in the establishment of the Personnel Development Program for United Way executives and staff.

In terms of contributions made by professional leaders to the United Way movement, Ralph Blanchard's provision for retirement needs has been fittingly complemented through the vision and energetic efforts of the National Executive in 1974 by the launching of a parallel program directed to the beginning and productive span of the United Way professional's career spectrum . . . a program designed to bring into play imaginative forces and effective facilities to improve and enhance the quality of their performance.

1974 Conferences

As more than 900 United Way professionals met in Los Angeles in March, 1974, for the National Biennial Staff Conference, they were gratified by the impressive gains made by United Way as it had moved into a position of greater visibility, strength and prestige since the launching of its rebirth and renewal program in 1970.

Speaking at the Recognition Luncheon where twenty-three professionals were honored for thirty years of United Way service, William Aramony made a progress report on the past four years.

Conference Chairman Richard E. Booth, Executive Director, United Fund of Greater New York, in his opening address stressed that "while the volunteer leader is . . . the backbone of (the) movement, it is up to . . . the United Way professionals to share . . . a leadership role in our organization . . . and in our communities." [15]

Two months later, nearly 850 Volunteer Leaders met in Chicago for sessions on United Way Campaigning, Planning and Allocating, and Communications. At the opening Conference Dinner, May 5, speaker Arthur M. Wood, Chairman of the Board, Sears, Roebuck and Company, in commenting on changes occurring in the traditional social services roles of government and the

Veteran United Way volunteer I. W. Abel, left, President, United Steel Workers of America, receives a Special Award from United Way of America Board Chairman Emeritus, Bayard Ewing, at the steelworkers convention in Atlantic City, 1974. Mr. Abel's volunteer activities cover a 30-year span from campaigner for the Canton, Ohio, Community Chest to Executive Board Member of the Allegheny County United Way in Pittsburgh. He is President of the Industrial Union Department, AFL-CIO, and member of the AFL-CIO Executive Board.

voluntary sector, pointed to the opportunities for the United Way to bring locally-tested, problem-solving methods to bear on national issues.

"As we meet here this week, one senses that the state of mind of our fellow Americans is one of uncertainty and confusion, and in some quarters of frustration and anger," Mr. Wood said.

"There is uncertainty as to what will happen in the marketplace as the cost of living increases for every American family.

"There is uncertainty on the political scene with many citizens questioning the ability of our chief executive to give the country strong leadership because of developments of the past year rising out of the Watergate investigations.

"There is concern in many cities that the problems of poverty, unemployment and housing are not being resolved and that progress toward solutions is too slow.

"It seems that we live from crisis to crisis and I sense that there is a strong desire in the nation for a period of economic, political and social tranquility.

"One aspect of solidarity in our country is the continuing involvement of citizen volunteers in working for the general good. The presence here of volunteer leaders who are involved in the United Way movement across the country is a good example of this determination to solve community problems by giving direction and leadership to human care services.

"I want to comment about the important organizational change that took place in 1970 to strengthen the national headquarters . . . to transform what had been a national service station, as one consultant called it, into an instrument for bringing United Way leadership, know-how and philosophy to bear on the urgent problems besetting communities. The new United Way of America is evolving in the direction set for it in 1970.

"Many of the problems with which local United Ways must contend, and many of the resources to deal with them, transcend geographic boundaries.

"The Federal government, national agencies, national corporations, national communications media and international labor unions are difficult, if not impossible, to deal with effectively . . . local community by local community. Thus United Way of America has become the extension of local United Ways to make important contacts with such organizations. It is the means for doing many things cooperatively which cannot be accomplished individually.

"One problem on which we have made such an application is Tax Reform. We helped bring into being and are providing leadership to the 501(c)(3) group, an organization of senior staff of a variety of national organizations with responsibility in the area of taxation plus some of the best legal minds in the field of taxation. This group developed and maintained close and cooperative relationships with the staff of the Congressional Joint Committee on Internal Revenue Taxation, the Assistant Secretary of the Treasury for Tax Policy and the Commissioner and senior staff of the Internal Revenue Service."

On the next day at the Annual Meeting of the National Congress of the United Way of America, the Alexis de Tocqueville Award was presented to the second recipient, Leslie L. Luttgens of San Francisco, first woman to head a major United Way organization. She served as President of the United Bay Area Crusade. Incorporated in 1972 by United Way of America, the Alexis de Tocqueville Society was created to recognize persons deemed to have rendered outstanding service as volunteers in their own communities or nationally, and thus to foster and promote voluntary community service, and a recognition of the value and importance of such service to the nation.

Following election of the Board of Governors of United Way of America by members of the Congress, James R. Kerr was reelected Chairman and Charles I. Stone, Seattle, Washington, attorney, was elected Board Vice Chairman and Chairman of the Executive Committee. Also elected Vice Chairmen were: Bayard Ewing, Providence, Rhode Island, and Charles F. Adams, Lexington, Massachusetts. Glenn E. Watts, Washington, D.C., was elected Secretary and James L. Knight, Miami, Florida, Treasurer.

Labor Participation

The naming of Douglas A. Fraser as general chairman of Detroit's 1974 United Way campaign brought into focus the importance of organized labor's participation in the United Way movement. Mr. Fraser was Vice President, United Auto Workers. He was the first union official to lead a campaign of Detroit's size. "Fraser's appointment to this volunteer position underscores the fact that all community elements unite and work together for the United Foundation, year-round," said Allen W. Merrell, UF Board Chairman. "Because it has always had the full support of organized labor, and its leaders were instrumental in the founding of the UF, we think it highly appropriate that we turn this year to a man who is as much a community leader as a labor leader," he declared.

Labor participation was one of the most significant developments in the history of United Way—and not only because it broadened the base of giving, but, perhaps, more importantly, because it brought Labor into United Way affairs at all levels. It gave emphasis to the principle that the United Way is all parts of the community working for common goals.

For its part, Labor's basic decision was to seek its health and welfare services in concert with the rest of the community, rather than setting up its own services.

Throughout the more than a quarter of a century of United Way-Labor relationships, union leaders have held high office in United Way. William Green, AFL President, and Philip Murray, CIO President, and later George Meany, served as Vice Chairmen, United Community Campaigns of America. Joseph A. Beirne, President, Communications Workers of America, was national President of the United Way in 1966 and 1967. Leo Perlis, Director, AFL-CIO Department of Community Services, has served several terms on the Board of Governors of United Way of America. Similarly, local labor officials have held leadership positions in local United Ways.

An updated Memorandum of Understanding between AFL-CIO Community Services Department and United Way of America was signed November 22, 1971 in Bal Harbour, Florida by George Meany, AFL-CIO President, and Bayard Ewing, United Way of America Board Chairman.

In addition to its contributions of time and service, organized labor is the largest group providing financial support for United Way, with donations amounting to one-third or more of the United Way campaign total, according to estimates by AFL-CIO Community Services.

State Organizations

The United Way from its beginnings to the present has been essentially a community centered "local rights" movement. It was 31 years since the first United Way campaign was held in Denver until the fledgling national organization called the American Association for Community Organization was formed, when 12 volunteer and professional representatives of nine local United Ways met in Chicago, February 22, 1918.

Since then both local United Ways as well as the national association, now United Way of America, have had strong, sustained growth. But organization at the state level has been sparse and uneven in United Way (see Index, Statewide Chests and Funds; Statewide Planning). State organizations vary widely in purpose, form and program. They can be grouped generally into three categories. The oldest group was concerned with joint planning and coordination of state and local social service programs. The first of these was the Ohio Council of Social Agencies created in 1919, forerunner of what is now the Ohio Citizens Council for Health and Welfare. This Council has an illustrious record of working for and achieving many advancements in social services in Ohio, often through state legislation. Other groups of this type include the present Wisconsin Council on Human Concerns, and in Canada, the Community Welfare Council of Ontario, established in 1946.

Other kinds of state organizations were concerned chiefly with fund raising. They first came into being during World War II as the offshoots of the National War Funds. Called State War Chests, those formed in North Carolina, Oregon, Virginia and Michigan still exist, though in some, their functions have undergone change. Another wave of fund raising state organizations was stimulated by the national United Defense Fund during the period of the Korean hostilities. Units were formed in Iowa, Kansas, West Virginia, Texas and again in Oregon and Michigan. North and South Carolina joined in the only bi-state organization to be formed and now dissolved, "Carolinas United." In Minnesota, the Charities Review Council, though not engaged in direct fund raising, examined and passed judgment on national and state agencies wishing to conduct campaigns in that state.

In Michigan, the state organization was responsible for making a milestone contribution to the advancement of the United Way movement throughout the country. To meet the problem of the increasing multiplicity of separate campaigns, Henry Ford II, then President of the Ford Motor Company, called a meeting of Michigan business and labor leaders for the formation in 1947 of a Michigan United Fund (see Chapter X). This was the first state organization to establish and campaign for quotas of both state and national health and welfare agencies. Under the impetus given by Henry Ford II, the state United Fund, now United Way of Michigan, struck the spark that ignited the Detroit Torch Drive in 1949, and from that the fire that swept the nation in the United Fund development of the Fifties.

A third group provided services to United Ways in small towns and rural areas throughout the state. Typical of these are United Way of California, founded in 1962, and Community Services of Pennsylvania, 1966, successor to a fund raising organization, Pennsylvania United Fund established in 1952, and the State Association for Community Services in New York, 1949. State organizations of this type offer consultation and information materials to smaller communities, and often represent all United Ways before state governmental bodies. United Way of California was especially effective in securing payroll deductions for state employees' contributions to all local United Ways. Distinguished by concern action and innovation in many areas, the Community Services of Pennsylvania has been responsible for securing substantial federal and state grants and contracts, i.e., in 1974 it argued for $903,000 from the Commonwealth of Pennsylvania

George Meany has been a long-time supporter of the United Way, personally, as well as officially as President of AFL-CIO. Among his many United Way activities he has served as Member of the Board of Directors of Community Chests and Councils, Inc., and as Vice Chairman of United Community Campaigns of America. His volunteer leadership to United Way was given special recognition when an oil portrait of him was presented at a dinner in his honor in New York in 1965.

to organize and manage the statewide alert for the Federal Supplementary Security Income Program, called the "Good Neighbor SSI Alert." It also created the pattern in 1973 for Volunteer Week which was so successful that it became the model for National Volunteer Week, now conducted annually in April by the National Center for Voluntary Action.

Until 1962, no direct organizational relationships had ever been formed between the various state organizations and the national United Way association. In that year, the United Community Funds and Councils of California was incorporated with an annual budget of $30,000 and an executive who had the status of a full-fledged staff member of the national United Way. Local United Ways in California paid dues only once to national which in turn assumed the costs of the state association. With the formation of the Regional system by United Way of America in 1972, the California state organization, along with Washington, was integrated into the Western Region with its staff responsible administratively to the United Way Regional Director. A similar relationship has been established between North Carolina and the Southeast Region of United Way of America. With aims, methods and activities of this type of state organization closely parallel and coordinated with those of the regional and national offices, this approach seems to provide a pattern for better stability and increased future growth for state organization.

National Budget Review

For 27 years prior to 1972, the National Budget and Consultation Committee reviewed and reported on selected national agency programs and budgets. The NBCC reports were informative and helpful, but did not appear to have direct impact on the income and program of national agencies. With the dissolution of NBCC in 1972, United Way of America took responsibility in 1973 and 1974 for the national agency review process through the Committee on National Agency Support. CONAS took an additional step not taken by NBCC in that it actually recommended for or against support of specific national agencies. Under the CONAS system, however, participation in the process is voluntary, and no guideline is provided as to the actual dollar support to be achieved, community by community or nationally.

In 1973, CONAS invited 49 national agencies to participate in its review process. Eighteen agencies responded affirmatively and were reviewed. CONAS recommended that fourteen be considered for local United Way support, and that three *not* be considered for local United Way support. The Committee was unable to make a recommendation on one agency, as a result of the organization's change in structure and program. Invitations for the 1974 CONAS review were sent to fifty-five organizations. Eventually, fifteen agencies were reviewed and reports made. Thirteen were recommended for consideration by local United Ways for support. The Committee also recommended that two national agencies not be considered for local United Way support, of which one was the United Service Organizations. Reaction in opposition to the CONAS decision from USO supporters was immediate, heavy, and articulate. In publishing its decision, CONAS reported that, "While . . . USO is a national agency whose goals, objectives and programs are important and worthwhile to the United States defense effort, CONAS believes that this agency's programs, especially the overseas ones, should be financed by other resources and *not* by local United Ways. Additionally, CONAS believes that many, if not all, of the USO domestic programs can be more appropriately provided by other existing United Way-funded agencies. After reviewing written material submitted by USO and meeting with agency representatives, CONAS believes that this agency *does not* meet the Committee's previously established criteria for local United Way funding. Therefore, CONAS recommends that the USO *not* be considered for financial support by local United Way organizations for 1975."

Following conferences with USO, Defense Department officials, local United Ways and others concerned, a Blue Ribbon Committee to undertake a study of the need for continued voluntary social services for the morale and welfare of the members of the U. S. Armed Forces, both in the U.S. and overseas, was appointed by James R. Kerr, Chairman of the Board of United Way of America. The study was also to analyze the need for USO-type services. The Honorable Samuel P. Goddard, Jr., Phoenix, former Governor of Arizona and a member of the Board of Governors of United Way of America, was named Chairman. Members included: Melvin Laird, former Secretary of Defense, representatives of business, labor and United Way volunteer leadership.[16]

An intensive world-wide study was conducted during 1974. The findings and recommendations of the Committee were based upon testimony and statistical information provided by the Department of Defense, National USO and local United Way organizations; and by meetings and interviews with hundreds of armed forces personnel of all ranks, local citizens, clergy and elected officials. Committee members made on-site visits to USO operations and military bases around the world.

The Study Committee members were unanimous in their findings that there was a need for services provided by a civilian voluntary agency to Armed Forces personnel in military-impacted areas in the United States and overseas.

The Committee concluded also that in order for USO to effectively meet the needs of service men and women, there must be improvement in management and administration of the organization.

Furthermore, the Committee recommended continued United Way support of the National USO. In addition, it urged increased Department of Defense support and improvement in the income that could be generated by local USO operations.

The Study Committee's Report of its findings and recommendations was approved by United Way of America on January 30, 1975.

Communications

One of the most dramatic breakthroughs in the United Way Rebirth and Renewal program was made by the Communications Division in the creation and

William Aramony visits with youngsters at Tokyo child care agency during first International Conference on United Fund Raising for Social Work Service, 1973.

development of audio-visual educational and promotional materials ranging from fine art and photography to motion picture and television films and multimedia presentations. In 1974 United Way film productions swept its field in honors and awards.

The International Film & TV Festival of New York awarded two gold medals—first place recognition for *The Long Journey,* starring Dean Jones, and the National Football League *Great Moments* TV spot series—to United Way of America. In Hollywood competition, the Independent Film Producers of America recognized *Little Boy Lost,* which starred David Janssen, with its gold Cindy; and in Ohio, the Columbus International Film Festival selected *Little Boy Lost* for its gold Chris Award, both first place prizes.

For excellence in radio public service spots, United Way's *The Big Parade* was selected from 5,000 national entries for the first place Andy Award of the Advertising Club in New York.

In another medium, the Saul Bass new United Way symbol won Art Direction Magazine's Creativity Award for 1972.

In a review of the United Way Communications program, *Channels,* publication of the National Public Relations Council, reported in January, 1975:

"In 1974, the United Way of America's National Media Program constituted the largest public service campaign in the nation, perhaps the largest in history, for a voluntary organization. In the airing of United Way spots with every televised National Football League game . . . 1,000 ads in national publications,

Floyd Little, Denver Broncos Running Back, with Paul Ogg, an adopted Vietnamese orphan, who was helped to overcome the cripping effects of polio by his new parents, and the United Way. This is a scene from one of the 39 Great Moments film series, 1975, in which United Way and the National Football League joined together for the second year to present great moments in both the careers of NFL stars and recipients of United Way services.

NFL's <u>very</u> special team

The great stars of NFL take pride in being part of a winning team: in their conference, and in marching to the League's Super Bowl victory.

One team, made up of stars from all the NFL teams, with players like Bob Griese, Franco Harris, Bob Trumpy and 36 others, is the *special NFL-United Way Public Service Team.*

These players contributed their time to help others through the United Way-NFL *Great Moments* Series on network radio and television. Across the three networks these players tell the stories of the millions of families and individuals helped by the 37,000 agencies of the United Way.

They bring you some of their great moments on the gridiron, and tell you how the United Way works to bring great moments to the lives of people in need.

You can join these players, and be part of the NFL-United Way team, yourself. By volunteering and supporting your local United Way, you can help to create a few great moments of your own.

Thanks to you, it works...for all of us...the United Way.

Don't miss the *Great Moments* series on your NFL broadcast network this season. Be part of the team that's always a winner...the United Way.

United Way

Beginning in 1974 and continuing in 1975 and 1976, United Way undertook what has become the largest public service campaign in the nation's history. In association with The National Football League, a comprehensive series of television and radio spots were broadcast in conjunction with all NFL games throughout the season, reaching over 80 million viewers each week. Entitled the "Great Moments" series, this mass media communications effort was the forerunner of the new United Way's media approach to telling the United Way story.

233

"Ladies and Gentlemen, a United Way volunteer of long standing..." With these words, Chairman of the Board James R. Kerr introduced the White House message from President Ford which was carried by the three major networks on September 5, 6, and 7, 1974.

96,000 car cards in public transportation, etc., etc., the United Way received more than $56 million in free public service advertising for its 2,240 local organizations. This is in addition to what locals generate through their own resources.

"How does the United Way do it? For one thing, they have an incredibly well-organized and well-designed communications program which is summarized in a 115-page catalog with more than 800 items available to local United Ways, including films, TV spots, radio spots, slides, photographs, multi-media presentations, brochures, signs, stickers, billboards, and on and on. They have a concept of service and a knowledge of fund raising that continues to excite the imagination and which illustrates what can be done when the commitment, the concept and the skill work hand-in-hand."

President Ford Speaks for United Way

Traditionally, the annual United Way campaigns have been launched by an all-network Presidential Broadcast.

"Ladies and gentlemen, a United Way volunteer of long standing, from the White House, the President of the United States." Thus did James R. Kerr, Chairman of the Board, United Way of America, introduce President Gerald Ford to 120 million television viewers in the 1974 kickoff for the United Way's first billion dollar campaign.

"I am speaking as one who has worked as a United Way volunteer in my own home town, and who knows what the United Way campaign can do," the President said.

"This one effort each year to raise funds to help people in need is of vast importance to you and to your community . . . and to the nation as well.

"The United Way symbolizes the best in us and in each of our communities. It brings together men and women from every part of the community—all working to help those who need help.

"This is the way to handle community problems . . . a uniquely American way. We care about our less fortunate neighbors. We are willing to work to make communities better. And you in your community know far better than anyone in Washington which of your neighbors need help and what is needed to make your community better. That's why the United Way serves so well . . . because it is an effort with a special goal and special campaign, designed for the community involved.

"Your pledge to United Way in your community provides the most effective, economical and efficient way to provide help.

"The volunteer effort of the United Way workers insures that more of your dollars go to serve people. Your pledge to the United Way campaign in your community is an investment in a better community . . . in a better nation and in a better world. I ask you to join in, to give your fair share, to make the United Way work for our fellow human beings this year, just as it has worked so well in the past," the President declared.

Communities in Change

The first half of the Seventies brought winds of change to United Ways in communities across the length and breadth of North America.

Characteristic of the many modifications made were:

1. the geographical outreachings of adjacent United Ways to join each other in larger, stronger, more productive areawide fund raising and planning organizations;

2. the looking inward at administrative and corporate United Way structures for the creation of new and improved organizational forms; and

3. developing innovative patterns of increased inclu-

siveness in new agency participation in the United Way fund raising system.

Led by Los Angeles, Cleveland, Toronto (see United Way in Canada, Chapter XVII), San Diego and Baltimore, structural changes in organization were made in greater or lesser degree in numerous communities. United Way of America's management services through MACSI, its Automated Data Processing Consultation program, and its "model guidance" through *Standards of Excellence for Local United Way Organizations,* assisted scores of local communities in bringing about structural changes that resulted in "tuning up" the performance of the United Way movement throughout the country. Most of these organizational changes were evolutionary in nature, although there were some communities in which radical shifts took place. One of these was in Cleveland, which had organized the first Community Chest type of organization in 1913. Now in a dramatic reorganization of landmark proportions, Cleveland combined into one superstructure; planning, allocating of funds and financing of all health and social services were provided through more than 150 member organizations in the establishment of the new Greater Cleveland United in 1971. Campaigns were to be conducted under the name of United Torch Drive.

In a sequel in 1972, Greater Cleveland United achieved a major breakthrough toward the concept of combining community fundraising for all health causes as well as the social services into an overall united campaign.

A new proposal drafted jointly between Greater Cleveland United and the Health Fund of Greater Cleveland was approved by both organizations. It called for conducting a two-phase community wide campaign. A broadly based first phase residential campaign for all United Torch Drive health and social service agencies would be held in the spring and a second phase of the campaign would solicit companies and employees in the fall.

The spring residential drive emphasized health causes, including existing Health Fund agencies, research-oriented United Torch Drive agencies, and local research money for cancer, heart, birth defects, multiple sclerosis, tuberculosis and other diseases.

The American Cancer Society, and the American Heart Association, did not agree to join the United Torch Drive or to participate in the two-phase campaign.

Ten retired United Way professional leaders met for two days (November 9 and 10, 1976) with National Executive William Aramony and at the invitation of host C. Virgil Martin, retired Chairman of the Board, Carson Pirie Scott and veteran United Way leader. They were the first participants in an audiovisual history of the United Way produced under the direction of national United Way Communications Vice President Mario Pellegrini.

Through ten hours of interview and discussion, their personal United Way experiences, observations, and philosophies were "preserved for posterity" via color, video tape recording, thus adding to United Way's documentary materials for its training and educational programs. (Left to right), William Aramony, Elwood Street, C.F. McNeil, Grace Blanchard, Lyman S. Ford, Raymond E. Baarts, Arch Mandel, William Kaufman, Dr. Ruth Becherer, C. Virgil Martin, Henry Weber, and Harry M. Carey.

E. Mandell de Windt, president of Greater Cleveland United, said, "We are extremely pleased with the action taken by the Health Fund. It represents a major breakthrough in keeping with the mandate from the Commission on Health and Social Services to make every possible effort to consolidate community campaigns of voluntary health and social services into a single joint annual campaign." [17]

Health Fund leaders hailed the proposal and called it the "newest of new looks in fund raising." William E. MacDonald, chairman of the Health Fund Board, said, "Torch Drive officials have proposed—and we have enthusiastically accepted—the elimination of their residential campaign in the fall of 1973 to be replaced by a mammoth unified effort in the spring of 1973. The new spring drive—the first in the country—will stress the specialized needs of the agencies that combat disease through research, public education and patient services." [18]

In another action of far-reaching nation-wide significance, the Welfare Federation of Cleveland changed its name to Federation for Community Planning and became the broad issue planning group for the area served by the United Torch Drive. The budget review and allocations functions for the Torch agencies, formerly handled by the Welfare Federation, had been shifted to Greater Cleveland United at the time of its organization the previous year.

In Los Angeles, United Way, Inc., adopted a new regional plan in a sweeping reorganization of structure in 1971, after more than 250 planning meetings had been held involving some 400 volunteers over a span of 30 months. Under the new plan, five operating regions, each with responsibilities for planning, budgeting, finance and fund raising were created. Each region has its own board of directors and staff, but United Way, Inc., remained a single united organization with major policy flowing from a corporate board for (a) maintaining the federation concept of raising monies (over $27 million) in all areas, and (b) spending monies where they are needed most.

One of the most significant aspects of the new plan was the addition of social planning and research through merger with the four previously independent planning councils in the Los Angeles area.

T. M. McDaniel, Jr., president of Los Angeles

United Way, Inc., called the decentralization of operation, "one of the most significant developments in federation in the nation."

Emerging from the Los Angeles and Cleveland reorganizational experience was the concept, new to United Way procedures in the larger metropolitan areas, of "in-house planning." The principle of placing the responsibility for planning and allocating along with fundraising for member agencies under the administrative aegis of a single United Way corporate body, instead of in a separate "Welfare Planning Council," rippled across the country. At the half-way mark in the seventies, it appeared that the trend toward "in-house planning" might well become the mode of the future. Simultaneously, welfare planning councils, with continuing United Way financial support, turned their attention to meeting the need for better coordination with other planning systems in the community, including municipal and regional councils for housing, health, transportation, recreation, etc. It was a time for examination in new patterns of community service. New structural forms began to emerge.

In Wayne County, Indiana, the United Way and the city of Richmond entered into an agreement to share equally in hiring a "social planner." The understanding provides for the creation of a five-member Social Services Planning Board, consisting of two appointees of the Mayor, two of the President of the United Way, and the City Judge or his appointee. The planner will

Harry M. Carey, retired United Way Executive, receives one of the medallions from William Aramony, National Executive, United Way of America, presented to ten "Old Timers" at a meeting at United Way of America's Alexandria headquarters, November 10, 1975.

be responsible to this body and "will be primarily involved in determining the relative priorities of the needs of the community, and the acquisition of other than local funds to set up and maintain social services."

Another turn in the United Way's direction of historical import was the move in key communities toward increasing inclusiveness of separate health drives into the overall United Way campaign. A plan of having just one solicitation in business and industry for both social services and all health agencies and causes, as orginated in St. Paul several years previously, received further impact by Greater Cleveland United's joint campaign arrangement with the Health Fund. Additional momentum to the single annual campaign objective was given by San Diego and Baltimore.

Major changes in the direction and structure of the United Community Services of San Diego County were made in 1971 following recommendations by a Citizens Study Committee. Reorganization was effected in "virtually every phase of UCS operations." [19] In furtherance of the "in-house" system, an internal planning division was set up to provide adequate information on which to base UCS allocations and budgeting decisions. Next the UCS changed its name to United Way, and then in 1974 the first combined campaign of the United Way and CHAD (Combined Health Agencies Drive) raised $7,541,223 for an increase of more than 10 percent over the aggregate amount raised by both United Way and CHAD in the previous years' separate campaigns.

Realignment of the United Way corporate configuration in the Baltimore area culminated in a first-time joining of forces with the Commerce and Industry Combined Health Appeal (CICHA) in 1974. In the campaign that followed $13,217,356 was raised for an increase of 12 percent above the total of the United Fund of Central Maryland and CICHA separate campaigns of the year before.

Tools for Accountability

United Way of America had been developing tools since 1971 for accountability and for proper reporting to donors, consumers, providers of service, government, etc. The reporting was aimed at finding out precisely what impact United Way money was having on solving people's problems. "No longer is it enough to talk about the worthiness of causes. It is necessary to measure how much causes are worth, so the development of tools is of central importance." [20]

The Alexis de Tocqueville Society was created by United Way of America and incorporated in Virginia in 1972. Its purpose is to recognize persons deemed to have rendered outstanding service as volunteers in their own community or nationally. The Society aims to foster and promote voluntary community service, and a recognition of the value and importance of such service to the nation.

The name was chosen because of de Tocqueville's admiration for the spirit of voluntary association and voluntary effort for the common good which he had observed in America, and about which he wrote enthusiastically. The directors of the Society are the members of the Board of Governors of United Way of America.

Recipients of the Alexis de Tocqueville Award have been: Bob Hope, Leslie L. Luttgens (Mrs. William F.), Henry Ford II and Charles Francis Adams on behalf of six generations of Adamses. Vernon Jordon, Jr., Executive Director, National Urban League, Inc. was selected by United Way of America Board of Governors on December 8, 1976 to be the 1977 recipient of the award for presentation on April 25, 1977.

De Tocqueville's book, Democracy in America, *published in 1835 after his journey to the United States, cites the prevalence of voluntarism in America.*

A set of interrelated tools for this purpose is being developed. When they are all in place, they will form a comprehensive integrated program for responsive, high performance community service.

United Way of America Services Identification System (UWASIS) was the first such effort. Then *Standards of Excellence* was produced followed by *National Standards for Information and Referral Services and Local United Way Allocations* in 1973. It took nearly a year to develop the latter system which produced the most complete picture ever as to where the funds go. The *Painful Necessity of Choice,* published in 1974, examined the conditions in local communities conducive to the use of priority planning approaches, the importance of proper implementation methods, and most important, the need to involve all participating agencies in the process.

Accounting and Financial Reporting, A Guide for United Ways and Not-for-Profit Human Service Organizations, released in late 1974, contains standards, models and directions for application by local United Ways. Useful for reporting United Way expenditures and income, it can also be employed in identifying the expenditures and income of the agencies to which the monies are allocated. It incorporates the revised *Standards of Accounting and Financial Reporting for Voluntary Health and Welfare Organizations.* It incorporates UWASIS. It allows for program budgeting and includes the latest accounting principles and practices promulgated by the American Institute of Certified Public Accountants in its *Audits of Voluntary Health and Welfare Organizations.*

The *Accounting Manual* is so presented that the principles and practices it delineates can be used either manually or with electronic data processing.

Budgeting, A Guide for United Ways and Not-for-Profit Human Service Organizations was published in 1975.

UWASIS II was published in 1976. It is a revision based on the experience of those who had applied the original publication in their operations. Future tool development plans include a guide to the development of policies and procedures on the admission and support of agencies and services. The second would deal with needs delineation and assessment. A third would cover performance assessment or evaluation. This would be, in a sense, the final task, the goal toward which all the other tools were directed—how to find out how much good United Way services and programs are doing.

In commenting on the United Way's total Program for Accountability, which he believed to be one of its highest priorities, William Aramony said, "Our current state of the art is such that no one has come up with a useable, acceptable tool for measuring program effectiveness. There is no guarantee that we can. We also recognize that such a tool, even if developed, may have limitations.

"We can measure effort, namely, how many sessions we hold, how many people we put into a project, how long clients spend in treatment and other quantitative criteria.

"But we have yet to identify a method of measuring the ultimate impact—for good or ill—on the people we serve. We think such an objective is worthy of a full effort.

"In forging these tools we must never forget that 'tools' do not make policy decisions—people do We are trying, therefore, to develop a way of looking at human service needs and at how we can account for the use of voluntary resources.[21]

Five Years After Rebirth and Renewal

The 1975 annual Volunteer Leaders Conference in Miami in April provided a showcase for the new United Way . . . the product of five years of successive breakthroughs via the Rebirth and Renewal Program. On no previous occasion had a United Way conference been favored by such a high level of distinguished leaders; by such a diversity of topics, vital to United Way progress; or by such ardent participation by the attendees.

Three main areas of United Way interests covered by 52 speakers were headed by Richard T. Baker for Campaign; J. Kenneth Kansas, Communications; and Samuel J. Silberman, Planning and Allocations. James R. Kerr was Conference Chairman. Keynote Speaker was A. W. Clausen, President, Bank of America NT&SA, and member United Way of America Board of Governors. He spoke on total partnership with the community, the new dimension in voluntarism.

"In the coming months, our human care network will face more than the usual range of problems," Mr. Clausen said. "That means for each of the communities we represent, the problems will be more serious and

Bob Hope, the first recipient of the Alexis de Tocqueville Award, accepts the ceremonial crystal from James R. Kerr, Board of Governors Chairman, United Way of America, April 10, 1973 at the Volunteer Leaders Conference in Chicago. Chicago Tribune Photo.

Two United Bay Area volunteers discuss the pertinency of Alexis de Tocqueville's observations of over 200 years ago to the United Way of today. Laurence D. Bolling, United Way of America Board of Governors member and Leslie L. Luttgens (Mrs. William F.) of San Francisco, recipient of the United Way's 1974 de Tocqueville Award.

A happy Henry Ford II holds the Alexis de Tocqueville Award presented to him at the 1975 Volunteer Leaders Conference in Miami. The award is United Way of America's highest recognition for volunteer achievement.

Mr. and Mrs. Charles F. Adams accept the Alexis de Tocqueville Award on behalf of six generations of Adamses at the opening dinner of the 1976 Volunteer Leaders Conference.

Vernon Jordan, Jr., Executive Director, National Urban League, Inc. was the 1977 recipient of the Alexis de Tocqueville Award.

pressing. But I think they can all be managed. Many of them will have to be managed by government. Yet, no matter how effective government programs are, they'll leave a tremendous vacuum, particularly in coping with the range of problems involving individual human needs. In this urgent and growing area, our private voluntary sector has a very important role to play. We have flexibility and diversity, a variety of funding sources, and the ability to respond to needs on a personal basis.

"Our rich tradition of voluntarism allows us to support programs that range from prisoner counseling, special education, meals for senior citizens, and methadone treatment to research and education in such diseases as sickle cell anemia, cerebral palsy, mental retardation, and alcoholism. In San Francisco alone, we have 183 United Way agencies that operate throughout five counties and provide services that touch the lives of one out of every three persons in our communities.

"Given our voluntary sector's unique ability to approach so many problems at the community level and on an individual basis, the issue that faces most of us

today is finding the best way to mobilize our resources and direct them toward human needs.

"If we're to realize our full potential, we need to build a volunteer structure that brings together men and women of every age, every circumstance, every ethnic background—not just people who tend to be remote from those who need help, but also people who are of the same backgrounds and in the same circumstances as the people whose problems we're trying to solve.

"The point I want to make is that people's problems may be different, but most of their basic goals are very similar. What we all want is to improve the total quality of life in our communities so that we can enjoy life together in a degree of peace and comfort. What we all need is each other.

"Fulfilling those needs calls for a true partnership. It requires that representatives from all sectors of our communities work together for the common benefit. It's my strongest hope that this partnership effort will be the future trend for our new dimension of voluntarism." [22]

A highlight of the conference was the presentation of the Alexis de Tocqueville Award to Henry Ford II, Chairman of the Board, Ford Motor Company, Detroit, "for his outstanding contribution in serving people through voluntarism and his personal commitment to community and nation." James L. Knight, Chairman of the Executive Committee, Knight-Ridder Newspapers, Inc., Miami, Florida, and Treasurer of United Way of America made the presentation, citing Mr. Ford's leadership in 1947-49 to transform the Community Chest movement into the United Fund concept; his membership on the Board of the United Foundation in Detroit; his service as National Campaign Chairman of Community Chests of America in 1948 and 1949; and his Chairmanships of the National Alliance of Businessmen and of the National Center for Voluntary Action.[23]

Following the Annual Meeting of the National Congress, the Board of Governors elected C. Peter McColough, Chairman. James R. Kerr, outgoing Chairman, was elected Vice-Chairman along with Bayard Ewing. Charles I. Stone was named a Board Vice-Chairman as well as Chairman of the Executive Committee. Glenn E. Watts was elected Secretary and James L. Knight, Treasurer.[24]

The Filer Commission

On December 2, 1975, the final report of the Commission on Private Philanthropy and Public Needs was delivered to the public. Known as the Filer Commission, in honor of its chairman, John H. Filer,[25] Chairman of the Board of Aetna Life and Casualty Company, the commission received strong support for its activities from congressional leaders. John D. Rockefeller, III, provided the initial start-up funds. Bayard Ewing, Vice-Chairman of the Board of Governors, United Way of America, served on the committee.

For over two years the Filer Commission conducted a broad, in-depth study of the importance of philanthropy to our society for the purpose of making recommendations regarding government incentives to private philanthropic initiative. The Commission produced over 80 studies covering a wide area of the philanthropic sector. In its final report, the Commission made 19 recommendations to Congress and to the public for the improvement of the philanthropic process.

As a direct result of the Commission's work, the United States Treasury Department established an Advisory Committee on Private Philanthropy and Public Needs. The 25-member committee is chaired by Douglas Dillon, noted national leader and former Secretary of the Treasury. William Aramony is a member of the Advisory Committee.

The objective of the Committee is to provide informed advice to the Treasury on tax and regulatory policies affecting private philanthropy and philanthropic activities, including donors, organizations, and beneficiaries.

1976—America's Bicentennial Year

United Way's 1976 Biennial Staff Conference was held in historic Boston, March 7-10, 1976. The largest and most successful staff conference in the movement's history, it was attended by over 1000 United Way people.[26]

C. Peter McColough, Chairman of the Board, United Way of America addressed the conference and stated, "We need a stronger link between the system and the service . . . between the institution and the individual. And that link—which must balance bigness with individual compassion and bureaucracy with individual perspective—is, of course, you. You and I belong to one of the few organizations that can address those

Tony Bennett, popular male vocalist, sings the United Way theme song, "There's Always Tomorrow" at the 1976 Biennial Staff Conference. Mr. Bennett made numerous personal appearances, gave concerts and appeared on national television for United Way as Chairman of the United Way "To The People" campaign.

(different human) needs. And that's the other, the enviable side of our coin. The side that makes the pressure, the discord, the change, and the uncertainty worthwhile." [27]

The star attraction of the conference was Tony Bennett who appeared as National Chairman of United Way's "To the People" campaign. This campaign was a year-round communications effort aimed at telling the United Way story through T.V., film, personal appearances and song. Mr. Bennett premiered a new United Way theme song, written by Sammy Cahn, with music by Torrie Zito, entitled "There's Always Tomorrow."

The 1976 annual Volunteer Leaders Conference was held in New Orleans with almost 1200 volunteers and professional leaders of local United Ways present. C. Peter McColough was Conference Chairman. At the opening session NFL Commissioner Pete Rozelle and football stars Roger Staubach and Bob Trumpy were honored for the support which the National Football

League and its players have provided United Ways through the "Great Moments" series.[28]

In keeping with the bicentennial theme of the conference, the Alexis de Tocqueville Award was presented to Charles Francis Adams, Chairman, Finance Committee, Raytheon Company and member, Board of Governors of United Way of America. The award was presented on behalf of six generations of Adamses. In his acceptance Mr. Adams said, "The speed and effectiveness with which we can adjust to changing times is the measure of our superior performance versus that of big government, which stands ever in the wings. If we as volunteers, cannot be wiser and more perceptive in meeting the needs of those we serve than the governmental process, then we are indeed in deep trouble.

"If objectivity in decision making does not better meet the interests of the people than judgments based on political considerations, then we are in even deeper trouble.

"Personally, I believe that in this comparison we can shine. Not only can we do our job more quickly, with less expense, and with a greater measure of compassion, but to this troubled and divided nation, the way we go about it can have a healing effect." [29]

The 1976 Annual Meeting of the National Congress of United Way of America was held in conjunction with the Volunteer Leaders Conference and featured a tandem volunteer and professional report. C. Peter McColough, Chairman of the Board of Governors, reported on major areas of progress in 1975 and tasks ahead.

One of the highlights of the 1976 Volunteer Leaders Conference was the presentation of plaques to National Football League representatives for the award-winning "Great Moments" series. The series appears on television in conjunction with the NFL broadcasts and is seen each weekend by more than 80 million viewers. (left to right) Bob Trumpy, C. Peter McColough, NFL Commissioner Pete Rozelle, and Roger Staubach.

The Joseph A. Beirne Community Services Award was established to honor the memory of one of the remarkable labor leaders of the twentieth century and to recognize labor leaders who have rendered outstanding United Way volunteer service. The first presentation of the award was made at the 1977 Volunteer Leaders Conference in Atlanta, Georgia. The recipient was Mrs. Dina G. Beaumont of Los Angeles, California.

Dina G. Beaumont, Vice President, District Eleven, Communications Workers of America, AFL-CIO, Los Angeles, California, was the 1977 recipient of the Joseph A. Beirne Award. Mrs. Beaumont was chosen as the first recipient of the award because of her outstanding volunteer service to the Los Angeles community.

He reported on achievements in the areas of resource development, inter-organizational politics and volunteer mobilization. William Aramony, National Executive, reported on specific activities in 1975, stressing that United Way of America has no life of its own but is, rather, an extension of local United Ways and the means by which they can do their business through cooperation with other communities.

Mr. Aramony outlined seven steps for the future, including: greater inclusiveness of people, programs and geography; investing in the capacity of the United Way to generate new support and fulfill its accountability responsibilities; achieving a breakthrough on the commitment of corporations to the United Way; areawide organization; strengthening and improving governmental-voluntary linkages; the development of a more acceptable basis for the movement's relationship to agencies and services; and the need for United Ways to become more of a community-wide problem solver and improvement force.[30]

As America's bicentennial year was drawing to a close, United Way was on the threshold of a dynamic future which would benefit all people.

NOTES

Chapter 18

1. *Executive Newsletter*, UWA, May 8, 1972.
2. *Executive Newsletter*, UWA, May 15, 1972.
3. *Executive Newsletter*, UWA, June 26, September 18, 1972.
4. *Executive Newsletter*, UWA, December 11, 1972.
5. *Proceedings of the 1973 Volunteer Leaders Conference*, p. 5.
6. Ibid, p. 19.
7. Ibid, p. 27.

8. Ibid, p. 35.
9. *Community,* UWA, Summer 1971, pp. 14-15.
10. *Proceedings, International Conference on United Fund Raising,* 1973-1974.
11. *Focus, United Way Voluntarism,* UWA, April 9, 1973.
12. *Focus, United Way Volunteers,* UWA, March 19, 1973.
13. William Aramony, *Rebirth and Renewal: A Progress Report,* April 1972, p. 12.
14. *Community,* UWA, Winter 1973, pp. 3-4.
15. Richard E. Booth, Opening Address, *The United Way Professional—You Make the Difference,* National Staff Conference, Los Angeles, 1974.
16. Blue Ribbon Study Committee Report, *On the Needs of U.S. Armed Forces Personnel for Continued Voluntary Social Services,* p. 11.
17. *Executive Newsletter,* UWA, March 20, 1972.
18. Ibid.
19. *Executive Newsletter,* UWA, May 17, 1971.
20. William Aramony, *Where is United Way Heading in Accountability—and Why?* UWA, December 1973.
21. Ibid.
22. A. W. Clausen, *Keynote Speaker,* UWA Volunteer Leaders Conference, April 24, 1975.
23. James L. Knight, *Presentation of Alexis de Tocqueville Award to Henry Ford, II,* UWA Tape Cassette, April 24, 1975.
24. *Executive Newsletter,* UWA, May 5, 1975.
25. *Commission on Private Philanthropy and Public Needs,* Brochure, p. 1.
26. *Executive Newsletter,* UWA, March 5, 1976.
27. C. Peter McColough, Speaker, 1976 United Way Staff Conference, Boston, Massachusetts, March 8, 1976.
28. *Executive Newsletter,* UWA, May 3, 1976.
29. Charles F. Adams, Acceptance Speaker, 1976 Volunteer Leaders Conference, New Orleans, Louisiana, April 25, 1976.
30. *Executive Newsletter,* UWA, May 3, 1976.

C. Peter McColough
Chairman of the Board of Governors,
United Way of America
Chairman of the Board & Chief Executive Officer
Xerox Corporation
Stamford, Connecticut

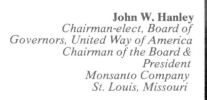

John W. Hanley
Chairman-elect, Board of
Governors, United Way of America
Chairman of the Board &
President
Monsanto Company
St. Louis, Missouri

Glenn E. Watts
Vice Chairman of the Board
and Chairman of Executive
Committee

President
Communications Workers of
America, AFL-CIO
Washington, D. C.

1976 BOARD OF GOVERNORS UNITED WAY OF AMERICA
Officers

Bayard Ewing
Vice Chairman of the Board

Attorney, Partner
Tillinghast, Collins & Graham
Providence, Rhode Island ▶

James R. Kerr
Vice Chairman of the Board

Chairman of the Board &
Chief Executive Officer
◀ AVCO Corporation
Greenwich, Connecticut

Stephen F. Keating
Secretary

◀ Chairman of the Board
Honeywell, Inc.
Minneapolis, Minnesota

A. W. Clausen
Chairman, Long Range
Planning Committee

President, Bank of
America NT&SA ▶
San Francisco, California

Mrs. Ernestine Carmichael
Treasurer

South Bend, Indiana ▶

John D. deButts
Chairman, National Corporate
Development Committee

◀ Chairman of the Board
American Telephone &
Telegraph Co.
New York, New York

William Aramony
National Executive
◀ Alexandria, Virginia

Clifton C. Garvin, Jr.
Chairman of the Board &
Chief Executive Officer
Exxon Corporation
New York, New York

Hon. Samuel P. Goddard, Jr.
Goddard & Ahearn
Phoenix, Arizona

Rosendo Gutierrez
President
PACE Engineering, Inc.
Phoenix, Arizona

Mrs. Ben W. Heineman
Chicago, Illinois

James L. Knight
Chairman of the Executive
Committee
Knight-Ridder
Newspapers, Inc.
Miami, Florida

Louis E. Martin
Vice President &
Editorial Director
Chicago Daily Defender
Chicago, Illinois

Avery Mays
Chairman of the Board
Avery Mays Construction
Company
Dallas, Texas

Mrs. Joseph N. Mitchell
Beverly Hills, California

Thomas A. Murphy
Chairman
General Motors Corporation
Detroit, Michigan

249

Capt. John J. O'Donnell
President
Air Line Pilots Association
Washington, D.C.

Leo Perlis
Director
Department of Community
Services, AFL-CIO
Washington, D.C.

Flaxie M. Pinkett
President
John R. Pinkett, Inc.
Washington, D.C.

Donald V. Seibert
Chairman and Chief
Executive Officer
J. C. Penney Co., Inc.
New York, New York

Augustus H. Sterne
Chairman of the Board
Trust Company of Georgia
Atlanta, Georgia

Charles I. Stone
Attorney, Senior Partner
Perkins, Coie, Stone,
Olsen & Williams
Seattle, Washington

Rev. Leon Howard Sullivan
Pastor
Zion Baptist Church
Philadelphia, Pennsylvania

Franklin A. Thomas
President
Bedford Stuyvesant
Restoration Corporation
Brooklyn, New York

J. C. Turner
President
International Union of
Operating Engineers,
AFL-CIO
Washington, D.C.

250

UNITED WAY PRESIDENTS

William C. White
President
Milwaukee Centralized Budget
of Philanthropies
President
American Association
for Community Organization
1918

Allen T. Burns
Director
Americanization for the
Carnegie Corporation
President
American Association
for Community Organization
1918-1919

Sherman C. Kingsley
Executive Secretary
Cleveland Community Fund
President
American Association
for Community Organization
1919-1920

W. J. Norton
Executive Secretary
Detroit Community Chest and
Community Union
President
American Association
for Community Organization
1921-1923

Benjamin F. Merrick
Partner
Travis, Merrick, Varnum
and Riddering
President
American Association
for Community Organization
1923-1924

Halsted L. Ritter
Attorney
Denver
President
American Association
for Community Organization
1924-1926

Henry G. Stevens
President
Iron Silver Mining Company
President
Association of Community
Chests and Councils
1926-1927

Clarence M. Bookman
Executive Director
Community Chest and Council
of the Cincinnati Area
President
Association of Community
Chests and Councils
1927-1928

J. Herbert Case
Chairman of the Board
Federal Reserve Bank,
New York
President
Association of Community
Chests and Councils
1928-1933

John Stewart Bryan
President & Publisher
Richmond Newspapers, Inc.
President
Association of Community
Chests and Councils
1933-1934

Frederick R. Kellogg
*Kellogg, Emery, Inness-Brown,
Brown, Black, Tappan,
Warfield and Scholl
President
Community Chests and Councils,
Inc.
1934-1935*

E. A. Roberts
*President
Fidelity Mutual Insurance
Company of Philadelphia
President
Community Chests and Councils,
Inc.
1943-1946*

Stillman F. Westbrook
*Vice President
Aetna Life Insurance Company
President
Community Chests and Councils,
Inc.
1935-1938*

Edward L. Ryerson
*Chairman of the Board
Inland Steel Company
President
Community Chests and Councils,
Inc.
1947-1950*

Dr. George Vincent
*President
Rockefeller Foundation
President
Community Chests and Councils,
Inc.
1938-1940*

Stanley C. Allyn
*Chairman of the Board
National Cash Register
Company
President
Community Chests and Councils,
Inc.
1950-1952*

Robert Cutler
*President
The Old Colony Trust Company
President
Community Chests and Councils,
Inc.
1940-1943*

Henry J. Heinz II
*Chairman
H. J. Heinz Company
President
Community Chests and Councils
of America
1952-1954*

Harry Clifford Knight
*President
New England Telephone
Company
Chairman of the Board and
Acting President
Community Chest and Councils,
Inc.
1942-1943*

Gerard Swope
*President
General Electric Company
Honorary President
Community Chests and Councils,
Inc.
1954-1959*

Albert J. Nesbitt
President
John J. Nesbitt, Inc.
President
Community Chests and Councils
of America
1954-1956

Ralph Lazarus
Chairman & Chief
Executive Officer
Federated Department Stores,
Inc.
President
United Community Funds
and Councils of America
1964-1965

James A. Linen
President
Time, Inc.
President
United Community Funds
and Councils of America
1956-1958

Joseph A. Beirne
President
Communication Workers of
America, AFL-CIO
President
United Community Funds
and Councils of America
1966-1967

John A. Greene
President
Ohio Bell Telephone Company
President
United Community Funds
and Councils of America
1958-1960

Walter H. Wheeler, Jr.
Chairman, Executive
Committee and Director
Pitney-Bowes, Inc.
President
United Community Funds
and Councils of America
1968-1969

Irving A. Duffy
Vice President
Ford Motor Company
President
United Community Funds
and Councils of America
1960-1962

Bayard Ewing
Partner
Tillinghast, Collins & Graham
President
United Community Funds
and Councils of America
1970
Chairman, Board of
Governors, United Way
of America

John S. Hayes
Chairman, Executive Committee
Washington Post-Newsweek
Company
President
United Community Funds
and Councils of America
1962-1964

James R. Kerr
Chairman of the Board
& Chief Executive Officer
AVCO Corporation
Chairman, Board of
Governors, United Way
of America

UNITED WAY NATIONAL CAMPAIGN CHAIRMEN

Newton D. Baker
Secretary of War
Founder, Cleveland Welfare
Federation
National Chairman
Mobilization for Human Needs
1932-1934

Honorable Prescott S. Bush
Partner
Brown Brothers, Harriman
& Company
National Chairman
National War Fund
1944

Gerard Swope
President
General Electric Company
National Chairman
Mobilization for Human Needs
1935-1936
National War Fund — 1945

Thomas S. Gates
President
University of Pennsylvania
National Chairman
Community Chests of America
1946

Charles P. Taft
Member
Taft, Luken & Boyd
National Chairman
Community Mobilization for
Human Needs
1937-1939

Henry J. Heinz II
Chairman
H. J. Heinz Company
National Chairman
Community Chest of America
1947-1951-1952

Charles Francis Adams
Secretary of the Navy
National Chairman
Community Mobilization for
Human Needs
1940

Henry Ford II
Chairman of the Board
Ford Motor Company
National Chairman
Community Chests of America
1948-1949

Tom K. Smith
Chairman of the Board
The Boatmen's National Bank
of St. Louis
National Chairman
Community Mobilization for
Human Needs
1941-1943

Charles E. Wilson
Chairman of the Board
General Electric Company
National Chairman
National Red Feather
Campaign
1950

Clarence Francis
Chairman
General Foods Corporation
National Chairman
United Community Campaigns
1953

Carrol M. Shanks
President
The Prudential Insurance
Company of America
National Chairman
United Community Campaigns
of America
1958

Harvey S. Firestone, Jr.
Honorary Chairman and
Director
Firestone Tire and Rubber
Company
National Chairman
United Community Campaigns
of America
1954

Richard R. Deupree
Honorary Chairman and
Director
Procter & Gamble Company
National Chairman
United Community Campaigns
of America
1959

J. P. Spang, Jr.
Chairman
The Gillette Company
National Chairman
United Community Campaigns
of America
1955

Oliver G. Willits
Chairman of the Board
Campbell Soup Company
National Chairman
United Community Campaigns
of America
1960

William M. Allen
Chairman of the Board
Boeing Company
National Chairman
United Community Campaigns
of America
1956

Benson Ford
Vice President
Ford Motor Company
National Chairman
United Community Campaigns
of America
1961

Charles G. Motimer
Chairman
General Foods Corporation
National Chairman
United Community Campaigns
of America
1957

Lee H. Bristol
Chairman of the Board
Bristol-Myers Company
National Chairman
United Community Campaigns
of America
1962

Mark W. Cresap, Jr.
President
Westinghouse Electric
Corporation
National Chairman
United Community Campaigns
of America
1963

C. W. Cook
Chairman and Chief Executive
General Foods Corporation
National Chairman
United Community Campaigns
of America
1967

John K. Hodnette
Vice Chairman, Board of
Directors
Westinghouse Electric
Corporation
National Chairman
United Community Campaigns
of America
1963

Orville E. Beal
President
The Prudential Insurance
Company of America
National Chairman
United Community Campaigns
of America
1968

Charles H. Brower
Chairman of the Board
Batten, Barton, Durstine &
Osborn, Inc.
National Chairman
United Community Campaigns
of America
1964

Gavin K. MacBain
Chairman of the Board
Bristol-Myers Company
National Chairman
United Community Campaigns
of America
1969

Walter H. Wheeler, Jr.
Chairman, Executive
Committee and Director
Pitney-Bowes, Incorporated
National Chairman
United Community Campaigns
of America
1965

James R. Kerr
President
AVCO Corporation
National Chairman
United Community Campaigns
of America
1970-1971

Milton C. Mumford
Chairman of the Board
Lever Brothers Company
National Chairman
United Community Campaigns
of America
1966

C. Peter McColough
Chairman of the Board
& Chief Executive Officer
Xerox Corporation
National Campaign Chairman
United Way of America
1972

NATIONAL EXECUTIVES
UNITED WAY
OF AMERICA

Professional leadership has been given to United Way by four National Executives. In addition to Allen T. Burns, 1926 to 1943; the others shown together here are (left to right) Ralph H. Blanchard, 1943 to 1960; Lyman S. Ford, 1960 to 1970; and William Aramony, National Executive since 1970.

UNITED WAY AWARD RECIPIENTS

RED FEATHER AWARD

1947	Gerard Swope, New York, N. Y.
1948	E. A. Roberts, Philadelphia, Pa.
1949	H. J. Heinz II, Pittsburgh, Pa.
1950	Philip M. Morgan, Worcester, Mass.
1951	Alex F. Osborn, Buffalo, N. Y.
1952	Stanley C. Allyn, Dayton, Ohio
1953	Edward L. Ryerson, Chicago, Ill.
1954	Mrs. Victor Shaw, Fairmont, W. Va.
1955	Robert Cutler, Boston, Mass.
1956	Albert J. Nesbitt, Philadelphia, Pa.

NATIONAL COMMUNITY SERVICE AWARD

1958	James A. Linen, New York, N. Y.
1960	John A. Greene, Cleveland, Ohio
1961	Ray R. Eppert, Detroit, Mich.
1962	Irving A. Duffy, Dearborn, Mich.
1963	Joseph A. Beirne, Washington, D. C.
1963	Edgar B. Stern, Jr., New Orleans, La.
1963	Oliver G. Willits, Camden, N. J.
1964	John S. Hayes, Washington, D. C.
1965	Benson Ford, Detroit, Mich.
1966	Ralph Lazarus, Cincinnati, Ohio
1967	Bayard Ewing, Providence, R. I.
1968	Walter H. Wheeler, Jr., Stamford, Conn.

NEWTON D. BAKER AWARD

1964	Robert B. Miller, Battle Creek, Mich.
1965	Dean Phillips, Columbus, Ohio
1966	The Very Reverend Robert F. Royster, South Bend, Ind.
1967	William H. Danforth, M.D., St. Louis, Mo.
1968	Frederic L. Ballard, Jr., Philadelphia, Pa.
1968	Daniel Klepak, Albany, N. Y.
1969	Mrs. Gerald Schmidt, Worcester, Mass.
1970	Mrs. A. W. Graessle, Jacksonville, Fla.

THE ALEXIS DE TOCQUEVILLE AWARD

1973	Bob Hope, Los Angeles, Calif.
1974	Leslie L. Luttgens (Mrs. William F.), San Francisco, Calif.
1975	Henry Ford II, Detroit, Mich.
1976	Charles Francis Adams on behalf of Six Generations of Adamses, Lexington, Mass.
1977	Vernon Jordan, Jr., New York, N. Y.

THE JOSEPH A. BEIRNE COMMUNITY SERVICES AWARD

1977	Dina G. Beaumont , Los Angeles, Calif.

INDEX

National Council of Defense, 39, 40, 86, 89
National Council on Community Foundations, 164
National Council on the Aging, 148
National Defense Councils. *See* National Council of Defense
National Emergency Services, Joint Committee on, 118, 119
National Federation of Settlements, 98, 101, 111
National Football League, 232, *233,* 242-43
National Foundation, 77, 109, 113, 114, 117, 123, 138, 146, 147, 151, 152, 186, 187, 195
National Fund for Medical Education, 140-41; Medical Research Program, 141, 148, 153
National Health and Welfare Retirement Association, 76, 96, 118, 228
National Health Council, 47, 104, 106, 159, 178
National Health Fund, 138
National Health Planning and Resources Development Act of 1974. *See* Social Security Act
National Information Bureau, 42, 46, 49, 51-52, 54, 59, 84, 91, 114, 152, 186, 195
National Institute of Immigrant Welfare, 94
National Institute of Mental Health, 146
National Jewish Welfare Board. *See* Jewish Welfare Board
National labor program. *See* Trade Unions
National Organization for Public Health Nursing, 94
National Quota Committee, 91-92, 93
National Recovery Administration, 76
National Recreation Association, 136
National Social Welfare Assembly, 102, 104, 111, 134, 143, 157, 159, 165, 181-82
National Social Work Council, 50, 62, 102
National Society for Crippled Children and Adults. *See* Easter Seals Society
National Standards for Information and Referral Services and Local United Way Allocations, 239
National Traveler's Aid Association. *See* Traveler's Aid Association
National Tuberculosis Association, 148, 152
National Urban League. *See* Urban League
National War Fund, 90, 92, 93-94, 96, 97, 102, 104
National Women's Committee, *68, 69*
Negroes, 170, 175, 211
Neighborhood Councils. *See* District Councils
Neighborhood Guild, 24

Nesbitt, Albert J., *134, 253,* 258
New Hampshire Social Welfare Council, 115
New Haven, Connecticut: Council, 146, 158; Foundation, 146
New Orleans, Louisiana, 35, 47, 60, 136
New York, New York, 17, 19, 20, 25, 39, 56, 76-77, 96, 225; Council, 142
New York, State Association for Community Services in, 115, 226, 230
Newer Federal Programs: Local Developments in the War Against Poverty, 173
Newmyer, Mrs. Leroy H., *130*
NFL *Great Moments* series, 232, *233,* 242-43
Nixon, Patricia (Mrs. Richard M.), 206, 218, *220*
Nixon, Richard M., *194,* 200
Nixon, Tricia, 206, *207*
Noble, Mrs., *68*
Nondiscrimination policies, 163-64, 166, 167, 175
Noonan, William J., *200*
Norfolk, Virginia, 124
North Carolina State War Fund, 97
North Carolina, United Way, 226
North Carolina War Chest, 230
Norton, William J., 23, 33, 34, 37, 38, 42, 46, 54, *251*
Noyes, Newbold, *59*

O

O'Connor, Basil, J., 109, 113, 114, 141, 146, 147, 152
O'Connor, J. J., 28
O'Donnell, John J., *250*
Office of Economic Opportunity, 164, 166
Ogg, Elizabeth, 146
Ogg, Paul, *233*
O'Grady, John, *71*
Ohio Citizen's Council for Health and Welfare, 106, 230
Ohio Institute for Public Efficiency, 106
Ohio State University, 46, *77,* 102
Ohio Welfare Council, 106, 226
Old Age and Survivors Insurance, 118
Olsen, Harold W., *180*
Omaha, Nebraska, 24, 136, 181
Oregon Chest, 106, 134, 135, 226, 230
Organized Labor. *See* Trade Unions
"Organizing and Financing Federations ond Councils of Social Agencies," 47
O'Ryan, William J., 21, *22, 23*
Osborn, Alex F., *124,* 258
Oshkosh, Wisconsin, 35
Oswald, John W., 5
Overseas relief. *See* Foreign relief
Overseas services, 39, 58. *See also* American National Red Cross; War chests

P

Painful Necessity of Choice, 239
Paisl, Mrs. *68*
Panama, 225
Paradis, A. A., 169
Parents Magazine, 102
Parris, Guichard, *193*
Pasadena, California, 89
Patrick, Gale. *See* Jackson, Mrs. Cornwell
Patterson, R. G., 77
Paulson: poster by, *128*
Payroll deductions, 94, 98, 155, 160, 163, 167, 169, 173
Peabody, Francis G., 24
Pearl Harbor, 88
Peat, Marwick, Mitchell and Company study, 2, 195-96, 200-201, 203
Pellegrini, Mario, *210, 222*
Pennsylvania, Community Services of, 122, 226, 230
Perkins, Donald S., 6
Perlis, Leo, 132, 152, 159, 230, *250*
Personnel Development program, 226-28
Personnel service. *See* United Way of America
Pfeiffer, Ralph A., 5
Philadelphia, Pennsylvania, 19, 42, 54, 64, 96, 174, 183; chest, 89; Council, 46-47
Philippines, 114, 225
Phillips, Dean, 258
Phillips, Mrs., *68*
Pierce, Franklin, 16
Pigott, Charles M., 6
Pilliod, Charles J., Jr., 6
Pinkett, Flaxie Madison, 5, 203, *250*
Pittsburgh, Pennsylvania, 26; Council, 26, 142; Fund, 60, 87, 135; Health Foundation, 139-40
Plain, George, 158, *185*
Planning. *See* Councils; Postwar planning; State organizations
Pomeroy, Hugh R., 134
Poole, John, *52, 59*
Pope, Gustavus D., 83
Posters: "Boy Scouts of America," *127;* "A bridge for humanity," *67;* "Celebrity," *209;* "Community Chest 1920," *34;* "GIVE," *125;* "Give the United Way," *166;* Hamilton, Ohio, 1918, *36;* "Happy family," *126;* "Have a heart," *48;* "He ain't heavy, he's my brother," *63;* Helping hands, *154;* "If you don't do it, it won't get done," *212;* "The little good guy," *161;* "1919 War Chest," *40;* Proud contributor, *142;* Rainbow and hand, *209;* "Rebuild," *73;* Red Feather, *88, 128;* "Save a life," *55;* "Share the American Way," *85;* "Suppose nobody cared?" *45;*